THE AVANT-GARDE FILM

THE AVANT-GARDE FILM

A Reader of Theory and Criticism

Edited by P. ADAMS SITNEY

ANTHOLOGY FILM ARCHIVES SERIES: 3

New York • New York University Press • 1978

Library of Congress Cataloging in Publication Data

Main entry under title:

The Avant-garde film.

(Anthology film archives series ; v. 3)

1. Experimental films—History and criticism—

Addresses, essays, lectures. I. Sitney,
P. Adams.

PN1995.9.E96A9   791.43'09   78-57645
ISBN 0-8147-7793-7
ISBN 0-8147-7794-5 pbk.

PREFACE

This anthology offers for the first time an extensive survey of the theoretical contributions of avant-garde film-makers and essays about their cinematic achievements. Several texts appear in print, or in English, for the first time here. Because of the diversity of the materials—manifestoes, letters, a scenario, program notes, lectures, interviews—and because of the stylistic peculiarities of some of the authors, no attempt has been made to standardize spellings, punctuation, or footnoting throughout the book. Each contribution conforms to its original manuscript or printed form.

I would like to thank the authors for their permission to reprint texts. *Film Culture, Daedalus,* Marie Epstein, Georges Borchardt, Mike Weaver, Mrs. John Benton, and The Vancouver Art Gallery generously assisted in securing permissions. The Museum of Modern Art Stills Archive, *Millenium Film Journal,* Fred Camper, The Ryerson Library of the Art Institute of Chicago, and above all Francene Keery provided illustrative material not already in Anthology Film Archives. Graduate and undergraduate students of Cinema Studies at New York University transcribed Peter Kubelka's lectures; Sue Ann Estevez and Steven Weisberg helped to edit and type them. Jonas Mekas and Marjorie Keller shared the proofreading. Steven Weisberg worked arduously on the early stages of this book and Susan Greene contributed to every phase of its production.

P.A.S.

For Raimund Abraham

CONTENTS

INTRODUCTION

1

Can there be a history of the independent cinema? Insofar as it calls itself *in*dependent or avant-garde, admirably introducing a negative element into its epithet, it reflects back upon another cinema, itself unnamed and undefined, against the darkness of which it shines. We certainly have histories of this other cinema, narratives of technological change, industrial growth, and national enclosures embroidered with the stories of an almost monomorphic hero called alternately Griffith, Chaplin, Méliès, Eisenstein, von Stroheim, Dreyer, Bresson. There is no scandal here: their very films could provide the models for the meticulous fictions of Sadoul, Mitry, Gregor and Patalas, Toeplitz, Wright.

If we are to take seriously the rejection of linear narrative which is nearly a defining feature of the independent cinema, how can we discuss the accumulated achievements of more than fifty years of film-making within such a framework? The occasion of editing this collection of theoretical and critical essays on the avant-garde film demands a reconsideration of this issue. The interrelationship between theoretical arguments and filmic practice in Peter Kubelka's work provides a starting point.

Kubelka's theory of cinema scrupulously avoids the rigidities of a written text. It has been enunciated for the most part over the past decade in a series of lectures, interviews, and above all academic courses in Europe and America. I have selected from transcripts of his numerous lectures at New York University passages which convey the gist of his ideas about "the metrical film." The original lectures were illustrated with films and loops; Kubelka often spoke while using an analysis projector and considered his gestures and intonations an essential part of his argument. Therefore the printed text is necessarily a very diminished version of his theory. I have also selected some brief statements from an interview he did with Jonas Mekas as a preface to the lecture materials.

Crudely synopsized we can say that Kubelka's theory stresses the importance of the static photogram (the single frame), while maintaining that the fundamental dynamic of cinema is not the illusion of movement but the "articulation" between individual photograms and between the images and the sound at the photogramic level. In the precisely metrical structures of *Adebar*, *Schwechater*, and *Arnulf Rainer*, these theoretical concerns find their practical origin. In the first two of these, visual references to fragmented and rigorously non-sequential actions (dancing, drinking) serve as foils for cinematic constructions which strenuously reject the intrusion of narrative time. In the third, *Arnulf Rainer,* the flickering of black and white photograms excludes even that brush with referentiality. It reorganizes the temporal experience of a brief sitting in the film theatre into a microrhythmical investigation of two axes of pure cinematic difference: black and white, sound and silence.

Most of what is called film theory can be bisected into an essentialistic quest for the irreducible basis of cinema and a series of descriptions—sociological, phenomenological, semiological—of the experience of viewing films as they already exist. The former tendency, of which Kubelka is a prime example, can be found chiefly in the writings of film-makers, while the latter represents the reflections on cinema by minds trained in the social sciences. Perhaps the most fecund constellations of theoretical work by film-makers came from the Soviet classic period and the avant-garde cinema which emerged after the Second World War and of which Kubelka's theoretical contribution forms a part.

Dziga Vertov, too, sought a radically new concept of cinematic time. For him the ecstasies of past, present, and future were political rather than chronological categories. As he repeatedly demonstrated in his films, often underlining the concept with intertitles, the only pastness accessible to a film-maker was the "reactionary" aspects of society; for him, religion, drunkenness, feudalism, and private capital were icons of pastness. All attempts to reconstruct unfilmed historical events, especially when attempted by conscious film-makers such as Eisenstein in *Potemkin* or *October,* earned his contempt, as fundamental misconceptions of the nature of temporal representation in film. The poles of past and future could be shown through images of capitalist and communist activity. The present was the field of rhetorical indeterminacy between shots which he attempted to describe with the musical metaphor of the "interval."

The concept of the "interval" is not fully elucidated within Vertov's writings, which are primarily either manifestoes or diaries. In the second Kino-Eye lecture he alludes to it obscurely. In the very early manifesto "We" (1922), he calls for the "Kinogram," the filmic equivalent of a musical scale which would abstractly delimit the possible figures of filmic construction. There the interval plays a major role:

> Kinokism is the art of organizing the necessary movements of objects in space by using a rhythmic and artistic ensemble which conforms to the material properties and the internal rhythm of each object.

> The Intervals (the transitions from one movement to the other), rather than the movements themselves, make up the material (the elements of the art of movement). The intervals carry the action towards its cinematic conclusion. The organization of movement is the organization of its elements, that is to say, of the intervals in a phrase. Each phrase includes an attack, a culmination, and a fall of

a movement (in one degree or another). A work is made out of phrases just as a phrase is built up from the intervals of a movement.

Eisenstein's continual quarrel with Vertov turned upon their different versions of the concept of "material" and of the essence of socialist cinema. Where Vertov seeks to discover the laws of cinema (the intervals) on the structural level and to utilize them for the foundation of a socialist ideology, Eisenstein looks to the relationship between film and its audience as the basis for the invention of ideological form. In the analogy of the locomotive (p. 17), he argues that revolutionary art will not emerge from "a 'quest' for forms corresponding to new content" (or what Vertov means by "the material properties and internal rhythms of each object."). Instead, the entire cinematic system of production must be reconceived according to socialist ideology, which corresponds to the factor of "steam" in the invention of the locomotive. In other words, this debate—which never formulated itself as such—entails Eisenstein's supposition that Vertov considers socialist cinema to be a special, albeit privileged, category within a larger more general theory of cinema. Vertov's response was that Eisenstein merely commercialized—and adapted to bourgeois narrative conventions—some of the results of the research of Kinokism.

In *The Man with a Movie Camera,* Vertov makes less use of this polemical conception of the temporal ecstasies than in most of his other films. Rather he postulates the simultaneity of three otherwise successive moments of the cinematic experience: filming, editing, projecting. As the representation of a day in a Soviet city, this film locates itself within the specifically avant-garde genre of the "city symphony" initiated by Cavalcanti with *Rien Que Les Heures* and brilliantly followed by Walter Ruttmann's *Berlin, Symphonie einer Grosstadt.* Yet unlike his predecessors, Vertov truncates the daily cycle, ending his portrait of the city in the evening when, as the very first shots of the film indicate, the populace goes to the cinema. Thus the literal time of watching the film opens to allow the rhetorical construction of a fictive day. Here the kinoki (cameramen, editors, projectionists) become the heroic technicians of an otherwise inaccessible vision of social organization.

Kubelka's *Unsere Afrikareise* shares with *The Man with a Movie Camera* a self-consciously metonymic style in which the referential continuity of adjoining shots is denied and replaced with an artificial ligature. Furthermore, Kubelka hyperbolizes the *ad hoc* status of the continuity by intricately synchronizing the images with sounds from obviously extraneous sources. Instead of replacing a mindless chronology with a politically viable temporality, Kubelka emphasizes both formally and thematically the eternality of the essential human order. One recalls, in fact, the parable of St. Augustine in the eleventh book of the *Confessions,* when he uses the recitation of a familiar psalm as a model for temporality. The reciter knows the whole of the psalm he speaks, while he utters each syllable, and after he has completed the prayer. Anticipation, action, and memory are perspectives on a temporal reality *sub specie æternitatis*. From the very same principles Kubelka repeatedly tells his audience that the authentic experience of his films comes once the viewer has memorized them the way one memorizes a familiar piece of music.

The formulations of both Kubelka and Vertov represent temporal strategies by which the avant-garde cinema declares its independence from the domination of chronology in narrative films.

2

The earliest impulses toward the establishment of an independent cinema arose from a desire to temporalize pictorial strategies by Cubist, Futurist, and Dadaist painters. The very last issue of Apollinaire's *Les Soirées de Paris* (1914) contained Leopold Survage's description of his ultimately unrealized film *Le Rythme Coloré*. From the same period both Kandinsky and Schoenberg conceived of film projects which were never executed. The text of Survage's "Le Rythme Coloré" has been translated, and the projects of Kandinsky and Schoenberg have been analyzed in the first book of the Anthology Film Archives Series, Standish Lawder's *The Cubist Cinema*. The earliest films actually completed by major figures of the "Modern" movement seem to have been lost or destroyed soon after they were shown; only stills remain today of *La Vita Futurista,* a collective effort involving Marinetti, Ginna, Balla and others. *The Futurist Cabaret Number 13* of Larionov and Burilik seems also to have disappeared.

The graphic film-maker repudiated the rich inheritance that film accepted from photography. The first film-makers, the Lumières and their cameramen, utilized with glory the deep space and receeding movement available to the camera lens, which had been ground in conformity with an idea of perspective emanating continuously from the Renaissance. The first graphic film-makers came to cinema from painting, especially from Cubism and geometrical abstraction. They believed that they could discover the essential in cinema only after they rejected the ease with which it recorded illusory depth. This was the reason many of them turned to animation. It was one route to the flatness of the modernist canvas.

Four central works of the graphic cinema in its initial stage deserve special attention here: *Rhythmus 21, Symphonie Diagonale, Le Ballet Mécanique,* and *Anemic Cinema.*

Hans Richter and Viking Eggeling worked and lived together when they made their first films. For both men, cinema seemed a natural extension of their scroll paintings. In 1920 they convinced U.F.A. to aid them with film experiments. Out of these experiments came Richter's *Rhythmus 21* and Eggeling's *Symphonie Diagonale.* For many years, informed taste preferred Eggeling's film to

Richter's; in their shared aspiration to achieve a musical construction from elementary plastic shapes, Eggeling's film achieves a complexity of repetition, inversion, and variation that is lacking in Richter's. Yet recently taste seems to have shifted; one finds critics preferring *Rhythmus 21* for its frank use of purely cinematic materials—the empty screen, black and white alternation, the disappearance and re-emergence of simple shapes.

The shift in taste reflects a serious change in the concept of cinematic form among avant-gardists over a fifty-year period. Naturally this will become more apparent as this history progresses. Briefly, one sees the birth, evolution, and decline of the musical organization of filmic time. Simultaneous to that decline is a renewed interest in the overall shape of a film. It is precisely in its elaboration of a shape that *Rhythmus 21* becomes a prophetic film.

It opens with the empty white screen. The edge moves from one side until the whole is black. That sweep is repeated from the other side; then the top and bottom edges converge on the center. Out of the alternations of full screen transformations of black and white emerges a white square which crosses the screen in various ways and dives in and out of its virtual vanishing point deep in the center. Through the multiplication of squares and the incorporation of negative images which again transform the black/white relationships, Richter gradually constructs a complicated composition reminiscent of a Mondrian. Although the image remains only briefly before the accelerated decomposition of the variations in the last moments of the film, one feels that the whole film has led up to this fleeting image. Its shape then suggests a slow crescendo and a rapid diminuendo, affirming throughout the square of the screen and the alternation of black and white as the essentials of cinema.

In his manifesto "The Badly Trained Sensibility," Richter reiterates and enlarges upon the position of Survage, who had written:

> A static abstract form is still not expressive enough. Whether round or pointed, oblong or square, simple or complex, it only produces an extremely confused *sensation*: it is only a simple graphic notation. Only when set in motion, undergoing change, entering into relations with other forms, is it able to evoke a *feeling*.

To this general thesis Richter adds the fascinating proposition that abstract film is able to achieve "feeling" through its unique temporality; for by divesting itself of photographic objects it reorients the work of "memory." The mind, free from associations which the sentimental cinema exploits, experiences time as feeling.

Fernand Léger's *Ballet Mécanique* sets itself several tasks: an anatomy of cinematic rhythm, comparing regular movements within a shot to rapid montage; the intensification of awareness towards objects, including the human body as an object; and a synthetic view of choreography of ordinary things and common actions (whence the title).

The optical space of the film is made shallow as a result of concentrating on objects, by means of closeups without establishing shots, masking out portions of the picture, the placement of objects against a shallow backdrop, and unusual angles of camera placement. The editing involves loop printing (repetition of the same shot without interruption), rapid intercutting of geometric forms, inversion, rapid intercutting of two views of the same object, animation of objects into crude "dances," and especially comparison of movements by juxtaposition.

The whole of the film evolves through a conflict between deep and shallow space, between moving and still images, in such a way that the longer rhythmic movements (the girl on the swing, the washerwoman climbing the steps over and over, the rotation of gears and pistons, the moving prismatic distortions) form a kind of visual consonance and the shorter flat images a dissonance.

An interesting example of the cinematic application of a standard cubist strategy occurs at the end * of this film when Léger plays with the headline "ON A VOLE UN COLLIER DE PERLES DE 5 MILLIONS." Clement Greenberg has described the evolution of the flattened cubist canvas: "The first, and until the advent of pasted paper, the most important device that Braque discovered for indicating and separating the surface was imitation printing, which automatically evokes a literal flatness." When the words first appear, we tend to read them as if they were written on the screen itself, without depth. Then Léger cut back and forth between three zeros in this sequence. The central zero is seen in closeup; then a long shot shows all three. The change of scale emphasizes the virtual depth between camera and image even though the white oval on a black base has no depth in itself. Furthermore, Léger returns to the zeros to dolly to and away, making doubly explicit the sense of camera depth. He also shows the writing upside down, and in fragments, to formalize its literal message.

In 1926 Marcel Duchamp enlisted the help of Man Ray and Marc Allegret to make a film of his rotoreliefs, mechanized disks with spiral lines and printing. The resulting film, *Anemic Cinema,* alternates a series of flat spirals which appear to recede or protrude from the screen when they move, with a series of puns printed spirally which appear perfectly flat as they are read. The issue of the relationship of the image to language, of which the Surrealists made much at the same time, becomes uniquely inflected. The sexual allusions in the puns tempt the viewer to read the spiral illusions as breasts, penises, vaginas, even feces. Yet this association is so deliberately tenuous that the very tendency to associate is

---

* Most versions of this film have this sequence in the middle, including the copies analyzed by Lawder in *The Cubist Cinema.* However, the print originally screened by Frederick Kiesler at the film's premiere has recently come into the possession of Anthology Film Archives. In this version the text occurs as an epilogue to the film.

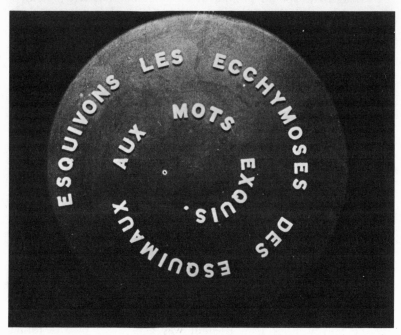

Anemic Cinema [Museum of Modern Art Stills Archive]

brought into question. Here cinema itself is represented as anemic: shallow, the play of optical illusions, indeed a toy for inducing effects within a spectator's imagination. "L'aspirant habite Javal et moi j'avais l'habite en spirale," reads one of the disks. The *je* or "I" here is not that of the film-maker or pseudonym Rrose Sélavy, but an empty phoneme vainly aspiring to a reference with which it can never make contact.

While eliminating rhythm and analogy which are so important in *Ballet Mécanique*, Duchamp created a work whose radical importance did not become apparent until the late 1960's when avant-garde film-makers began to reconsider the relationship of images to words.

3

These four crucial works by Eggeling, Richter, Léger, and Duchamp either repudiate or reduce to a paradoxical status the authority photography has had in maintaining the Renaissance conception of haptic space. Furthermore they ignore the privileges of diachronic causality as a model for filmic construction. Instead they articulate a purely cinematic temporality, called "rhythm," which either excludes or subverts mimetic representation.

Although the spatial prejudices of the manufactured system of lenses and registration which are the givens of cinematic representation could be overcome by the techniques of animation and distortion characteristic of the graphic cinema, the temporal reconditioning of the mechanism was more problematic. The sheer successiveness with which the camera records images inscribes a linearity within the very act of cinematic recording. From the beginning, Lumière's cameramen realized the comic or startling potential of the simple reversibility of that succession: they cranked the projection of divers at the Baths of Diana so that they arose from the un-splashing water and flew to the diving board. As early as 1915, the psychologist Hugo Munsterberg conceived of the dramatic potential in the reordering of the camera's automatic succession:

We might use the pictures as the camera has taken them, sixteen in a second. But in reproducing them on the screen we change their order. After giving the first four pictures we go back to picture 3, then give 4, 5, 6, and return to 5, then 6, 7, 8, and go back to 7, and so on. Any other rhythm, of course, is equally possible. The effect is one which never occurs in nature and which could not be produced on the stage. The events for a moment go backward. A certain vibration goes through the world like the tremolo of the orchestra.

By the mid-twenties Jean Epstein was captivated by the formal possibilities of manipulating different speeds of recording. It is remarkable that despite these theoretical insights, no film-maker made radical use of the independence of otherwise successive photograms within a shot before Peter Kubelka made *Schwechater* (1958), where the individual photograms of a series of simple gestures, of pouring and drinking, are organized in a rhythmical, rather than representational, manner. Until that moment the fundamental attack on the linearity of filmic time took place at the level of the shot change rather than photogramically.

Jean Epstein himself was one of the most interesting figures in film history. Initially a poet, he made forty-one films between 1922 and 1948; yet only one, *La Chute de la Maison Usher* (1928) remains available in American distribution. In it he combined two Poe stories, "The Fall of the House of Usher," and "Ligeia" to depict the darkest aspect of the artistic imagination through a Pygmalion myth in reverse, where the painting draws the life of the beloved model. No other film of this period so powerfully uses the visual representation of sound. Here the Orphic music of the artist, who plays a guitar, and the forces of nature shift continually between cause and effect, initiation and inspiration, delusion and actuality. Epstein portrays a hopelessly obsessive aesthetic vision as a wild confusion of mind and materiality through the use of differing degrees of slow motion.

Slow motion becomes the vehicle through which sound effects are visualized. A considerable emphasis in Epstein's theoretical work (he wrote seven brilliant books, all untranslated into English) is placed on the different speeds of the camera. The constitution of an object and its narrative function, he held, is dependent upon the speed at which it is filmed. The climax of *Usher* illustrates this principle in several ways: the intensity of the wind is visualized through the speed of rustling drapery and of waves on the lake; while the mood within the chateau is rendered by the slow turning of the pages of a book (as it is read by the owner's guest, whose deafness is a foil to the elaborate sound imagery), or the superimposed reverberations of a guitar string as it breaks, and the superimposed hammering of coffin nails as it echoes in the artist's mind.

In his masterful *La Glace à Trois Faces* (1927) Epstein demonstrated his inventiveness with narrative forms. He chose a simple story by Paul Moran as his vehicle; in it a playboy breaks dates with three different women to take a fatal drive by himself. Epstein uses four different cinematic styles to represent the perspectives of the four characters. At the time the film was released he published the essay "Event Art," in which he wrote:

> And two women, unknown to each other, by means of sixty feet of film, are brought together in the eye of the viewer, and there only is their true note sounded: just as the notes of a chord separated by a half-octave surrender their musical significance only in the ear of the musician.
>
> Banality is the least relative sign of truth. This studied, searched out, decomposed, multiplied, detailed, applied banality will give the

cinematographic drama a striking human relief, a hugely increased power of suggestion, an unprecedented emotive force.

The accelerated or slowed-down events will create their own time, the time proper to each action, to each character, our time. In elementary school, the first compositions are written in the present tense. The cinema tells everything in the present, right down to the subtitles. As they learn more grammar and rhetoric, the students begin to mix pasts and futures in their stories, bringing them into harmony. The fact is that there is no real present; today is a yesterday, perhaps an old one, which obliquely bears a tomorrow, perhaps a distant one. The present is an uncomfortable convention. In the midst of time, it is an exception to time. It escapes the chronometer. You look at your watch: the present, strictly speaking, is gone already, and strictly speaking, is there again. It will always be there from one midnight to the next. I think and therefore *I was*. The future "I" bursts into a past "I"; the present is nothing more than this instantaneous and incessant molt. The present is only a meeting.

Cinematography is the only art that is capable of representing it as such.

A careless motorist seems an insignificant character; a swallow on the wing, even more so; their meeting: event.

This tiny spot engraved by the bird's beak on the man's forehead, had against it the will of three hearts, the miraculous vigilance of love, all the probabilities of the three dimensions of space, all the chance of time.

But it took—it's the proper word—place.

Supersaturation freezes the crystal in an instant. So it is with the drama, like the egg at the fingertips of the naked magician, come out of nothing, of everywhere. All around, characters and actions, submissively fall into order. Toward the future lies a false track which in its turn will undergo the surprising intersection with the absolute. Toward the past, the idyll, read backwards, is tragedy. The episodes each find their place, in order, deduced, bound together, comprehensible, understood. *Exactly—the actors intimate— that's why we were there.* As in the beautiful syntax of a Latin sentence, from the final verb, you come back to the subject.

The superabundance of musical, linguistic, and temporal models suggested in this brief passage is characteristic of Epstein's early theoretical writings. He was fundamentally an avant-garde figure, although he was never comfortable within any avant-garde "movement." In the two early texts I have selected for this anthology, he writes of the essence of cinema and of the avant-garde. His ideas overlap in both essays, as he is attempting to expand and illuminate the concept of "photogénie" which his predecessor Louis Delluc introduced into French film theory. For Epstein, the photogenic, or what is essentially cinematic, demanded a dialectical relationship to any given technique, which he considered merely contingent, and entailed the recognition of interrelationships among space, time, and material things within the radically idealistic structure of filmic illusion. In his later texts, he demonstrated his philosophical training by bringing the ideas of the Pre-Socratics and Spinoza to bear on film theory, showing how the relativity of camera speeds could underline the paradoxes of both atomism and pantheism.

The tendency which I have somewhat arbitrarily called "subjective" (to distinguish it from the graphic) raises a series of questions about the character of cinematic representation while operating within the spatial and temporal conventions of the dominant cinema, often to subvert them. Drawing its model from oneiric activity, the subjective cinema needs photographic illusionism to constitute one of its essential moments; the other being the discontinuity of montage. Three examples of silent Surrealist cinema will illustrate this tendency; *Etoile de Mer* by Man Ray and Robert Desnos, *La Coquille et le Clergyman* by Germaine Dulac, and *Un Chien Andalou* by Salvador Dali and Luis Buñuel.

Etoile de Mer operates through a series of polarities which variously contradict and converge upon each other; word/image, conventional photography/anamorphosis, and images and words in opposition to their referents. Early in the film the title "Les dents des femmes sont des objets si charmants . . ." is followed ironically with a shot of a woman's legs. The comic substitution of legs for teeth manifests a deeper allusion to the vagina dentata, a mythic obsession which seems to motivate many of the images of the film from the initial shot of an opening doorway photographed through stippled glass so that it suggests a female sexual organ, through an otherwise unaccountable scene of impotence in which the contemplative hero bids "Adieu" to the woman he is pursuing the moment she strips herself before him, to finally, the image of a living starfish, which he holds in a glass cylinder, as a metaphor for the vagina dentata.

The first title, "Les dents des femmes . . ." completes itself "Qu'on ne devrait les voir qu'en rêve ou à l'instant de l'amour." Thus the model of the dream is immediately introduced into this film. The relationship between the film experience and dreaming, as well as the privileged access of cinema to representing the dream work, are persistent themes of the avant-garde film. In the American films of the 1940's this will become the major mode of independent filmmaking. Man Ray and Desnos however are not content to stop at the dream suggestion. In the rest of the film they gradually dissect the junctions of picture and text. When the titles announce that the woman of the film is "belle comme une fleur de verre" the poetic text puns upon itself (verre/vers) and gestures toward the mediation of the stippled glass through which most of the film is anamorphically recorded and even towards the latent sheets of glass in all lenses.

The texts from Germaine Dulac that I have selected here represent for the first time in English a survey of her contributions to film theory, and in particular, her formulation of the concept of pure cinema. When she made *La Coquille et le Clergyman* (1927) she was entering a crucial stage of her film-making career. Later that same year she completed the much more artistically successful film, *L'Invitation au Voyage*, which like her earlier *La Souriante Madame Beudet* (1923) impressionistically explores a woman's erotic day-dreams and her dissatisfaction with her daily life. The following year she realized three important short films, *Disque 927* and *Thèmes et variations* (two abstract montages of images inspired by classical music, which I have not been able to view in their entirety) and the slow-motion nature study *Germination d'un Haricot*. In 1929 she made another abstract film, this time inspired by Debussy, *Etude Cinégraphique sur une Arabesque*.

In *La Coquille et le Clergyman*, Germaine Dulac attempted to do justice to a script by Antonin Artaud. Artaud seems to have detested the film. Together with some Surrealist friends he caused a commotion at its opening and had to be removed from the theatre. Nevertheless one would not surmise from his writings on cinema the reputed degree of his rejection of the film. In the essay "Cinéma et l'abstraction," he praised the actors and thanked Dulac for her interest in his script, "which seeks to penetrate the essence of cinema and does not pay the slightest heed to art or life."

Of the scenario itself he wrote in the same essay: "It does not tell a story, it develops a series of mental states, which proceed one from the other like thought deduced from thought without reproducing a logical chain of events. From the collision of objects and gestures real psychic situations deduce themselves between which the cornered intellect seeks a subtle escape." Dulac employed slow motion, split images, and optical distortions in her adaptation of the scenario about a priest's displaced lust for a beautiful woman who comes to his confessional.

Artaud had no patience for the exploration of pure cinema. The article I have selected for this anthology, "Sorcery and the Cinema," affirms the power of raw cinema, even unenhanced by the technical options of transformation through the camera, to assume a central role in art, at the moment when the symbolical power of language ("son pouvoir du symbole") was dissolving, by repudiating narrative and seeking a "subtle," "secret," and internalized order among images.

The implicit dialogue between the texts of Dulac and Artaud approximates the exchange between Vertov and Eisenstein and anticipates the theoretical debates within the American avant-garde cinema. On the one hand, there is a vision of a pure or essential cinema, the pursuit of which would constitute a radically new genre for film. On the other hand, some theoreticians seize upon the idea of an important and revolutionary change in art as a whole for which cinema would be the perfect vehicle. Interestingly both positions appropriate metaphors of music and language to justify their claims.

Un Chien Andalou is one of the purest examples of Surrealist cinema, which rejects the exploitation of imagery engendered by the camera. Robert Desnos, who was a film reviewer as well as a poet, used the occasion of its premiere to attack Epstein, Gance, L'Herbier, and the idea of an avant-garde cinema in general. He gave it a higher status than *Entr'Acte* or *L'Etoile de Mer* (both of which he admired) and considered it among the highest achievements of the cinema, along with the films of Chaplin, Stroheim, and Eisenstein, as a work "indisputably human, sane, and poetic."

In *Un Chien Andalou* the examination of cinematic principles is shifted completely to the level of temporality. It is as if the camera had the same access to the visible world as a window pane. In fact, in the middle of the film, when the protagonist looks lustfully down upon the androgyne hit by an automobile, he presses his face against the upper storey window from which he is watching her. The window as a barrier through which the visible world enters but which cannot be transgressed is an icon of Buñuel's and Dali's conception of cinema. Like the major Surrealist painters, especially Magritte, they accepted three-dimensional illusionism as the "rational" ground for irrational juxtapositions. In this film the juxtapositions take place sequentially but are edited so as to appear, through the second illusionism of narrative montage, simultaneous. The strategies of metaphor, synecdoche, and metonomy by which the simultaneity is sustained become the structural models of the film's formal development. For instance, the opening of the film elaborates a visceral metaphor in which a thin cloud passing before the moon is substituted for an image of a razor slicing a woman's eye. However, immediately after the metaphoric substitution which suggests, without representing, the horrible operation, the film-makers show us the vitreous fluid flowing out of the eye. The metaphor has called attention to its own failure as a substitute and yet has provided the moment for a subtler substitution in which a cow's eye, in close-up, can be substituted for the woman's eye. We see, then, in immediate succession an antithetical metaphor, whose very calmness evokes terrible violence, followed by an even more violent synecdoche.

The figure of synecdoche is thematically analyzed in the middle of the film when the protagonist is seen contemplating his hand. A following shot shows the hand alone with ants crawling out of a hole in the palm. This synecdochical illusion engenders a series of metaphors (a sea-urchin and a woman's armpit) ending in an image of a crowd of people gathering outside on the street around the androgyne like ants around the hole. The supervising policeman gives the hermaphrodite a severed hand, itself a metaphor for a synecdoche.

4

Le Sang d'un Poète, Jean Cocteau's first film, bridges the transition from an avant-garde cinema centered in Paris to one dominated by Americans. For of all the independent films from Europe this one had the most influence on those who would revive the avant-garde cinema toward the end of the Second World War. Two aspects of Cocteau's film give it this privileged position: its manifestly reflexive theme, and its ritual. The film opens with an allegory of the relationship of the authorial persona to the temporality of cinematic representation. We see Cocteau, surrounded by the klieg lights of a movie studio, blocking his face from the camera with a classical dramatic mask, which foreshadows the moment in the film when the film-maker will declare in a handwritten title that he is trapped in his own film; yet what we see of him then is still another mask, this time fashioned after his own profile. The declaration of the enigmatical distance between the authorial self and his mediating persona is coordinated with a bracketing device that affirms that the film transpires in no time, or in the instant between two photograms. We see a towering smokestack begin to crumble, an image reminiscent of many of the Lumières' one-shot films. At the end of the film the smokestack completes its fall.

The Hôtel des Folies Dramatiques which the poet explores after crossing the threshold of the mirror is a series of rooms, accessible only to sight through the keyhole. In each a principle of cinematic illusionism is illustrated with the naive exuberance of Méliès films which Cocteau must have first encountered in his childhood. The assassinated Mexican is revived in reverse motion; camera placement allows us to see a girl clinging to walls and ceiling; finally, a hermaphrodite is constructed of flesh, drawn lines, and a roto-relief in Duchamp's style so that it is not only an illusionary blending of male and female characteristics but a figure synthesized from the very arts which feed into cinematic representation. The myth of the poet that Cocteau elaborates moves freely among centuries and between childhood and maturity.

The temporal ambiguity that Cocteau postulated between any two consecutive frames of a continuous shot operated independent of the camera which photographed that shot. In Maya Deren's reworking of that suspended temporality, account would be taken of the status of the camera in cinematic metaphors of reflection. She did not do this as Vertov had done and as many would begin to do in the 1960's by introducing the film-making apparatus into the imagery of the film. Her early, and best, films dwell instead upon the temporal and spatial complexities of representing the self in cinema. In *Meshes of the Afternoon,* which she made with her husband, the film-maker Alexander Hammid, there is a moment after the heroine, played by herself, has fallen asleep when she dreams of seeing herself. She stands before a large window, looking out upon a bright California landscape in mid-afternoon, with her hands pressed against the glass. A reverse shot from outside shows her hair blended with the reflection of off-screen trees, her hands defining the barriers of the glass, and her eyes in a distracted, almost narcissistically inward gaze. The montage will establish that she is watching herself through the window repeating with symbolic displacement the very entrance to her house which preceded her sleep. Here the window, as a metaphor for cinematic representation, has neither the amorphous presence of Man Ray's distorting lens or the barrier quality of the window in *Un Chien Andalou;* it is, rather, a mirror. For Deren, and subsequently for most of the American independent film-makers who followed her, film-making was essentially a reflexive activity.

In many of the American films of the 1940's the reflexive relationship between the authorial subjectivity and the Selfhood represented in the film was mediated simply by the film-maker's crossing over to become his own central actor. Deren did this in three of her first four films. Yet more significant than this elementary transformation of the fiction into psychodrama was the elaborate structure of metaphors by which these films comment upon the problematic status of their imagery and their temporal structures. In her last essay, "Cinematography: The Creative Use of Reality," she formulates a reflexive relationship between all photographic representation and the world in the passage in which she writes of the "implicit double exposure" which the mind makes in recognizing the reference of a photographic image. In *Meshes of the Afternoon,* the mirror metaphor has an entire morphology: she pursues a black figure who turns out to have a mirror for a face; at the climax of the film, a knife that had menacingly recurred several times before, reflects her face just before she plunges it into the face of her lover; finally that violent attack turns out to be a stab not at his flesh but at its reflection in still another mirror. Throughout Deren's work the cinematic image has the fragility of a mirror image.

At Land works out more meticulously the temporal status of this imagery. In that film, Deren portrays herself as washed out of the backward rolling sea. Once on the shore, she begins a quest through several contrasting landscapes, ostensibly in search of some stable sexual identity. As she moves from one landscape to another, the compositions and the allusions to off-screen space are so coordinated as to make those disparate spaces seem continuous. In fact, with *A Study in Choreography for Camera,* she generated an entire short film from this principle: the stretch, spin, and leap of a dancer through radically different spaces is portrayed as one continuous gesture. Implicit in such spatial paradoxes is the recognition of temporal disjunction between the time of filming and the time of representation. In *At Land,* this disjunction becomes thematic at the end of the film. There is a retrograde recapitulation of the principal scenes of the film in each of which the heroine is looking off-screen.

She introduces a new shot between each of these repeated elements showing the same heroine in approximately the position that the camera must have occupied to take the earlier one. A corresponding off-screen glance thus links the two versions of the same spatial field in an illusionary exchange of looks. Here she has not only pushed the metaphor of the mirror into a formal mechanism, but she has also accounted for the temporary omniscience of the camera and prepared the way for a final image in which the problematics of cinematic representation find a culminating metaphor. The shot begins with her feet as she runs along the sand of the beach where she first was seen; as the camera pans from her footprint to her running figure she has travelled much farther than the time of the pan could allow. Here through an elementary trick of stopping and starting the camera the temporal instability of the most elementary cinematic successiveness (that within the shot) is demonstrated. Furthermore the choice of imagery is significant. For a footprint is an indexical sign (in the trichotomy of C.S. Peirce); that is, it both signifies the passage of the runner and it simultaneously seems to have been *caused* by that runner. A bullet hole is another indexical sign; so indeed is a photograph. Photography, and therefore cinema, seldom fully escapes from the seduction of the indexical, which postulates at some earlier time the phenomenal presence of a camera to its object. The ambiguity of this polarity and its problematical "presence" in past time is the very theme of Deren's *At Land*.

5

Maya Deren called herself a Classicist to distinguish her theoretical position from both the Surrealists and the practitioners of the graphic cinema (which she felt was nothing more than a form of painting in cinema). For her the central contribution of cinema was its temporal dimension. For her this meant accepting the conventions of spatial representation according to the dictates of the traditional lens and registration apparatus as the very ground for cinema. She wrote: "If cinema is to take its place beside the others as a full-fledged art form, it must cease merely to record realities that owe nothing of their actual existence to the film instrument." Also, "The impartiality and clarity of the lens—its precise fidelity to the aspect and texture of physical matter—is the first contribution of the camera." Its other and more fundamental contributions allow for the transfiguration of temporal complexes. The polemical position was first answered in the American context by the work of Sidney Peterson.

After an initial collaboration with the poet James Broughton on the film *The Potted Psalm* (1946), Peterson made a series of films under the limited sponsorship of the California School of Fine Arts where he taught what was probably the first class in avant-garde film-making. *The Cage* (1947), the first film to emerge from that situation, combined the subgenres of the city symphony and what I have called "the trance film" in my long study of the American avant-garde film *Visionary Film*. By "trance film" is meant those subjectivistic films in which a protagonist wanders through a menacing landscape, as if entranced, in quest of an epiphany of sexual identity. In *The Cage* a young painter dislodges his eyeball while attempting to expand his realm of vision. The subsequent imagery of the film alternates between a view of San Francisco from the point of view of the freely wandering eyeball, and the allegory of its pursuit by the wounded painter, his girlfriend, and a malevolent doctor. What is most interesting about the film is the way in which the theme of consciousness as pure vision, which has been part of the American aesthetic tradition since Emerson and which dominates much of the theory of Abstract Expressionism, receives its filmic treatment. The liberated eyeball experiences a fundamentally temporal disorientation; it is incapable of seeing sequentially; it even sees forward and backward motion simultaneously. Peterson cinematically explores the postulate that temporality is a bodily rather than visual function.

One of his most successful films, *Mr. Frenhofer and the Minotaur* (1949) combines elements of Balzac's novella *Le chef d'oeuvre inconnu,* Joycean interior monologue, and the imagery of Picasso's "Minotauromachie." The rhythmical intercutting of elliptical scenes from the story, as well as shots of two characters *reading* the story, images from the etching, and a continual monologue of puns, allusions, displacements, and metaphors, makes for a system of shifting levels of reference in a complex interplay between the passions of artists and the passions depicted in their art; between the act of modeling as a paradigm of film acting, and the representation of the model in painting, film, and dream. The shifting images are visually unified by the consistent use of anamorphic photography.

Peterson described his ambitions in making *Mr. Frenhofer and the Minotaur* thus:

> It was my decision to do a thing about the Balzac story, taking seriously as the theme of the story the conflict between Poussin's Classicism and its opposite. So strained through my mind it became really a way of exploring the conflict stated in Rousseau's remark to Picasso: "We are the two greatest painters; you in the Egyptian manner, and I in the modern."

In the dialectic of the history of the American avant-garde film, Peterson reformulated the Picasso-Rousseau distinction as one between himself and Deren. He refused to accept the clarity of the conventional lens as a value. Instead he insisted upon a cinema in which the very space of representation was invented by the filmmaker. Thus in his ironic rendering of the Balzac story Frenhofer's palimpsestic destruction of the portrait of the ideal woman becomes a visionary forecast of Abstract Expressionism, while the fantastic imagery of Picasso's etching became another form of neo-classical idealism.

Broughton's filmic practice has tended to overlap with his activity as a poet and director of plays. Several of his films are organized with the economy and frontality of a theatrical production. This is not to say that Broughton is unaware of the specificity of cinema: in *Mothers' Day* he concentrates upon the temporal disjunctions between memory and its cinematic representation. The film takes the form of a family album in which the narrator attempts to reconstruct both his own childhood memories of his mother and the myth she has told of her courtship and marriage. Throughout the film the temporal figures continually shift into psychological metaphors. For example, the first image of the mother framed in the upper storey window of an old house is followed by an image of a similar house in an advanced stage of destruction. The coupling of the shots emphasizes the irrevocable loss of time while at the same time the mother is identified with the empty facade of the structure. All through the film, the mother's children are represented as adults playing children's games; here again the temporal bind in which the narrator can only picture the children as grown-ups blends into the metaphoric perspective of childish adults.

Broughton uses the cinema for both the evocation and the analysis of an ironic nostalgia. In *Mother's Day,* the cinematic tropes, the costumes from various periods, the representation of children's games by adults, and the formal association of the whole film with a family album, all serve to undermine the *presence* of the images and to locate the film in the mind of a remembering subject.

In many of his subsequent films, such as *The Adventures of Jimmy; Loony Tom, The Happy Lover; Four in the Afternoon;* and *This is It,* the interplay of verse or prose narration with the imagery creates comparable disjunctions of time. Broughton, like his contemporary Willard Maas, was poet before he became film-maker and also like him he believed that Cocteau's *Le Sang d'un Poète* provided the essential model for the avant-garde film of the future: a welding of montage and poetic language.

In his notes to *Mother's Day,* Broughton emphatically aligns himself with the position of Maya Deren, even including her favorite metaphor of choreography, against the Dionysiac cinema of Peterson ("camera trickery"). In his cyclic films, *Four in The Afternoon, The Bed, The Golden Positions,* Broughton incorporates choreographic movements into comic schemata of essential life rituals.

6

Kenneth Anger too has worked within the spatial framework of the dominant cinema. His first publicly screened film, *Fireworks,* describes a double dream in sado-masochistic homosexual imagery.

Significantly, a photograph occupies a central and paradoxical position within the film as both the source and residue of the dream. An opening passage of the protagonist held in the arms of a sailor, followed by a scene of the same protagonist waking, suggests that the former was his dream. This seems to be reinforced by the fact that a photograph, showing the same image as the dream, lies by his side, as if the source of his nocturnal masturbational fantasy has become "animated" in his sleep. Yet as the waking day proceeds, its mimesis veers progressively towards ironic displacements: for a match is substituted a bundle of burning sticks; for a heart, a metallic meter; for semen, cream; for a penis, a roman candle. The internal evidence then suggests that we are still within the oneiric model even before we see the final image of the protagonist still sleeping. What terminates the dream and allows us to see the sleeping figure unmediated by his own imagination is the burning of the very photograph which seemed the source of the dream. Here the space and time of the dream coincide with the duration of the photograph as a fetishistic object occupying a twilight area between an experience of dubious authenticity and the awakening into a full present which is continually postponed.

The filmic dream constituted for Anger, as it had for Deren, a version of the perceptual model that generated most of the subjec-

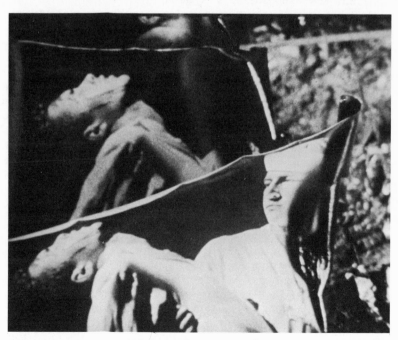

Fireworks: *the burning photograph.*

tive films of the American avant-garde. Whenever that model is operating, a subject/object polarity is established so that the camera's relationship to the field of its view reflects the functioning of a receptive mind to the objects of its perception. The metaphor of the dream permits the reflexive gesture of duplicating the presence of the film-maker (subject) or his mediator in front as well as behind the camera. The introduction of photographs or other iconic representations as objects of the camera's gaze merely adds another reflexive turn within the model without altering it. Thus *Mother's Day* postulates an organizing consciousness involved in some variant of nostalgia. Likewise the anamorphosis of Peterson's films pointed to a radically askew perspective grounded in a being upon whom the psychological and intellectual tensions of each film converged. As long as this model dominated the forms of this mode of film-making, the works it generated hovered near a solipsistic reduction of psychology to a transcendant self and a dialectically opposed Otherness, and naturally excluded were either the possibility of elaborating an interplay of several developed characters or the formal recognition of the mediating presence of a film viewer.

One of the most subtle and nuanced inflections of this model, and one which had enormous influence, was manifested in the cinema of Marie Menken. In a remarkable series of disarmingly unpretentious films she demonstrated a rhythmic inventiveness perhaps previously unmatched in the cinema. In *Notebook* she stored fragments from all phases of her cinematic career, from the mid-Forties to the late Sixties. There we can see how, at a time when most of her contemporaries were invoking the Dionysian imagination in their invented imagery, she was exploring the dynamics of the edge of the screen and playing with distinctions between immanent and imposed rhythm. The early and exquisite "Raindrops" dramatizes the subtle wit of Menken's version of the perceptual model. As she waits behind the camera for a drop of rain on the tip of a leaf to gather sufficient mass to fall, we sense her impatience and even anxiety lest the film will run out on her; so an unseen hand taps the branch forcing the drops to fall. Tampering in this way with an otherwise straight-forward observational film is characteristic of Menken, who cheerfully incorporates the extraneous reflection of herself and her camera, even her cigarette smoke, into an animated film and who makes the very nervous instability of the hand-held camera a part of the rhythmic structure of several films.

In *Arabesque for Kenneth Anger* she offers her fellow film-maker a version of his earlier *Eaux D'Artifice*. There Anger had made a water-dominated counterpart to his initial fire ceremony, *Fireworks*. A figure in a Baroque dress emerges from a fountain, which evokes a penis in orgasm, in flight or pursuit through fountains of the Tivoli gardens. The entire film was tinted a deep blue, and suggested the night passage of a frail psyche through an overpowering and menacing landscape until her eventual metamorphosis back into a fountain. Menken in contrast filmed a visit to the Alhambra in midday, achieving a comparable deep blue tone through the deceptively naturalistic choice of light sources and conventional blue-sensitive film stock. The spiraling flight of a pigeon among the roofs of the Alhambra provides her with an initial rhythmical figure and a metaphor for her wildly eccentric camera movements. Against this she plays the second metaphor, again deceptively naturalistic, of architecture reflected in a pool; a metaphor for the cinema's reduction of spatial configurations to a shimmering two-dimensional surface. The circles and swirls that her revolving camera imposes upon the Moorish structures can then be found translated into the rings that drops of water make in the pools reflecting the same buildings. This delicate mesh of observation and imposition which appears in almost all of Menken's films, inspired Stan Brakhage, who radicalized it and systematically explored its potential for the articulation of a new form within the avant-garde cinema.

7

Brakhage's *Anticipation of the Night* takes up the opening of *Meshes of the Afternoon* and elaborates it in terms of a Petersonian consciousness. We see those parts of the body which a subject sees of himself: the shoulders, the legs, and especially the outlined image it projects as the shadow. The shadow man of *Anticipation of the Night* leaves his home at the beginning of the film and encounters a series of sights of the natural and human universe as stations of imaginative loss which ultimately lead to his suicide at the end of the film.

In this film Brakhage fully achieves for the first time a dialectical fusion between the image represented on the screen and the film-maker/subject's reaction to it. By constantly moving the camera in imitation of the movement of the eyes and the fluctuations of attention, and by editing the movements in rhythms that suggest both the sudden and the gradual intrusions of memory and anticipation on the flux of the present, Brakhage mediates the visual world without a mediator. In his subsequent lyrical films the shadow man will disappear and the montage will directly represent vision and thought.

According to Brakhage's theory, vision has at least three aspects. The first is open eyesight which is a continual flux of focus and movement, sensuously probing the actual world that manifests itself before the eyes. The entire cinematic tradition, he would claim, had ignored this mode of primary seeing before him. Secondly he describes "brain movies" as images of the past or fantasies which briefly emerge before the visual imagination as if filmed from a fixed tripod. In this respect he is close to the brilliant early theories of Hugo Munsterberg, who claimed that cinema did not record the actual world so much as the reflective processes of the mind. Finally Brakhage would include the representation of "closed eye vision," the phosphenes which appear when we close our eyes in moments of intense psychological stress. All three modes of seeing merge together in his lyrical films.

Reading Gertrude Stein, Brakhage found a narrative mode which corresponded to his theory of vision and which guided his theory of temporality. All of Brakhage's lyrical films operate upon the fiction of a man, the film-maker, looking upon a natural sight and responding to it imaginatively. That encounter is always conceived as a crisis and the moment of the crisis provides the present tense and ground for the temporal ecstasies. For Brakhage the cinema is primarily a visual medium with no direct means of representing a past which has not been recorded on film, and certainly no future. He rejects the fictional dramatic film and bases his concept of temporality upon the discontinuity between shooting and editing.

At the beginning of his theoretical book, *Metaphors on Vision*, Brakhage was to write:

> Imagine an eye unruled by man-made laws of perspective, an eye unprejudiced by compositional logic, an eye which does not respond to the name of everything but which must know each object encountered in life through an adventure of perception. How many colors are there in a field of grass to the crawling baby unaware of "Green?" How many rainbows can light create for the untutored eye? How aware of variations in heat waves can that eye be? Imagine a world alive with incomprehensible objects and shimmering with an endless variety of movement and innumerable gradations in color. Imagine a world before the "beginning was the word."

Early in *Anticipation of the Night* the shadow man attempts to imaginatively reconstruct the adventure of grass to a preverbal infant. The camera moves through leaves and grass, encounters and pursues a rainbow, explores the tactility of ground movement and ultimately reveals the mediation of a crawling child whom the shadow man observes. The very structure of the sequence as hysteron-proteron, in which the childlike vision is imitated before the child is seen, suggests the ultimate failure of the imaginative attempt. Somewhat later the film-maker sees children delighting in the rides of an amusement park at night and tries to participate in their rapture, moving his camera in sympathy with their whirling movements. Finally, near the end of the film he sweeps over the sleeping bodies of children. Their stasis emphasizes the isolated consciousness of the film-maker. In this final and most extravagant attempt at recapturing the freshness of their vision he tries to imagine their animal dreams. Here the recovery is the strongest in the film, perhaps because it is without an external guiding gesture, but it too fails with the breaking of dawn and its implicit reduction

of the entire quest for renewed vision to a nightly cycle. The hand
of the shadow man fastens a rope to a tree and hangs himself.

8

By the early 1960's those forms I have been describing no longer
seemed to satisfy the most ambitious film-makers. They began the
elaborate mythic structures that equated the dialectics of individual
consciousness with the elemental struggles of gods, demi-gods, much
as the Romantic poets, Blake, Shelley, Hölderlin, and Hugo had
done. The major works of this phase, such as Anger's *Scorpio Rising*,
Markopoulos' *The Illiac Passion*, Harry Smith's *Heaven and Earth
Magic*, Jack Smith's *Flaming Creatures*, Brakhage's *Dog Star Man*,
and Jacobs' unfinished *The Sky Socialist* substitute archetypal conflicts for narrative exposition. The plurality of figures they present
as gods or titans are interiorized beings, and although the drive
towards the mythopoeia represents an attempt to overcome the
solipsism of the trance film and the lyrical film where the perspective is reduced to a negative selfhood and a menacing landscape (or
otherness), the resulting films for the most part offer fragmented or
unresolved myths which incorporate metaphors of their own failure
to escape solipsism.

Each of the central works of the mythopoeic phase presents its
own mode of mythology and its own strategy for questioning the
authority of its mode. Kenneth Anger's *Inauguration of the Pleasure
Dome* (first version, 1954) depicts a convocation of Egyptian and
Hellenic deities under the control of a Magus and a "Scarlet
Woman" from the mythopoeic imagination of his chosen master,
Aleister Crowley. From the opening ritual of waking and dressing,
the film acknowledges the *ad hoc* nature of its divine personifications. It is both the making new of ancient myths and a contemporary masquerade. The turning point of the film, the poisoning of
Pan and his subsequent *sparagmos,* coincides with the assuming of
new masks and the compounding of guises.

Only the first of Jack Smith's three major films, *Flaming Creatures, Normal Love* (begun 1963), and *No President,* was defini-
tively completed and distributed. All three exploited the chemical
changes that occur in film stock not used until long after the recom-
mended time range for exposure. Smith derived this heightened
textural ambiguity from seeing Ron Rice's picaresque portrait of a
beat poet, Taylor Mead, in *The Flower Thief.* However, he carried
it to an extreme that Rice had not exploited. By costuming his
actors in black and white gowns before flagrantly artificial white
backdrops, he capitalized upon the tendancy of outdated film stock
to wash toward whiteness. In the color film *Normal Love,* a comparable pastel effect was achieved by elaborating an imagery that
would coincide with the tendencies of outdated color material.

While Anger's *Scorpio Rising* describes the limitations of the

mythopoeic imagination by grounding it in Hollywood and historical archetypes, *Flaming Creatures* offers a more complexly ironic
version of the dialectic play of imagination and nature. In the
pivotal scene of the film an act of imagination, or more exactly of
the fancy, engenders a physical convulsion: the camera responds
to a comic orgy by gyrating in sympathy to it; yet before the orgy
is over, an earthquake occurs and the same spastic movement is
presented again as a response to the natural disaster.

A very different relationship between editing and mythopoeia can
be found in the long films of Gregory Markopoulos from this period.
In his early films *Psyche* and *Swain,* he had used impressive montages of recapitulation as an organizational principle in the former
and as the climax of the latter. *Twice a Man,* Markopoulos' version
of the myth of Hippolytus, employs a complex schema of memory
within memory and a shifting mediation in the minds of four
figures.

The ambiguous movement between recollection and prolepsis in
this film is grounded in the very structure of the editing of every
shot. Rather than directly splice one shot to the next and build his
dynamics on the stress accent of the point of change, as in the
classical montage of Eisenstein, Markopoulos will introduce one or
two frames of the forthcoming shot before the "present" shot is
completed; he also allows a series of brief flashes from the former
shot to recur periodically as echoes after the former shot has ended
its dominance. Thus one image breaks into the next in a moment of
vibrating fusions of past, present, and future time. With this structure operating throughout the film, Markopoulos can introduce
metaphors and complexly bracketed themes into his montage; he
can also shift easily to extended passages of recapitulation.

The film-maker saw in this system an affirmation of the priority
of montage over spatial transfiguration in the tradition I have associated with Maya Deren. In a crucial essay, "Towards a New Narrative
Film Form," * he joins her in rejecting the use of filters, anamorphosis, or any other means of transforming the elementary spatial
givenness of the cinematic image. He extends her commitment to the
immanent aesthetics of the filmic material in a direction she never
took, when he points out that the fact that all films are a strip of
still, rapidly changing, frames has been "understood only as a
photographic necessity." He emphasizes that rather than being a
contingent fact about cinema it is the potential source of its primary
structures. The elaboration of the operations of the single frame
then became the focus of Markopoulos' later theoretical work.

The Romantic myth of a divided and reunited Selfhood is the
subject of Harry Smith's *Heaven and Earth Magic.* There a female
figure is injected by a magician with a substance that simultane-

---

* Unfortunately, he has refused the right to anthologize his essays, following
the publication of his impressive collection *Chaos Phaos* (Temenos Press,
Florence 1971).

ously makes her ascend to heaven and divides her body. The mental landscape of heaven is envisioned in a series of cyclic attempts to reconstitute her, ending with both her and the magician being swallowed by a titanic figure. After they descend through his body in an elevator they are defecated by him, whole again, on earth.

Smith's film is the major instance of an animated mythopoeic film and also the example from this phase that most fully uses combined sound and image to attest to its fictionality. At the very beginning of the film, as the magician brings into the frame the basic elements out of which the woman will be initially constituted, we see him exit on screen right and then reenter from screen left as if he had walked around the back of the screen. Similar acknowledgements of the illusion of animation occur throughout the film. Figures move along arbitrary imagined lines against the back of the screen until suddenly a bridge will appear and they are bound to cross it as the only possible line of movement in the field of vision.

As a work of the graphic cinema Smith's film has a fundamental orientation toward the reorganization of spatial illusion. He wittily acknowledges this near the opening of the film when the magician pulls a photograph of a watermelon patch into the frame. The photograph has a horizon in Renaissance perspective, but the frame of the film does not. He takes a watermelon out of the photograph for his manipulation in the more ambiguous black field of the film.

When Smith speaks of sources for his mythopoeia, MacGregor Mather's presentations of the Kaballah, Wilner Penfield's open brain surgery on epileptics, and especially D. P. Schreber's *Memoirs of My Nervous Illness,* a link between radical myth-making as an exploration of the complexities of the self and paranoia manifests itself. Brakhage's major work on cinematic myth-making, *Dog Star Man,* (1961-64), also presents a radically individualized spatial field and explores divided consciousness and its self-inflicted torments.

I have discussed the intricate reflection on myth and time in this film at length in my book *Visionary Film.* The making of *Dog Star Man* occupied a crucial period in the development of Brakhage's exceptionally influential theories. His book, *Metaphors on Vision,* was edited and published during this period, even though some of its texts go back to the mid-Fifties. Here Brakhage articulated, in his involuted punning prose, the most radical version we have yet had of the Emersonian strain in American film theory. Cinema, according to Brakhage, aspires to the representation of the full range of optical sensations experienced by the film-maker, in active vision, in memory, and even with the eyes closed. The opening chapter of the book is reprinted here. Readers interested in film theory are urged to work through the whole volume, which is dense and complex, published by *Film Culture.*

Much of the complexity of Brakhage's writings derives from the ironies of formulating in words a theory of the interference of language with vision. One strategy he has used to control this problem has been to mediate his text with profuse allusions and quotation of poetry (as the place where language is most self-aware). In the letter to Yves Kovacs, he reinterprets the influence of Surrealism by bringing it into alignment with recent American poetics. The complementary question of the relationship of film to music dominates the letter to Ronna Page.

Bruce Baillie's major films occupy a region between the early lyrical films of Brakhage and the mythopoeic cinema that followed. *To Parsifal, Mass, Quixote,* even *Castro Street* and *Valentin de las Sierras,* are heroic poems without heroes. The characteristic strategy of Baillie is to find an image of exaltation or liberation—in the movement of a train, a flying spaceman, a motorcyclist, or a particularly sympathetic and usually aged face—which is at first valorized and emphasized by carefully selected music or an intricate mixture of natural and musical sounds. Yet the more sinister implications of these metaphoric vehicles are seldom far removed. In *Mass* and *Quixote* this tension within the imagery is polarized by an explicitly political structure and the ironic use of filmic quotations (from advertisements and commercial films) which specifically attribute a negative value to cinematic representation. *Castro Street* and *Valentin de las Sierras* lack the social context of the earlier films and rely more heavily on the ability of sensuous imagery to convey the antithetical structures of meaning. In fact, it is as they veer toward the apogee of this sensuousness that the contradictory movement is initiated: in *Castro Street* it is the slow movement of the train through a field of flowers that raises the polarity of natural and mechanical consciousness which is deceptively couched in the center of the film; while in *Valentin de las Sierras* the close loving attention to the wrinkled flesh of the ancient guitarist, whose song gives the film its title, reveals that he is blind. His blindness intensifies the pathos of his song and underlines the optical scrutiny of the wandering film-maker, who in this film presents himself as entering on horseback, but unseen, the village he records in a rich texture of close-up synecdoches. In his very attention to detail the film-maker seems to be avoiding any direct glance that would acknowledge his presence; in place of a self-image, he offers us the moving shadow of the horse which brings him to and away from his subject.

9

While Deren, Broughton, Peterson, Markopoulos, and Brakhage were mining their Surrealist, Dadaist, and Constructivist sources for a cinematic vocabulary with which to formulate crises of the self, another group of young American artists turned back to the geometrical abstraction of the Germans in the 1920s to revive the graphic cinema. Oskar Fischinger's presence in Hollywood during these years was a mediating influence. So was that of Len Lye in

New York. Along with Ruttmann, Richter, and Eggeling, Fischinger had been one of the originators of the geometrical style in film-making. Unlike all the others, he continued that work until the 1950s. The coming of sound helped him to realize his theories of synchronization between music and image. Lye, a New Zealander, may have been the first film-maker to paint images directly on film (others had certainly tinted shaped outlines before him). His work in England throughout the 1930s marks the highpoint of the fusion of kinetic montage with abstract color dynamics in the cinema.

The young Californian graphic film-makers Harry Smith, John and James Whitney, and Jordan Belson variously drew inspiration from Fischinger's mesh of geometry and melody and Lye's erratic vibrant colors and pulsing rhythms. Smith's early cinema was an attempt to translate music into color and shape. In 1950 he experimented in reversing this proposition by showing four films with a live jazz band. They responded to the images in a jam session as if to a leading instrument. The Whitneys developed a synthesizer which could simultaneously generate picture and sound. In their theoretical formulation of this synthesis, they saw their work as a reconciliation of the positions of Mondrian and Duchamp, the Neo-Platonic purist and the anti-aesthetic ironist. Belson eventually pushed his abstraction to the boundaries of representation where geometrical shapes mediate between suggestions of macro-cosmic and micro-cosmic imagery, for instance between an eye and galaxy or between a cluster of stars and swarm of bees.

Another powerfully influential figure was the collagist and box maker Joseph Cornell. His films were rarely seen until the late 1960s, but they were very important to those who did manage to see them. His collage films of the late Thirties, *Rose Hobart* and the "Children's Party" series, which he made by reediting other commercial films, are the masterpieces of their kind. Only Bruce Conner, who had not seen them, made collages of comparable intensity (*A Movie, Cosmic Ray, Report*) more than twenty years later. Larry Jordan assembled the "Children's Party" series according to Cornell's instructions in the late 1960s. His own graphic films testify to Cornell's influence as a cutout collagist. Jordan brilliantly animated cutout figures against both fixed and shifting backdrops. Unlike the Polish film-makers Lenica and Borowcyzk who practiced a similar technique, Jordan eschewed literalism. His collage films *Hamfat Asar, Gymnopedies, Duo Concertantes, Our Lady of the Sphere,* and *Orb* are allusive evocations of visionary ecstasies and terrors, organized through delicate rhythmic patterns of transformation.

Robert Breer's animation evolved from flat work (*Form Phases,* 1953) through a mixture of flat and shallow movements (cutouts alternating with crumpled papers, a mechanical mouse, bits of hand painting) in *Recreation* (1957) to a complex fusion of cartoon, collage, single frame changes, and live photography in *Fist Fight*

(1964). In this film he also incorporated a sense of the film-making process when he lifted the camera off the animation stand and walked outside with it, filming his feet as he went, to take a shot of the sun. Breer has moved between poles of synthesis and purification. In *Blazes* he created a spectacular barrage of fast images by shuffling a series of calligraphic designs and filming them over and over in different random sequences. *66* (1966) explores the formal options of flat colored shapes in an animation that works with extremely fast changes and unusually long holds in an eccentric alternation. *69* (1969) presents a similar set of options, explored and fragmented, with a new element of illusory depth. In *70* (1970), he abandoned shape, and sprayed areas of white cards with colored dyes. The film animates these unbounded color areas, fusing the free texture of the hand-painted film with the control of the frame by frame animation. In *Gulls and Buoys* and *Fuji*, the tension between animation and actual photography manifests for him a new form. Using a rotoscope technique, which ultimately dates back to Emile Cohl's invention, Breer freely copies, in crayon and ink, isolated details of originally photographed material (seascape scenes, a Japanese train ride). However unlike traditional rotoscopers like Cohl and MacKay, Breer chose to emphasize elementary cinematic dynamics in the photography, by utilizing zoom shots, panning, hand-held camera, or by shooting from a train window, and incorporating single frame editing, and then allowing the freest possible hand strokes in the copying. The results are two cinematic iconic texts which mysteriously refer to an indexical original, "lost in translation."

10

Wavelength reformulated the central analogy of the American avant-garde: *the camera as a model of cognition,* by veering away from Brakhage's attempt to translate the mechanical traces of the filmic process into optical and physiological functions. In Snow's film the camera and its lens maintain their status as physical tools while allowing for an interpretation as a complex model for perception. This tension within the structure of metaphor may be what Snow meant by "the beauty and sadness of equivalence" in his note on the film for the Fourth International Experimental Film Festival Catalogue, where he wrote: "I was thinking of planning for a time monument in which the beauty and sadness of equivalence would be celebrated, thinking of trying to make a definitive statement of pure film space and time, balancing of 'illusion' and 'fact', all about seeing."

The film begins with an act of pure recording as if the camera were a completely passive *tabula rasa* instrument capable of preserving without distortion the impress of the exterior world. The image shows an empty loft and the sound records the street noise outside of it. When people enter the loft carrying a bookcase we hear them in synchronization. But soon after, the natural sound is suspended and replaced by an artificially generated sine wave. On the visual track flashes of pure color, transitions to negative, slight superimpositions occur. Thus both the sound and picture recording instruments begin to generate their own subject matter.

The problematics of "equivalence" include the alternation of day and night which occurs suddenly, twice in the film, without disturbing the relentless forward zoom. During the day the metaphorical link between the recording instrument (camera) and its object (the room, *camera* in Latin) was emphasized by changes in the intensity of the light: when the interior of the room darkened, the street scene outside became visible as if the windows were the camera lens. When the details within the loft received illumination the exterior was burned out. At one point two people turn on a radio, which is an "equivalent" machine for gathering and translating sound waves. The Beatles "Strawberry Fields" is heard while the film-maker responds by shooting through a pink filter.

The first transition to night is accompanied by the violent entry of an intruder who collapses on the floor. When night returns after another day passage, a woman enters, looks toward the body (we have zoomed past it by now) and telephones for help. After she leaves, her image repeats in flashes of black and white superimposition, as a ghostly reminder of the immediate past echoing within the room. From this point the zoom proceeds into a still photograph of waves pinned on the wall.

The next to last shot is another superimposition. The closeup of the waves is placed over an image which frames the photograph on the wall. The temporal movement of the zoom is thereby represented in the compound image. By increasing the light on the photograph and fading out the framed image, Snow simulates the ultimate final movement in purely optical terms. In doing so, he reminds us that the zoom lens, unlike the moving camera, is static and represents virtual movement through the shifting optics of two lenses.

The trajectory of *Wavelength* is initially mechanical, then a fusion of mechanism and the humanized presence of the film-maker. But after the telephone call it provides a metaphor for a superhuman authority. At the middle stage, when the film-maker is co-present with this machine, Snow incorporates the strategies of Andy Warhol whose long takes of a man eating a mushroom (*Eat*), or of a building (*Empire*) and arbitrary zooming about in the room where someone is delivering a confessional monologue (much of *The Chelsea Girls*) were themselves deflations of the metaphor of the camera as an eye or the mind.

Wavelength might be construed as a complex reaction to both the early and the late Warhol styles: the fixed camera and the impulsive zoom. Warhol's unbudging camera was at first a radical dehumanization of the tactics of earlier film-makers within the American avant-garde. He recognized, at least implicitly, that their way of making cinema was closely bound to the aesthetics of Abstract Expressionism which he had been dehumanizing in his paintings. His shift to film-making involved an attack on the same front in a different medium. However as he became involved in making cinema, Warhol seems to have found himself possessed by the work of Jack Smith. Under Smith's influence, he slowly turned from the dialectically cold presentation of affective or at least private gestures (sleeping, getting a haircut, kissing, eating, etc.) to a cinema that focused on unstable psychologies and sadistically induced paroxisms of confession by its very refusal to be affected, as Stephen Koch has brilliantly analyzed in his book, *Stargazer*.

A subsequent filmic structure investigating the nature of the zoom lens was Ernie Gehr's *Serene Velocity*. The spatial illusion that Gehr analyzes is so radically reduced that it can no longer contain any human activities. Gehr set up a camera in the corridor of an academic building and photographed, one frame at a time, changing the exposure for each frame, phrases four frames long. Between each of the phrases he changes the position of the zoom lens. In the course of the film he moves from two close zoom positions in the middle of the lens' range to its extremes of distance and closeness. The only articulation of temporal movement within the imagery of the film is the gradual breaking of dawn, seen in the brightening of a window in a door at the end of the corridor in the last minutes of the film. For a viewer, the film describes a rhythmic crescendo; for although neither the camera position, nor the spatial field before it, changes, the illusionary movement of the zoom, from what appears to be a pulsing vibration, to a strenuous push-pull effect, creates increasingly greater optical tension and the concomitant effect of gradually destroying the spatial illusion by emphasizing the orthogonals of the corridor as a two-dimensional grid with each increment of the zoom ratio.

In his later film *Still*, it is the camera position that remains still while the ostensibly temporal difference between scenes shot from the same position, in clusters of superimposition, provides the structure of the film. Furthermore, by varying the light intensity of different layers of superimposition, Gehr can render the people and vehicles which pass before the optically "solid" cityscape with varying degrees of transparency. Thus the temporal flux which introduces differences in color and horizontal movements (and occasional diagonals as people cross the street) as *ad hoc* ephemera in a relatively shallow theatre is limited by the frontal mass of building facades at a right angle to the camera. A version of the same principle can be seen in Ken Jacobs' *Soft Rain*. There the film-maker shoots out a window over low rooftops, onto a city street with cars and people passing. A piece of black paper, hung in front of the lens, occupies an ambiguous optical space, as if it might be a windowshade. The projecting wall of a building next to the

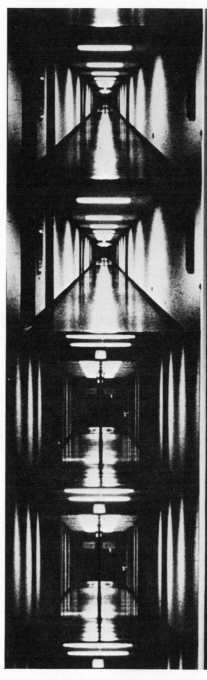

Serene Velocity

rooftops forms a perfect line from one edge of the frame to its geometrical center, but the eccentric angle of its photography calls attention to the very disparity between a geometrical and an illusionary reading of the space. The title of the film directs our attention to a drizzle on the threshold of perceptibility which becomes, according to the film-maker's intention, confused with the grain of the film. Finally a temporal pattern is manifested by the exact repetition of the same roll of film three times. However, the viewer must perform a deliberate act of memorizing arbitrary sequences of human and automobile movements, after the first roll has ended, in order to determine for certain whether or not the three rolls are indeed a repetition or three different takes of the same scene. In both *Still* and *Soft Rain* the absence of camera movement and the arbitrary patterns of movement help to establish an authority for the exterior scenes which is only gradually undermined when the active understanding of the viewer is engaged in spotting and following-up clues embedded in the image. The unusually long duration of the shot (within the standards of the dominant cinema) contributes to engaging the viewer's understanding by disengaging his sensual involvement with the illusionary image.

11

Brakhage's critique of the tripod has been part of his attack on the very resistance of filmic materials to conform to the subtleties of the representation of cognition. In *Metaphors on Vision* (1963) he wrote:

And here, somewhere, we have an eye capable of any imagining. And then we have the camera eye, its lenses grounded to achieve 19th century Western compositional perspective (as best exemplified by the 19th century architectural conglomeration of details of the "classic" ruin) in bending the light and limiting the frame of the image just so, its standard camera and projector speed for recording movement geared to the feeling of the ideal slow Viennese waltz, and even its tripod head, being the neck it swings on, balled with bearings to permit it that Les Sylphides motion (ideal to the contemplative romantic) and virtually restricted to horizontal and vertical movements (pillars and horizon lines) a diagonal requiring a major adjustment, its lenses coated or provided with filters, its light meters balanced, and its color film manufactured, to produce that picture post card effect (salon painting) exemplified by those oh so blue skies and peachy skins.

In the subsequent paragraph he offers the following remedy to the tripod: "One may hand-hold the camera to inherit worlds of space." Michael Snow chose to structure his film ←→ according to the very horizontal and vertical limitations of the tripod Brakhage had condemned. In *La Région Centrale* he utilized that "major adjustment," an equatorial mount, to present a hitherto unknown mode of camera movement that would not imitate eye or body movements. The back and forth movement of the tripod in ⟷ scans a classroom in which human activities, such as sweeping, reading, window washing, boxing, passing a ball, and conversation, reflect the dominant movement of the camera. It is a reversal of the camera/subject relationship Warhol established. Yet as the film progresses, the movement picks up speed, transforming the illusion of the room from one of physical, haptic space where human activity can occur to a purely optical space, like that of *Serene Velocity*. At the apogee of velocity the direction of the movement shifts to the vertical axis and gradually slows down. In the coda of the film, the forward and backward succession of the filmstrip itself becomes thematic as the film is run in both directions at once in superimposition, defining a uniquely cinematic space and time.

The spiraling, panning, twisting camera of *La Région Centrale* explores a barren portion of the Canadian landscape, which of course is one aspect of the title; the other, more obscure "région centrale" would be the blind spot so close to the camera which, despite the astonishing flexibility of the mount, remains outside the field of vision. The invisible center corresponds ironically to the subjectivity postulated behind the camera in the previous aesthetics of the American avant-garde just as the shadow of the mount corresponds to the shadow of the film-maker's body in films such as *Meshes of the Afternoon* or *Anticipation of the Night*.

Within the avant-garde cinema where the exigencies of the marketplace have no power in determining the content and form of films, the currents of film history cross over one another with elaborate complexity. Film-makers respond to each others' work in a given period and across time. Thus a crooked line can be traced from Maya Deren through Stan Brakhage to George Landow and Hollis Frampton and then back to Brakhage which would provide as viable a historical model as the chronological and theoretical grid I have been elaborating. In this case we should examine the attitude of each film-maker to the fictional self and the imagined viewer.

The paradox of iconic imagery which ends *At Land* (the footprints recorded in sand in super-human time) became the central motif of Brakhage's *Blue Moses,* one of his rare sound films and probably his most explicitly polemical film. An actor directly confronts the film audience by addressing the camera. His language is both seductive and intimidating: "Don't be afraid! We're not alone. There's the cameraman . . . or was . . . once . . . what can I say?" Through language the temporal ambiguities of the presence of the film-maker to the world he views *via* the camera, in relationship to the later moment of projection is underlined. The pretext for the actor's address is the frightening appearance, now obscured, of footprints in a desolated woods: "She wondered about the tracks. They're hopelessly obscure now . . . 'someone's been running here!' she said. You'll notice the space—between, I mean . . . tracks."

'What on earth would anyone be running from—or to . . . here?'
"You see what she means . . . or meant." The montage of the film,
which cuts among shots of the actor in various disguises, shows the
continuity of sentences across impossible time spans and thereby
thematizes the invisible time of editing. *Blue Moses* returns to
a trope from *At Land* to parody both *L'Avventura* and *L'Année
Dernière à Marienbad,* which were being taken as very important
cinematic achievements at that time by critics who thoroughly
rejected the native avant-garde cinema.

The title of the film must derive from the sublime speech of
Jehovah to Moses (*Exodus* xxxiii, 20-23) denying the patriarch the
possibility of seeing His face. The actor of Brakhage's film mimics
both the role of Moses and of Jehovah in this encounter to declare
the impossibility of an unmediated "presence" within the temporal
and representational intricacies of cinema.

Landow's *Remedial Reading Comprehension* condenses both the
Brakhage and Deren films and displaces their polemical thrusts. At
the beginning of the film a woman is seen dreaming. She looks re-
markably like the young Deren in her somnambulistic trance films.
Her dream involves the ambiguity of the pronoun "you" in a cinematic context. Where Brakhage emphasized the controlling presence
of the film-maker ("Don't be afraid! There's a film-maker behind
every scene—in back of ev-er-y wo-rd I spe-ak—behind you, too, so
to speak—no! Don't turn around. It's useless.") Landow shows
himself *running* under the text which makes the viewer, the "you,"
the organizing consciousness of the film rather than the film-maker.

The comparable involvement of the viewer in Frampton's *Zorns
Lemma* is answered by Brakhage's *The Riddle of Lumen.* The
alphabetical game which the viewer is invited to join in, implicitly,
while watching Frampton's film, leads to a thematic exploration of
the tensions between names and sights. Brakhage answered Frampton's puzzle with a "riddle" of his own. The only direct allusion to
the word/image problem is a shot of a child, in the middle of the
film, reading a book which illustrates things next to their names to
teach the alphabet. The Latin of the title is a more oblique allusion
to the Grosseteste text Frampton translated for his film. *The Riddle
of Lumen* is didactic insofar as it proposes a wide range of optical
options which link one shot to the next: shape, density, color, depth,
internal rhythm (the external or montage rhythm is steady, almost
metronomic), along axes of similarity or contrast. The single organizing principle of the film, which the viewer is invited to guess, is
contained in the title: light.

12

A significant departure from the cognitive model began to emerge
in the late Sixties, which is relevant to this scheme. It proposes the
difference between two texts, a species of translation, as the reflexive

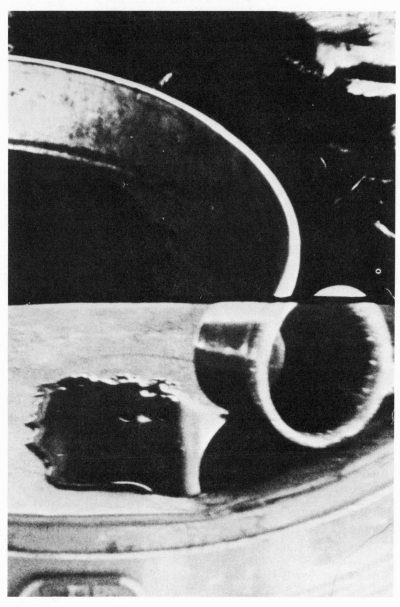

The Riddle of Lumen: *two sequential images.*

model for cinema. Breer's *Gulls and Buoys* and *Fuji* are good examples of this type of organization. Ken Jacobs' *Tom, Tom, the Piper's Son* begins and nearly ends with a 1905 film of the same title. Jacobs refilmed the original, isolating details, effecting repetitions, reversals of motion, shifts of scale and attention. It is a brilliant piece of didactic aesthetics, enlarging the viewer's attention to the original film when it is repeated near the end. Also incorporated into the "translation" are rests for the eyes and a violent rupture in the texture of the film.

The exploration of imageless textured surfaces as more than a setting for geometrical or photographed imagery became the conscious concern of several film-makers in the late 1960's. Brakhage's achievements in creating metaphors for the experience of closed-eye vision were as catalytic in this manifestation as the central works of the graphic cinema until then. Among the more recent and purer examples of this are Ernie Gehr's *History* (1970), made by enlarging and emphasizing the grain in a strip of film, and then extending that complex granular pattern over forty minutes of miniscule changes; Hollis Frampton's *Palindrome* (1969), in which patterns are created in color by the chemical erosion of the film; and the continuing work of Paul Sharits. From *Ray Gun Virus* (1966) to *N:O:T:H:I:N:G:* (1968) he worked with variations on the flicker film in color. With *S:TREAM:S:S:ECTION:S:ECTION:S:S:ECTIONED* (1970) he repeated images of flowing water so often and so quickly that they lost any sense of depth while a series of vertical scratches on the surface of the film affirmed a place even more literal and flush with the screen than the flattened water surface.

The early films of Hollis Frampton elaborated a lexicon of tropes which culminated in the synthesizing vision of *Zorns Lemma*. *Surface Tension* introduced writing on the screen, counterpointing and "translating" a text previously spoken, and the first of his internal clocking mechanisms, this time a digital clock recording "real time" which is ironically accelerated by the time-lapse photography. *Palindrome* made the chemical patterns of raw color film stock the visual material of the film itself, and he organized these patterns in a form which contrasted the frozen image with illusions of metamorphosis. The title of the film, coming from the Greek, "running backwards," denotes a form, or a word, which is the same backwards or forwards. The palindrome has been differently used by George Landow and Michael Snow as I shall elaborate below. Later in *Artificial Light* the polarities of sameness and difference took the form of a repeated cluster of shots in illusory depth, flattened and obscured by scratching, painting, superimposition, etc.

Frampton has remained intensely, at times painfully, aware of his historical position as a film-maker. His films constitute a dialogue both with the films of his contemporaries and the critical categories in which they have been seen. *Zorns Lemma* summarizes and parodies the quests of the graphic cinema. Beginning with a blank screen while a voice reads from the Bay State Primer, he grounds his film in the heritage of Peter Kubelka, whose *Arnulf Rainer* was a remote model for the metrical pulse (twenty-four frames long) which dominates Frampton's film. When the *Primer* ends, the soundtrack goes silent for about forty minutes while we see series after series of images, each one second long, and each containing a word filmed in a deep spatial context (signs in store windows, graffiti, names on passing trucks). The montage arranged the shots in alphabetical order. By occasionally mixing collages with the actual street signs he compounds the paradoxes of reading and perceiving depth which had been an essential trope of the graphic film since Léger's *Ballet Mécanique*. Furthermore, he gradually eliminates letters from the series, replacing them with finite or infinite acts (e.g. tying a shoe vs. waves of the sea rolling backwards). The anticipation of the eventual replacement of all the letters is a subtle version of the clock from *Surface Tension;* it is one of the ways in which the viewer gauges how far the film has progressed and how much longer that section will last.

The structure of *Zorns Lemma* continually puts itself in question. The opening recitation and the initial sequence of words suggests that alphabetical order is the common denominator of the film. But the replacement shots challenge that notion. A final section shows a single deep shot of two people trudging through a field of snow. There is obviously no alphabetic operation here. On the soundtrack a chorus of women's voices read a translation of Grosseteste's essay on light. What this section shares with the rest of the film—its real common denominator—is the pulse of one second, now transferred from the images to the sound, and "clocked" by a ticking metronome which signals each voice to read from the Neo-Platonic text.

The serial film, *Hapax Legomena,* taking its title again from the Greek, meaning those words which only occur once in ancient texts, is another megastructure incorporating concentric, eccentric, parallel, and tangential structures within it. Again the critical and historical issues are dissected. In (*nostalgia*) the time it takes for a photograph to burn (and thus confirm its two-dimensionality) becomes the clock within the film, while as Frampton plays the critic, asynchronously glossing, explicating, narrating, mythologizing, his earlier art, and his earlier life, as he commits them both to the fire in a labyrinthine structure.

The tension between reading and perceiving in depth becomes the undersubject of *Poetic Justice* as the film one sees (reads) shares only a room in common, perhaps not even that, with the film one reads about. In *Special Effects*, Frampton explores a critical issue that informed many of Stan Brakhage's *Songs:* can a film be made about the minute variations and fluctuations that occur at the edge of the screen? Frampton reduced the image to a bordered frame (a reduction of the screen shape itself) and made his film by shaking the camera before the image.

As a theoretician Frampton has focused his wit upon the fundamental issues of language, narrative, history, and autobiography in
cinema. I have selected for this anthology a lecture he prepared on
the formative power of light in cinema and an essay on narrative.
They are representative of his writings: he approaches the central
problems of film theory as if they were puzzles, not to be solved by
a head-on encounter, but to be reformulated as intellectual exercises. As such his essays are both stylistically and thematically antithetical to the important texts of Brakhage—who was the most
influential theoretician at the time Frampton came of age as a
film-maker—for Frampton conceives of language not as a prison for
restricting the perceptions but as a meta-cinematic tool for reorient-
ing and enlarging the primary visual imagination. In this respect he
is an heir of Marcel Duchamp.

In George Landow's *The Film That Rises to the Surface of Clari-
fied Butter* the intertextual model devolves upon two cartoonists
and the monsters they animate. The entire film has been rephotographed, with dirt deliberately allowed to accumulate, to underscore the illusionary status of both parts of the film, live photography and animation. The problematics of original and secondary
texts determines the double structure of *What's Wrong with this
Picture?* In the first part we see a kinescopic "translation" of a video-
tape, in which the spontaneous dialogue of the original interview
has been printed out and is superimposed over the image, often
obscuring it. In the second part, Landow remade a mundane instructional film, allowing moments of interference such as superimposition and negative to intrude. By including the original film as
well as the remake Landow displaces the mimetic model from the
imitation of a hypothetical situation to that of the surface qualities
of that film and its gestures as facts.

In *Wide Angle Saxon*, Landow parodies Frampton's (*nostalgia*)
by incorporating a screening of the hypothetical *Regrettable Redding
Condescension* by Al Rutcurts (a pseudonymous anagram for
"Structural") into his film. Within the hilarious argument of Landow's film this screening constitutes a negative moment in the conversion of a man to Christianity. While clapping after a screening
of the boring film, out of politeness, the hero suddenly recalls a
passage from the New Testament and decides to change his life.
Wide Angle Saxon is an elaborate study of compulsive errors and
displaced images, influenced by Freud's *The Interpretation of
Dreams* and *The Psychopathology of Everyday Life* with sequences
illustrating the palindromes "Malayalam" and "A Man, A Plan, A
Canal: Panama!" The film-maker locates the moment of conversion,
which he bases on the irreversible historicality of Typology, within
a cinematic context of reversible, asequential, repetitive structures.

Michael Snow's extravagant 267 minute long *Rameau's Nephew
by Diderot (Thanx to Denis Young) by Wilma Schoen,* an encyclopedic exploration of image/language and image/sound relation-

ships, also contains a filmic palindrome, but of a very different order. The camera first zooms back from a group of people having a polite conversation about flatulation. However the unintelligible language they speak derives from reading their scripts backwards, and trying to pronounce the texts engendered by literally reversing the letters of each word. Snow then reversed the strip of film, without turning it upside-down, so that as he zooms back to the original position their sentences approach a threshold of intelligibility. The discussion of flatulence becomes an analysis of metaphor and a joke on Brakhage: "Is this the fart of vision?" "Without recourse to metaphor or simile could you describe the scent?" "Well, it's getting stronger." "Shit, it smells like shit." "A crude metaphor." "For what?" "Dog, cat, moose, rabbit, chicken, cow, human . . . what kind?" "All the bowels are on that list . . . U.O.I.E.A."

Rameau's Nephew is a film of separate scenes interconnected by an elaborate nexus of internal references (every time the expression "for" or "four" occurs it is marked on the screen, for example) and radiating external allusions to all of Snow's previous works and to many other films. Near the end there is a climactic philosophical essay on the inability of a film to define its own ontological status: several characters in a hotel room discuss and perform acts of language and sex and try to prove that there is a "veri-table table" in the room. One of them offers a solution by destroying the table with a hammer, but even then it returns in superimposition (so that it can no longer support a glass when they try to place one on it) to confound their demonstrations. The previous organization of the script and the subsequent reorganization of the editing regularly enters the film as a barely submerged theme. For instance, in the long hotel sequence some notes of a trumpet are substituted in the soundtrack for a voice. A character immediately refers to this montage alteration when he observes, "I didn't know you spoke trumpet." As a whole this is a *summa* of the possibilities of sound montage avant-garde film-makers began to explore in the late Sixties and throughout most of the Seventies with the ironic interaction of words and images.

A considerable amount of the practical and theoretical work in this domain began to occur in Europe in the Sixties and eventually flowered in strong independent film movements in England, Germany, and Italy. A comparable historical development could be traced in Japan. An adequate account of that history lies outside the scope of this book, although it can be found in Malcolm Le Grice's *Abstract Film and Beyond*.

THE AVANT-GARDE FILM

DZIGA VERTOV:

Selected Writings

FROM THE MANIFESTO OF THE BEGINNING OF 1922

You—cinematographers:
directors without occupation and artists without occupation, flustered cameramen
and scenario writers scattered the world over,
You—the patient public of the movie houses with the tolerance of mules under the load of served emotions.
You—the impatient owners of the not-yet-bankrupt movie theaters, greedily snapping up the scraps off the German table, and, to a lesser extent, the American table—
You wait,
Debilitated by memories, you day dream and pine for the MOON of the new six-reel feature . . .
(nervous persons are asked to close their eyes),
You wait for what will not happen and what you should not expect.
My friendly warning:
Don't bury your heads like ostriches.
Raise your eyes,
Look around—
There!
Seen by me and by every child's eye:
Insides falling out.
Intestines of experience
Out of the belly of cinematography
slashed
By the reef of the revolution,
there they drag
leaving a bloody trace on the ground, shuddering from terror and repulsion.

All is ended.

DZIGA VERTOV

RESOLUTION OF THE COUNCIL OF THREE 10/IV–1923

Resolution on the cine-front: Consider not in favor.

First Russian productions shown us, as expected, are reminiscent of the old "artistic" models in the same way that the NEP-men remind us of the old *bourgeoisie.*

Projected production schedules for the summer, here and in Ukraine inspire no confidence.

Possibilities of wide experimental work is in the background.

All efforts, all sighs, tears, and hopes, all prayers are to her—the six-reel cine-drama.

Therefore, be it resolved, that the Council of Three, not waiting for the admission of Kinoks to production and, in spite of the desire of Kinoks to realize by themselves their own projects, forgoes for the moment the right of authorship and decrees:

publish immediately for broad distribution the general basis and credos of the impending revolution through the Movie newsreel, for which purpose Dziga Vertov is hereby directed, along the lines of party discipline, to publish these passages from the book, *Kinoks Revolution,* which describe the substance of the revolution.

Council of Three

Carrying out the resolution of the Council of Three of April 10, 1923, the following excerpts are published:

1.

Watching the pictures that came from the West and from America, taking into account the information we have on the work and searching abroad and here—I come to the following conclusion:

Verdict of death, decreed by Kinoks in 1919, to all motion pictures without exception, is in effect to this day.

The most careful inspection does not reveal a single picture, a single searching, that tries correctly to unserfage the camera, now in pitiful slavery, under orders of an   LEGALIZED MYOPIA imperfect shallow eye.

We do not object if cinematography tunnels under literature, under theater; we fully approve the utilization of the cinema for all branches of science, but we recognize these functions as accessory, as offshoots and branches.

The fundamental and the most important:

Cinema—the feel of the world.

The initial point:

The utilization of the camera,   WAY FOR THE MACHINE as a cinema eye—more perfect than a human eye for purposes of research into the chaos of visual phenomena filling the universe.

The eye lives and moves in time and space, perceiving and recording impressions in a way quite different from the human eye. It is not necessary for it to have a particular stance or to be limited in the number of moments to be observed per second. The movie camera is better.

DOWN WITH
16 PHOTOGRAPHS
PER SECOND

We cannot make our eyes better than they have been made, but the movie camera we can perfect forever.

To this day, the cameraman is criticized if a running horse moves unnaturally slowly on the screen (quick turn of the camera) or, conversely, if a tractor ploughs too fast (the slow manipulation of the camera crank).

ACCIDENTAL
SYNTHESIS AND
CONCENTRATION
OF MOTION

These, of course, are incidental, but we are preparing a thoughtout system of these incidents, a system of apparent abnormalities that organize and explore phenomena.

To this day, we raped the movie camera and forced it to copy the work of our eye. And the better the copy, the better the shot was considered. As of today, we will unshackle the camera and will make it work in the opposite direction, further from copying.

DO NOT COPY
FROM THE EYES

Out with all the weaknesses of the human eye.

MACHINE AND
ITS CAREER

We hereby ratify the eye, which is groping in the chaos of motions for a movement of its own and in its own right; we validate the eye with its own measurement of strength and in potentiality before the self-ratification.

2.

. . . to induce the viewer to see in a way that is best for me to show. The eye obeys the will of the camera and is directed by it to that sequence of moments of action that best brings out a cinema-phrase, the sequence that raises and lowers dénouement with the greatest brilliance and speed.

System of the Continuity of Actions

Example: Shooting a boxing bout not from the point of view of a member of the audience, but on the basis of showing off as best as possible the sequence of holds of the boxers.

Example: Shooting a group of dancers—but not from the point of view of the audience, sitting in an auditorium and having in front of it scenes of a ballet.

For the viewer of a ballet haphazardly follows the whole group, or incidental performers, or some legs— a series of scattered observations, different for everyone in the audience.

THE MOST INEFFICIENT,
THE MOST UNECONOMICAL
RENDITION OF A SCENE
IS THE THEATRICAL
RENDITION

The movie viewer cannot be presented with this. The system of consecutive actions demands filming the dancers or the boxers in a way which would account for consecutive events with certain details and actions forced upon the viewer, so that there is no chance for him to miss these.

The camera drags the eyes of the viewer from hands to legs, from legs to eyes, in a way that is the most efficient. It organizes the parts into an edited orderly study.

3.

You are walking on a Chicago street today in 1923, but I make you nod to comrade Volodarsky, who is, in 1918 walking down a street in Petrograd; he acknowledges   MONTAGE IN TIME your greeting.   AND SPACE

Another example: They are lowering the coffins of national heroes (shot in Astrakhan in 1918), they fill in the graves (Cronstadt, 1921), cannon salute (Petrograd, 1920), memorial-service hats come off (Moscow, 1922). These actions go together even in the ungrateful, not specially filmed, material (see *Kino-Pravda, No. 13*). Crowds greeting Lenin in different places, in different times are also in this category (see *Kino-Pravda, No. 14*).

. . . I am eye. I am builder.   HUMAN RACE OF
I implanted you, a most re-   KINOKS COUNCIL OF
markable chamber which did   THREE. MOSCOW, HALL
not exist until I created it to-   OF INTERVALS TODAY-
day. In this chamber, there   TODAY APRIL
are twelve walls, photographed   3
by me in various parts of the   REPORT BY DZV ON
world. Manipulating shots of   THE THEME
walls and details, I have suc-   CHAMBRE
ceeded in arranging them in   CINEMA-PHRASE
an order that pleases you and   BEGINNING 8:30 P.M.
in constructing correctly a cinematic phrase, which is the room.

I am eye. I have created a man more perfect than Adam; I created thousands of different people   ELECTRIC YOUNG MAN in accordance with previously prepared plans and charts.

I am eye.

I take the most agile hands of one, the fastest and the most graceful legs of another, from a third person I take the handsomest and the most expressive head, and, by editing, I create an entirely new perfect man.

. . . I am eye. I am a mechanical eye.

I, a machine, am showing you a world, the likes of which only I can see.

I free myself from today and forever from human immobility, I am in constant movement, I approach and draw away from objects, I crawl under them, I move alongside the mouth of a running horse, I cut into a crowd at full speed, I run in front of running soldiers, I turn on my back, I rise with an airplane, I fall and soar together with falling and rising bodies.

This is I, apparatus, maneuvering in the chaos of movements, recording one movement after another in the most complex combinations.

Freed from the obligation of shooting sixteen–seventeen frames per second, freed from the frame of time and space, I coordinate any and all points of the universe, wherever I may plot them.

My road is toward the creation of a fresh perception of the world. Thus, I decipher in a new way the world unknown to you.

....

. . . Let us agree once more: The eye and the ear. The ear peeks, the eye eavesdrops.

Distribution of functions.

Radio-ear-edited, "Hear!"

Cinema-eye-edited, "See!"

There it is, citizens, in the first place instead of music, painting, theater, cinematography, and other castrated outpourings.

In a chaos of movements running past, streaking away, running up and colliding—only the eye enters life simply. The day of visual impressions is past. How to convert the impressions of the day into a functional whole—into a visual study? To film everything that an eye has seen will result in a jumble. To edit artfully what had been photographs would result in a greater clarity. It would be better yet to scrap the annoying rubbish. Thus we get organized memoirs of impressions of a simple eye.

ORGANIZATION OF OBSERVATIONS BY A HUMAN EYE

A mechanical eye—that's the movie camera. It refuses to use the human eye as if the latter were a crib-sheet; it is attracted and repelled by motion, feeling through the chaos of observed events for a roadway for its own mobility and modulation; it experiments, extending time, dissecting movement, or, on the contrary, absorbing into itself the time, swallowing years and, thus, diagramming some processes unattainable to the normal eye.

DECOMPOSITION and CONCENTRATION of VISUAL PHENOMENA

. . . In aid to the eye-machine is the Kinok, the pilot, who not only steers the apparatus, but also trusts it in experiments in space and in whatever may follow. Kinok, the engineer, directs the apparatus by remote control.

BRAIN

This concerted action by the liberated and perfected apparatus and the strategy-making brain of man—directing, observing, compensating, will result in an unusual freshness, and even the most commonplace will become interesting.

••

. . . They are many who, hungering for spectacles, lost their pants in theaters.

They run from weekdays, run from the "prose" of life.

And yet the theater is almost always only a scabby surrogate of this very life plus an idiotic conglomerate from balletic contortions, musical squeaks, clever lighting effects, stage sets (from those smeared on to those constructed) and sometimes good work from literary masters perverted by all this hogwash.

Some theater overseers enlist help: bio-mechanics (a good pursuit by itself), cinema (bestow it honor and glory), literatures (not bad by themselves), constructions (some are not bad), automobiles (how can we not respect them?), rifle shooting (dangerous and impressive thing in the front lines). But, on the whole, not a goddamn thing comes out of it.

Theater and nothing else.

Not only no synthesis but no orderly mixture either.

Could not be otherwise.

We, Kinoks, resolute opponents of premature synthesis ("To synthesis at the zenith of accomplishment"), understand that to mix the crumbs of achievements is to have the infants perish from crowding and disorder.

In general—

ARENA IS SMALL

Please come into life.

Here we work—craftsmen of seeing—organizers of visible life, armed all over with the maturing eye. Here work the master-craftsmen of words and sounds, the most skillful editor-cutters of the heard life. To them, I also dare slip over a mechanical ever-present ear and megaphone—radio telephone.

This is

NEWSREEL
RADIO NEWS

I promise to wangle a parade of Kinoks in Red Square in case the futurists come out with No. 1 of their edited newsreel.

Neither the newsreel of "Pathé" nor of "Gaumont" (newspaper chronicle) nor even the Kino-Truth (political chronicle), but a real Kinok-type of a chronicle—a dashing survey of visual events deciphered by the movie-camera, fragments of actual energy (as against theatrical energy), with their intervals condensed into a cumulative whole by the great mastery of an editing technique.

Such structure of a cinematic thing allows a development of any theme—be it comical, tragic, or anything else.

It is all a matter of juxtaposition of one visual moment with another, all a matter of intervals.

This unusual flexibility of edited structure allows to introduce into a movie continuity, any political, economic, or any other motif.

Therefore

As of today cinema needs no psychological, no detective dramas,

As of today—no theatrical productions shot on film,

As of today—no scenariozation of either Dostoyevsky, or Nat Pinkerton.

Everything is included in the new concept of the newsreel.

Into the confusion of life, hereby decisively enter:

1) The Eye, disputing the visual concept of the world by the human eye and offering its own "I see" and

2) Kinok-editor, who organizes, for the first time, what had been so perceived into minutes of life structure.

(1923)

CREATIVE PLANS, TESTIMONIALS, IDEAS

1. If *Kino-Pravda* is truth shown by means of the cinematic eye, then a shot of the banker will only be true if we can tear the mask from him, if behind his mask we can see the thief.

2. The only way we can divest him of his mask is by concealed observation, by concealed photography: that is, by means of hidden cameras, supersensitive film and light-sensitive lenses, infrared film for night and evening shooting, noiseless cameras. Constant readiness of the camera for filming. Immediate shooting of a perceived object.

Not in the theater, but in life, the thief plays the role of the cashier in order to rob the cash register. Or else the confidence man plays the role of a doting suitor to seduce and, then, rob a woman. Or else the hustler plays the simpleton in order to fool his victim. Or else the prostitute plays the-girl-with-a-bow to make a fool of the nincompoop. Or else the hypocrite, the flatterer bureaucrat, the spy, the bigot, the blackmailer, the contriver, etc., who hide their thoughts while playing one role or another, take their masks off only when no one can see them or hear them. To show them without their masks on—what a difficult task that is, but how rewarding.

3. All this when a man plays someone else's role in life. But if we take a professional actor, playing a role in the theater, to film him through the "Kino-Eye" would be to show the agreement or disagreement between the man and the actor, the correspondence or lack of correspondence between his words and his thoughts, etc. I am reminded of one actor who was playing in one of the old silent

films. Dying from wounds in front of the camera, showing suffering
on his body and face, he was at the same time telling an anecdote
which was amusing everyone—apparently showing off his ability to
act while not feeling the emotions he was portraying. If the con-
vulsions of the wounded man could have been recorded for sound,
then in place of moans we would hear, to our astonishment, something directly opposite to what we were seeing on the screen: words
with double meaning, jokes, giggling . . .

Apparently, the actor had to die so many times before the camera
that it had become automatic; he did not have to use his mind to
act. His mind was free to tell jokes. This—the ability to dissimulate,
to affect two identities—seemed quite disgusting to me at the time.

To show Ivanov in the role of Petrov, as seen through the "Kino-
Eye," would be to show him as a man in life and as an actor on the
stage; not trying to pass off acting on the stage as life, and vice
versa. Complete clarity. Not Petrov in front of you, but Ivanov
playing the role of Petrov.

4. If a fake apple and a real apple are filmed so that one cannot
be distinguished from the other on the screen, this is not ability,
but incompetence—inability to photograph.

The real apple has to be filmed in such a way that no counterfeit
can be possible. The real apple can be tasted and eaten, while the
artificial one cannot—a good cameraman can understand this easily.

(1944)

Translated by Val Telberg

KINO-EYE, LECTURE I

The history of Kino-Eye has been a relentless struggle to modify
the course of world cinema, to place in cinematic production a new
emphasis of the "unplayed" film over the played film, to substitute
the document for *mise en scène*, to break out of the proscenium of
the theater and to enter the arena of life itself.

Let me attempt to sum up the results obtained in this direction
by the Kino-Eye.

1. The manifesto of the "Kinoks" on the cinema, free from the
actors, was published and later developed and popularized in a
number of articles and in several public discussions.

2. In order to confirm the contents of the manifesto, there were
produced and exhibited about 100 films without actors. These were
of a wide variety, from primitive newsreels to extremely complex
documentary films of the "cinethings." We can cite, for example,
the *Weekly Reels, History of the Civil War, Calendars of Goskinof,*
and the *Cine-Translations*. Outstanding among those films, which
were responsible for heavy blows at the theatrical cinema, must be
mentioned: *The Struggle Under Tzarism, Life Caught Unaware,
Lenin's Truth, Forward Soviets!, The Sixth Part of the World, The
Eleventh Year,* and, finally, *The Man with a Movie Camera.*

Among the films produced by some of my pupils may be mentioned: *Moscow Nursery, For the Harvest, A Holiday for Millions.*

3. We have developed a language, proper to the cinema, special methods of shooting and montage, which are not those of the enacted film. The language of the film has become absolutely distinct from that of the theater and literature. We have created the conception of *documentary cinematography.*

4. We have established an experimental studio for the recording of facts, and later *Pravda* on July 24, 1926, published plans for a "factory of unplayed film," a "factory of facts," that is to say, pure documentary.

5. At an open meeting that took place in Moscow in 1924, followers of Kino-Eye revealed the existence of a directive by Lenin that pointed out the necessity of changing the proportion of fact-films on film programs. Finding support in this directive, the followers of Kino-Eye declared that they demanded an immediate reorganization of all Soviet film production and exhibition; they requested an internal apportionment, that is to say, a certain proportion between the theatrical cinema, the enacted film, the cine-plaything on the one hand, and, on the other, the cinema which is not played, the cine-eye, the fact-film.

This proposal was boldly called the "Leninist Film Proportion." Attempts were made to publish the proposal in the cinematographic press. N. Lebedev, the editor-in-chief of the only movie magazine appearing at that time, *Kino-Journal,* returned the manuscript to me, declaring that he protested the term "Leninist Film Proportion" and that he was against this attempt to utilize an "accidental" phrase by Lenin, and to present it as a sort of testimonial directive. The proposal of the "kinoks," rejected by the cinema press, was nevertheless published later by *Pravda* on the 16th of August, 1925. The very term itself, "Leninist Film Proportion," was not current for very long, and it is only today, in 1929, that it has been taken up again.

6. Kino-Eye has exerted considerable influence on the theatrical film, the language of which it has modified. More and more, our cinema has borrowed the methods of Kino-Eye, superficially, at least, to create what is known as the "art" film. We cite as examples *Strike, Potemkin,* and others. These borrowings have been sufficient to arouse attention and have created quite a stir at home as well as abroad in the domain of the theatrical, enacted film.

Nevertheless, these directed films, the methods of which were superficially taken from Kino-Eye, present only a particular and incidental facet of the Kino-Eye movement, the spread of which continued uninterrupted.

7. Kino-Eye has exerted a considerable influence on almost all the arts, notably in the sphere of music and literature. We will recall here that in their manifesto of the unplayed film, the exponents of Kino-Eye asked workers in the word, workers in letters, to initiate

the oral chronicle, radio chronicle. We recall that following this, in *Pravda* in 1925, N. Ossinski asked that literature engage itself upon the road traced by Kino-Eye, that is to say, that it attempts to present facts—documentary elements—in an organic form.

"Vertov is right," wrote O. Brik in *Soviet Cinema*, No. 2, 1926, and he demanded of photography that it follow the example set by Kino-Eye. "It is necessary to get out of the circle of ordinary human vision; reality must be recorded not by imitating it, but by broadening the circle ordinarily encompassed by the human eye."

In their earliest declarations on the subject of the sound film, which was not yet even invented then but which was soon to come, the Kinoks, who now call themselves the "Radioks," that is, followers of Radio-Eye, traced their path as leading from the Kino-Eye to the Radio-Eye; in other words, leading to the sound Kino-Eye transmitted by radio.

A few years ago I wrote an article entitled "The Radio-Eye" which appeared in *Pravda* under the general heading "Kino-Pravda and Radio-Pravda." I stated in that article that Radio-Eye was a means of abolishing distances between men, that it offered an opportunity for the workers of the world not only to see themselves, but to hear themselves SYNCHRONOUSLY.

The declaration of the "Kinoks" provoked at the time most passionate discussions in the press. I remember a long article by Fevralski, "Tendencies in Art and Radio-Eye." I recall a special publication, *Radio*, which devoted one of its issues exclusively to Radio-Eye.

The followers of Kino-Eye, not confining themselves solely to the development of the unplayed film, were preparing themselves to work on the Radio-Eye, the talking and sound film without the play of actors.

Already in *The Sixth Part of the World*, the subtitles are replaced by an oral theme, by a radio theme, contrapuntally adapted to the film. *The Eleventh Year* is already constructed like a *visual* and *sonal* cine-thing, that is to say, that the montage was done *in relation not only to the eye, but also to the ear*.

It is in the same direction, in passing from Kino-Eye to Radio-Eye, that our film *The Man with a Movie Camera* was mounted.

The theoretical and practical work of the *kinoks-radioks* (differing in this respect from theatrical cinematography, which has found itself caught off-guard) have run ahead of their technical possibilities and, for a long time, have been awaiting a technical basis the advent of which will be late, in relation to Kino-Eye; they await the Sound-Cine and Television.

Recent technical acquisitions in this area lend powerful arms to the partisans and workers of *documentary sound cinegraphy* in their struggle for a revolution in the cinema, for the abolition of play, for an October of Kino-Eye.

From the montage of visual facts recorded on film (Kino-Eye) we pass to the montage of visual and acoustic facts transmitted by radio (Radio-Eye).

We shall go from there to the simultaneous montage of visual-acoustic-tactile-olfactory facts, etc.

We shall then reach the stage where we will surprise and record *human thoughts,* and, finally

we shall reach to the greatest experiments of direct organization of thoughts (and consequently of actions) of all mankind.

Such are the technical perspectives of Kino-Eye, born of the October Revolution.

(Excerpts from a lecture given in Paris in 1929)

KINO-EYE, LECTURE II

Kino-Eye is a victory against time. It is a visual link between phenomena separated from one another in time. Kino-Eye gives a condensation of time, and also its decomposition.

Kino-Eye offers the possibility of seeing the living processes in a temporally arbitrary order and following a chosen rhythm, the speed of which the human eye would not otherwise be able to follow.

Kino-Eye avails itself of all the current means of recording ultra-rapid motion, microcinematography, reverse motion, multiple exposure, foreshortening, etc., and does not consider these as tricks, but as normal processes of which wide use must be made.

Kino-Eye makes use of all the resources of montage, drawing together and linking the various points of the universe in a chronological or anachronistic order, as one wills, by breaking, if necessary, with the laws and customs of the construction of a cine-thing.

In introducing itself into the apparent chaos of life, the Kino-Eye tries to find in life itself an answer to the questions it poses: To find the correct and necessary line among the millions of phenomena that relate to the theme.

Montage and a Few Principles of Kino-Eye

To make a montage is to organize pieces of film, which we call the frames, into a cine-thing. It means to write something cinegraphic with the recorded shots. It does not mean to select pieces to make "scenes" (deviations of a theatrical character), nor does it mean to arrange pieces according to subtitles (deviations of a literary character).

Every Kino-Eye production is mounted on the very day that the subject (theme) is chosen, and this work ends only with the launching of the film into circulation in its definitive form. In other words, montage takes place from the beginning to the end of production.

Montage being thus understood, we can distinguish three periods:

First period: The "Montage Evaluation" of all the documents that are directly or indirectly related to the chosen theme (manuscripts, various objects, film clippings, photographs, newspaper clippings, books, etc.). As a result of this montage, which consists in picking and grouping the most precious documents or those simply useful, *the plan indicated by the theme* becomes crystallized, appears more evident, more distinct, more defined.

Second period: "Montage Synthesis" of the human eye concerning the selected theme (montage of personal observation or of reports by the information-gatherers and scouts of the film). *Plan of shots,* as a result of the selection and classification of the observations of the "human eye." At the moment when this selection is made, the author takes into account the indications of the thematic plan as well as peculiarities of the "machine-eye" of Kino-Eye.

Third period: "General Montage," synthesis of the observations noted on the film under the direction of the "machine-eye." Calculation in figures of the montage groupings. Unification of homogeneous pieces; constantly, one displaces the pieces, the frames, until all shall have entered a rhythm, where all the ties dictated by the meaning shall be those which coincide with the visual ties. As a result of all these mixtures, of all these displacements and of all these reductions, we have a kind of visual equation, a visual formula. This formula, this equation, which is the result of the general

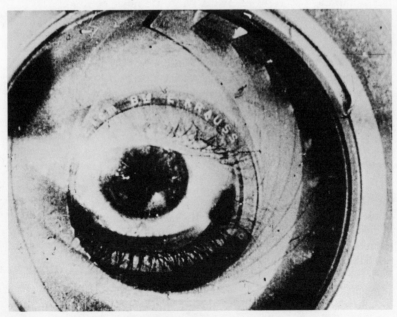

The Man with a Movie Camera: *the visualization of the film-eye metaphor through superimposition*

montage of the cine-documents recorded on the film, is 100 per cent
the cine-thing: I see, I cine-see.

Kino Eye is:

montage, when I select a theme (to pick a theme among a possible thousand);

montage, when I keep watch over the execution of the theme (of
a thousand observations, to make a proper choice);

montage, when I establish the order of exposition of what has
been shot according to the theme (of a thousand possible combinations to select the most adequate, basing one's self as much upon
the qualities of the filmed documents as upon the requirements of
the chosen theme).

The school of Kino-Eye requires that the cine-thing be built
upon "intervals," that is, upon a movement between the pieces,
the frames; upon the proportions of these pieces between themselves, upon the transitions from one visual impulse to the one
following it.

Movement between the pieces—spectacular interval—spectacular
relations between the pieces. According to Kino-Eye: a great complexity, formed by the sum total of the various relations of which
the chief ones are: (1) relations of planes (small and large); (2)
relations of foreshortenings; (3) relations of movements within the
frame of each piece; (4) relations of lights and shades; (5) relations
of speeds of recording.

Starting with this or that combination of relations, the author of
the montage determines: the duration of each piece in meters for
each of the images, the duration of projection of each distinct
image. Moreover, at the same time that we perceive the movement
that determines the relation between images, we also take into consideration, between two adjoining images, the spectacular value of
each distinct image in its relations to all the others engaged in the
"montage battle" that begins.

To find the most convenient itinerary for the eyes of the spectator
in the midst of all these mutual reactions, of these mutual attrac-
tions, of these mutual repulsions of images among themselves, to
reduce this whole multiplicity of intervals (of movements from one
image to the other) to a simple spectacular equation: to a spectacular formula expressing in the best possible manner the essential
theme of the cine-thing, such is the most difficult and important task
of the author of montage.

This theory which has been called the "theory of intervals" was
launched by the "kinoks" in their manifesto *WE,* written as early
as 1919. In practice, this theory was most brilliantly illustrated in
The Eleventh Year and especially in *The Man with a Movie
Camera.*

(1929)
(*Film Culture,* No. 25, Summer 1962)
Translated by S. Brody

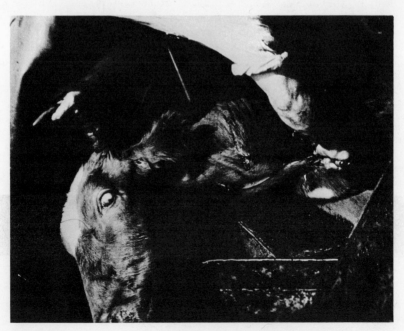

Strike: *the massacre of the strikers intercut with the slaughter of a cow.*

SERGEI EISENSTEIN:

On the Question of a Materialist Approach to Form

The unanimous, warm reception which the press has given *Strike,* and the very nature of its evaluation means we may acknowledge *Strike* as a revolutionary victory not only in itself, but also as an *ideological victory in the realm of form.* This is particularly significant now, when many are so fanatically prepared to persecute a work for its form, branding it *"formalism"* and preferring to it . . . a total lack of form. In *Strike,* in fact, we have the first instance of revolutionary art where form proved to be more revolutionary than content.

And the revolutionary novelty of *Strike* is certainly not the result of the fact that its subject—the revolutionary movement—was historically a mass movement rather than an individual one, nor is this the source, let us say, of the lack of plot, the absence of a hero, and the other things which characterize *Strike* as the "first proletarian film." Instead its novelty lies in the fact that *a correctly established formal method of approach* for revealing a vast amount of historical-revolutionary material in general was advanced.

Historical-revolutionary material—*the "industrial" past* of contemporary revolutionary reality—was taken for the first time from the proper *point of view:* an examination of its characteristic episodes as stages of a single process from the point of view of their "industrial" essence. To reveal the logic of production and to set forth the technique of methods of struggle as a "living" flowing process, without any unbreakable rules except that of having an ultimate goal, devices which are varied and formed at every given moment depending on the conditions and correlations of forces in a given phase of struggle, having shown it as saturated with everyday life—this is the formal requirement which I put before the Proletcult in defining the content of the seven parts of the cycle "Toward Dictatorship."

It is quite obvious that the specific nature of the actual *character* (mass character) of this movement does not as yet play any role in constructing the logical principle just stated, and it is not *mass character* that defines it. The form in which the content is treated as a function of its subject matter—in our case the device of montage of a scenario applied here for the first time (that is, the construction of the scenario not on the basis of any conventional laws of drama, but in exposing the content through techniques determining the construction of montage as such in general, for example, in the organization of newsreel material *), and the very correctness of establishing a point of view toward the material— turned out to be, in the given case, *the result of a basic formal realization of the material presented*—of the director's basic formal reviving "trick," determined (historically) in the first place.

In terms of asserting a new form of film phenomenon as the result of a new view of the social imperative (crudely formulated: "the underground"), the director of *Strike* went by the path always typical of a revolutionary assertion of the new in the realm of art— by the path of the *dialectical* introduction into a series of materials, of devices of treatment not characteristic of this series, but belong- ing to another contiguous or opposite series. Thus the "revolutioniz- ing" of the aesthetics of theatrical forms which have been changing before our very eyes for the last twenty-five years were marked by the absorption of external signs of "neighboring" arts (consecutive dictatorships: of literature, painting, music, exotic theaters in the era of stylized theater, and of the circus, superficial tricks of film and others—subsequently). In addition, there arose the fertilization of one series of aesthetic phenomena by another (including even the role of the circus and sports in terms of revitalizing the actor's profession). The revolutionary quality of *Strike* is expressed in the fact that it has taken the revitalizing principle not from a series of "artistic phenomena," but from a series of *directly utilitarian phenomena*—specifically, the principle of construction to present in film the exposition of production processes—a selection signifi- cant in its going beyond the bounds of the aesthetic circle (which is quite logical for my works, which in any case are oriented on the basis of principles which are never in the realm of aesthetics, but in the realm of the "meat chopper"), but even more by the fact that *the sphere* which was sought for correctly *materialistically speaking*, was one whose principles alone can *determine the ide- ology of forms of revolutionary art, just as they determined revolu-*

---

* It is interesting, however, to note that because of this in the actual tech- nique of exposition in *Strike* and the other [unrealized] parts of "Toward Dictatorship," the moment of an actual scenario was missing and there is a jump: the theme is a montage sheet, which is completely logical in terms of the montage aspect of the work.

tionary ideology in general—heavy industry, factory production and forms of the production process.

In speaking of the form of *Strike,* only very naive people may talk of "contradictions between the ideological demands and formal deviations of the director"—while it is time it became clear to at least some people that form is defined much more profoundly than by one or another more or less successful external "trick."

Here one can and must no longer speak about a "revolutioniza-tion" of forms, in the given case of film, for this expression has no positive meaning in terms of production—but about a case of revo-lutionary film form in general, because it is definitely not the result of phony "quests," nor a "synthesis of an excellent mastery of form with our content" (as Pletnev writes in *The New Spectator*) [1925, No. 5]. *Revolutionary form is the product of correctly discovered technical devices of making concrete a new view and approach to material and phenomena—*to a new class ideology. This approach is the true renovator *not only of social significance, but also of the material-technical essence of film* which is revealed in the so-called "our content." It is not by "revolutionization" of the forms of a large coach that a locomotive is created, but by the correct technical calculation of the practical discovery *of a revolutionary form of energy which had not existed before—*steam. Not a "quest" for forms corresponding to new content, but the logical *realization of all phases of technical production of producing art in correspon-dence* to the "new *form* of energy"—*the ruling ideology—*will pro-duce those forms of revolutionary art which up until the very last moment everyone still *wants to* "guess at" *spiritually.*

Thus the principle of approach set forth and the point of view established by me in film production of historical-revolutionary material was recognized in *Pravda* to be correct as such material-istically speaking, as one would expect by a *Communist,** who designated the (formal!) approach "even Bolshevik"—but not by *professional film critics* (who cannot see further than their nose, that is, no further than my "eccentricity.") Recognized, even in spite of the film's weakness in program and subject matter—the lack of material which adequately describes the technique of the Bolshevist underground and of the economic premises for a strike which, of course, is a great flaw in the *subject-ideological* part of the content; although in the given case it is perceived only as "not an all-sided exposition of the production process" (that is, the process of struggle). My principle did define, also, a certain unnecessary pointedness of forms simple and severe in themselves.

*Mass Character—*the *second conscious* director's trick—as is evi-dent from the above, is logically still not compulsory: and actually, out of the seven parts "Toward Dictatorship" which is impersonal throughout, only two have a mass character. It is not accidental

---

* A reference to Mikhail Koltsov's review of *Strike,* in *Pravda,* 14 March 1925.

that *Strike*—one of them, which is *fifth* in the order of the series—
was chosen to be *first*. *Mass character* material is proposed as the
most clearly *capable* of asserting the stated ideological principle of
an approach to form in developing the given solution, and as *sup-
plementing the dialectic opposition* of this principle to the *material
based on plot and individualism of bourgeois cinema*. It is also
formally established consciously by the construction of a logical
antithesis to the bourgeois West with which we are in *no way competing*, but to which we are *opposed* in every way.

An approach based on mass character leads to a maximal intensification of emotional captivation of an audience which is decisive
for art in general, and for revolutionary art even more so.

Such a cynical analysis of the bases of *Strike*'s construction, perhaps somewhat debunking the beautiful words about its "elemental
and collective creation," puts under it a more serious and practical
basis and affirms that a formal approach carried out *correctly* in
terms of Marxism results in a production both ideologically valuable
and socially necessary.

This all provides a basis for giving to *Strike* that name with which
we are accustomed to noting revolutionary turns in art—October.

Strike—is the October of film.

October, which even has its own February, for what else are
Vertov's works if not the "overthrow of the autocracy" of fictional
cinema and . . . nothing more. It is a question here only of my
single predecessor—*Kinopravda*. *Kinoglaz* [Cinema Eye], which
appeared when the shooting and part of the montage of *Strike* were
already finished, could not have had an influence—nor could it
essentially *influence anything* since *Glaz* is a *reductio ad absurdum*
of technical methods valid in a newsreel—in Vertov's pretense that
they are *sufficient* for the creation of a new cinema. Actually *this is
only an act of limiting to one particular form* of cinematography:
one *shot* made by the "running of one camera."

Without denying a certain degree of genetic connection with
Kinopravda (both in February and in October they shot with
machineguns—the difference is at whom!), indeed it, like *Strike*,
proceeded from industrial newsreels. Still I consider it necessary
to point to a *strong fundamental difference*, that is, the *difference
in method*. *Strike* does not "develop the methods" of *Kinopravda*
(Khersonsky) and is not an "experiment to graft several methods
of the construction of *Kinopravda* to artistic cinema" (Vertov). And
if one can point to a certain *similarity* in *external form* of construction, then it is in the most essential part—in the *formal method of
construction—that Strike is in direct contrast to Kinoglaz*.

Let us begin with the fact that *Strike does not pretend to be an
escape from art, and in this lies its strength*.

In our opinion the *work of art* (at least in the two spheres of it
in which I work—theater and film) is above all *a tractor replough-
ing the spectator's psyche in given class conditions*.

The productions of the Kinoks [Cinema Eyes] do not have such a quality nor such an intention, and, they are, I think, as a result of a certain "mischievousness" of its producers which is somewhat unsuitable to the epoch—the *negation* of art instead of a *materialistic realization,* if not of its essence, then, in any case, of the possibility of its *utilitarian application.*

Such frivolousness puts the Kinoks into a rather funny position, since, in a formal analysis of their work, one must conclude that their works certainly and very definitely belong to art, and *what's more, to one of the least ideologically valuable expressions of it— to primitive impressionism.*

It is from a montage of pieces of real life (with the impressionists —of real tones) *whose effect is not calculated, that Vertov weaves the carpet of a pointillist painting.*

Of course, this is the most "cheerful" view of *easel* painting, and even in terms of themes is about as "revolutionary" as—AKhRR, which is proud of their Wanderers quality.* This accounts for the success of the "Kinopravdas," which are always *topical,* that is, are *thematically effective,* and not of *Glaz,* whose themes are less satisfactory and which, therefore, except for primitive propaganda moments in it (in its majority) *fails because of weakness in its formal effects.*

Vertov takes from his environment that *which* impresses *him,* and not that *with which,* in effecting the viewer, he will plough through the viewer's psyche.

Practically speaking, the difference of our approaches is most clearly apparent in a small amount of material which coincides in both *Strike* and *Glaz,* which Vertov almost considers to be plagiarism (there is so little material in *Strike* that one would have to borrow from *Glaz!*)—in particular in the slaughterhouse which has been stenographically recorded in *Glaz* and produces a bloody impression in *Strike.* (It is this extremely strong impression—"without white gloves"—which has created 50% of its opponents.)

Like a good impressionist, *Kinoglaz,* with notebook in hand (!), runs after things as they are, *without bursting rebelliously into the inevitability of the static nature of the causality of their connection, without overcoming this connection because of an authoritative social-organizing motif, but submitting to its "cosmic" pressure.* In fixating its external dynamism, Vertov masks the static nature of the pantheism delivered by him (in politics it is a position characterizing opportunism and Menshevism) into dynamism by devices of alogism (here purely aesthetic: winter/summer in *Kinopravda* No. 19) or simply short films of montage pieces and obediently re-

---

* The Wanderers is a group of Realistic painters who in 1870 formed the Society of Wandering Exhibitions. They painted realistic depictions of the lower classes and were concerned with social reform. AKhRR was an organization of painters in the '20s and '30s that promoted naturalistic painting.

producing it piecemeal in the dispassionate fullness of its balance.*

Instead *Strike* snatches pieces from the surroundings *according to conscious, willful premeditation* calculated on a basis of (*once having brought them down on the viewer in a suitable juxtaposition*) *subduing it* by suitable association to a *certain final ideological motif.*

This certainly does not mean, however, that I do not intend to eliminate from my works remnants of the theatrical element which do not organically fit in with film, and perhaps even the very *apogee of willful premeditation—"the performance,"* because of the main thing—*directing—the organization of the viewer through organized material*—in the given case, in film, is possible not only through the *material* organization of effective phenomena being shot, but through *optical* organization—by the mode of shooting. And if in *the theater* the director, *through his treatment,* recuts the *potential dynamics* (or statics) of the playwright, the actor, and the rest into a *socially effective construction,* then here, in *film, by selection of treatment,* on the basis of montage he recuts *reality* and real phenomena *in a similar arrangement.* This is what *directing* really is, and it has nothing in common with the *dispassionate depiction* by the Kinoks, with the fixation of phenomena, with not going further than *fixating the attention* of the viewer.**

---

* In the final analysis, it is interesting to introduce one example of Vertov's static quality from the most abstractly *mathematically* successful montage episodes—the raising of the flag over the pioneer camp (I do not remember in which of the *Kinopravdas*). [*Kinoglaz*] This is a striking example of a solution not in terms of the *emotional dynamics* of the actual fact of raising the flag, but in terms of a *static examination* of this process. Besides *this* characterization being felt directly, what is symptomatic here in the actual technique of montage is the use in the majority of short film pieces of *static* (and even *contemplative*) *close-ups,* which, of course, by virtue of their 3-4 frame units are hardly capable of being dynamic on the inner-frame level. But here in this particular example (and one must note that in general this device is very wide-spread in the Vertov "manner"), we have apparently brought into focus ("the symbol") of the interrelationship of Vertov and the external world investigated by him. What is present is a montage "make-up job" in the dynamics of static pieces.

Attention must also be called to the fact that this is a case of personally shot montage material, that is, a montage combination for which the director is *fully* responsible [SME].

** To be fair we must note that Vertov has made attempts of another organization of material—of *effective* organization—in particular in the second part of *Leninist Kinopravda* (January 1925). True, here it was displayed only in the form of groping on paths of emotional "tickling"—in the creation of "moods" without any account for their application. When Vertov will leave this first stage of mastery of effect and learn to provoke the necessary states in his audience and, in assembling them, to furnish this audience with ammunition set up ahead of time, then . . . there will hardly be a discrepancy among us, but then Vertov will stop being the kino-oko [cinema eye] and will become a director and even, perhaps . . . "an artist."

It is then that one will be able to ask a question about someone's use of certain methods (but then—whose? and—which?!), because only then can one *seriously* speak about any kind of Vertovian methods, which actually come down to merely the stated intuitive device of the practice of his constructions (probably hardly realized by Vertov himself). It is impossible to call *devices of practical skill a method.* Theoretically the doctrine of "social vision" is no more than the incoherent montage of pompous phrases and of "commonplaces" strongly giving way in terms of montage to that simple montage "sleight of hand," which he tries extremely unsuccessfully to "socially" substantiate and exalt.

Kinoglaz is not only a symbol of *vision*, but also the symbol of *contemplation*. We do not need, however, to *contemplate*, but to *act*.

We do not need *Kino-glaz* but *Kino-fist*.

Soviet film must smash skulls! And it is not with a "united view of millions of eyes will we fight the bourgeois world" (Vertov)— we must quickly put a million lamps under these millions of eyes!

To smash skulls with kino-fists, to smash to ultimate victory and now, under the threat of the inroads of "everyday reality" and Philistinism into the revolution, to smash as never before!

Open the road to the kino-fist!

(First published in *Kino-zhurnal ARK*, 1925, No. 4-5) Translated by Roberta Reeder. Ms. Reeder would like to thank Victor Terras and Jay Leyda for their valuable suggestions on this translation.

HANS RICHTER:

The Badly Trained Sensibility

'The Badly Trained Sensibility'
By Hans Richter

First published in 'G' in June 1924

They say feelings are conceived in sleep and, hatching themselves out, just appear! It is simply not true. Feeling is just as precisely structured and mechanically exact a process as thinking; it is just that our awareness of this process, or rather its IDENTITY, has been lost. So modern man is excluded from a whole sphere of perception and action.

The loss of this sphere is more pointed in film than in any other form concerned with evoking the full range of our feelings. As it has no traditional assumptions film is capable of extending sentimental indulgences to preposterous lengths.

The cinema as we have it today gives no indication of the range of possibilities open either to PHOTOGRAPHY or to MOVEMENT. Still without a well-defined aesthetic, it does not understand that creative form (schöpferische Gestaltung) is the control of material in accordance with the way we perceive things. Not knowing how our faculties function film does not realise that this is where its job really lies. Instead, the screenplays of today strain for theatrical effects.

By film I mean visual rhythm, realised photographically; imaginative material coming from the elementary laws (Elementaren und Gesetzmässigen) of sensory perception. The film illustrated here falls into this category.

Not to be content with picture-postcard views, not to find the usual love-scene, the happy-ending with virtue rewarded, the same old arrangement of legs, arms, heads in plush drawing-rooms and royal courts— but, instead, to see movement, organised movement, wakes us up, wakes up resistance, wakes up the reflexes, and perhaps wakes up our sense of enjoyment as well.

This film gives memory nothing to hang on. At the mercy of "feeling", reduced to going with the rhythm according to the successive rise and fall of the breath and the heartbeat, we are given a sense of what feeling and perceiving really is: a process—movement. This "movement" with its own organic structure is not tied to the power of association (sunsets, funerals), nor to emotions of pity (girl match-seller, once famous—now poor—violinist, betrayed love), nor indeed to "content" at all, but follows instead its own inevitable mechanical laws.

The vitality of this "movement", in itself a wonderful phenomenon, can just as easily lie untapped as become an addition to man's resources. But we must be in a position to exert control over this process to make this area of feeling as accessible to judgment as other areas of volition. This is a development of the sensibility which has eluded our grasp until now. Three crucial aspects define the extent of the method; the chief ways in which the process is built up. Here I am grateful to Viking Eggeling upon whose experiments my work is based.

A. Example of a unified form of movement.

Continuous flow, syncopated by an uneven accompanying rhythm — jerky — effect

The forms grow ⎫
fall apart ⎬ changing from
are fused completely ⎭
light : dark
horizontal : vertical
large : small
quick : slow
etc.

brought together again by a sense of relations

The single "sensuous shape", the "form", whether abstract or representational, is avoided. This film is concentrated on the process of movement.
— and □ (1/1, 1/2, 1/3,) serve as the simplest, most economical formal means by which movement is defined spatially; the essential elements of the set of relations horizontal:vertical are made dominants as the □ are built up. So the form is not arrived at arbitrarily, and improvisation is ruled out. Both rhythm and formal content are built up stage by stage within a definite frame-work.

H R

GREATEST CONTRAST:

1.　　　　　　　　　　　　　To attain perceptible differences, whether it be a matter of visual or auditory impressions, or of flights of imagination, contrasts must be clearly made. Things without differences have no fixed limits—and are imperceptible. The greatest possible contrast defines the greatest possible perceptibility.

×　　　**CLOSEST RELATIONSHIP:**

2.　　　　　　　　　　To appreciate these differences means recognising the large number of separate elements as parts of a whole. It means perceiving affinities, relationships. Just as separation is necessary for perception to impose limits on what is perceived, so combination is necessary for the fusion of what is perceived.

THEIR MUTUAL INTERACTION:

3.　　　　　　　　　From the way the two aspects of contrasting and relating depend on each other, their mutual interaction, comes feeling. This is the way of the creative process.

Film allows this quite elementary procedure to be followed in several ways. Whatever kind of film ("abstract", adventure, or some form yet unknown) is produced is unimportant compared to the SOUND STRUCTURAL BASIS OF OUR GENERAL IDEA, upon which depend the coherence and intensity of our feelings. As far as coherence and intensity are concerned, large claims may be made!

What flourishes today as "feeling" is easy submission to uncontrollable emotions about the hero, chaste maiden, and smart businessman (as above). This sensibility, some kind of mad thing made up of feelings preserved from past, and unreal, centuries, dominates and distorts our vision of the world.

Our perceptive faculties have become flabby, our breathing has become restricted; our sensibility—unable to develop—has become more a weakness than a strength.

On the whole, the modern European regards all this as a mere preoccupation with "form".

That is just where he is wrong.

The development of such a soundly based approach is not confined to introducing some novel or "superior" line of art-goods, but touches at the root of basic questions about the evolution of the psyche, which originally had a certain "thinking power" now lying fallow. This "thinking power" enables the sensibility to exercise its powers of judgment and of action. It provides the whole man with powerful means of action indispensable to his general sense of direction.　Hans Richter (trans. M.W.)

B.　Examples of the different types of expressive means—where 'formal' aspects remain.

a)　**Position**　Type of movement $\left\{\begin{array}{l}\text{as surface: space} \\ \text{as beat: flow (Gleiten)}\end{array}\right.$

b)　**Proportion**　Type of movement　=rest: play
Position, etc.

c)　**Light distribution**　Number
Proportion, etc.

NOTES

"Die schlecht trainierte Seele" first appeared in *G—Zeitschrift für elementare Gestaltung*, no. 3, June 1924, pp. 34–37, in a format which we have tried to render approximately here. Mies van der Rohe is said to have financed the type-setting on the first occasion! There were five issues of *G* (short for Gestaltung—creation, the formative process), all of which were edited by Richter, helped by Mies and Werner Graeff. One issue of particular interest to us contained a description by Hausmann of his Optophone. No. 5–6 was given over to film.

I have rendered 'Seele' in the same way that I translated 'etat d'âme' in Survage's manifesto—by 'sensibility'. It seems the modern equivalent, though should be taken to mean more than physical sensitivity. Richter's connections with the De Stijl group remind us that sensibility for them would include spirit. The illustrations are all from *Rhythmus 21*, with the exception of **B** b) which is from *Rhythmus 23*.　　　　　　　　M.W.

(*Image*, October 1965)
Translated and designed by Mike Weaver.

JEAN EPSTEIN:

The Essence of Cinema

Submitting to the interview of a
journalist one day, I had to respond to several questions destined
in this journalist's mind, I believe, to penetrate the mystery of the
cinema's identity. The first of these questions was: "For you, is
cinema documentary above all else?" And I replied: "No. The documentary is only a small part of cinema."

The journalist's second question was: "Is large-scale production
an essential feature of the cinema for you?" I responded: "No. Large-
scale production is only a part of the cinema; I attribute little importance to it." He continued his questions, for a journalist is never
short of questions; therefore he also asked me: "Are films stylized in
the cubist or expressionist manner the essence of cinema for you?"

This time my response was more categorical: "No. That is nothing
more than a subordinate property of cinema and almost represents
a corruption of this property." I believe that the extreme stylization
of the set is capable of destroying a film's equilibrium for the sake
of a single, entirely secondary element of the film: the set, towards
which all attention is attracted at the expense of the cinema properly speaking. Do you remember the saying which was part of the
program of the Théâtre d'Art Libre at its birth: "The word creates
the decor as it does everything else."? Well, I believe that the artistic cinema, which is in the process of being born, would have the
right to insert in its program this formula: "The cinematic gesture
creates the decor just as it does everything else."

The journalist questioned me further: "Are realist films the
essence of cinema for you?" This time I didn't answer him at all,
for I confess not to know what realism is in matters of art. It seems
to me that if an art is not symbolic, it is not an art. . . .

Therefore, I said that neither documentary, nor large-scale production, nor expressionism, nor realism is the essence of cinema. By

saying this, I don't mean that certain films classified in these diverse genres are not really beautiful films. I simply want to say that the documentary, expressionist, or realist aspects of these films are no more than accessory features of the cinematic structure. For inexperienced eyes, these features, even while subordinate, are often more apparent than the cinematic substance itself, and they may thus misunderstand its real importance. When a dish is too peppery, it is the pepper that you are most conscious of, but it isn't the pepper that nourishes you.

We have thus reviewed some cinematic condiments, some condiments of *photogénie*. We thus return again and forever to the question: "What are the aspects of things, of beings and of souls which are photogenic, aspects to which cinematic art has the duty of limiting itself?"

The photogenic aspect is a construct of spatio-temporal variables. That is an important formula. If you prefer a more concrete translation, here it is: *an aspect is photogenic if it changes positions and varies simultaneously in space and time.*

(1923)
Translated by Stuart Liebman

La Chute de la Maison Usher [Museum of Modern Art Stills Archive]

JEAN EPSTEIN:

For A New Avant-Garde

I just want to say this: that one must love cinema and hate it at the same time—love it as much as hate it—and this alone proves that the cinema is an art with a very well-defined personality of its own. The difficulty lies above all in the choice of that which is rightfully hateful in it. And if this choice is difficult, it is because it must be revised at extremely short intervals.

Indeed, the best friends of an art always end up becoming infatuated by their principles. And because art in its transformation goes beyond its rules at every moment, these best friends of old become the worst enemies of tomorrow, fanatics devoted to worn-out methods. This continual overturning of loyalties characterizes the evolution of all the arts at every stage.

It is thus today at last—at last but a little too late—that some methods of cinematic expression, still considered as strange and suspect a year ago have become à la mode. Being in fashion has always signalled the end of a style.

Among these methods we can chiefly enumerate the suppression of subtitles, accelerated editing, the importance accorded to and the expressionism of the sets.

The first films without subtitles were made almost simultaneously in America and in Germany. In America it was a film by Charles Ray, La Petite Baignade (The Old Swimmin' Hole), distributed and titled here though only after much delay. Retreating before the novelty of the fact, the distributors were careful to add about fifteen subtitles to the film. In Germany, it was Scherben by Lupu Pick. I haven't come here to make apologies for the so-called "American" title—incorrectly named, for it is, alas, often French too—which, prior to the image explains to the spectator what he is about to see in the next image, then afterwards tells him a second time in case he neither saw nor understood. Certainly, the suppression of the title as a new method has had its value, not entirely in and of itself but as a useful one among others. And Lupu Pick, who must be considered the master of the film without titles, showed us last season a kind of cinematic perfection, that is, *The Night of St. Sylvester,* perhaps the most filmic film that has ever been seen, in whose shadows an extreme of human passions was seen on film for the first time. Moreover, the theory which is at the base of the film without titles is evidently logical: the cinema is made to narrate with images and not with words. Only, one should never go to the extremities of theories; their extreme point is always their weak point where they give way. For one can't deny that watching a film absolutely free of subtitles is, for psychological reasons, disconcerting; the subtitle is above all a rest for the eye, a punctuation for the mind. A title often avoids a long visual explication, one that is necessary but annoying or banal. And if one had to limit oneself to films without titles, how many otherwise beautiful scenarios would become unrealizable. Finally, there are numerous kinds of information which I still believe more discreet to provide in a text than in an image; if one must indicate that an action takes place in the evening, maybe it would be better simply to write it than to show a clock face with the hands stopped at nine o'clock.

Obviously, a subtitle in a good film is no more than a kind of accident. But on the other hand, isn't advertising a film by specifying that it is without subtitles like praising the poems of Mallarmé because they do not have punctuation?

Rapid editing exists embryonically in the gigantic work of Griffith. Yet it is to Gance that the honor goes for having so perfected this method that he deserves to be considered as its inspired inventor. *La Roue* is still the formidable cinematic monument in whose shadow all French cinematic art lives and believes. Here and there, attempts are being made to escape from its hold and its stamp; it is still difficult. And if I persist in calling attention to this point, it is so that what I am about to say in a moment can not in any way be construed as a criticism of *La Roue*. It contains, moreover, elements far more noble, more pure, more moral than the discovery of the rapid editing technique which seems to me nothing more than an accident in the film. But if in *La Roue* this is a very happy accident, how unfortunate it becomes in so many other films. Today, rapid editing is abused even in documentaries; every dramatic film has a scene, if not two or three, made up of little fragments. 1925, I predict, will inundate us with films which will correspond exactly to our cinematic ideal of 1923 down to the most superficial detail. 1924 has already begun and in a month four films using breakneck editing have already been shown. It's too late; it's no longer interesting; it's a little ridiculous. Wouldn't our contemporary novelist be ridiculous if he wrote his works in the symbolist style of Francis Poictevin where, invariably, the word "memory" (*souvenir*) was written "remembrance" (*resouvenance*) and "despair" (*désespoir*) as "desperation" (*désespérance*)?

If one must say of a film that it has beautiful sets, I think that it would be better not to speak about it; the film is bad. *The Cabinet of Dr. Caligari* is the best example of the abuse of sets in cinema. *Caligari* represents a serious corruption of cinema: the hypertrophy of a subordinate feature, the stress on an "accident" at the expense of the essential. It is not chiefly about the shoddy expressionism "ready made for thirty francs" of *Caligari* that I want to speak, it is about the principle of a film which is hardly anything more than photographs of a group of sets. Everything in *Caligari* is a set: first of all the decor itself, next, the character who is as painted and tricked up as the set, finally the light—an unpardonable sacrilege in cinema—which is also painted, with shadows and half-lights illusionistically laid out in advance. Thus the film is nothing more than a still life, all the living elements having been killed by strokes of the paint brush. Along with a thousand other things, cinema has borrowed sets from the theater. Little by little, if it is viable by itself, the cinema will pay back its debts and this debt as well. The work of painters will not succeed in renewing the cinema, any more than it renewed the theater. On the contrary, the work of painters cannot but succeed at impeding the normal development, straight and pure, dramatic and poetic, of the cinema. Painting is one thing, the cinema something else entirely. If the "Théâtre d'Art" declared at its birth: "The word creates the decor as it does everything else . . .", the "Cinéma d'Art" now being born declares: "The gesture creates the decor as it does everything else." In cinema, stylized sets should not and cannot be. The decor of the fragments of those few films which approach true cinema is ana-tomical, and the drama which is played in this intimate physique is superlatively ideal. In closeup, the eyelid with the lashes that you count, is a set remodeled by emotion at every instant. Beneath the lid appears the gaze which is the character of the drama—and which is even more than a character: it is a personality. Through imperceptible movements whose religious secret no emotional microscopy has yet been able to reveal, the circle of the iris spells out a soul. Between the tuft of the chin and the arc of the eyebrows an entire tragedy is won, then lost, is rewon and lost again. Lips still pressed together, a smile quivers off-stage, towards those wings which is the heart. When the mouth finally opens, joy itself flies out.

If I criticize three techniques particularly abused by modern cinema, methods which now enjoy a belated vogue, it is because these methods are purely physical, purely mechanical. The mechan-ical period of cinema is over. The cinema must henceforth be called: the photography of illusions of the heart.

I remember my first meeting with Blaise Cendrars. It was at Nice where Cendrars was then assisting Gance in the production of *La Roue*. We were speaking about cinema and Cendrars told me:

"*Photogénie* is a word . . . very pretentious, a bit silly; but it's a great mystery!" Gradually, much later, I understood what a great mystery *photogénie* is.

Each of us, I suppose, may possess some object which he holds onto for personal reasons: for some, a book; for some, perhaps a very banal and rather ugly trinket; for someone else, perhaps a piece of furniture without value. These objects—we do not consider them as they are. To tell the truth, we are incapable of seeing these objects. What we see in them, through them, are the memories and emotions, the projects or the regrets which we have attached to these things for a more or less lengthy period of time, sometimes for forever. Now, this is the cinematic mystery: an object such as this with its personal character, that is to say, an object situated in a dramatic action that also possesses a photographic character, reveals anew its moral character, its human and living expression when reproduced cinematically.

I imagine a banker waiting at home for bad news from the stock exchange. He is waiting for a free line to telephone. The call is delayed. Closeup of the telephone. If the shot of the telephone is well presented, well written, it is no longer a mere telephone that you see. You read: ruin, failure, misery, prison, suicide. And in another atmosphere, this same telephone will say: sickness, doctor, help, death, solitude, grief. And at still another time this same telephone will cry gaily: joy, love, liberty. All this may seem extremely simple; they may be considered childish symbols.

I confess that it seems very mysterious to me that one can thus charge the simple reflection of inert objects with an intensified sense of life, that one can animate it with its own sense of life. I confess, moreover, that it seems much more important to me to concern ourselves with this phenomenon of cinematic telepathy than to cultivate two or three almost purely mechanical methods too exclusively.

M. Jean Choux, the film critic of the newspaper *La Suisse*, has written à propos of *Coeur Fidèle* the lines which I reproduce below which do not apply to this film alone.

"Apotheosis of closeups. Oh, these faces of men and women displayed so harshly on screen, solid as enamel and more powerfully sculptural than the Michelangelesque creatures on the ceiling of the Sistine! To see a thousand immobile heads whose gazes are aimed at, monopolized and haunted by a single enormous face on the screen towards which they all converge. Such a terrifying tête à tête. An idol and the crowd. Like the cults of India. But here the idol is living, and this idol is a man. From these closeups an extraordinary meaning is emitted. The soul is isolated by them, just as one isolates radium. The horror of living, its horror and mystery, is proclaimed. This pitiful Marie, this Jean and this Little Paul, don't they have any other purpose than to be this Marie, this Jean and this Little Paul? It's not possible! There must be something else."

Certainly there is something else.

The cinema heralds it.

(*A lecture delivered at the Vieux Columbier theater on December 14, 1924*)

Translated by Stuart Liebman

GERMAINE DULAC:

From "Visual and Anti-visual Films"

The great pity, as far as film is concerned, is that, though a uniquely visual art, it does not at present seek its emotion in the pure optic sense. Every cinematic drama, whether created by forms of movement or by human beings in a state of crisis, *must* be visual and not literary, and the impression retained, the essence of the creative idea or the driving feeling must emerge uniquely from the optical harmonies.

There was a time, not long ago, when the cinema was not madly seeking, as it is today, for its own meaning beyond the errors of interpretation in which the industry had enveloped it. It was happy with a traditional sort of form, letting its technique evolve to a high level of perfection without concern for its higher esthetic.

By its technique, I mean the scientific side of its material expression: photography. By its esthetic, I mean the inspiration utilized by the technique to produce expression on the level of the spirit.

And if the great masters in the evolution of film admitted that the ideas of lighting, optics and chemistry with which it was surrounded could be transformed, being at the mercy of progress, they decidedly rejected the idea of a parallel spiritual evolution.

Thanks to the combination of ribbons of sensitive film and the right machine, we had in our hands the means of photographing life and recording its various manifestations and movements. To photograph was to aim the lens at tangible forms, with a specific intention or to a specific end, and a fool would he have seemed who, beyond these precise forms, had spoken of photographing visual harmonies.

Every new technical discovery was modifying, is still modifying and becoming part of the conditions of the possibilities of vision. One discovery changes proportions by means of new lenses or prisms, digging through the visual planes to make an impression upon our sight; another, in improving the sensitivity of the film, makes it possible to capture the nuances and subtleties of color and to render their contrasts in a white, a black and a gray capable of caressing the eye. Others, perfecting the lighting, make it possible to send out to the eye radiations which touch it more powerfully. If machines decompose movement and set out to explore the realm of the infinitely small in nature, it is in order to visually reveal to us beauties and dramas that our eye, a feeble lens, does not perceive.

A horse, for instance, leaps a barrier. With our eye we judge his effort synthetically. A grain of wheat sprouts; it is synthetically, again, that we judge its growth. Cinema, by decomposing move- ment, *makes us see*, analytically, the beauty of the leap in a series of minor rhythms which accomplish the major rhythm, and, if we look at the sprouting grain, thanks to film we will no longer have only the synthesis of the movement of growth, but the psychology of this movement. We feel, visually, the painful effort a stalk ex- pends in coming out of the ground and blooming. The cinema makes us spectators of its bursts toward light and air, by capturing its unconscious, instinctive and mechanical movements.

Visually, movement, with its rhythms, its right angles and its curves, brings us into contact with a complex life.

And so, as we see, every technical cinematographic discovery has a very clear meaning: it improves the visual impression. Cinema tries to make us see *this*, to make us see *that*. Constantly, in its technical evolution, it appeals to our eye in order to impress our understanding and our sensitivity. It seems then, from its scientific basis, that cinema must address itself uniquely to sight as music addresses itself uniquely to hearing.

I am constantly repeating these words: *visual, visually, sight, eye*. Now, there is a huge contradiction here. If, in its technique, cinema is uniquely visual, it has nevertheless come about that in its moral esthetic it scorns the purely visual, the image, in favor of merely reproducing forms of expression where the image may perhaps have a role, but not the most important.

For example, the cinema records photographic shots, not to move *visually*, but to tell or to embellish plots which were not essentially created to be seen, but to be read or heard.

Instead of focusing on the value of the image and its rhythms, today's films focus on the dramatic action. There is a world of difference between mute dialogue and the music of silence.

Up until now the cinema has tended more to be a mute dialogue than to be music. Take a scene where two actors are talking to each other. The silent expressiveness of their faces will be the only visual element. But alas, in the dramatic cinema, events count for more than expressions.

The cinematographic instrument, then, in its scientific possibili- ties, is conceived for one purpose, but cinematic inspiration is pursuing a different one. Where is the truth? I believe it is in the instrument that has created the seventh art.

But why, you ask me, this duality of goals? Because of the fundamental error which dominated the first scenarios, which were imbued with the preconception that a dramatic action could not develop otherwise than in the manner of a novel or a play, that is, by means of specific events rather than by means of suggestiveness of expression.

Human action, since that was what they wanted to bring to life, consisted of gestures, of catching comings and goings, races, battles, and since it was necessary to find a pretext to support this external action, they said to themselves, "Let's adapt literary and dramatic works to the cinema, perfectly safe works which have already earned their popularity." From this came the contemporary cinema.

When they come to us, the directors, and ask us to do a film, the producers don't say to us, "Do you have a visual idea? Do you have a visual theme, according to which your scene can develop visually?" What they say to us is, "Adapt such and such a play that's full of action, or such and such a novel that's had a big printing, and put that on the screen," and they look for the story, turning away from the visual and falling into the literary.

And from this comes the stagnation of the cinema. From this comes the fact that the seventh art, an ample, magnificent and new mode of expression, seems in most of its productions to be stricken with sterility, and fills us with disillusionment and sometimes with bitterness. It's that the screen, far from capturing on the whiteness of its canvas *visual tones*, is content to reflect only forms which I would call *anti-visual*.

To be visual, to reach the feelings through harmonies, chords, of shadow, of light, of rhythm, of movement, of facial expressions, is to address oneself to the feelings and to the intelligence by means of the eye.

A deaf creature could never hear anything but the internal music which sings inside him, and can in no case perceive the sound waves which come from outside, or find joy in them.

In the same way, a blind man could not logically be struck by visual forms which are not part of his previous experience. Now I'm perfectly willing to argue that, as cinema stands today, a blind man could take pleasure in a filmed work. It would only require that someone sit beside him and explain to him the active sense of the images. Here's the young male lead, he's tall and blond, he's sitting in a garden in the moonlight, he's alone and seems to be waiting for someone. Here comes the young female lead running in. She comes up to him. Embrace. Nearby, in the garden, the traitor is watching. I can assure you that the blind man, as he listens to this narrative, will get the sense of the film; that is, he'll follow the story and get from the show at least 50% of what he would have gotten by seeing it.

Now a real film can't be able to be told, since it must draw its active and emotive principle from images formed of unique visual tones. Can you tell a painting? Can you tell a sculpture? Of course not. One can only evoke the impression and the emotion they inspire.

Works for the screen, in order to be worthy of the profound meaning of cinema, should not consist of a story, either—the power of the image alone should be the active principle and take precedence over every other quality.

In making a film, they push the story first and place the image in the background, which is to say they give theatre precedence over cinema. When the relationship is reversed, then cinema will begin to live according to its own meaning. It is the struggle of the image, taken in the profound sense of its orchestration, against literature.

The whole problem of cinema is in this word: visualization.

I will not seem paradoxical, then, when I say to you:

The future belongs to the film that cannot be told.

I'll explain what I mean.

Visual impact is ephemeral, it's an impression you receive and which suggests a thousand thoughts. An impact similar to that created by a musical chord.

The cinema can certainly tell a story, but you have to remember that the story is nothing. The story is a surface.

The seventh art, that of the screen, is depth rendered perceptible, the depth that lies beneath that surface; it is the musical ungraspable.

Whether it's a matter of a face, a geometrical form, an evolving line, it is movement, in all its richness, rendered by the rhythm of its curves, of its right angles, that creates the drama. A body that stretches out or contracts in a total movement. A grain of wheat that sprouts, the horse's leap, visual and silent movements of the same bearing, the same general lines. So it's not the extravagance of literary imagination that makes the film. The film is something much more simple. The expressiveness of a face, to have its full value, must not be divided between one shot and the next.

A grain of wheat that sprouts does not change place, it rises up; a horse's leap is accomplished in a very limited space, and all the same, in all three situations, there is movement, more movement, believe me, than in a chase . . . let's not confuse agitation and movement.

This idea necessarily leads certain filmmakers to envision for some of their works unity of action and unity of place; they feel that in this concentration and in this continuity the visual dramatic movement will have more power, more value. An estheticism utterly opposed to the American theory of combined actions and fragmented visions.

The more we get rid of the plot to go in the direction of visual cinema, the more we will work for the seventh art.

This conception entails a necessary revision of cinematic themes.

Plot film or abstract film, the problem is the same. To touch the feelings through the sight and to give, as I have already said, predominance to the image, pushing aside that which cannot be expressed by it alone. The image can be as complex as an orchestration since it may be composed of combined movements of expression and light.

Visual cinema: these two words coupled together seem a redundancy. In the future, perhaps, but not now. . . . At this moment cinema is anti-visual. Let us make it visual and sincere. This is the very first great reform to attempt.

(*Le Rouge et le Noir*, July, 1928)
Translated by Robert Lamberton

GERMAINE DULAC:

The Essence of the Cinema: The Visual Idea

I will be concerned, in these few pages, not with discussing technique, but rather with discussing the moral essence of the cinematic art, an art born of our own time, and for which we must make an effort, in order to avoid the misunderstanding which so often meets unexpected revelations.

We know that that which is will have another face tomorrow, and we are already trying to pick out the features of this new face in the mist of the future. Yesterday's truth at first obscures tomorrow's, before giving way to it, but we, a generation committed to progress, refuse to remain in its shadow.

This liberal spirit in which our period prides itself is, in fact, scarcely applied outside the realm of science. One discovery is always made possible by another, and this process makes us more receptive to novelty. In the realm of pure ideas, this liberalism is not so grand, we must admit, in spite of the coquettishness with which we sport it.

Occasionally, an idea with no precedent springs from a prophetic brain, with no preparation, and we are surprised. We do not understand it and we have difficulty accepting it. Should we not, then, contemplate this idea religiously, from the moment it appears to us in the light of its dawn, contemplate it with a fresh intelligence, stripped of all tradition, avoiding reducing it to our own level of understanding, in order, on the contrary, to raise ourselves up to it and expand our understanding with what it brings us? But the overpowering tradition is there to scorn and turn to ridicule everything new.

The Cinema provides conclusive proof of this capsule theory.

When, thirty years ago, the Lumière brothers had perfected the discovery which made it possible to capture life in its movement, the entire world bowed down before the mechanical invention.

The sensitivity of the photographic images each recording a stage in the movement, and by their multiplicity making it possible to reconstitute the entire movement . . . everyone found the accomplishment marvelous. People became interested in the invention and improved it. The movie camera came to be as a scientific instrument, a precision recording device.

When, many years later, artists, people who work with ideas, discovered that the cinema had a soul, an intellectual meaning which made it possible for it to leave the scientific realm and enter that of art, with hitherto unknown powers and forms, the Tradition was roused.

For many centuries, there had been only six arts: painting, music, poetry, sculpture, dance, architecture. One would certainly have had to be a fool to pretend to add a new member to this magnificent company. Another art? What an aberration! Was it necessary, and did artists need it to express themselves? . . . The human sensibility already had abundant means of expression, and a new art springing up beside the others seemed something useless and insane.

Nevertheless, a caste of artists has been born which is unwilling to express its sensibility and its intelligence in any of the pre-existing forms. They are neither writers nor dramatists nor painters nor sculptors nor architects nor musicians, they are Filmmakers, for whom the art of movement, as contained in cinema, is a unique form of expression. These practitioners of a new art do not view the cinema from the usual perspective of the crowd, and if they allow themselves to be drawn into making concessions to the taste of the public, in submitting to economic pressures, they feel they have committed treason.

And this is the reason why, for some time, enthusiastic Filmmakers have been preaching their Faith, both aloud and in writing, trying to convince—lest the works born from their efforts meet with disastrous failure, for I must add, in parentheses, that a failure is not permitted in an undertaking which involves enormous amounts of capital, unless some Maecenas . . . . , but that's only a dream, and what we must do is to convince the public (without whom we are helpless to do anything) that its taste, its demands, are not in line with the spirit of cinema.

From the beginning, people got used to a bad kind of cinematic optic, and when the Filmmakers noticed the mistake and tried to lead the crowd in a new direction, the crowd refused, and the error perpetuates itself.

The Cinema, as we conceive it today, is nothing but the mirror of the other arts. Well, it is too big a thing to remain only a mirror, it must be freed from its chains and be given its true personality. In its technique, nothing links it to the pre-existing arts.

No doubt it is accepted that the external goal of the cinema is to reproduce visually a movement in its total period: it does not, like sculpture or painting, reproduce the single instant of a gesture, it completes it and follows it in its evolution. Sculpture, painting, decoration, architecture, grown old in their immobility, are nothing to it, and I will even say that photography is nothing but a means of expression for it, its pen and ink, not its thought.

If, at this moment, I think of interior movement, I think of literature (poetry, drama, novel) and also music.

A play is movement because there is constant evolution in the characters, the events, the facial expressions. The novel is also movement: the revelation of ideas which succeed one another, emerge and interact, playing against one another. And poetry is movement, reflecting successive impressions, contrasting and linking together sensations, states of the soul.—The words, in literature, can be seen as the elements of a movement which is recreated by the sentence. Music is movement, too, developing in ever-changing, always living harmonies.

We accept, then, that literature in its various forms, dramatic art and music are arts of movement, like cinema.

Others before me made this connection, when the Lumière brothers' invention was first perfected, and it turned out to be a disastrous connection which falsified from its very foundation the new means of artistic expression the inventors were putting in our hands. The mechanical instrument was out in front of internal perception and the discovery was exploited commercially without any attempt to see if it contained an artistic potential, if a new form of expression was latent within it, like some unknown substance.

At that time, I repeat, the Filmmakers, that is, the artists who feel the need of dynamic expression in movement, were not yet born into the intellectual world. Since the instrument was ahead of the creative spirit and the form had gotten ahead of the art, practical minds had the idea of putting visual movement at the service of already existing movements, of literature, of dramatic and novelistic conceptions. Instead of envisioning the art of movement in itself, they confused it with agitation, with change of place. They saw in it only the means of multiplying the scenes and sets of a play, of extending the stages of the theatres out to the horizon and reinforcing the dramatic action by changes of perspective.

As for music, no one even thought about it. Music was an art of sensations which were too abstract. Its only use was accompanying films.

From that point on, in the intellectual world, Cinema was put in its place. It became a new means of expression for novelistic or dramatic literature, and since cinema was movement, it was confused with the interrelating of actions, of situations, it was put in the service of the "story to tell" and since visualized stories demand a frame, a setting, so the static arts of architecture and painting followed after the literary idea and lept upon the poor cinema, taking it for a beast that would easily be domesticated. What could it use from them? Nothing. Nothing but sets, which were not even made for it. For cinema, which is moving, changing, interrelated light, nothing but light, genuine and restless light can be its true setting.

Cinema, considered (or rather unconsidered) from this point of view, was nothing but an entirely secondary intellectual novelty, and as such was ranked among the lower-grade forms of expression. Thus condemned to servitude, it was unable to grow, and in spite of all the beautiful accomplishments it offers us (which all the same are perhaps not in its own spirit) it remains stifled.

Thus, even today, cinema has not achieved its real place as an intrinsic art. The public, suspicious *a priori* of every innovation, and coming to the support of tradition, has filed it between theatre and literature; lucky it hasn't been treated as a substitute for painting, architecture or sculpture!

Now cinema is not composed of any of the elements of these arts. It is unjustly held prisoner in the framework of [the past],[1] chained, reduced to outdated conceptions, when what we should be doing is to search, in what it offers us, for the expansion of our sensitive being in an unexplored form.

The cinema is a new art, and even in the forms which tradition and the industry have imposed upon it its contributions are of the first importance.

One of its first characteristics is its educational and instructive power; in documentaries we see film as a sort of microscope with which we are able to perceive, within the realm of reality, things we would not perceive without it. In a documentary, in a scientific film, life appears before us in its infinite detail, its evolution, all that the eye is normally unable to follow.

Among others, there is a slow-motion study of the blooming of flowers. Flowers, whose stages of life appear to us brutal and defined, birth, blooming, death, and whose infinitesimal development, whose movements equivalent to suffering and joy are unknown to us, appear before us in cinema in the fullness of their existence.

When we were children and were taught natural history, we were told about bees and how they lived. We looked at the motionless images in our books but all of that was very distant for us, a land open only to the imagination. With cinema, no more unexplored countries! No more barriers between us and things! No more barrier beween our spirit and truth in its subtlety! Moreover, scientifically, cinema casts upon everything it records a clear light which banishes errors and distortions.

The cinema is an eye wide open on life, an eye more powerful than our own and which sees things we cannot see.

Truth, subtlety, logic, the grasping of the ungraspable; undeniable contributions; cinema decidedly has its own place, and an eminent one, since it teaches us things which, without it, we would not know. And starting from an entirely scientific and material

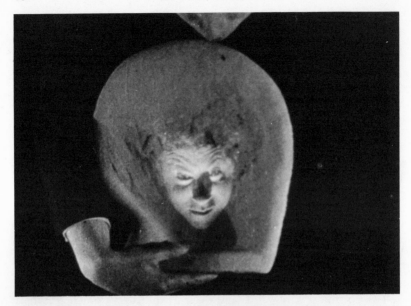

La Coquille et le Clergyman [Museum of Modern Art Stills Archive]

foundation, we can build the theoretical structure of a new art, the art of the *visual idea* with its roots in nature, in reality, and in the imponderable.

The films created in each country are marked with their point of origin; they have nationalities. But we penetrate beyond local customs to the spirit, to the soul, because cinema with its stories that are often infantile and make us shrug our shoulders has performed the magnificent task of extending our spirit in the direction of the human, of teaching us to see the major outlines and ignore the details. It simplifies our spirit, by elevating it.

In the imaginative realm, then, it has brought inspiration down to that which men have in common among them, and submitted it as well to those rules of synthesis which lead toward the great illumination, those rules of logic which determine that one point in a movement must, harmoniously, make way for another.

Cinematic methods, which concentrate impressions, have accustomed the most rebellious spirits to a kind of rapidity of movement which is found in contemporary literature and theatre. This is to establish the fact that neither literature nor theatre, which dilute impressions and inspirations, have influenced cinema, but on the contrary they have been influenced by it.

Can we not deduce from this that, since literature and theatre, which have wanted to enter into and still do enter into the visual idea, have had to submit to the laws of the cinema, it is because they are not fit to collaborate with us? And, particularly, when a director must draw his inspiration from a novel or a play, what he takes most often from this novel or play is the suggestion that is *not* realized in the words or the events, and he creates a new work alongside the previously created one.

Should not cinema, which is an art of vision, as music is an art of hearing, on the contrary lead us toward the visual idea composed of movement and life, toward the conception of an art of the eye, made of a perceptual inspiration evolving in its continuity and reaching, just as music does, our thought and feelings?

An art made of truth and nuances, radiating the imponderable! An art which does not have its limits set by a lump of clay, a piece of canvas, lines which come to an end, words which trap life, the tight channel of a sentence stifling feeling.

Only music can inspire this feeling which cinema also aspires to, and in the light of the sensations that it offers we can get a sense of those that the cinema of the future will give us. Music, too, lacks defined limits. Can one not conclude, in the light of things as they are, that the visual idea, the theme which sings in the hearts of filmmakers has far more to do with musical technique than with any other technique or any other ideal?

Music, which creates this sort of beyond of the human feelings, which records the multiplicity of the states of the soul, plays with sounds in movement just as we play with images in movement. This helps us to understand what the visual idea is: the artistic development of a new form of sensibility.

The integral film which we all hope to compose is a visual symphony made of rhythmic images, coordinated and thrown upon the screen exclusively by the perception of an artist. A composer does not always take his inspiration from a story, but most often from a feeling, a perception.

Debussy's *Le Jardin sous la Pluie,* or Chopin's "goutte d'eau" prelude, for example, are the expressions of a soul pouring forth, reacting among things.

There is no story there except that of a soul which feels and thinks, and nevertheless our feelings are reached. The heart of the composer sings in the notes, which, perceived in turn by the audience, cause the emotion to be born in them. In the same way the sensitivity of the filmmaker can express itself through a superimposition of light and movement, the sight of which will move the soul of the viewer.

The cinema which, like Proteus, takes on so many varied forms, is also capable of remaining just what it is today. Music accompanies many plays and poems, but music would never have been music if it had been confined within this union of notes, words and action.

There is the symphony, pure music. Why should the cinema not have its symphony as well?

The character is not the center of importance in a scene, but the relationship of the images to one another, and as in every art it is not the external fact which is really interesting, it is the emanation from within, a certain movement of things and people, viewed through the state of the soul. Is that not the essence of the seventh art?

Today the inspiration of the filmmaker is held down.

Every work of art is essentially personal. Unfortunately, film-makers do not have the right to express themselves; they must put their own sensitivity at the service of works which are already well known, since the public does not accept, alas, any but a certain kind of film, so far.

Among the viewers a few love the cinema for its future possibilities. They will understand. Many others love the cinema in its present state and it is to them that I wish especially to speak, because it is a terrible mistake to keep this beautiful art prisoner, an art whose future is so much greater than the miserable little stories we make it tell.

And I will have finished when I have said it one more time: Our ideal is far beyond our accomplishments; you must help us to liberate the cinema from its shackles and create a pure cinema.

(*Les Cahiers du Mois,* No. 16/17, 1925)
Translated by Robert Lamberton

NOTE

1. There seem to be one or more words missing in the original at this point, probably representing a typesetter's error. I have translated what appears to be the sense of the passage.—Trans.

GERMAINE DULAC:

The Avant-Garde Cinema

The works of the cinematic avant-garde:
their destiny before the public and film industry

We can use the term "avant-garde" for any film whose technique, employed with a view to a renewed expressiveness of image and sound, breaks with established traditions to search out, in the strictly visual and auditory realm, new emotional chords. The avant-garde film does not appeal to the mere pleasure of the crowd. It is at once too egoistic and too altruistic. Egoistic, because it is the personal manifestation of a pure thought; altruistic, because it is isolated from every concern other than progress. The sincere avant-garde film has this fundamental quality of containing, behind a sometimes inaccessible surface, the seeds of the discoveries which are capable of advancing film toward the cinematic form of the future. The avant-garde is born of both the criticism of the present and the foreknowledge of the future.

The cinema is an art and an industry. Considered as art, it must jealously defend its purity of expression and never betray that purity in order to convince. But it is also an industry. To make a film and distribute it require money, a lot of money. The photographic film which receives the image is expensive, its processing costly. By itself, every visual or audio element used corresponds to a figure, a fixed expense. The electricity required for a beautiful lighting effect can only be had for money, and for another example, there is the lens. The list would be a long one, were I to go on.

The film industry produces commercial films, films made with a concern for reaching the public at large, and it produces mercantile films as well. By mercantile films should be understood those which make every concession to pursue a simple economic goal, and by commercial films those which, taking the greatest possible advantage of cinematic expression and technique, sometimes produce interesting works while still working toward a reasonable profit. That is where the union of industry and art occurs.

From the commercial cinema emerges the total work, the balanced film for which the industry and the avant-garde, separated in their two camps, both work.

In general, the industry does not attach itself zealously to the contribution of art; the avant-garde, with its opposite impulse, considers nothing else. Whence the antagonism.

❋   ❋   ❋

The avant-garde and the commercial cinema, that is, the art and the industry of film, form an inseparable whole.

But the avant-garde, which is essential to the evolution of film, has most of the public and all of the producers against it.

The various avant-garde schools have attempted:

1. To free the cinema from the hold of the existing arts;
2. To bring it back to the considerations essential to it: movement, rhythm, life.

Historic Evolution.

Since Louis Lumière's mechanical discovery, cinema has always excited research by filmmakers, on the level of the spirit, parallel to that of the inventors. Wasn't Méliès, in his day, an avant-garde filmmaker, substituting the spirit of cinema for the spirit of photography? [1]

❋   ❋   ❋

It is rather upsetting to consider the simple mentality with which the public received the first cinematic presentations. First of all, for the public, the cinema was a photographic means of reproducing the mechanical movement of life. They were happy with the sight of a train arriving in a station, without dreaming that, therein, lay hidden a new contribution offering a means of expression to the sensibility and the intelligence.

The capture of life-movement envisaged as simple photographic reproduction became, before every other effort, an outlet for literature. Animated photographs were assembled around a composed, fictive action; the life angle was abandoned and only the literature angle kept in view. And so the cinema entered into the cerebral domain of narrative movement. A theatrical work is movement. The novel is also movement, because there is an interlocking and succession of situations, ideas, feelings, which interact with one another. The human being is movement, because he moves, he acts. From deduction to deduction, from confusion to confusion, rather than study in themselves, for their intrinsic value, the ideas of movement, of the image and its rhythm, they turned the cinema into a photographed stage show. They took it as an easy means of multiplying the episodes and settings of a drama, of reinforcing and varying the theatrical or novelistic situations of the story with the help of endless cuts, using an alternation of artificial sets and natural backdrops.

The years passed, improving the means of execution and affirming the film sense, the direction the filmmakers had taken. The narrative cinema evolved, completely arbitrary and novelistic. The plot was wrapped in realistic forms and the emotions reduced to proportions which were strictly true and human.

The logic of an event, the precision of a frame, the correctness of a pose constituted the basic structural parts of the new cinematic technique. Moreover, along with composition, expressive pacing intervened in the organization of the images and gave birth to rhythm, although, in spite of the visual sense which was beginning to dawn, the story "for the story" won out.

The shots no longer succeeded one another independently, tied together by nothing more than a title, but came to depend on each other with a moving and rhythmical psychological logic.

Before long, they thought of photographing the unexpressed, the invisible, the imponderable, the human soul, the visual "suggestive" emerging from the precision of photography. Above the facts, a line of feelings was sketched out, harmonic, dominating people and things.

From this the psychological film logically emerged. It seemed childish to put a character in a given situation without evoking the realm of his interior life, and so they added to his movements the perception of his thoughts, his feeling, his sensations. With the addition to the bare facts of the drama of the description of the multiple and contradictory impressions in the course of an action—the facts no longer existing in themselves, but becoming the consequence of a moral state—a duality imperceptibly entered, a duality which, to remain in equilibrium, adapted itself to the cadence of a rhythm, to the dynamism and pace of the images.

And the avant-garde activity began. The public and most of the film industrialists had accepted realism; confronted with the developed and isolated play of emotional and perceptual elements, they rebelled. The cinema must, according to their theories, belong exclusively and dryly to the drama created by the situations and the facts, and not to the drama provoked by the conflicts of minds and hearts. They fought against impressionism and expressionism without realizing that all the research undertaken by the innovators of the day was enlarging the domain of pure action, of emotion set free by "psychological projections and analysis of atmosphere." [2]

Abel Gance's *La Roue* marks a great step forward. In this film, psychology, gestures, drama became dependent on a cadence. The characters were no longer the only important factors in the work,

but rather the objects as well, the machines, and the length of the
shots, their composition, their opposition, their framing, their harmony. Rails, locomotives, boilers, wheels, pressure gauge, smoke,
and tunnels act through the images along with the characters; a
new drama burst forth made up of raw emotions and of lines of
development. The conception of the art of movement, and of
systematically paced images came into its own, as well as the
expression of *things* magnificently accomplishing the visual poem
made up of human life-instincts, playing with matter and the imponderable. A symphonic poem, where emotion bursts forth not
in facts, not in actions, but in visual sonorities. Imperceptibly,
narrative storytelling, the actor's performance lost some of their
isolated value, in favor of a general orchestration made up of
planes, rhythms, frames, angles, light, proportions, contrasts, harmony of images.

"To strip the cinema of all those elements which did not properly
belong to it, to find its true essence in the understanding of movement and visual values: this was the new esthetic that appeared
in the light of a new dawn." [3]

The definitive rise of the avant-garde

It was about 1924 when the undertakings and experiments of a
few courageous directors split off from commercial production to
become what is called avant-garde production. The divorce between these two forms of production became necessary because
the public could not accept certain innovative scenes in the films of
the day, passionately involved as they were in the convolutions of
the plot. These passages, moreover, were officially suppressed, if
they crept into the finished work, either by the producers or by the
theatre-owners, who were anxious to spare the audience the shock
or the displeasure brought on by a new technique of expressive
images.

And so there were, from then on, avant-garde production and distribution. Minimal production; limited distribution. Production
which was minimal because the experiments did not find, in order
to multiply, the capital which is continually necessary to any stable
cinematic effort. And the avant-garde, detached from motives of
profit, marched boldly on toward the conquest of the new modes
of expression which it felt would serve to expand cinematic thought,
with nothing to fall back on, materially or morally, but with faith.
It studied the expansion it wanted, analysing the possibilities, determined to make the expression of every being, of every object,
moving. It scorned neither the infinitely large nor the infinitely
small. Within pure cinematic means, beyond literature and theatre,
it sought emotion and feeling in movement, volumes and forms,
playing with transparencies, opacities and rhythms. It was the era
of pure cinema which, rejecting all other action, wanted to cling

only to that which emerged directly from the image, "in the attempt to give a strictly personal expression of the universe." [4]

Pure cinema did not reject sensitivity or drama, but it tried to attain them through purely visual elements. It went in search of emotion beyond the limits of the human, to everything that exists in nature, to the invisible, the imponderable, to abstract movement. It was this school which set forth in various forms, both ironic [5] and sensitive,[6] the expression of movement and rhythm, liberating these from the novelistic situation, in order to allow the idea, the criticism or the dramatic action, to burst forth suggestively. The proofs to be given were:

1. That the expression of a movement depends on its rhythm;
2. That the rhythm in itself and the development of a movement constitute the two perceptual and emotional elements which are the bases of the dramaturgy of the screen;
3. That the cinematic work must reject every esthetic principle which does not properly belong to it and seek out its own esthetic in the contributions of the visual;
4. That the cinematic action must be *life*.
5. That the cinematic action must not be limited to the human person, but must extend beyond it into the realm of nature and dream.

The essential givens of pure cinema might be found in certain scientific writings, those which discuss, for example, the formation of crystals, the trajectory of a bullet, the bursting of a bubble (a pure rhythm, and what a moving one! wonderful syntheses), the evolution of microbes, the expressiveness and lives of insects.

Was not cinema potentially capable of grasping with its lenses the infinitely large and the infinitely small? This school of the ungraspable turned its attention to other dramas than those played by actors. More than anything else, it was attacked because it scorned the story to latch onto suggestive impression and expression and because it enveloped the viewer in a network, not of events to follow, but of sensations to experience and to feel. Today we find the influence of this school expressed very clearly in the actions of certain beautiful films which are accessible to every taste, such as *The General Line [Old and New]* (transformation of cream into butter and the movement of the mechanical churn) and Dovzhenko's *Earth* (the rain fertilizing the soil and running over the flowers and fruit). Alongside of the pure cinema school, certain visual composers set out to treat nature itself in new rhythms, transforming abstract reveries into concrete and living realities. With them, the cinema expanded its stock of rhythmic truths.[7]

All these contributions of the avant-garde were instinctively absorbed by the commercial cinema, slowly, and without a revolution. While the pure cinema remained deliberately abstract, other audacious works inspired by it applied its techniques to more direct feelings, in general using that technique toward ends which met with less resistance.

❋   ❋   ❋

Conclusion

To sum up, the avant-garde has been the abstract exploration and realization of pure thought and technique, later applied to more clearly human films. It has not only established the foundations of the dramaturgy of the screen, but researched and cultivated all the possibilities of expression locked in the lens of a movie camera.

Its influence is undeniable. It has, so to speak, sharpened the eye of the public, the sensitivity of the creators, and broken new ground in enlarging cinematic thought in its totality.

The avant-garde, let us repeat, is a living ferment; it contains the seeds of the conceptions of future generations, which is to say, progress.

The cinematic avant-garde is necessary to the art, and to the industry.

(*Le Cinéma des Origines à nos Jours*, Ed. du Cygne, 1932)

Translated by Robert Lamberton

NOTES

1. In the case of Méliès, the French play on words, *esprit* = spirit *and* wit, is important, though impossible to translate. —Tr.
2. *Das Kabinett des Dr. Caligari, Coeur Fidèle, La Souriante Madame Beudet, El Dorado.*—Surprising though it may be, it was enlightened producers who made such undertakings possible at this period.
3. Germaine Dulac, *Les Esthétiques et Les Entraves*, Librairie Félix Alcan, 1927.
4. Jean Tédesco.
5. Fernand Léger's *Ballet Mécanique*, Hans Richter's series of films, René Clair's *Entr' acte*.
6. Viking Eggeling's absolute films, Ruttmann's *Opus I-IV*, Henri Chomette's *Reflets du Lumière et de Vitesse, Cinq Minutes de Cinéma Pur*, Deslaw's *La Marche des Machines*, René Clair's *Essais en Couleurs* and *La Tour*, Joris Ivens's *Le Pont*, Germaine Dulac's *Arabesques, Disque 927*, and *Thèmes et Variations*.
7. Jean Grémillon's *Tour au Large*, Dimitri Kirsanoff's *Brumes d'Automne*, Joris Ivens's *Regen*, Marcel Carné's *Nogent, Eldorado du Dimanche*, Jean Vigo's film of social criticism A *propos de Nice*, Victor Blum's mountain film *Wasser*, Ruttmann's *Melodie der Welt*, Caballeros's *Essence de Verveine*.

Omitted passages have been indicated by three asterisks.

ANTONIN ARTAUD:

Sorcery and the Cinema

One continually hears that the cinema is in its infancy and that we are only hearing its first babblings. I dare say I do not understand this viewpoint. The cinema came into existence at an advanced stage in the development of human thought and benefits from this development. Doubtless it is a means of expression whose technical development still has some way to go. One can imagine several improvements which, for example, would give the camera a stability and a mobility which it does not have. One day soon we shall probably have a three-dimensional cinema, even color cinema. But these are accessories which cannot add much to the substratum of the cinema itself which is a language in its own right just as much as music, painting, and poetry. In the cinema I have always distinguished a quality wholly peculiar to the secret movement and material of images. There is one element of cinema that is unpredictable and mysterious, which one does not find in other forms of art. It is a fact that even the driest and most banal image is transformed on the screen. The smallest detail, the most insignificant object take on a meaning and a life which is theirs alone, aside from the meaning of the images themselves, or the thought they translate and the symbol which they constitute. By isolating the objects, cinema gives them a life of their own which becomes increasingly independent and detaches them from their ordinary sense. A leaf, a bottle, a hand, etc. are imbued with a quasi-animal life which begs to be used. Then there are the distortions of the camera, the unforseen use it makes of the things one gives it to record. The moment the image vanishes, a detail to which one had not paid attention catches fire with a singular force, and profoundly changes one's impression. There is also a kind of physical intoxication which the rotation of the images communicates directly to the brain. The mind is thrilled irrespective of any representation. This virtual power in the images searches out in the depths of the mind possibilities as yet unused.

The cinema is essentially the revealer of a whole occult life with which it puts us into direct contact. But we must know how to divine this occult life. There are far better means than through the play of superimpositions for divining the secrets which animate the depths of consciousness. Raw cinema, as it is, in the abstract, exudes a little of this trance-like atmosphere, eminently favorable for certain revelations. To use it to tell stories, an exterior action, is to deny its best resources, to go against its most profound goal. That is why I think the cinema is made primarily to express matters of thought, the interior consciousness, not by the play of images but by something more imponderable which restores them to us in their direct material, without interpositions, without representations. The cinema has arrived at a turning-point in human thought at the very moment when language loses its power to make symbols and the mind tires of the play of representations. Clear thought does not suffice for us. It situates a world utterly used up. Clarity is what is immediately accessible, but that is what encloses life in a hard and impenetrable crust. One begins to see that this over-familiar life which has lost all its symbols is not the whole of life. And today is a great age for sorcerers and saints, greater than ever before. A whole imperceptible substance takes shape and tries to reach the light. The cinema is bringing us nearer to this substance. There can be no cinema unless it translates dreams or whatever pertains to the realm of dreams in waking life. It might as well be the theater. But the cinema, a direct and rapid language, has no need for a slow and ponderous logic to live and flourish. The cinema will come closer and closer to fantasy, which we come to see more and more as really the only reality, or else there will be no more cinema. Or soon it will end up like painting and poetry. What is certain is that most forms of representation have had their day. That is why for quite a while already good painting has only served to reproduce the abstract. It is therefore not only a matter of choice. There will not be one art of film which represents life and another which represents the process of thought. For life, what we call life, becomes more and more inseparable from the mind, as the forces active in the depth of the self rise to the surface like outcroppings, which the cinema can translate more aptly than any other art, since stupid order and customary clarity are its enemies.

The Seashell and the Clergyman is part of this search for a subtle order, a hidden life which I have wished to make plausible, as plausible and real as the other.

To understand this film it is enough to look deeply into one's self. To abandon oneself to plastic, objective, and attentive examination of the inner *self* which was to this day the exclusive domain of the "Illuminated."

(1927)
Translated by P. Adams Sitney,
incorporating several generous
suggestions from Schuldt.

JOSEPH CORNELL:

Monsieur Phot
(seen through the stereoscope)

The voices will be silent and the rest of the picture will be in sound.

New York City about 1870. A park on a winter afternoon. In front of a large equestrian statue, the base of which is protected by an iron picket fence, stands a row of nine street urchins facing the camera. One holds a basket of clean laundry, another stands beside a harp. The recently melted snow has left puddles of water among the car tracks in the foreground.

The urchins are giving their attention to a photographer and his apparatus shown at almost close-up distance on the left edge of the field of vision. His high silk hat is lying by his paraphernalia on the wet cobblestones.

Some bickering among the boys causes the photographer to emerge from under his black sheet, and he threads his way fastidiously through the puddles to the group of urchins. The photographer is heavily bearded in the style of his time and his manner is one of excessive politeness. He is wearing a wing collar and formal afternoon dress.

Close-up of photographer and boys. His politely remonstrative gestures reveal that he must have absolute order and quiet from them.

Original scene. The polite photographer picks his way back to his camera and goes under the black sheet again.

At this point we are permitted to view the scene through the lens of the polite photographer's black box. Perfect order prevails among the urchins, when, at regular intervals, a group of pigeons fly monotonously five or six times in and out of the field of vision. Then the photographer is interrupted by a passing horse-car.

(From now on the film will be in color).

Before there is time to press the bulb, a pheasant of gorgeous plumage runs excitedly into the scene. The urchin with the laundry

chases it, disappearing for a moment or so with his basket at the
left, then taking his place in line again.

Quiet again prevails when suddenly the basket of laundry seems
to have become animated and the above mentioned pheasant
finally extricates itself from a train of white linen. It flutters in the
air striking with its beak at the boys who shield their faces pitifully
with their arms but do not fight back.

Close-up of boys and bird. The photographer strides into the
scene and beats off the pheasant with his silk hat. The urchins
bestow upon him looks of heart-rending gratitude. The polite
photographer helps to reassemble the linen. (Here ends the passage
in color).

On returning to his camera, the photographer must wait patiently
for a horse-car to pass slowly. The scene is still viewed through his
camera. Calm again reigns when the urchin with the harp seats
himself quietly on a stool and begins playing Reynaldo Hahn's
lovely "Si mes vers avaient des ailes!" The others stand attentively
and are not distracted by the music.

Close-up of the photographer emerging as in a trance from the
black sheet. His eyes are moist and he is deeply moved. He remains
frozen for awhile in an attitude of gentle ecstasy. Fadeout into the
original scene without the view through the photographer's camera.

The urchin at the harp is the sole survivor of the group. He continues to play as the polite photographer industriously packs his
apparatus. He then dons his hat (he wears no overcoat), shoulders
the apparatus, and, waiting for another horse-car to pass, carefully
crosses the puddles toward the boy. He stops for a moment and
turns toward the back of the harp player who is oblivious of his
presence.

Close-up of the head and shoulders of the photographer looking
down upon the urchin in tenderest compassion, tears streaming
down his cheeks and spotting his immaculate white wing collar.

Original scene. The photographer goes on his way past the
statue into the distance. The playing continues. It is becoming
dark. Snow is beginning to fall.

An hour later. It is now so dark that we can but barely distinguish the boy at the harp through the falling snow.

Another hour later. Complete darkness except for a few street
lights in the distance. The rippling music of the harp sounds like a
fountain playing into water. The bleakness of the past two hours
has been punctuated by the passing of an occasional horse-car.
We hear the far-off approach, see what we can of a dimly lighted
interior through the snow covered windows, and hear the distant
crunching of the heavy wheels swallowed up by the night.

Just as the sound of one of these cars fades, the voice of a rich
mezzo-soprano floats out upon the night air, singing in French the
melody, "Si mes vers avaient des ailes!" which is superbly accompanied by the harp.

With the song ended, there is to be noted a change in the playing of the music. With each repetition there is more feeling poured into the execution, until a more transcendently beautiful interpretation is scarcely imaginable. The music stops suddenly. Complete silence. After some moments a horse-car is heard approaching, passing, and swallowed up again by the night. The snow is still falling.

        ✿   ✿   ✿

The huge parlor of a hotel of the Victorian period. Windows the height of the room line the walls on each side. The floor is covered with figured carpet. Large, elaborate chandeliers and ornate decorations give the impression of a ballroom. In the foreground, to the left, is a piano with a dust cover. Morning sunlight is streaming in through the windows on the left and a Sunday calm reigns.

On the left edge of the field of vision, seated in a chair which is half turned toward the camera, is discovered the sole occupant of the vast hall, the polite photographer. He wears formal morning clothes and is examining some photographs.

Close-up looking over the photographer's shoulder. The first photograph we are permitted to view is one of the horse-car of the previous scene; the urchins are peering out of the windows and some pigeons are resting upon the horses' harness, while the harp and basket of laundry repose on the car roof. Another photograph reveals the former park scene covered with snow up to the hoofs of the statue of the horse, giving the effect of the horseman riding through the snow. The harp is lying over the rider with all its strings broken, so that it looks as if the rider's outstretched hand had just struck the last note on the wrecked instrument. As the

photographer has lingered over this photograph the tender and
poignant passages from Strauss' "Tales from the Vienna Woods"
have been heard. The photographer displays considerable emotion.

(The film will be in color from now on).

The next photograph is a close-up view of the gorgeous pheasant
aflutter among the white linen. At this point, to the end of the
episode, will be played that section of Stravinsky's "Fire-Bird"
which so marvelously suggests the bird's flight into the distance.

In the meantime a maid in an immaculate, starched white uniform has entered the background on the left, working toward the
photographer with a feather duster. As she nears him, she
brandishes the duster, (the feathers of which are identical in size
and color to the pheasant) so vigorously around her white uniform
that the amazing coincidence causes the photographer to jump to
his feet, dropping the collection of pictures. The maid pays no
attention to him and in a few moments exits to the right, dusting
as she goes.

Close-up of head and shoulders of photographer. There is a
nonplussed expression on his countenance and perspiraton trickles
down his face dropping upon his immaculate white collar.

Original scene. The photographer turns in the direction of the
maid and follows her with his eyes. Then he gathers up his pictures and slowly seats himself again. (Here ends the passage in
color and the Stravinsky music).

Through the doorway at the end of the hall there enters a young

man in concert clothes. He is accompanied by an attendant who removes the dust cover from the piano and then retraces his steps. They pay no attention to the photographer who is likewise undistracted by their presence.

The young man seats himself at the piano and strikes some very grand chords. He is an artist of the pigeon-flight school. At first one supposes that he is just warming up, but this sort of preliminary playing seems to be all of which he is capable.

Suddenly a breeze or strong draught causes the chandeliers to start jangling like Japanese wind bells, filling the hall with very agreeable music. They are supplemented with incidental music from the orchestra, Tschaikowsky's "Danse de la Fée Dragée", charmingly appropriate. The pianist looks up angrily and waits for this impromptu concert to stop. After a minute or so of impatience, he makes a rapid exit through the doorway. The attendant reappears, replaces the dust cover, and exits. He is not surprised at the music of the chandeliers.

The photographer becomes suddenly alert as the music ceases very gradually. He glances up curiously. His countenance is benign and serene. He gathers his photographs and walks slowly towards the other end of the room, along the windows at the left.

The reflection of the chandeliers in the mirror at the end of the room catches his eye.

Close-up of the photographer on the left edge of the field of vision, looking into the mirror. By means of a fade-out the reflection of the chandeliers in the hall becomes the chandeliers in the interior of . . .

A large, sumptuous glass and china establishment seen through plate glass windows. (This episode opens with color).

Slightly to the left of the center of the window is discovered the urchin of the harp peering into the depths of this forest of exquisite glass and ceramics.

Suddenly from somewhere inside, the gorgeous pheasant darts into view. It flies at terrific speed in and out of the chandeliers and pieces of priceless glassware as if they were branches of his native wood. At times it swoops gracefully past the counters, grazing the pieces by a hair's breadth. When it flies slowly, the boy traces the movements with his finger on the plate glass.

As the bird nestles in one of the glass pieces or vases to rest awhile there is heard some music which engages the attention of the urchin. It sounds like distant harp music. The urchin becomes tense as he recognizes its source.

Close-up of a fountain at the rear of store. It is made of thin blown glass and through its fantastic shape water plays into a glass basin. The music caused by the falling drops of water is strongly reminiscent of the haunting waltz of Debussy, "La plus que lente". The close-up has permitted us to realize better the fairylike and supernatural atmosphere of the glass store. In this miraculous setting we feel that anything might happen. We are so enchanted that two or three minutes of the close-up, just as it is, do not seem too long. Suddenly the fountain stops playing and there is a tense, nervous silence of about half a minute; then a violent fluttering and beating of wings, mingled with the rolling of a snare-drum, which also continues for about half a minute. Several deafening reports of a gun are heard in rapid succession, accompanied by the pandemonium of a million pieces of falling glass.

Original scene outside the window. The urchin, shading his eyes with his hands, is searching for the cause of the fracas since the whole scene seems just as peaceful and undisturbed as ever.

Fade-out into the hotel parlor before the mirror. The camera moves back enough to take in the doorway. We now discover the cause of the preceding disturbance. The pianist stands in the doorway with an old-fashioned gun in his hand, surveying the debris of the glass from all the chandeliers which is scattered on the carpet. There is a distracted and slightly remorseful look upon his face.

The photographer walks through the doorway, turning to the left. Each is oblivious of the other.

Original view, long shot from the other end of the hall.

The pianist lays his gun against the wall and slowly advances to the piano. He is bravely restraining his emotion, which is on the point of overcoming him. He removes the dust cover and slowly walks to a pile of the shattered glass. He covers the pile of glass very carefully with the dust cover. Then to the tender and poignant passages of "Tales from the Vienna Woods" he walks slowly toward the doorway and exits.

A street corner at night, at which time it takes on an appearance of supernatural beauty. Enclosed by a low latticework fence are two lamp posts placed among life-sized marble statues of women in classical poses. The bluish light from the gas flames gives the statues the appearance of figureheads on old ships, illumined by phosphorescent seas. Snow is falling.

Within this enclosure the urchin of the harp is discovered restored to his beloved instrument, from which issues the strain of "Si mes vers avaient des ailes!" with a new significance. At times the notes sound like sobs heroically stifled. There is an occasional passerby who takes no notice of the playing. An occasional horse-car is heard in the distance.

The selection is played through about three times, becoming softer with each repetition.

The scene is one of inexpressible serene and satisfying beauty. Fade-out.

EPILOGUE

The epilogue will be entirely in color and the action carried out as in a ballet.

An old-fashioned stage setting seen through a portal. There is an aisle through the center, flanked by a row of decorative lamp posts behind which is dense foliage reaching to the ceiling. Seated by each lamp post is an urchin at a harp.

The action commences with the urchins playing ensemble an ineffectual ballet selection, such as Linke's "Glowworm". When they finish they applaud vigorously, bravos and whistles mingling with the applause.

As the applause dies out, we hear being played by the unseen orchestra the kind of soft string music that accompanies a stage mermaid as she reposes in a glass tank filled with water and non-chalantly reads from a book and devours a piece of fruit.

As the music continues, there emerges from the background a form. As it approaches down the aisle, it is seen to be a camera on wheels behind which is the polite photographer on roller skates, under his black sheet. As they near the footlights, the black sheet flies into the air. The photographer grabs wildly at it several times, almost losing his balance each time. He finally grasps the sheet as the gorgeous pheasant flies out from under it, but in so doing crashes to the floor. The camera continues on its course, toppling over the footlights out of view into the orchestra pit. There is a glorious sound effect as the camera lands in a drum, upsetting triangles, glockenspiels, etc., and causing false, bewildered notes by the frightened musicians. The music ceases.

The urchins leave their harps and hurry to the aid of the photographer. They help him to his feet and support him to prevent another mishap as he exits to the left. In the meantime, four of the urchins with violins have seated themselves apart and expertly play the scherzo movement from Debussy's string quartet.

The urchins all return now to their harps. The harpist nearest the footlights suddenly breaks into a short solo, the invigorating "Tic-Toc-Choc" of Couperin. He is applauded.

The regular lights now go off and the lamp posts become illuminated. In the dimmer light, we notice that something has appeared on the left side of the stage in the foreground. The regular lights go on again. The new object on the stage turns out to be the piano and pianist of the ballroom scene. The pianist's back is toward us. On the shiny black piano stands a large magnificent, highly polished glass dome enclosing a pheasant of brilliant plumage in a natural setting. An attendant is just leaving the stage with a dust cover.

The pianist goes through some gyrations of the hot-cha school of singing, thumb-licking, rope-weaving, etc. The urchins give him their attention as he starts striking impressive chords in his affected manner. They become bored, however, and in less than a minute drown him out with an infectious galop of 1870 vintage. The pianist rises angrily. The urchins stand and meet his gaze.

As the pianist rises, the photographer appears at the right wearing his high silk hat and pointing a gun toward the piano. The photographer fires, demolishing the glass bell. The lights go out instantly and there is complete silence.

When the lights of only the lamp posts go on after some moments there remains nothing to be seen but snow falling on baskets of clean laundry scattered in the aisle and stretching into the distance.

(1933)

The illustrations are copies of the images Cornell inserted in his typed copies of the text. They are placed in approximately the same places they occur in the original.
Courtesy of The Ryerson Library of The Art Institute of Chicago and Betty Cornell Benton.

MAYA DEREN:

Cinematography:
The Creative Use of Reality

The motion-picture camera is perhaps the most paradoxical of all machines, in that it can be at once independently active and infinitely passive. Kodak's early slogan, "You push the button, it does the rest," was not an exaggerated advertising claim, and, connected to any simple trigger device, a camera can even take pictures all by itself. At the same time, while a comparable development and refinement of other mechanisms has usually resulted in an increased specialization, the advances in the scope and sensitivity of lenses and emulsions have made the camera capable of infinite receptivity and indiscriminate fidelity. To this must be added the fact that the medium deals, or can deal, in terms of the most elemental actuality. In sum, it can produce maximum results for virtually minimal effort: it requires of its operator only a modicum of aptitude and energy; of its subject matter, only that it exist; and of its audience, only that they can see. On this elementary level it functions ideally as a mass medium for communicating equally elementary ideas.

The photographic medium is, as a matter of fact, so amorphous that it is not merely unobtrusive but virtually transparent, and so becomes, more than any other medium, susceptible of servitude to any and all the others. The enormous value of such servitude suffices to justify the medium and to be generally accepted as its function. This has been a major obstacle to the definition and development of motion pictures as a creative fine-art form—capable of creative action in its own terms—for its own character is as a latent image which can become manifest only if no other image is imposed upon it to obscure it.

Those concerned with the emergence of this latent form must therefore assume a partially protective role, one which recalls the advice of an art instructor who said, "If you have trouble drawing the vase, try drawing the space around the vase." Indeed, for the time being, the definition of the creative form of film involves as careful attention to what it is not as to what it is.

Animated Paintings

In recent years, perceptible first on the experimental fringes of the film world and now in general evidence at the commercial art theaters, there has been an accelerated development of what might be called the "graphic arts school of animated film." Such films, which combine abstract backgrounds with recognizable but not realistic figures, are designed and painted by trained and talented graphic artists who make use of a sophisticated, fluent knowledge of the rich resources of plastic media, including even collage. A major factor in the emergence of this school has been the enormous technical and laboratory advance in color film and color processing, so that it is now possible for these artists to approach the two-dimensional, rectangular screen with all the graphic freedom they bring to a canvas.

The similarity between screen and canvas had long ago been recognized by artists such as Hans Richter, Oskar Fischinger, and others, who were attracted not by its graphic possibilities (so limited at that time) but rather by the excitements of the film medium, particularly the exploitation of its time dimension— rhythm, spatial depth created by a diminishing square, the three-dimensional illusion created by the revolutions of a spiral figure, etc. They put their graphic skills at the service of the film medium, as a means of extending film expression.*

The new graphic-arts school does not so much advance those early efforts as reverse them, for here the artists make use of the film medium as an extension of the plastic media. This is particularly clear when one analyzes the principle of movement employed, for it is usually no more than a sequential articulation—a kind of spelling out in time—of the dynamic ordinarily implicit in the design of an individual composition. The most appropriate term to describe such works, which are often interesting and witty, and which certainly have their place among visual arts, is "animated paintings."

This entry of painting into the film medium presents certain parallels with the introduction of sound. The silent film had attracted to it persons who had talent for and were inspired by the exploration and development of a new and unique form of visual expression. The addition of sound opened the doors for the verbalists and dramatists. Armed with the authority, power, laws, tech-

---

* It is significant that Hans Richter, a pioneer in such a use of film, soon abandoned this approach. All his later films, along with the films of Léger, Man Ray, Dali, and the painters who participated in Richter's later films (Ernst, Duchamp, etc.) indicate a profound appreciation of the distinction between the plastic and the photographic image and make enthusiastic and creative use of photographic reality.

niques, skills, and crafts which the venerable literary arts had accumulated over centuries, the writers hardly even paused to recognize the small resistance of the "indigenous" film-maker, who had had barely a decade in which to explore and evolve the creative potential of his medium.

The rapid success of the "animated painting" is similarly due to the fact that it comes armed with all the plastic traditions and techniques which are its impressive heritage. And just as the sound film interrupted the development of film form on the commercial level by providing a more finished substitute, so the "animated painting" is already being accepted as a form of film art in the few areas (the distribution of 16 mm. film shorts of film series and societies) where experiments in film form can still find an audience.

The motion-picture medium has an extraordinary range of expression. It has in common with the plastic arts the fact that it is a visual composition projected on a two-dimensional surface; with dance, that it can deal in the arrangement of movement; with theater, that it can create a dramatic intensity of events; with music, that it can compose in the rhythms and phrases of time and can be attended by song and instrument; with poetry, that it can juxtapose images; with literature generally, that it can encompass in its sound track the abstractions available only to language.

This very profusion of potentialities seems to create confusion in the minds of most film-makers, a confusion which is diminished by eliminating a major portion of those potentialities in favor of one or two, upon which the film is subsequently structured. An artist, however, should not seek security in a tidy mastery over the simplifications of deliberate poverty; he should, instead, have the creative courage to face the danger of being overwhelmed by fecundity in the effort to resolve it into simplicity and economy.

While the "animated painting" film has limited itself to a small area of film potential, it has gained acceptance on the basis of the fact that it *does* use an art form—the graphic art form—and that it does seem to meet the general condition of film: it makes its statement as an image in movement. This opens the entire question of whether a photograph is of the same order of image as all others. If not, is there a correspondingly different approach to it in a creative context? Although the photographic process is the basic building block of the motion-picture medium, it is a tribute to its self-effacement as a servant that virtually no consideration has been given to its own character and the creative implications thereof.

The Closed Circuit of the Photographic Process

The term "image" (originally based on "imitation") means in its first sense the visual likeness of a real object or person, and in the very act of specifying resemblance it distinguishes and establishes the entire category of visual experience which is *not* a real object or person. In this specifically negative sense—in the sense that the photograph of a horse is not the horse itself—a photograph is an image.

But the term "image" also has positive implications: it presumes a mental activity, whether in its most passive form (the "mental images" of perception and memory) or, as in the arts, the creative action of the imagination realized by the art instrument. Here reality is first filtered by the selectivity of individual interests and modified by prejudicial perception to become experience; as such it is combined with similar, contrasting or modifying experiences, both forgotten and remembered, to become assimilated into a conceptual image; this in turn is subject to the manipulations of the art instrument; and what finally emerges is a plastic image which is a reality in its own right. A painting is not, fundamentally, a likeness or image of a horse; it is a likeness of a mental concept which may resemble a horse or which may, as in abstract painting, bear no visible relation to any real object.

Photography, however, is a process by which an object creates its own image by the action of its light or light-sensitive material. It thus presents a closed circuit precisely at the point where, in the traditional art forms, the creative process takes place as reality passes through the artist. This exclusion of the artist at that point is responsible both for the absolute fidelity of the photographic process and for the widespread conviction that a photographic medium cannot be, itself, a creative form. From these observations it is but a step to the conclusion that its use as a visual printing press or as an extension of another creative form represents a full realization of the potential of the medium. It is precisely in this manner that the photographic process is used in "animated paintings."

But in so far as the camera is applied to objects which are already accomplished images, is this really a more creative use of the instrument than when, in scientific films, its fidelity is applied to reality in conjunction with the revelatory functions of telescopic or microscopic lenses and a comparable use of the motor?

Just as the magnification of a lens trained upon matter shows us a mountainous, craggy landscape in an apparently smooth surface, so slow-motion can reveal the actual structure of movements or changes which either cannot be slowed down in actuality or whose nature would be changed by a change in tempo of performance. Applied to the flight of a bird, for example, slow-motion reveals the hitherto unseen sequence of the many separate strains and small movements of which it is compounded.

By a telescopic use of the motor, I mean the telescoping of time achieved by triggering a camera to take pictures of a vine at ten-minute intervals. When projected at regular speed, the film reveals the actual integrity, almost the intelligence, of the movement of the vine as it grows and turns with the sun. Such telescoped-time photography has been applied to chemical changes and to physical metamorphoses whose tempo is so slow as to be virtually imperceptible.

Although the motion-picture camera here functions as an instrument of discovery rather than of creativity, it does yield a kind of image which, unlike the images of "animated paintings" (animation itself is a use of the telescoped-time principle), is unique to the motion-picture medium. It may therefore be regarded as an even more valid basic element in a creative film form based on the singular properties of the medium.

Reality and Recognition

The application of the photographic process to reality results in an image which is unique in several respects. For one thing, since a specific reality is the prior condition of the existence of a photograph, the photograph not only testifies to the existence of that reality (just as a drawing testifies to the existence of an artist) but is, to all intents and purposes, its equivalent. This equivalence is not at all a matter of fidelity but is of a different order altogether. If realism is the term for a graphic image which precisely simulates some real object, then a photograph must be differentiated from it as *a form of reality itself*.

This distinction plays an extremely important role in the address of these respective images. The intent of the plastic arts is to make meaning manifest. In creating an image for the express purpose of communicating, the artist primarily undertakes to create the most effective aspect possible out of the total resources of his medium. Photography, however, deals in a living reality which is structured primarily to endure, and whose configurations are designed to serve that purpose, not to communicate its meaning; they may even serve to conceal that purpose as a protective measure. In a photograph, then, we begin by recognizing a reality, and our attendant knowledges and attitudes are brought into play; only then does the aspect become meaningful in reference to it. The abstract shadow shape in a night scene is not understood at all until revealed and identified as a person; the bright red shape on a pale ground which might, in an abstract, graphic context, communicate a sense of gaiety, conveys something altogether different when recognized as a wound. As we watch a film, the continuous act of recognition in which we are involved is like a strip of memory unrolling beneath the images of the film itself, to form the invisible underlayer of an implicit double exposure.

The process by which we understand an abstract, graphic image is almost directly opposite, then, to that by which we understand a photograph. In the first case, the aspect leads us to meaning; in the second case the understanding which results from recognition is the key to our evaluation of the aspect.

Photographic Authority and the "Controlled Accident"

As a reality, the photographic image confronts us with the innocent arrogance of an objective fact, one which exists as an independent presence, indifferent to our response. We may in turn view it with an indifference and detachment we do not have toward the man-made images of other arts, which invite and require our perception and demand our response in order to consummate the communication they initiate and which is their *raison d'être*. At the same time precisely because we are aware that our personal detachment does not in any way diminish the verity of the photographic image, it exercises an authority comparable in weight only to the authority of reality itself.

It is upon this authority that the entire school of the social documentary film is based. Although expert in the selection of the most effective reality and in the use of camera placement and angle to accentuate the pertinent and effective features of it, the documentarists operate on a principle of minimal intervention, in the interests of bringing the authority of reality to the support of the moral purpose of the film.

Obviously, the interest of a documentary film corresponds closely to the interest inherent in its subject matter. Such films enjoyed a period of particular pre-eminence during the war. This popularity served to make fiction-film producers more keenly aware of the effectiveness and authority of reality, an awareness which gave rise to the "neo-realist" style of film and contributed to the still growing trend toward location filming.

In the theater, the physical presence of the performers provides a sense of reality which induces us to accept the symbols of geography, the intermissions which represent the passage of time, and the other conventions which are part of the form. Films cannot include this physical presence of the performers. They can, however, replace the artifice of theater by the actuality of landscape, distances, and place; the interruptions of intermissions can be transposed into transitions which sustain and even intensify the momentum of dramatic development; while events and episodes which, within the context of theatrical artifice, might not have been convincing in their logic or aspect can be clothed in the verity which emanates from the reality of the surrounding landscape, the sun, the streets and buildings.

In certain respects, the very absence in motion pictures of the physical presence of the performer, which is so important to the theater, can even contribute to our sense of reality. We can, for example, believe in the existence of a monster if we are not asked to believe that it is present in the room with us. The intimacy imposed upon us by the physical reality of other art works presents us with alternative choices: either to identify with or to deny the experience they propose, or to withdraw altogether to a detached awareness of that reality as merely a metaphor. But the film image—whose intangible reality consists of lights and shadows beamed through the air and caught on the surface of a silver screen—comes to us as the reflection of another world. At that distance we can accept the reality of the most monumental and extreme of images, and from that perspective we can perceive and comprehend them in their full dimension.

The authority of reality is available even to the most artificial constructs if photography is understood as an art of the "controlled accident." By "controlled accident" I mean the maintenance of a delicate balance between what is there spontaneously and naturally as evidence of the independent life of actuality, and the persons and activities which are deliberately introduced into the scene. A painter, relying primarily upon aspect as the means of communicating his intent, would take enormous care in the arrangement of every detail of, for example, a beach scene. The cinematographer, on the other hand, having selected a beach which, in general, has the desired aspect—whether grim or happy, deserted or crowded— must on the contrary refrain from overcontrolling the aspect if he is to retain the authority of reality. The filming of such a scene should be planned and framed so as to create a context of limits within which anything that occurs is compatible with the intent of the scene.

The invented event which is then introduced, though itself an artifice, borrows reality from the reality of the scene—from the natural blowing of the hair, the irregularity of the waves, the very texture of the stones and sand—in short, from all the uncontrolled, spontaneous elements which are the property of actuality itself. Only in photography—by the delicate manipulation which I call controlled accident—can natural phenomena be incorporated into our own creativity, to yield an image where the reality of a tree confers its truth upon the events we cause to transpire beneath it.

Abstractions and Archetypes

Inasmuch as the other art forms are not constituted of reality itself, they create metaphors for reality. But photography, being itself the reality or the equivalent thereof, can use its own reality as a metaphor for ideas and abstractions. In painting, the image is an abstraction of the aspect; in photography, the abstraction of an idea produces the archetypal image.

This concept is not new to motion pictures, but its development was interrupted by the intrusions of theatrical traditions into the film medium. The early history of film is studded with archetypal figures: Theda Bara, Mary Pickford, Marlene Dietrich, Greta

Garbo, Charles Chaplin, Buster Keaton, etc. These appeared as personages, not as people or personalities, and the films which were structured around them were like monumental myths which celebrated cosmic truths.

The invasion of the motion-picture medium by modern playwrights and actors introduced the concept of realism, which is at the root of theatrical metaphor and which, in the a priori reality of photography, is an absurd redundancy which has served merely to deprive the motion-picture medium of its creative dimension. It is significant that, despite every effort of pretentious producers, directors and film critics who seek to raise their professional status by adopting the methods, attitudes, and criteria of the established and respected art of theater, the major figures—both the most popular stars and the most creative directors (such as Orson Welles)—continue to operate in the earlier archetypal tradition. It was even possible, as Marlon Brando demonstrated, to transcend realism and to become an archetypal realist, but it would appear that his early intuition has been subsequently crushed under the pressures of the repertory complex, another carry-over from theater, where it functioned as the means by which a single company could offer a remunerative variety of plays to an audience while providing consistent employment for its members. There is no justification whatsoever for insisting on a repertory variety of roles for actors involved in the totally different circumstances of motion pictures.

Photography's Unique Images

In all that I have said so far, the fidelity, reality, and authority of the photographic image serve primarily to modify and to support. Actually, however, the sequence in which we perceive photography —an initial identification followed by an interpretation of the aspect according to that identification (rather than in primarily aspectual terms)—becomes irreversible and confers meaning upon aspect in a manner unique to the photographic medium.

I have previously referred to slow-motion as a time microscope, but it has its expressive uses as well as its revelatory ones. Depending upon the subject and the context, it can be a statement of either ideal ease or nagging frustration, a kind of intimate and loving meditation on a movement or a solemnity which adds ritual weight to an action; or it can bring into reality that dramatic image of anguished helplessness, otherwise experienced only in the nightmares of childhood, when our legs refused to move while the terror which pursues us comes ever closer.

Yet, slow-motion is not simply slowness of speed. It is, in fact, something which exists in our minds, not on the screen, and can be created only in conjunction with the identifiable reality of the photographic image. When we see a man in the attitudes of running and identify the activity as a run, one of the knowledges which is part of that identification is the pulse normal to that activity. It is because we are aware of the known pulse of the identified action while we watch it occur at a slower rate of speed that we experience the double-exposure of time which we know as slow-motion. It cannot occur in an abstract film, where a triangle, for instance, may go fast or slow, but, having no necessary pulse, cannot go in slow-motion.

Another unique image which the camera can yield is reverse motion. When used meaningfully, it does not convey so much a sense of a backward movement spatially, but rather an undoing of time. One of the most memorable uses of this occurs in Cocteau's *Blood of a Poet*, where the peasant is executed by a volley of fire which also shatters the crucifix hanging on the wall behind him. This scene is followed by a reverse motion of the action—the dead peasant rising from the ground and the crucifix reassembling on the wall; then again the volley of fire, the peasant falling, the crucifix shattering; and again the filmic resurrection. Reverse motion also, for obvious reasons, does not exist in abstract films.

The photographic negative image is still another striking case in point. This is not a direct white-on-black statement but is understood as an inversion of values. When applied to a recognizable person or scene, it conveys a sense of a critically qualitative change, as in its use for the landscape on the other side of death in Cocteau's *Orpheus*.

Both such extreme images and the more familiar kind which I referred to earlier make use of the motion-picture medium as a form in which the meaning of the image originates in our recognition of a known reality and derives its authority from the direct relationship between reality and image in the photographic process. While the process permits some intrusion by the artist as a modifier of that image, the limits of its tolerance can be defined as that point at which the original reality becomes unrecognizable or is irrelevant (as when a red reflection in a pond is used for its shape and color only and without contextual concern for the water or the pond).

In such cases the camera itself has been conceived of as the artist, with distorting lenses, multiple superpositions, etc., used to simulate the creative action of the eye, the memory, etc. Such well-intentioned efforts to use the medium creatively, by forcibly inserting the creative act in the position it traditionally occupies in the visual arts, accomplish, instead, the destruction of the photographic image as reality. This image, with its unique ability to engage us simultaneously on several levels—by the objective authority of reality, by the knowledges and values which we attach to that reality, by the direct address of its aspect, and by a manipulated relationship between these—is the building block for the creative use of the medium.

The Placement of the Creative Act and Time-Space Manipulations

Where does the film-maker then undertake his major creative action if, in the interests of preserving these qualities of the image, he restricts himself to the control of accident in the pre-photographic stage and accepts almost complete exclusion from the photographic process as well?

Once we abandon the concept of the image as the end product and consummation of the creative process (which it is in both the visual arts and the theater), we can take a larger view of the total medium and can see that the motion-picture instrument actually consists of two parts, which flank the artist on either side. The images with which the camera provides him are like fragments of a permanent, incorruptible memory; their individual reality is in no way dependent upon their sequence in actuality, and they can be assembled to compose any of several statements. In film, the image can and should be only the beginning, the basic material of the creative action.

All invention and creation consist primarily of a new relationship between known parts. The images of film deal in realities which, as I pointed out earlier, are structured to fulfill their various functions, not to communicate a specific meaning. Therefore they have several attributes simultaneously, as when a table may be, at once, old, red, and high. Seeing it as a separate entity, an antique dealer would appraise its age, an artist its color, and a child its inaccessible height. But in a film such a shot might be followed by one in which the table falls apart, and thus a particular aspect of its age would constitute its meaning and function in the sequence, with all other attributes becoming irrelevant. The editing of a film creates the sequential relationship which gives particular or new meaning to the images *according to their function;* it establishes a context, a form which transfigures them without distorting their aspect, diminishing their reality and authority, or impoverishing that variety of potential functions which is the characteristic dimension of reality.

Whether the images are related in terms of common or contrasting qualities, in the causal logic of events which is narrative, or in the logic of ideas and emotions which is the poetic mode, the structure of a film is sequential. The creative action in film, then, takes place in its time dimension; and for this reason the motion picture, though composed of spatial images, is primarily *a time form.*

A major portion of the creative action consists of a manipulation of time and space. By this I do not mean only such established filmic techniques as flashback, condensation of time, parallel action etc. These affect not the action itself but the method of revealing it. In a flashback there is no implication that the usual chronological integrity of the action itself is in any way affected by the process, however disrupted, of memory. Parallel action, as when we see alternately the hero who rushes to the rescue and the heroine whose situation becomes increasingly critical, is an omnipresence on the part of the camera as a witness of action, not as a creator of it.

The kind of manipulation of time and space to which I refer becomes itself part of the organic structure of a film. There is, for example, the extension of space by time and of time by space. The length of a stairway can be enormously extended if three different shots of the person ascending it (filmed from different angles so that it is not apparent that the identical area is being covered each time) are so edited together that the action is continuous and results in an image of enduring labor toward some elevated goal. A leap in the air can be extended by the same technique, but in this case, since the film action is sustained far beyond the normal duration of the real action itself, the effect is one of tension as we wait for the figure to return, finally, to earth.

Time may be extended by the reprinting of a single frame, which has the effect of freezing the figure in mid-action; here the frozen frame becomes a moment of suspended animation which, according to its contextual position, may convey either the sense of critical hesitation (as in the turning back of Lot's wife) or may constitute a comment on stillness and movement as the opposition of life and death. The reprinting of scenes of a casual situation involving several persons may be used either in a prophetic context, as a *déjà-vu;* or, again, precise reiteration, by inter-cutting reprints, of those spontaneous movements, expressions, and exchanges, can change the quality of the scene from one of informality to that of a stylization akin to dance; in so doing it confers dance upon non-dancers, by shifting emphasis from the purpose of the movement to the movement itself, and an informal social encounter then assumes the solemnity and dimension of ritual.

Similarly, it is possible to confer the movement of the camera upon the figures in the scene, for the large movement of a figure in a film is conveyed by the changing relationship between that figure and the frame of the screen. If, as I have done in my recent film *The Very Eye of Night,* one eliminates the horizon line and any background which would reveal the movement of the total field, then the eye accepts the frame as stable and ascribes all movement to the figure within it. The hand-held camera, moving and revolving over the white figures on a totally black ground, produces images in which their movement is as gravity-free and as three-dimensional as that of birds in air or fish in water. In the absence of any absolute orientation, the push and pull of their interrelationships becomes the major dialogue.

By manipulation of time and space, I mean also the creation of a relationship between separate times, places, and persons. A swing-pan—whereby a shot of one person is terminated by a rapid swing away and a shot of another person or place begins with a rapid swing of the camera, the two shots being subsequently joined in the blurred area of both swings—brings into dramatic proximity people, places, and actions which in actuality might be widely separated. One can film different people at different times and even in different places performing approximately the same gesture or movement, and, by a judicious joining of the shots in such a manner as to preserve the continuity of the movement, the action itself becomes the dominant dynamic which unifies all separateness.

Separate and distant places not only can be related but can be made continuous by a continuity of identity and of movement, as when a person begins a gesture in one setting, this shot being immediately followed by the hand entering another setting altogether to complete the gesture there. I have used this technique to make a dancer step from woods to apartment in a single stride, and similarly to transport him from location to location so that the world itself became his stage. In my *At Land,* it has been the technique by which the dynamic of the *Odyssey* is reversed and the protagonist, instead of undertaking the long voyage of search for adventure, finds instead that the universe itself has usurped the dynamic action which was once the prerogative of human will, and confronts her with a volatile and relentless metamorphosis in which her personal identity is the sole constancy.

These are but several indications of the variety of creative time-space relationships which can be accomplished by a meaningful manipulation of the sequence of film images. It is an order of creative action available only to the motion-picture medium because it is a photographic medium. The ideas of condensation and of extension, of separateness and of continuity, in which it deals, exploit to the fullest degree the various attributes of the photographic image: its fidelity (which establishes the identity of the person who serves as a transcendant unifying force between all separate times and places), its reality (the basis of the recognition which activates our knowledges and values and without which the geography of location and dislocation could not exist), and its authority (which transcends the impersonality and intangibility of the image and endows it with independent and objective consequence).

The Twentieth-Century Art Form

I initiated this discussion by referring to the effort to determine what creative film form is not, as a means by which we can arrive eventually at a determination of what it is. I recommend this as the only valid point of departure for all custodians of classifications, to the keepers of catalogues, and in particular to the harassed librarians, who, in their effort to force film into one or another of the performing or the plastic arts, are engaged in an endless Procrustean operation.

A radio is not a louder voice, an airplane is not a faster car, and the motion picture (an invention of the same period of history) should not be thought of as a faster painting or a more real play.

All of these forms are qualitatively different from those which preceded them. They must not be understood as unrelated developments, bound merely by coincidence, but as diverse aspects of a new way of thought and a new way of life—one in which an appreciation of time, movement, energy, and dynamics is more immediately meaningful than the familiar concept of matter as a static solid anchored to a stable cosmos. It is a change reflected in every field of human endeavor, for example, architecture, in which the notion of mass-upon-mass structure has given way to the lean strength of steel and the dynamics of cantilever balances.

It is almost as if the new age, fearful that whatever was there already would not be adequate, had undertaken to arrive completely equipped, even to the motion-picture medium, which, structured expressly to deal in movement and time-space relationships, would be the most propitious and appropriate art form for expressing, in terms of its own paradoxically intangible reality, the moral and metaphysical concepts of the citizen of this new age.

This is not to say that cinema should or could replace the other art forms, any more than flight is a substitute for the pleasures of walking or for the leisurely panorama of landscapes seen from a car or train window. Only when new things serve the same purpose better do they replace old things. Art, however, deals in ideas; time does not deny them, but may merely make them irrelevant. The truths of the Egyptians are no less true for failing to answer questions which they never raised. Culture is cumulative, and to it each age should make its proper contribution.

How can we justify the fact that it is the art instrument, among all that fraternity of twentieth-century inventions, which is still the least explored and exploited; and that it is the artist—of whom, traditionally, the culture expects the most prophetic and visionary statements—who is the most laggard in recognizing that the formal and philosophical concepts of his age are implicit in the actual structure of his instrument and the techniques of his medium?

If cinema is to take its place beside the others as a full-fledged art form, it must cease merely to record realities that owe nothing of their actual existence to the film instrument. Instead, it must create a total experience so much out of the very nature of the instrument as to be inseparable from its means. It must relinquish the narrative disciplines it has borrowed from literature and its timid imitation of the causal logic of narrative plots, a form which flowered as a celebration of the earth-bound, step-by-step concept of time, space and relationship which was part of the primitive materialism of the nineteenth century. Instead, it must develop the vocabulary of filmic images and evolve the syntax of filmic techniques which relate those. It must determine the disciplines inherent in the medium, discover its own structural modes, explore the new realms and dimensions accessible to it and so enrich our culture artistically as science has done in its own province.

(Reprinted by permission of *Daedalus*, the Journal of the American Academy of Arts and Sciences, Boston, Massachusetts. Winter 1960, *The Visual Arts Today*.)

SIDNEY PETERSON:

Cine Dance and Two Notes

So far as I know, no one has ever
shot even a fragment of ballet at 100,000 frames per second, even
though by this simple device one minute of shooting would be extended to more than 69 hours of performance. It would be like
watching the hour hand of a clock move. The only possible audience would be the performers themselves, and not even the most
narcissistic would be able to take all 69 hours.

I mention this fantastic possibility only because slow motion has,
almost from the beginning, been the most obvious technical device
(instant lyricism) for producing results that have gratified dancers
and pleased cameramen. Witness Arnold Genthe's remarks about
the films shot of Isadora Duncan's older pupils—Anna, Irma, and
Lisa.* "Without benefit of any of the apparatus available to motion
picture operators today, they were purely an experiment. At that
time all efforts to record the dance on the screen had failed. The
smooth coherence of dance rhythm was always lacking." So Genthe
slowed up the action, and Anna Pavlova said, "Isadora told me that
they are the only dance pictures she has seen on the screen which
are smooth, fluent and harmonious." After viewing the pictures, the
great Russian and her husband were both enthusiastic about the
way "the harmony of the dance movements" had been maintained.

Their enthusiasm, however, did not result in more films. "No
good dance motion picture was ever taken of Pavlova," Genthe
lamented. "It is sad to realize that no motion pictures of Isadora
Duncan's dances exist, nor are there any of Nijinsky. The art of
the dancer is a fugitive thing and the only way it can be preserved
as an inspiration and guide for future generations is through the
cinema. That there are no such memorials to these three incom-
parable artists is a sin of omission to be charged against the motion
picture industry of their day."

It is difficult to know which is worse in this case, the sin of omis-

---

* As I Remember (New York, 1936), pp. 177-78.

sion or the probable sin of commission. At least, in the absence of such memorials, the legends survive, undisturbed by the atrocities that would almost certainly have been committed in the name of dance film. It is inconceivable that the results, even in slow motion, would have served as an inspiration or guide to another generation. It is not a question merely of "smooth coherence of dance rhythm," but of a conflict of media in a composite medium, which had its own already well-established hierarchy.

If dancing were basket-weaving, there would be no problem about its being relegated to the role of subject matter in a cinematic or televised message. The main difficulty arises, I believe, because dance too is an art of the moving image. It does not relate to film as, for example, scene painting relates to theatre. It is, in effect, a competing medium. Discussing the combining of the specific characteristics of various media, Rudolf Arnheim suggests that "there must be artistic reasons (no mere longing for memorials) for such a combination: it must serve to express something that could not be said by one of the media alone. . . . A composite work of art is possible only if complete structures, produced by the media, are integrated in the form of parallelism. Naturally such a double track will make sense only if the components do not simply convey the same thing." *

Film has the problem of divesting itself of much that it has accomplished; of, in effect, starting over from scratch, returning to a time when it still had choices in the directions it might take, when it had not yet discovered its potentiality as a narrative or dramatic medium.

The important thing here is the realization that the art of the moving image did not commence with Fred Ott sneezing for Thomas Edison with the help of a jar of red pepper, any more than it commenced with Loie Fuller doing her famous *Bat Dance* in somebody's back yard for an anonymous cameraman. Both were practitioners of an art as old as humanity, if not older. Obviously their successors should look at old movies, for guidance if not inspiration.

But film-makers should, I think, start taking some fresh looks at all that part of their art which preceded the invention of the machinery they employ. The advantages of a longer tradition for the purposes of departures are patent. There were so many rejected possibilities during the period of frantic invention, so many aborted achievements. For example, what ever happened to the so-called "trick film," which had its inception with Georges Méliès and disappeared almost completely after World War I?

I raise this point partly because of the very real success of Maya Deren's *Choreography for Camera* with dancer Talley Beatty—a "trick film" if there ever was one—and partly because the associa-

---

* *Film as Art* (Berkeley, 1957), pp. 215-16.

tion of tricks and magic with the art of the moving image is as old as the art itself. It was no accident, but a kind of historic necessity, that made Méliès a magician before he became a film-maker. Three hundred years earlier, Porta had demonstrated the relationship of the screen to magical effects in his *Natural Magic*, a sixteenth-century best-seller. And three hundred years before that, Roger Bacon had done it all with mirrors. Seventeenth-century Italian stage machinery belonged to the same tradition. Torelli was known as *il gran stregone*, the great wizard. The Transformation Scenes of British pantomime were more of the same.

Beatty's celebrated leap had its origins, not in film, but in the so-called Dumb Ballet of the English stage, of which *Fun in a Bakehouse* and *Ki Ko Kookeeree* were examples. *The Oxford Companion to the Theatre* calls the Leap "the supreme test of the trick player" throughout all that part of the nineteenth century when it flourished. In this sense, Miss Deren (whose leap Beatty's really was) with her leap joined Méliès and a company that included—not Taglioni, Grisi, or Cerrito—but Grimaldi, the Lupinos, the Conquests, and those extraordinary "entortillationists" and "zampillerostationists," the Hanlon-Lees.

When one considers how much used to be done with how little, it is appalling to realize how little is now being accomplished with how much. Torelli would have given his left arm to have been able to produce effects that can now be achieved easily with any simple hand camera. It is not likely that the aesthetic problems involved in the making of dance film are going to be solved by harassed TV directors or by a film industry concerned almost exclusively with values that automatically reduce the moving image to the level of subject, employing formulas such as girl meeting girl who breaks leg or the romance of the exuberant hoofer who cannot restrain himself from jumping on tables. Too much of the machinery is in the hands of naïve naturalists. Witness the amazing decision to film *West Side Story* on the West Side. The point is not worth laboring.

The stupendous past and a Pisgah future are clearly in the hands of experimentalists, who have nothing to lose by their pains. The traditions of the art of the moving image are as broad as they are long. All that is required is a little imagination and learning. It's all there, as ready-made as Duchamp's urinal signed Mutt, awaiting resurrection, along with the sense of wonder that seems practically to have disappeared from stage, screen, and studio.

(*Dance Perspectives* #30, 1967)

NOTES ON TWO FILMS

THE CAGE (1947) Directed by Sidney Peterson. Photography by Hy Hirsh. Production by Workshop 20, California School of Fine Arts.

Since THE CAGE is, among other things, a kind of philosophic essay in the vernacular of film, it may not be improper to describe it as non-Aristotelian. It is based on an aesthetic derived from what Professor Boas has called the self-evident proposition that a work of art is what it is both because of the artist who makes it and the person who sees and interprets it, the conception, in short, that the Aristotelian absorption of works of art into the natural order instead of into the so-called order of human nature, was a mistake. The circumstances of its Workshop origin called for a work conspicuously of the human order, non-abstract, objective in detail, making full use of the camera's uncanny ability to parody the incomprehensible integration of human experience with the inclusiveness of a vision untrammeled by the prejudicial intellect. Hence the pursuit of the abstract on the level only of the idea tending, in accordance with its own nature and the nature of its attachments, toward abstraction. Hence, too, the suggestion of a rationale that may be easily mistaken for surrealist or even psychiatric, not to say psychotic. THE CAGE was not intended to be a portrait of a schizophrenic in air-conditioned confinement. It has about as much to do with Bunuel-Dali as the eggcase of a female cockroach has to do with Hieronymus Bosch. It may look like, act like, but it's not. What is involved is a complicated equation of ideas and images, the whole point of the solution of which is that X is allowed to continue to remain X, equal to itself only. So much for the philosophic, not to say mathematical aspect. Besides being a balanced equation, THE CAGE is a somewhat comic fable and as such may be deciphered as easily as a last month's bill.

If half a century from now somebody falls off a ladder as a result of a sudden realization that the gradual coming into focus of a plaster bust in the opening shot represents the history of art from blur to plug hat, thus disposing in four feet of film of the absurd tradition that the aesthetic impulse is a dolled-up version of the involitional mimicry of butterflies and shellfish, the producers of the film cannot, of course, be responsible. Such compressions of meaning are inseparable from the non-Aristotelian position. Furthermore, it seems reasonable to suppose that most of THE CAGE's obscurities, such as they are, may be safely disregarded except by those who have a taste for such things. I merely wish to point out that the period of incubation for an idea caught from a film (or anything else) may be a lifetime and it is entirely unnecessary for an audience to break out in a rash of significations before the lights go on.

Workshop 20 was established at the California School of Fine Arts in order to give a few painters some collaborative experience in a medium with which they were familiar only in the ordinary way; a medium, moreover, peculiarly free of the aborting influence of styles and periods of painting too often serving as points of departure for rather unfresh experience. It was felt that the use of a production of a film as a device for the discovery of significant imagery in the everyday appearances of things might result in some discoveries which, if made, would be of use to painters. The advantages of film for pedagogy in general are too well known to repeat. The special advantages of a sort of cinematic pedagogy in depth for people who will, if the pedagogy is successful, eschew every form of it, have still, for the most part, to be explored. Certainly the making of THE CAGE by no means exhausted the possibilities in that direction.

"Minotauromachie," etching by Pablo Picasso (1935) [Museum of Modern Art]

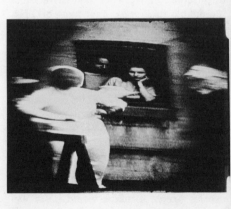

Mr. Frenhofer and the Minotaur

MR. FRENHOFER AND THE MINOTAUR (A Workshop 20 Production. Directed by Sidney Peterson. Based on Balzac's *Chef d'Oeuvre Inconnu*). In this film version of an early 19th century treatment of a late 17th century theme the story is strained through the mind of a minor character and in the process receives a liberal admixture of a 20th century treatment of a myth that was old before the start of the Christian Era. Here Poussin, the protagonist of *The Unknown Masterpiece,* is done over again according to that part of Nature most suitably expressed in the form and lack of form of an interior monologue. And to the mixed triviality and even mawkish sentimentality of (Balzac's) somewhat Hollywoodan approach to the subject of a quest for the absolute has been added a mild Joycean flavor of verbal disintegration. The visual distortion is a way of getting away from the usual literalness of the unmodified camera's vision of a literalness that tends to address the captured image as such to the upper reaches of the mind. The diffusion of the image is an attempt to catch the quality of what Henry James called "the projected light of the individual strong temperament in fiction—the color of the air with which this, that or the other painter of life more or less unconsciously suffuses his picture . . . something that proceeds from the contemplative mind itself, the very complexion of the mirror in which the material was reflected." James identifies Balzac's air as "rich and thick, a mixture of sun and shade, more somber and thicker and representing an absolutely greater quantity of 'atmosphere', than we find prevailing within the compass of any other suspended frame." The fidelity of the film's "atmosphere" is certainly greater than its adher(ence) to the plot of the original story. The intrusion of elements taken from Picasso's Minotauromachy is by way of contrast to and modification of Balzac's rather simple acceptance of the worship of painting as consisting of a devotion to naturalism and of deviation from that veneration as being a form of madness. In the labyrinth in which F. is supposed finally to have lost himself there is also, of necessity, a minotaur and, also of necessity, a Minotauromachy. As for the detail of MR. FRENHOFER, its interpretation should be on another level entirely. Thus the recurring "Kitty" is a reference to Catherine Lescault, the subject of the unknown masterpiece, but though Catherine is Kitty and Kitty Catherine, both are equally something else and so on. This is not complicated, merely diffuse, a sort of indefinite intellectual extension of quantitative atmosphere whereby we are not led to conclude at the film ends, where it starts, but in some vast labyrinth of endless reference where it is also possible to encounter Minotaurs which are simply monsters, picassoidal or otherwise, which we should have the courage to recognize after first, of course, discovering them.

P.S. 1977—With hindsight I find the invitation to a diffuse and indefinite intellectual extension a curious anticipation of Barthes' *scriptible* approach to another Balzac story: *Sarrasine*—so long ago. -S.P.

(Reconstructed from remains of an original program note)

JAMES BROUGHTON:

Two Notes on Mother's Day

Note One:

From the beginning I accepted the camera's sharply accurate eye as a value rather than a limitation. The camera's challenge to the poet is that his images must be as definite as possible: the magic of his persons, landscapes, and actions occurring in an apparent reality. At this point something approaching choreography must enter in: the finding of meaningful gesture and movement. And from the beginning I decided to make things happen head on, happen within the frame, without vagueness, without camera trickery—so that it would be how the scenes were made to happen in front of the lens, and then how they were organized in the montage, that would evoke the world I wanted to explore.

The subject matter of *Mother's Day* cannot, certainly, be considered specialized. Most of us have had some experience of childhood, either by participation or by observation. But do we remember that children are often incomprehensibly terror-stricken, are always ready to slip over into some private nonsense-ritual, or into behavior based upon their misconception of the adult world? Furthermore, what about the "childish behavior" of grownups, their refusal to relinquish childhood misconceptions, or to confront the world they inhabit?

Although this film is, then, by its very nature, a nostalgic comedy, it eschews chronological accuracy in either the period details or the dramatic events. It has been one of the cliches of cinema since the days of cubism that the medium allows the artist to manipulate time: to cut it up, retard or accelerate it, and so forth. In *Mother's Day* historical time may be said to stand still. Periods and fashions are gently scrambled. The device is deliberate: for with this film we are in the country of emotional memory, where everything may happen simultaneously.

This is because the basic point of vision of the film is that of an adult remembering the past (and the past within the past): projecting himself back *as he is now*, and seeing his family and his playmates at his present age-level, regarding them with adult feelings and knowledge, and even projecting them forward into his present-day concerns.

But also there is, as it were, a double exposure of memory in the film. Though its springboard is the remembering of childhood, it more deeply involves the mother's remembering of her own life: her desires and regrets toward her own playmates, her disappointments in marriage, her envy that her children take over her romantic illusions on their own terms and inevitably leave her behind.

Since this is a film about families, about privacy and society, it repeatedly uses the image of the circle and, as Parker Tyler has pointed out, the object revolving on a fixed axis. The use of headgear (about which I am so often questioned) is merely an extension of these visual metaphors.

The choice of actors all of relatively the same age to act the parts of both children and grown-ups was a means of maintaining throughout the film that uncertain borderland of conflict between being a child and being a grown-up, as well as to implicate the world of the mother in the world of infantile daydream—she being, in the case of this particular family album, perhaps the biggest child of them all. The only exceptions to this casting—the figures of two older women—are projections of her fear of time and of possible event.

Note Two:

The subject matter in *Mother's Day* is both cultural and personal. I make these distinctions because the themes of two of my books meet and cross in this film. In my verse play, *The Playground,* I have pictured adults acting like children within a frame of reference to our social and psychological "childish behavior:" the refusal to confront the world we live in. And in *Musical Chairs* I have presented in a series of poems a record of the inner state. The subtitle of that volume is "A Songbook for Anxious Children."

In *Mother's Day* I deliberately used adults acting as children to evoke the sense of projecting oneself as an adult back into memory, to suggest the impossible borderline between when one is child and when one is grown-up, and to implicate Mother in the world of the child fantasies as being, perhaps, the biggest child of them all—since she, in this case, has never freed herself from narcissistic daydreams.

Since this is a film about mothers and children, about families and forms of social experience, it is dominated by the circle, and—as Parker Tyler pointed out—by the object revolving on a fixed axis.

The hats are another (and more graphic) means of referring to finding what shoe to fit for following in parental footsteps, as they also serve nicely as traditional symbols for changes in fashion and social changes.

The visual style of *Mother's Day* is based on play. The film is concerned with aspects and aftermaths of play. The spirit of play is the key to the order of images, for the actions—even when they are dealing with the most unfrivolous matters—are conceived in terms of play.

The objects which the persons find in their world, explore, reject, or use in their rituals, are to be thought of as toys: the paraphernalia of play. Like all playthings they are as actual as they are symbolic. They are toys in the game everyone plays or tries—the long, busy game of growing up.

The play of a child can be profoundly serious, or a devilish mockery, or a light-hearted improvisation. And adults (like Mother) play just as hard, but more obsessively and with less happy results all around.

A toy is a real thing, but it is also whatever property for the imagination one may want to make it. And the world is full of objects of wonder revolving about the questing and puzzled eyes of the newcomer to it, suggestive of many mysteries and destinies, and for him to use or make what he can of them: the toys of our lives. We have toys at all our seven ages, though we may not acknowledge them so.

(1948)

JOHN AND JAMES WHITNEY:

Audio-Visual Music

I

Each individual who has identified himself with the abstract film medium has begun from scratch and devised every detail of his technical means. Inevitably, form under this circumstance has been preeminently interrelated with technique. Form is weak or it flowers just so well as the means are integrated. The perfection of means, however, does not proceed along a simple forward path of progress, because this art is not a science with a rationale more than any other. And it is actually a very new thing that so much technology must be brought to bear upon an art form as it is in the field of the cinema. Perhaps the abstract film can become the freest and the most significant art form of the cinema. But also, it will be the one most involved in machine technology, an art fundamentally related to the machine.

In our work, we have continuously sought an equilibrium between technical limitations and creative freedom. We have partially achieved it, lost it again, and now search for it once more at a higher level. Our first film made with an optical-printer but without sound, is a case in point; the equipment and the state of our general technique determined a set of limitations which have never since been so circumscribed. Yet within those limitations was found an area of freedom open to creative manipulation which has never again been so vast. This film rapidly acquired unity and simplicity.

With our expanded means, including sound, today we endeavor to reestablish that equilibrium. This, we believe, has become possible as we accept the technical means at our disposal as adequate and proceed to widen the area of freedom within discovered and accepted limitations. The films produced over the five year period since our first, seldom have been completed before their value to us as experiments were negated by new experiments following a new approach to form and with altered and sometimes improved equipment. Thus, they frequently manifest one technical quality or another that is subtly out of order with their formal organization. Still, they are better described as exercises than experiments, for they are rehearsals for a species of audio-visual performances that we can very well visualize now.

II

It is a commonplace to note that film and sound today have become a permanent unity. We are attracted by the prospects of an idiom as unified, bi-sensorially, as the sound film can be.

Naturally, we have wanted to avoid weakening that unity, which would be the very essence of an abstract film medium.

It occurred to us that an audience could bring with it its own disunifying distractions in the form of numerous past associations and preconceptions were we to use previously composed music in relation to our own abstract image compositions. We, therefore, tried the simplest, least common, primitive music we could find. But another source for disunity became apparent. In this case, the dominant source of distraction was a contradiction between the origins (the players, instruments, time, place, etc.) of this kind of music and our animated image.

Thereafter, little thought was given to any other consideration than to search for a method of creating our own sound by some means near as possible to the image animation process, technically and in spirit.

III

The sound track of all our films to date was created synthetically by the device which came into being as a result of these conclusions. Without attempting to describe it in detail here,* its principle resembles less a musical instrument than certain devices used for charting the rise and fall of ocean waves. Pendulums instead of waves create the ebb and flow movement. This motion is greatly demagnified and registered on a narrow space of the motion picture film provided for a sound track. No sound is needed to produce these patterns on the sound track. The patterns themselves generate tones in the sound projector. The instrument has a selection of some thirty pendulums adjusted in frequency relationship to each other so as to form a scale. They can be swung singly or in any combination.

We value the instrument despite certain distinct limitations for an assortment of reasons. An immediate practical one is that it as much as provides us with a means where otherwise there would be none at all. Sound recording of original music even at the 16 mm.

---

* A description can be found in *Hollywood Quarterly;* Vol. 1, No. 1.

scale is prohibitively expensive and presents enormous difficulties for the amateur.

Some other reasons have to do with adaptability of the instrument to our purposes. In composing the sound, we seek to exploit a spatial quality characteristic of the instrument which reinforces that effect of movement in space which we seek to achieve in the image. Since both image and sound can be time scored to fractions of a single motion picture frame, there is opened a new field of audio-visual rhythmic possibilities. The quality of the sound evokes no strong image distraction such as was observed in other music. Consequently, the sound is easily integrated with the image. The scale of the instrument is adjustable to any intervals we may choose including quarter tones and smaller. This permits use of graduated ascending or descending tonal series. They correspond in quality of feeling and variability to certain types of image series, such as, for example, an enlarging or diminishing shape, an ascending or descending shape, or a color series.

In concluding this section it should be observed that there is for us perhaps more personal freedom than is possible in any other motion picture field today. Our sound and image technique provide a complete means accessible to one creator. We believe in the future of the abstract film medium as one differing from the others in that it demands none of the large scale collaboration typical in present motion picture fields.

IV

We seek to extend certain principles which have evolved over the past forty years by the work and thought of such men as Marcel Duchamp and Piet Mondrian.

During this time, in painting, spatial limitations of the particular, human, real world have generally given way to a concern with a conceptual simultaneity of space-time. Mondrian sought "a truer vision of reality" by destroying the particular of representation, thus liberating space and form in terms of equilibrium.* By a mechanical destruction of the particular we believe it possible to approach anew this problem. We seek a new equilibrium—an equilibrium on a temporal frame as in music. And we seek a balance of contrasting plastic *movements*.

Obviously Western Art forms have been no less determined and limited by their accepted creative means than our work is limited and its character is determined by our mechanical means. Our very realm of creative action is implicit in the machine. Emphasis is necessarily upon a more objective approach to creative activity. More universal. Less particular. More so by virtue of the inherent impersonal attribute of the machine. We discern a creative advan-

---

* See *Plastic Art and Pure Plastic Art* by Piet Mondrian; Wittenborn & Co., New York.

tage here similar to that deliberately sought after by both Mondrian and Duchamp however opposed their respective points of view; Duchamp, an anti-artist, and Mondrian, seeking a purity of plastic means.

But the machine is yet a poorly integrated, clumsily handled invention else man would not be face to face with his destiny by it today. Personal contact with new creative fields by way of the machine would hardly be worth struggling after were it not for the tremendous variety of new clay to be found there, its universality and its close kinship with modern experience.

Our animating and sound producing devices do not respond to our touch as a musical instrument responds to the virtuoso. Aside from our own admitted inexperience there are clear-cut historical reasons for this. The devices of art and music which have made Western Art forms possible, originated in antiquity and have evolved slowly paralleling the life of that culture. The introduction of the machine in such proportions as has taken place only in this century constitutes a quantitative change effecting a distinct qualitative revolution. The motion picture camera is no more an improved paint brush than our sound track device is an improved musical instrument.

It is our opinion that the work and ideas of Marcel Duchamp with his underlying principles, against hand painting, and, a studied exploitation of the mechanisms of chance, make a significant esthetic contribution to the advancement of this "qualitative revolution." Perhaps his concept of irony provides a clue to the whole future of machine realized art. He defines his meaning of irony as ". . . a playful way of accepting something. Mine is the irony of indifference. It is a meta-irony."* Our own experience has been that this corresponds very closely to the correct philosophical disposition by which the resources of the machine may be accepted and employed.

(*Art in Cinema*, San Francisco Museum of Art, 1947)

---

* See *View* Magazine. Duchamp Number, Series V No. 1.

P. ADAMS SITNEY:

Harry Smith Interview

Smith: The dating of my films is difficult because I had made the first one, or part of that, in 1939. It was about twenty-five years ago, although it says forty years in the *Film-Makers Cooperative Catalogue*, because, at different times, I have posed as different ages.

Sitney: When were you born?

I never give that information out. I would like to say that I'm the Czar of Russia. My mother always claimed to be Anastasia. That's how I got Mr. R. interested in these things. This interview has to be severely cut down. Like no names, Mr. R., you know, or something.

I had drawn on film for quite a while, but exactly which one is #1 I don't know. It was made something between 1939 and, I would say, 1942 at the latest. Later, I was very disappointed to find out that Len Lye had done it. Naturally, I was horrified when either Dick Foster or Frank Stauffacher showed up with a book one day and told me that not only had Len made hand-painted films, but he had done 16mm ones. Then later somebody in San Francisco, whose name I forget (he was the Harley-Davidson agent), got like stimulated by me and made 8mm hand-painted films.

#1 was made by taking impressions of various things, like cutting up erasers or the lid of a Higgins Ink bottle. That's where I derived all the circular shapes. There's a kind of cork on the top of it. I dipped it in the ink and squashed it down on the film; then, later, I went over the thing with a crow-quill pen. However, the colors aren't too good in that film. I can't remember how long it took to make it, because I'd made a number of others. I had a considerable number of films that have not been printed at all. Undoubtedly less than half of my stuff is in my possession now.

Were the early films made on 16mm?

No, on 35mm. After I made #1, I met the Whitney Brothers through Frank Stauffacher and Dick Foster. Foster was the one

who had really started the Art in Cinema Society because he had
been in New York and had met film-makers there. But, later, he
and Stauffacher fell out; so I took over Foster's position. They sent
me down to Los Angeles to look for films.

A sketch for the projection system of *No. 18 (Mahagonny)*. Films will
be projected in the four central rectangles, while texts and numbers
will appear in the other enclosed areas.

I had been going to the University of Washington studying an-
thropology. I was a teaching assistant there occasionally. (I still
love Drs. Gunther and Jacobs.) I was never a good student, at all.
I led a very isolated youth. My father had run away from home at
an early age to become a cowboy. I think that at that time his
grandfather was the Governor of Illinois. They were a wealthy
family. My great-grandfather, General John Corson Smith, was
aide-de-camp to General Grant during the later Civil War. My
mother came from Sioux City, Iowa; but my grandmother had had
a school that was supported by the Czarina of Russia in Sitka,
Alaska, although she moved around. The Czarina still supported
those operations for years, and that's what led to my mother's
being Anastasia. My father destroyed every single shred of information on her when she died. I never saw him again. The last
time that I saw my father, I was like a heroin addict. I might have
been sixteen or seventeen. I left on the bus for San Francisco after

the funeral. I had to get back to get a hold of the connection. My
father was crying. . . . What I started to say was that they lived in
separate houses. My grandfather came to Washington and founded
the Pacific American Fisheries with his brother, which is the largest
salmon canning combine in the world. They killed off all the salmon
in Washington. They still have twenty some canneries in Alaska.
They fished everything else out of British Columbia and Washington years ago. This doesn't have much to do with my films. It's all
true. My father may still be alive. I haven't contacted him in years,
although he tried to find me by various means. He found out that
my films were being shown at the Art in Cinema Society and tried
to discover where I was. He finally did find out where I was and I
sent him one of those "Tree of Life" drawings. I never did hear from
him again. He was evidently very smart; he had taught me about
alchemy. He was interested in that sort of thing. On about my
twelfth birthday he gave me a whole blacksmith's shop. (They were
stuck with various canneries that had been built up during the
First World War. The whole thing over-expanded.) Most of my
childhood was spent in a fairly elaborate place in Anacortes, Washington. There was nobody there at that time except my father who
was something of a ne'er-do-well. My great-grandfather must have
been pretty interesting. At one point, he said, "I am leaving for a
five-year tour of Tibet." After the Civil War, the Masons split into
two groups—one of them was led by Albert Pike, who wrote *Morals
and Dogma of the Scottish Rite;* the other one, the Knights Tem-
plar, were refounded by my great-grandfather. Any time that the
Masons have a parade on Fifth Avenue, they always have a float
that shows my great-grandfather founding this thing. He traveled
all over the world and initiated people like the King of Hawaii and
King Edward the Seventh into that business. When I was a child,
there were a great number of books on occultism and alchemy always in the basement.

   Like I say, my father gave me a blacksmith shop when I was
maybe twelve; he told me I should convert lead into gold. He had
me build all these things like models of the first Bell telephone, the
original electric light bulb, and perform all sorts of historical experiments. I once discovered in the attic of our house all those illuminated documents with hands with eyes in them, all kinds of
Masonic deals that belonged to my grandfather. My father said I
shouldn't have seen them, and he burned them up immediately.
That was the background for my interest in metaphysics, and so
forth. My mother described mainly events from when she was
working in the school in Alaska my grandmother had run. For example, one day she hadn't been able to get into the place where
she was living: It was so cold, her hands started to freeze and she
was unable to unlock the door. She went out into the woods where
she saw all the animals performing ceremonies. She told me many
times about that because it must have been a wonderful thing.

That was somewhere on the Yukon River. Hundreds had gathered together and were leaping over each other by moonlight. They were running around in little circles in different places. Of course it all could be explained in terms of bio-mass, or what is that thing called? There is some way that the animals have certain ranges and interrelate with one another. It was evidently some special thing. The authority on these things, Tinbergen, points out that animals do absolutely every single thing that humans do except make fire.

Very early, my parents got me interested in projecting things. The first projections that I made were from the lamps of a flashlight. In those days, flashlights had lenses on the front of them; that couldn't have been much later than in 1928.

What I really started to say was that, due to the vast amount of buildings and things that had no use after there were no more salmon in the Fraser or the Columbia, my parents lived in separate houses from the time I was about ten until I left home at the age of eighteen. They had communication between their houses by ringing bells. They'd meet for dinner. My father wanted to play the piano and the guitar. He was interested also in drawings and things; he was the one who showed me how to make that "Tree of Life" geometrically. I mostly lived with my mother. I performed what might be considered sexual acts with her until I was eighteen or nineteen maybe. No actual insertion or anything, but I would always get up in the morning and get in bed with her because she had a long story she would tell me about someone named Eaky-Peaky. She was a really good story teller. My posture is derived from trying to be exactly her height; for she was shorter. I think that the first time she went to Alaska must have been kind of strange because it was right after or during the Gold Rush. Both my parents were there at that time. There were various people on this boat going to the Gold Rush. One of them, for example, was suffering from withdrawal from morphine and thought she had worms under her flesh. She was lying there saying, "The worms! the worms!" The other was some kind of whore who was hanging her tits out the porthole and saying, "Come on, boys, milkshake, five cents a shake." I don't know how my father got there. They somehow met there. They met somehow.

So anyhow, the first projections that I made were negatives that my mother and father had taken in Alaska. I had thousands of those, enormous masses of this stuff. I can remember the amazement that I felt when I took the lens of the flashlight and was able to see one of the snow scenes on the walls of the hall.

My mother evidently had a number of boyfriends as my father was never there. He was always in Alaska doing something. She would park me in movies, most of which I can't remember. They were all silent movies. That's what got me interested in them. Sure, she was off doing something else; maybe not with boyfriends. I did meet a few of them; that's how I met Aleister Crowley. Probably he's my father, although I don't want to say that. There's a question as to whether he is or Robert James Smith is. She had fallen in love with Crowley when he was in this country in about 1918, while he was living on some islands in Puget Sound north of Seattle. Then he showed up a few more times, probably—I don't know when they were—in 1927 or sometime—that can be determined from books on his travels. I can remember meeting him at least once; he showed me a clam neck hanging out of a cliff; he had a black turtle-neck sweater on. He was not any kind of sissified character like they say. He was a really handsome, muscular person. My mother would sneak off to see him. He was there twice as far as I can remember; she met him when he was running naked down the beach in 1918.

She would leave me in a theater. I saw some good films there, which I wish it were possible to locate again. I saw one, for example, which was pretty good in which bad children put caps into the spaghetti at a fancy Italian dinner. (That was one of the first sound films that I ever saw.) When the people chewed their spaghetti there was a BAAAKH; that was about all that was on the soundtrack. The mouth would fly open, and false teeth would go across the dinner table, and so forth. They consistently took me to see Charlie Chaplin and Buster Keaton. I can remember being horrified when Keaton (in *The General*) gets caught in the bear trap, though my parents thought that was so funny. I was never able to understand why it was funny, but they kept taking me back to it day after day after day. Mainly, I liked serials. I didn't particularly like Charlie Chaplin or Buster Keaton. Of course, I appreciate them now.

I was still going to school, which was an interesting school; what was that called? The Western Washington School of Education. The head of it later got busted for Communism. I liked it because they had a glass beehive in the middle of the classroom that had a chute running out through the window so we could study the bees at work. It was an unpleasant place because they kept accusing me of stealing things like money. On the day that Admiral Byrd was visiting, somebody said Miss Rich, who was my principal, was going to take us to see Admiral Byrd; and I said, "Oh, kick Miss Rich in the pants." It was horrible, because I said this to the person next to me, and the person next to me said it to the person next to him, "Harry said, 'kick Miss Rich in the pants.'" And he said it to the next one. I saw this thing go around, back and forth across the room. It finally got to the teacher, so, naturally, I was kept home when everybody else went to see Admiral Byrd; although, strangely enough, I met him in a Mannings later that day.

I saw all those Fu Manchu movies; they were some of my favorites. There was also some serial that had a great big spider about the size of this room, which would be chasing Pearl White down through tunnels. That thing scared the shit out of me, but I probably had erections during it, it was so terrifying. I was very interested in spiders at about the age of five. I discovered a lot of them in the Columbine vines. Also I remember meeting my grandfather (my mother's father) who was also pretty interesting because he had followed a particular friend of his—he had been born in Kentucky, I don't know where, some place like that and followed the Union troops north after the Civil War. I remember he and his friend had long white beards with yellow streaks down the front of them. I had thought that egg had run down them. They had been eating eggs, see, and the egg had run down the middle of their beards.

This is the college education that I got . . . I was never able to pass the entrance examination in English. Despite the fact that I should have a Ph.D. at this point on all other bases but that. I just could not diagram sentences. I was sort of an instructor at one point at the University of California. I went to the University of Washington first. I was never too well liked there. The war had ended, and there was all this anti-Communism; what they call witch hunting was going on, and my favorite teacher was . . . you see, I got connected with the World Friends Service Committee at that point. I began working with the Japanese that were being kicked off the West Coast. The day after Pearl Harbor, all the Japanese were arrested and sent to camps in some horrible desert, I forget where that was. They sure came back in condition! We finally got one Japanese back to Seattle who was a midget and wore a monocle—a girl, who was going to deliver a lecture in some church; I forget what that thing was called—the Fellowship of Reconciliation, that was it. I barely escaped the Communist plots, I think. It was pretty funny: We rented this church for her to give the lecture in, and nobody came, not one person. There, I'm stuck with this girl that is completely confused. I was also involved with a lot of Jewish refugees that were going to the University of Washington then, ranting about people being thrown into incinerators and so forth in concentration camps. It was an interesting period: I wish they'd have another war; I liked it.

There's confusion in the notes for the *Catalogue* because I tend to glamorize, saying that I did such and such at a much earlier age than I did it. The reason I moved to Berkeley from . . . how did that happen? Anyway, I went to Berkeley on some little trip from Seattle with someone named Kenneth, I forget what his last name was. I'd met him in a bookstore. He said, "I'm leaving for Berkeley, do you want to go?" So I went to Berkeley. This was supposed to be for over the weekend. However while I was there I ran into someone named Griff B. He turned me on to marijuana. So naturally when I got back to the University of Washington, where I was about to become a teaching assistant, it was impossible to stay there after having smoked pot. The stuff that is given in the *Cata-*

logue that was used on different films is slightly inaccurate. I've never experienced the real heroin-addiction thing. In the place where I lived, the Fillmore district of San Francisco called Jackson's Nook, two people died; I mean, there was a number of people staggering out into the back yard and dropping dead. When my mother died, there were a lot of guns around the house, because they'd always had them while they were in Alaska, both my mother and father. I took all that stuff back with me. It led to a rather exciting life in San Francisco at that point. My mother was dying in the hospital of what Ronald J. once called terminal diarrhea. She died the day after I left. I was like a heroin addict at that point. The symptoms were not very serious though; I was not lying on the floor frothing at the mouth; I had a stomach ache and a runny nose and that sort of thing.

I was mainly a painter. The films are minor accessories to my paintings; it just happened that I had the films with me when everything else was destroyed. My paintings were infinitely better than my films because much more time was spent on them. I can show you slides of them. I don't have any slides that were made since about 1950. That's a painting that was made of the score for one of the films that were shown. That's like the scenario for the last movement of one of those color films.

My first film was made by imprinting of the cork off an ink bottle and all that sort of thing, as I said before. The second one was made with Come-Clean gum dots, automatic adhesive dots that Dick Foster got for me. It's like a paper dot with gum on the back. The film was painted over with a brush to make it wet, then with a mouth-type spray gun, dye was sprayed onto the film. When that dried the whole film was greased with vaseline. Of course this was in short sections—maybe six foot long sections. Anyway they would be tacked down. With a pair of tweezers, the dots were pulled off. That's where those colored balls drop and that sort of stuff. Being as it was pulled off, it was naturally dry where the dot had been and that part which had been colored was protected by the vaseline coating at this point. Then color was sprayed into where the dot had been. After that dried, the whole film was cleaned with carbon tetrachloride.

The next one was made by putting masking tape onto the film and slitting the tape lightly with a razor blade and a ruler, and then picking off all those little squares that are revolving around. I worked off and on on that film for about five years pretty consistently; I worked on it every day at least. I may have abandoned it at one point for three months or six months at the most.

Mrs. S. who owned the house in Berkeley gave me a room in exchange for mowing the lawn and trimming the ivy. I had developed a theory that the ideal diet was a mixture of butter and sugar—a pound of sugar and a pound of butter mixed together. I became so weak, though, that I was unable to get out of bed for a long time.

Except some girl, Panthia L., would come up some mornings and scramble an egg and give it to me; or I'd go down to the supermarket and steal avocados, butter and sugar.

Were the early abstract films at all influenced by your childhood interest in the occult?

Sort of. But mainly by looking in the water. I lived a kind of isolated childhood. I said my parents were living in different houses and would only meet at dinner time. They'd set up this fancy five-storey art school, at which there were really only two students—sometimes there were four students. With Mrs. Williams, I studied at least from maybe 1932 to 1942; I must have studied with her for ten years. She gave lessons two or three times a week during that period, which consisted of drawing things. She'd lay out a cylinder or a ball or an egg-shaped thing which we were supposed to draw on a piece of paper and then lay a piece of glass over that and trace the drawing with a grease pencil, then hold it up and see if it looked exactly the same.

#1 took a very long time. Either a day or a week. Then #2—which was much longer than the form it is in now: It was actually at least half an hour long—it was cut down to match a recording by Dizzy Gillespie, which I believe is called "Guacha Guero." It took maybe a year to make. Then on the next one I worked on about five years, then I gave up that particular style. There were maybe eight years of it. I developed certain really complicated hand-painting techniques of which I made only short versions. For example, painting the whole film a certain color and then smearing vaseline on it; and then taking a stylus and scraping designs off. It is possible to get a lot of spirals and curvilinear designs which I was never able to get by cutting off the masking tape; then spraying bleach into the place where the groove was. I made short samples of that sort of material. As I say, less than half of all that stuff is in my possession at this point. I also made alternate versions of a great number of scenes. Sometimes, in order to demonstrate how it was done, I made up special reels that partially had the masking tape still left on, and partially the first . . . Anyway, there are thousands of feet that were never printed, and several entire very long films. Many of those films are missing totally. I never edited at all, except to cut them down—except that second one, which shows the balls falling. Like I say, it was at least 1,200 feet long originally. It was then cut down to a hundred feet to make it match "Guacha Guero." What Jonas Mekas calls "The Magic Feature" (#12) was originally about six hours long, and then it was edited down, first to a two-hour version, and then down to a one-hour version. There was also an enormous amount of material made for that picture. None of the really good material that was constructed for that film was ever photographed. There was a Noah's ark scene with really fantastic animals. I started out with the poorer stuff. The really good things were supposed to be toward the end of the film, but, being as the end of the film was never made . . .

On that Oz film, that expensive one, of course, I had quite a few people working; so that all kinds of special cut-outs were made that were never photographed. I mean really wonderful ones were made! One cut-out might take someone two months to make. They were very elaborate stencils and so forth. All of my later films were never quite completed. Most of the material was never shot, because the film dragged on too long.

Those two optically printed films were made for the Guggenheim Foundation. The three-dimensional one was made from the same batch of stencils as the color one. First, I got a camera from Frank Stauffacher, which is when those two films were made: The first is called *Circular Tensions* (#5); I forget what the other one is called. The black and white one (#4) preceeds that.

The black and white film (#4) begins with a shot of—

—a painting. It is a painting of a tune by Dizzy Gillespie called "Manteca." Each stroke in that painting represents a certain note on the recording. If I had the record, I could project the painting as a slide and point to a certain thing. This is the main theme in there, which is a-doot-doot-dootdoot-doot-doottadootdoot; those curved lines up there. See, ta-doot-doot-doot-doot-dootaloot-dootaloot, and so forth. Each note is on there. The most complex one of these is this one, one of Charlie Parker's records, I don't remember the name of it. That's a really complex painting. That took five years. Just like I gave up making films after that last hand-drawn one took a number of years, I gave up painting after that took a number of years to make; it was just too exhausting. There's a dot for each note and the phrases that the notes consist of are colored in a certain way or made in a certain path. The last paintings that I made were realistic things connected with the Tower of Babel. There was an extraordinary one of the control room of the Tower of Babel, which was built into a railway car leaving it. That painting was derived from a scene in Buster Keaton's film *The General,* where he chops out the end of the box car. A special film was projected onto the painting so that all the machinery operates.

In a number of cases I've made special screens to project films on. All those so-called early abstract films had special painted screens for them. They were made of dots and lines. All those things disappeared.

When I went to Oklahoma last year, I decided to devote my attention to the Indians. I really was honored to be able to record those things from the Indians. I decided to devote the rest of my life to that one thing. It was an unusual opportunity, because the Kiowa Indians are extremely conservative. They hadn't really been studied very much. Through various reasons, I got involved with them so that they told me all their myths and everything. It seemed better to devote the conclusion to that. That's why I'm living in this hotel room. Despite the fact that I can't afford the hotel room—it's fifty dollars a week—I am more or less able to spend my time doing that one thing. It is a very elaborate series of records, you know. We're devoting far too much time to accessory subjects. Naturally, I sort of goof on everything I'm doing.

I'm very puzzled about your fascination to visualize music.

That is an interesting question, isn't it? I don't know. When I was a child, somebody came to school one day and said they'd been to an Indian dance and they saw somebody swinging a skull on the end of a string; so that I thought, Hmmmm, I have to see this. I went to that. Then I fell in with the Salish around Puget Sound for a long time. I sometimes spent three or four months with them during summer vacation or sometimes in the winter, while I was going to high school or junior high school. It all started in grade school. In an effort to write down dances, I developed certain techniques of transcription. Then I got interested in the designs in relation to the music. That's where it started from. Of course! It was an attempt to write down the unknown Indian life. I made a large number of recordings of that, which are also unfortunately lost. I took portable equipment all over that place long before anyone else did and recorded whole long ceremonies sometimes lasting several days. Diagramming the pictures was so interesting that I then started to be interested in music in relation to existence. After that I met Griff B. and went to Berkeley and started smoking marijuana, naturally little colored balls appeared whenever we played Bessie Smith and so forth; whatever it was I was listening to at that time. I had a really great illumination the first time I heard Dizzy Gillespie play. I had gone there very high, and I literally saw all kinds of colored flashes. It was at that point that I realized music could be put to my films. My films had been made before then, but I had always shown them silently. I had been interested in Jungian psychiatry when I was in junior high school. I found some books by Jung in the Bellingham Library. The business about mandalas and so forth got me involved. I would like to say I'm not very interested in Jung anymore: It seems very crude now.

Incidentally, this whole thing can probably be printed, if you want to print it for me, like some kind of poem. In that way, this constant shifting back and forth can be eliminated.

Later I borrowed a camera from Hy Hirsh. He had a pretty good camera, a Bell and Howell model 70-something, and had seen my films. The San Francisco Museum showed that one of the grille works (#4) that precedes *Circular Tensions*, and he came up and spoke. That's when I asked for a camera. I've never owned a camera; I've usually just borrowed one, then pawned it. That's always an embarrassing scene; trying to explain to the person where his or her camera is. I can remember Frank Stauffacher saying to me, "Now you haven't pawned the camera, have you?" He said this jokingly, but it was pawned. Usually, people get their cameras back, eventually. My later films were made with one that belonged to Sheba

Ziprin. The *Mysterioso* film (#11) and the long black and white film (#12) were shot with her camera, which is now in a pawn shop in Oklahoma City. The main parts of my film in Oklahoma last year were shot on a camera that belonged to Stuart Reed. That camera is in a barber shop in Anadarko, Oklahoma, where Mr. A.'s Wollensak also is, unfortunately.

After I first stopped making films, I made those paintings that you point at. Unless you've seen those, it's hard to describe what they really are. They are at least as good as the films. I'd been able to hear Charlie Parker and Thelonious Monk, both of whom had come to San Francisco, but wanted to make one final thing, another painting of Thelonious. When I came to N.Y.C., I realized that it would be impossible to make it in the form of a painting, because his music was so complex, and it would be better to make a film. I hadn't made films for at least five years by then. #10 was a study for the *Mysterioso* film. Generally speaking, those films were made by trying to collect interesting pictures, cutting them out, and then filing them. I had enormous files possibly only 2 or 3 per cent of which was shot. I had worked on this one thing for twenty years, having collected a lot of that stuff before; but then, when I left San Francisco, I gave it to Broughton, because I felt that he might do something with it; but he obviously never did.

After I came here I started filming again. Toward the end, I had everything filed in glassine envelopes: any kind of vegetable, any kind of animal, any kind of this that and the other thing, in all different sizes. Then file cards were made up. For example, everything that was congruent to that black and white film (#12) was picked out. All the permutations possible were built up: say, there's a hammer in it, and there's a vase, and there's a woman, and there's a dog. Various things could then be done—hammer hits dog; woman hits dog; dog jumps into vase; so forth. It was possible to build up an enormous number of cross references.

This was all written on little slips of paper, the file cards—the possible combinations between this, that, and the other thing. The file cards were then rearranged, in an effort to make a logical story out of it. Certain things would have to happen before others: Dog-runs-with-watermelon has to occur after dog-steals-watermelon.

I tried as much as possible to make the whole thing automatic, the production automatic rather than any kind of logical process. Though, at this point, Allen Ginsberg denies having said it, about the time I started making those films, he told me that William Burroughs made a change in the Surrealistic process—because, you know, all that stuff comes from the Surrealists—that business of folding a piece of paper: One person draws the head and then folds it over, and somebody else draws the body. What do they call it? The Exquisite Corpse. Somebody later, perhaps Burroughs, realized that something was directing it, that it wasn't arbitrary, and that there was some kind of what you might call God. It wasn't just chance. Some kind of universal process was directing these so-called arbitrary processes; and so I proceeded on that basis: Try to remove things as much as possible from the consciousness or whatever you want to call it so that the manual processes could be employed entirely in moving things around. As much as I was able, I made it automatic.

I must say that I'm amazed, after having seen the black-and-white film (#12) last night, at the labor that went into it. It is incredible that I had enough energy to do it. Most of my mind was pushed aside into some sort of theoretical sorting of the pieces, mainly on the basis that I have described: First, I collected the pieces out of old catalogues and books and whatever; then made up file cards of all possible combinations of them; then, I spent maybe a few months trying to sort the cards into logical order. A script was made for that. All the script and the pieces were made for a film at least four times as long. There were wonderful masks and things cut out. Like when the dog pushes the scene away at the end of the film, instead of the title "end" what is really there is a transparent screen that has a candle burning behind it on which a cat fight begins—shadow forms of cats begin fighting. Then, all sorts of complicated effects; I had held these off. The radiations were to begin at this point. Then Noah's Ark appears. There were beautiful scratch-board drawings, probably the finest drawings I ever made—really pretty. Maybe 200 were made for that one scene. Then there's a graveyard scene, when the dead are all raised again. What actually happens at the end of the film is everybody's put in a teacup, because all kinds of horrible monsters came out of the graveyard, like animals that folded into one another. Then everyone gets thrown in a teacup, which is made out of a head, and stirred up. This is the Trip to Heaven and the Return, then the Noah's Ark, then The Raising of the Dead, and finally the Stirring of Everyone in a Teacup. It was to be in four parts. The script was made up for the whole works on the basis of sorting pieces. It was exhaustingly long in its original form. When I say that it was cut, mainly what was cut out was, say, instead of the little man bowing and then standing up, he would stay bowed down much longer in the original. The cutting that was done was really a correction of timing. It's better in its original form.

#13 had all the characters out of Oz in it. That was assembled in the same way: I naturally divided Oz up into four lands because Oz consists of the Munchkins, the Quadlings, the Gillikins, and the Winkies; and then the Emerald City is in the middle; that is where the wizard's balloon had landed. I had built that thing many times as a child. I had fairly severe hallucinations, and I had built something called my Fairy Garden for many years. I actually used to see little gnomes and fairies and stuff until I was seven or eight. It's a typical psychic phenomenon; I mean, I wasn't nutty or anything; all children see that stuff. Up until I was eighteen or so, I worked hard on my Fairy Garden and then started building Oz. It was a

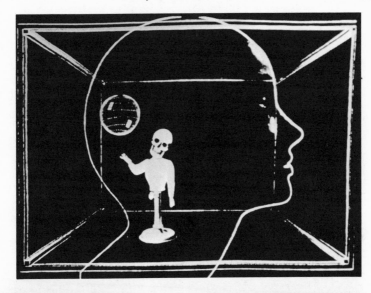

No. 12 (Heaven and Earth Magic): *an image from the film (above) and one of the framing masks through which it was to be projected.*

fairly large place, because we had blocks and blocks of property in Anacortes. I built Oz a number of times; the final form, though, was for this film. It was to be a commercial film. Very elaborate equipment was built; the animation stand was about the size of a floor and exactly fourteen feet high. Oz was laid out on it, then seven levels, built up. It was like the multiplane camera of Disney, except that I was using a Mitchell camera that moved around. That's how I got into so many difficulties. Van Wolf had not paid rent on the camera, which was a thousand dollars a week. He was the producer, but he was taking far too many pills to do much but try to wiggle out of situations that developed. He got various people to pay for it: Huntington Hartford, Harry Phipps, Peggy Hitchcock, Elizabeth Taylor, and so forth invested in the film.

It was divided into different things. I ditched the Munchkins, Quadlings, Gillikins, and Winkies in their original form. What I was really trying to do was to convert Oz into a Buddhistic image like a mandala. I can't even remember what those lands were. One of them was Hieronymus Bosch Land: All of Bosch's paintings were carefully dissected. Another one was Microscopia taken from the books of Haeckel, who was the Viennese biological artist and very wonderful. The things he made are just marvelous; he picked out every possible grotesque object that there was. There was another land that was entirely made out of flesh. Enormous vistas for miles were made out of naked people from dirty mags. That would have been a nice film! Most of my material was prepared for it, and over six hours of tests were shot to get the apparatus to operate correctly. Only the little piece in the drawer there was ever synchronized to the music. In this particular section, the Ballet Music from *Faust*, the Tin Woodman performs magic before leaving for the Emerald City. The sound track was made up for the whole film.

Dr. Leary had me interested in that black-and-white film (#12), although, you realize, that *Heaven and Earth Magic*, whatever it's called, was a color film at that point. It ran through a special machine that projected slides. This is the first one that occurs: As the first head is on the screen, the slide of the same image is projected around it. There was a fader that obscured the screen out at the edges. You don't realize that it's an oblong image; it's just that there's another head the same as this—that's the telephone operator who made the greatest number of phone calls in the United States in some particular year. Where everything dissolves into the bridge, you see it's taking place on the moon; when the machinery is all operating, it's inside a watermelon. The slides themselves run through another color apparatus, and the seats in the theater were to be on some kind of electrical contact or rubber pads so that, as the audience looked at the film, if a certain number of them would lean in one direction, that would activate little lights in the projection booth which indicated that the audience who were in dentist chairs, watermelons, and so forth, were thinking about a watermelon or about a dentist chair, and so forth. Then I would slip that slide in, since any one of the slides could go with any portion of the film. They are now in an order that was convenient. It was an attempt to employ feed-back phenomena. It was executed to a degree in Steinway Hall. Mr. Phipps set up a sort of presentation there. The whole thing was set up, and I arbitrarily guessed what the audience was thinking of from their responses. We didn't have any special chairs for them to sit in though.

I never did finish that sentence about the relation of Surrealism to my things: I assumed that something was controlling the course of action and that it was not simply arbitrary, so that by *sortilège* (as you know, there is a system of divination called "sortilege") everything would come out all right. #14 was made on this basis. Although I kept a record that such and such was shot in such and such an area of the screen, it was completely arbitrary.

Was it your decision to leave the Kodak leader between rolls of film?

I stole that idea from Andy Warhol. Everything that was shot was put in. A great number of images are missing. The stuff to which the most effort was devoted doesn't even show at all. A very large amount of material for some reason just isn't on the film. Peter Fleischman, who made that last film with me, and I spent weeks shooting objects that must have been all underexposed. I assumed, when Ansco said that the film had a rating of 300, that it did have a rating of 300. It doesn't; it has a rating of, perhaps, 100. Most of what was shot at the beginning and the end of the film disappeared because of that. The central portion was not developed for a long time; it was left lying around in the hot weather for about six months, so that it faded out and became white. I like the effect of the thing: It's all black at the beginning and the end, white in the middle; it looks good. Mr. Casper at Filmtronics made extremely good prints of the middle part. They are better than the original, but, nonetheless, it didn't come out anything like I'd expected it to.

I started to get people for a film some months ago . . . how did that start? I think I asked Andy if he wanted to make a film, and he said, "Yeah!" So I said, "Look, can I have $300?" He said, "Yeah." Who was it I asked next? I think Jack Smith. Then Robert Frank. At that point, it seemed ridiculous to make an underground movie, but to make a really elaborate superunderground movie for showing in neighborhood theaters. That would be the only one I would make. The project keeps bogging down, basically because I haven't been able to find anybody that knows enough about films in regular theaters. Arthur and Hugh Young have the money for it. I called them in a drunken condition and asked them for two million dollars, and Arthur said they perhaps would do it if they thought there were any possibility of producing an actual thing. In fact, I called them last Wednesday or Tuesday again, and they have been waiting all this time to look at films. They are interested in astrology. It is necessary to get some handsome producer to produce the film; not to produce money but to decide whether it's to be a short feature, or a short, like a Bugs Bunny length, so it can be distributed in first-run theaters.

It would be like a trip around the world. Various people would come in. It would be marvelous; for instance, if Andy were able to supervise maybe a twenty-minute color picture of Mount Fuji, but with a really good cameraman and technicians and everything so it would be really his beauty. Stan Vanderbeek was going to work on it. What he would do would be to go to northern Australia and animate aboriginal bark paintings. It would be produced eventually. Mr. Young once sent me a lavish check because he didn't like *Taras Bulba*. I'd called him the night before asking for money to go to Hollywood to try to salvage the Oz film. He said, "No, no, no, no, we're going to the movies, we're going to the movies, we don't have any time to talk with you now, Harry. And we're not interested in films. And anyhow you're drunk. You're calling me a fart." However, the next morning, a check did come in the mail, and he wrote, "We didn't like *Taras Bulba* at all, and we decided to see if you could do better." However, I took the money and went to Miami Beach to see Peter's mother, instead of going to Hollywood. I've been afraid to phone them for a long time.

I don't think I'll make any more animated films. They're too laborious and bad for the health. Sitting under those lights for hours is terrible. I've made enough of those; just like I've made enough hand-drawn films. I would like to make an "underground" movie that could be shown everywhere in little towns, because it was seeing art films, or whatever they used to call them, that first got me interested in these things. Now there must be lots of kids all over the world that would make films if they saw some of the things that are being made now.

There was another very good series of films I saw during the late 1920's. It always started with coming up to a door that had a little grille work in it, a mysterious little thing; the going in there, through it. Isadora Duncan was in one of those. You'd go through this door, and then there would be some Turkish or Chinese exotic operations. Those and the Fu Manchu movies were the ones that influenced me most. Naturally, I would like to make some kind of artistic film that would be helpful to the progress of humanity. And that's the best one I can think of. There's no doubt in my mind that eventually someone is going to make a so-called underground movie that will revive Hollywood as Kenneth Anger writes of it.

(*Film Culture* No. 37, Summer, 1965)

HARRY SMITH:

On *Mahagonny*

[On June 3, 1977 P. Adams Sitney interviewed Harry Smith on his monthly Arts Forum program on WNYC-FM. It was to have been the first of three interviews. However the station terminated the plan because of negative public response to the initial program. This is an edited and annotated version of that program. The voice is that of Harry Smith, except where questions from P.A.S. are indicated.]

Visionary cinema is confused with film. The only preliminary thing I would like to say is that I assume that the radio audience is familiar with the works of Claude Levi-Strauss regarding the Stop sign and the Go sign, the raw and the cooked (animals being cooked and eaten by men). I would particularly suggest page 96, and then you can throw away *The Raw and the Cooked*. A knowledge of Noam Chomsky is also necessary. Chomsky's *Aspects of the Theory of Syntax* should be looked at, at least. It is his doctoral thesis, and probably the most brilliant one Harvard has had since Sixteen something. Then, of course, the listener should know a little about Wittgenstein. In that case it's not necessary to take the cellophane off the book before you throw it away.

You should ask some questions, but please explain first that the answers have no connection with the questions unless the up and down is binom . . . binomially . . . (mispronounciations being the raw/cooked part). As a matter of fact, as you leave your home tonight examine the fire hydrants to see if they are still painted red and green the same way they were.

PAS: I find the bibliography puzzling, but perhaps some will find it illuminating. I would like you to tell us about the work you have been doing on your film, *Mahagonny*, the principles upon which you have been making it, and the way in which you plan to exhibit it.

Jung's theories regarding synchronicity have recently turned out to be true. For a long time it was thought that Jung was merely some kind of shill that had been placed there just to see exactly how far the public would go in belief. But now empirical proofs have arrived from the University of California. I can't go into that. Get the latest issue of *The Journal of the American Society of Psychical Research* (April 1976) and you will find out that what you believed was going to happen, happened. For example, this evening Prof. Sitney thought we were going to be late, and he arranged it perfectly.

PAS: Yes, we were a little late getting to the studio. I see we are having a very easy time getting off the subject.

Mahagonny? We just did it. The theory of *Mahagonny* is the Three interacting with the Four: as we all know, three times four is twelve, and three plus four is seven; so consequently there are twenty-two songs. The first lines being: "Wanted: fugitives from Justice, the widow Begbick, Fatty the bookkeeper (or is the word translated "procurer"?), and Trinity Moses." If my listeners have been following the Mideastern situation lately, they will understand why Trinity Moses later impersonates God, when they realize how there was a war between the Mohammedans and the Jews which turned into *them* uniting against the Christians; that's the raw/cooked thing carried to the second binomial juncture.

The first lines being: "Wanted", the last lines, after it goes through things like

You can sponge his face with vinegar,
But you cannot help a dead man;
You can cut out his tongue,
But you cannot help a dead man.

the final lines are: "There is no hope for you, or ourselves, or anyone." Careful examination of the film, *The Harder They Come,* would be necessary. The only person in that film who is not Jamaican is the recording engineer, who is oriental.

PAS: The connection between your film, *Mahagonny,* and *The Harder They Come* escapes me.

Well, we're hoping to open the film in Zurich. I think that will explain the connection, it being more important to live *Mahagonny* than to see *Mahagonny.* It is constructed on all sides: The first thing that happens is, of course, the personification of the widow Begbick as the Three, as opposed to the Four. The Three being money, sex, and, as it says, whiskey ("Show me the way to the next whiskey bar.") But in the original it is: "Show me the way to the next pretty boy." The widow Begbick is running brothels from the place where they are in Florida at that point, "with the desert ahead and the sheriff behind." Trinity Moses represents money ("the next little dollar"). This is then compounded with four things, which I will tell you later.

PAS: What will be the imagery?

Imagery never exists as such. It is determined by what people are told the image is going to be. There is a very interesting study of how people look at a picture. In this case Hokusai's wave is taken; and the first forty-six scans more or less follow the picture of the wave as it breaks over Fuji. The last forty-six scannings are of a random nature, regarding what the individual desires. Now, these studies will demonstrate what is printed on the screen. The book, *Eye Movements and Psychological Processes* (ed. Richard A. Monty, John W. Senders, 1976), goes into the fact that if there is a picture of some people going into a door while others are sitting at a table, and now if the words, "How much money do they have?" are said or printed, the eyes move over the clothing or the furniture. But, naturally, if the question is "How old are they?", people look at the faces; "What do they work at?" they maybe look at the hands. The fact is that the fovea cuts out most of what we see and that the brain constructs an image out of almost nothing (which is, of course, why Hapatia was dragged onto an altar and her flesh scraped off with seashells). Because when one of the people I mentioned earlier was proved to be real, naturally the whole world became real. Otherwise we would be afraid of falling through the floor, and going to China. People don't like that; it's an eight thousand mile jump.

In *Mahagonny* four different images are being projected at once, more or less as a commentary on Duchamp's Large Glass. In the showing of *Mahagonny* people's passions are played upon. I have made a close examination of the tables in the Minnesota Multiphasic Personality Inventory, where the questions are classified according to, let us say, verbal root, or nominal roots . . . although this time . . . Oh never mind. Gladys Reichart pointed out long ago that in languages as divergent as Navaho and Indo-European (of course, Edward Sapir cut her throat for that) the word "Sun", referring to the thing in the sky, has a different connotation (in one case it being connected with redness and blood, *a la* the Pampas of Argentina) . . . I think you are not very far from a fool, Prof. Sitney. There is just this microphone between us. That is connected with a joke regarding going to Little Rock: "Well, I don't know how to get there, but there's a hell of a big one down in the field of Aunt Martha's."

PAS: Will there be words projected on the screen in your film?

Yes. There are a number of words. They were made by a number of people. Although basically the ones I'm using were done by Mason Hoffenberg. Word frequency counts have been made of things like Mayan, the Enochian words in *The Calls of the Thirty Aethers* that Dr. Dee wrote down in the window seat while Sir Edward Kelley looked into the Olmec mirror. There are a number of other cases where words that were automatically compounded by automatic machinery are being projected. Of course, anything that happens to have twenty-two forms in it is being projected on other screens. There are basically five movie projectors and about twelve slide projectors. That is why we are moving to Switzerland; it has more electricity than anywhere else.

The major screen is a boxing ring from the original set of *Mahagonny,* that is from "The Little Mahagonny" that was given along with some things by Schoenberg, Hindemith, etc., I believe, at Baden-Baden, perhaps in 1923. The twenty-two statements by the announcer will, of course, be translated into some language or other. Then the twenty-one forms of Death that are in the *Codex Lauds,* which along with the *Liverpool Codex* was brought back from Poland by Dr. Dee and Sir Edward Kelley (it contains things like a man shot in the eye), and then, of course, the Tarot cards will be included. I have recently been fortunate enough to see Robert Wang's paintings that have taken him so many years to make for Israel Regardie of the cards for the Hermetic Order of the Golden Dawn. They are being made public for the first time on one of the screens.

The original set of *Mahagonny* had a boxing ring with a pool table in the middle of it and some chairs. In our case it was more expedient to put the boxing ring against the wall, and put the four pool tables under the boxing ring so that they could all be lit independently. The boxing ring itself should be lit from behind. As much as possible the general Expressionist mode of constructing features has been followed. But due to the fact that everyone in my listening audience merely considers Expressionism to be second-rate drawing, we had had to add a *little* of Claes Oldenburg, Jim Rosenquist, and so forth.

PAS: Some years ago, you projected for me excerpts from *Mahagonny* on a single projector, masked by a series of gels. The imagery seemed to alternate between pictures of people, animation, outdoor scenes, and interiors. What relation would that version have to your present plans?

Of course, over the past decade a large number of projections of *Mahagonny* have been made under various circumstances. That particular one was experimenting with shape in relation to response. The best response to a film, as Prof. Sitney knows, is if the audience goes to sleep; it's *really* been successful; they have entered into the film fully. That particular projection apparatus still exists, with the gels and things. However, it is being done differently at this point. With the four screens being used, naturally, instead of having to block off the lower left hand corner when the words "Look Out" are printed in Urdu or something, we merely black one screen out. However a certain amount of masking is being used to get horizontal or diagonal groups of things.

Any one reel is made up of twenty-four units in palindrome form: P.A.S.A.N.A.S.A.P. and so on. Every other scene is animation [A]. Every first scene on a reel is people [P], then animation, and then something like a generalized image [S] as opposed to a portrait, which is really what P stands for, and then an animation, and then a nature scene of some sort [N], such as photographing the Morgan Bank to get the pockmarks made when the milkwagon blew up loaded with dynamite. (They still get nervous despite the fact that there are no anarchists around. They get nervous on Wall Street. They began closing bronze doors at the mere sight of a camera.) There are twenty-four shots in each of twelve reels, adding up to two gross or two hundred and eighty shots.

I hope your listeners realize at this point why I wanted to edit this tape. I was dragged out of bed. Some idiot that I hope The Mighty Sparrow writes a song about had taken my reds and wouldn't give them back until six o'clock. I took so much speed at noon that I just hope the program is over soon.

The main object of those mask shots was to get light behind individual images that you looked at. Long, long ago in Nineteen Fifty—something I gave an elaborate light show. It was 1956 or something, I don't know when, in Steinway Hall. I originally projected slides around what some idiot, not realizing that the number 12 is somehow equivalent to heaven and earth, called *Heaven and Earth Magic;* they're always unable to accept numbers. That's only natural because once you begin to study numerology every number has a meaning; so it breaks down entirely, except for the number 18, for which I can't figure anything except film #118, which is a postcard size film, which disappeared about 1830. Oh where was I? Yes, it will be the first time the Matterhorn has had an active eruption for years.

PAS: Are you saying that your film will make the Matterhorn erupt?

Now *you're* doing it. So that the experiments that were done earlier with colored light in relation to motion are really very close to some very interesting drawings I've seen recently that were made by Schiller and Goethe examining a color wheel and getting differential impressions. It's funny how that once the behaviorists —and Gardner Murphy if you're listening to your radio forgive me, but you were *nasty* to me when I was a conscientious objector, and I won't forgive you—got off that, it has now come back to, like, red *does* mean a more violent activity than green . . . You know, it is different to get "red in the face" than it is to have the "blues".

Mahagonny has required all of my energy, many hundred thousand dollars; at this point it is running about two thousand a month just to keep going, with no food or clothing allowed out of these two thousand dollars I'd like to add, and the rent is always behind. It is funny what it gets spent on.

A peculiar little book on Goethe has recently come out, listing all the translations of *Faust*. His main things revolve around the problem: Is it I that is looking at the thing? or is it the thing which is projecting itself to me? This, of course, is again why Hapatia was scraped to death as she was riding her chariot on her way to her father's, Plotinus', school. The point is that Plato's notion that the eye projected a beam that went, in this case, through the electric light beam and to a variety of other places, while we believe that it is something else that lights the room; this is again the problem that Goethe had. (The only reason I mention *Faust* is that the United Nations publishes an odd little book at this point, for something like $23.00, that lists, I think, eighteen hundred versions of *Faust*, translated from e.g. Armenian into Welsh.) Goethe goes over that same business in his argument with Newton, or later with his business about the plant: Is it I that is looking at the colors? or are the colors shining on me? Is it I that differentiates the signature of one plant from another? or is it the plant that determines the signature? The relationship between the *is*, *was*, and *will be* comes in here; the *is* being so infinitely small, and both the *was* and *will* being constructed out of projections of the other one, the future being a construction of the past, and the past being an attempt to correlate what is sometimes perceived as the *now* with a way of operating in the future. I don't know! What P. Adams wants me to do is to ask for money. Well, I won't. So I don't have much to say about *Mahagonny* except that I'm making it in my autumn years. I've been cooked enough; the leaves are falling off!

Four screens are to be used and rhythmic patterns will occur between the length of the scenes. The general form of twenty-four interlocked shots is the same, backwards and forwards. Individuals in the audience will have their attention directed to one particular part of the counterpoint at each minute. Peter Kubelka wanted to open it in Vienna: "You can use my castle and my Steenbeck!" But I was afraid they'd understand German there. The whole point of *Mahagonny* is to translate not the story which is trivial (it is handled much better in *Happy End*) but to translate Brecht's indecision. For you must understand that although a lot of people think that Brecht was a Communist, it wasn't exactly that way. He was caught in the middle where he either had to jump along with the Nazis or he had to jump along with the Communists. There wasn't any dream king like Ludwig II drowning himself. One of the best examples of cooking something is the column that runs up the main stairwell in the ridiculous castle that Lufthansa Airways now makes just a tiny airshot. God, what a fantastic piece of marble carved like a papyrus or something tied together, going up to blue things among stars and I don't know . . . All these questions can be looked up in a book called *Theatrum Vitae Humanae* by J. J. Boissard (Metz, 1596). The original decision was to translate an opera into an occult experience. And I hope Prof. Sitney now understands the relation of occlusion to sleep. Or why one should sleep through movies. In this case, *you can't do it* if you come to *Mahagonny*! What was that play Ludwig did in which he flooded the theatre? Of course, D'Annunzio did it in one of his plays; but that was mere chance. There was a war scene, and bombs were being set off; the theatre filled with smoke; the audience rioted, but fortunately at that moment, he writes in his diary, a cannon blew a hole in the wall and they escaped from the stage. It is just the same old stunt; it is just like the Globe Theater, only we're electrifying it this time.

I have to talk to Andy Berler of CAPS, because I was supposed to finish *Mahagonny* by April Fools Day. The public service contract has not been fulfilled. Well, the point is, Mary and Andy if you hear this, the greatest public service that I could have pulled at the time was to disappear, and I did it! After twelve years I moved out of the Chelsea Hotel to a secret location on the Lower East Side or some side. My public service is to leave people alone and have them leave me alone, and to work on the most elaborate mathematical tables regarding *Mahagonny*. I would like to say, Andy, that somebody gave me considerably more money than the CAPS grant to show *Mahagonny* free. It is going to be in a black room with a boxing ring, and millions of volts of electricity brought in, and there won't even be any chairs! Nobody's going to want to look at a thing that long: it is two hours and twenty minutes without an intermission. I would like to say that anyone I know, or have ever seen, or am likely to meet, is going to be excluded. They are *not*, after the way they treated me, are treating me, or they're going to treat me, going to be allowed to see anything that will give them happiness. No! I'm saving it for things like playboy, no-good, tin kings of Bolivia, that have been having special tablecloths woven for thirty years. They are the ones that can see it. If Barbara Hutton is alive, she can see it, and that's it!

CAREL ROWE:

Illuminating Lucifer

The title, L-U-C-I-F-E-R R-I-S-I-N-G, rises in vibrating fiery letters from the waves of the ocean. Throughout *Lucifer* neon calligraphy and animated symbols flash, sometimes simultaneously matted into the landscapes of ancient Egypt. Often these electrified talismans break into the material like signals from lost civilizations: picture-writing erupting through layers of history. *Lucifer*'s universe is populated with signaling gods and alchemical symbols. The work, at this stage, is largely concerned with communication between Isis (Myriam Gibril) and Osiris (Donald Cammell), through the forces of nature; this communion of natural elements provokes meteorological reactions in preparation for Lucifer's arrival: lightning issues forth from the staffs and emblems of these radiant deities; nature replies with rosy dawns, whirlpools, and emissions of molten rock. The sun goes into eclipse. Intercut with an endless torchlight procession, Lilith (Marianne Faithfull) climbs the prehistoric stairway to a Celtic shrine where, as goddess of the moon, she supplicates the sun. The sun rises directly in the center of the solstice altar; its rays part to reveal a scarlet demon within the round hole of the rock: the blazing astrological symbol of Mercury (god of communication and ruler of magicians) appears. A magus (Kenneth Anger) stalks around his incandescent magic circle in invocation to the Bringer of Light (cf. Murnau's *Faust*.) Outside the smoking circle a Balinese fire demon (symbol of sacrifice) materializes, the magus bows before the idol, a globe of phosphorescent lightning shudders across the screen and Lucifer, resplendent in satin L-U-C-I-F-E-R jockey jacket, arises from within the circle. In response, nature throws a celebration of volcanic eruptions and avalanches of snow, and, ultimately, an electrical storm over Stonehenge. Isis and Osiris, the happy parents (or Lucifer-as-Horus) stride through the colonnade at Karnak to greet their offspring and a feldspar-colored saucer sails at us from behind the stone head of Ramses II.

After six years of self-imposed exile in London, Kenneth Anger is touring the US with a retrospective of his work and the première of the first third of his first feature, *Lucifer Rising*. This work-in-progress is a remake and continuation of the sabotaged "Love Vision" of *Lucifer* begun seven years ago in San Francisco. The original was to have been about "today's new tribes of teenagers, turned-on children—teeny-boppers and adolescent hippies" and featured a set of living Tarot tableaux. Today's version of *Lucifer* is as much a departure from its predecessor as it is from the major body of Anger's work. But his previous works can still be understood as pointing the way to this grander, more expansive vision which is less demonic, more divine.

Georges Sadoul speaks of Maya Deren and Kenneth Anger as the "two most important names in the development of the New American Cinema." Both were forerunners of a generation of visionary film-makers (Brakhage, Harrington, Markopoulos) who began their work in the mid-forties. Recent critical work attempting to draw parallels between the films of Deren and Anger through their mutual preoccupation with mystical ritual is misleading. Deren's interest in the occult as a system for depicting an interior state moved away from surrealist psychodrama and toward a fascination with combining the elements of a given ritual to structure the narrative material. Influenced by classical aesthetics, she experimented with trans-temporal continuities and discontinuities found in the cinematic structure. With Deren the narrative form orders the subconscious into a design; ritual is used to impose an ideal order on the arbitrary order of art and the chaotic order of the world. The interior event is presented as a matrix out of which a pattern is made, and this pattern of ritual elements is combined to form the overall structure. Historically, it is useful to view Deren as a forerunner of the works of Alain Resnais or the experimental structuralists of today, such as Frampton, Wieland, or Snow, rather than to see her work as simply a part of the "trance film" trend in the early American underground.

Anger's use of ritual is quite different, his narrative model is constructed through a comparative analysis of myths, religions, and rituals and their associations external to their respective systems. His two works which give greatest evidence of this are *Inauguration of the Pleasure Dome* (1954-1966) and, as examined later in this survey, *Scorpio Rising* (1964).

Deren was concerned with occultism as a classicist, interested in recombing its ritual orders within a system. Anger, a romanticist, sees occultism as a source of hermetic knowledge. For Anger, "Making a movie is casting a spell." He claims "Magick" as his lifework and "the cinematograph" for his "Magick weapon." He dubs the collection of his works "The Magick Lantern Cycle," has adopted Aleister Crowley as his guru, sees his films to be "a search for light and enlightenment" and sees Lucifer not as the devil but as "Venus —the Morning Star." To date, all of his films have been evocations

or invocations, attempting to conjure primal forces which, once
visually released, are designed to have the effect of "casting a
spell" on the audience. The Magick *in* the film is related to the
Magickal effect of the film *on* the audience.

As a prestidigitator Anger somewhat parallels Méliès: a magician making transformations as well as reconstructions of reality.
As a symbolist operating within the idealist tradition he has a turn-
of-the-century fascination with ideal artificiality: in *Lucifer* he
causes certain landscapes to reveal themselves at their most magical
by both capturing the moment and capitalizing upon it, showing a
rare moment of nature, albeit enhanced through technical effects
(such as the hand-tinting and the spellbinding "star machine" which
was built at the Chicago Art Institute to play red and green pentagrams over the screen and audience at his most recent presentations
of *Lucifer*). Not a surrealist who puts blind faith in his own dream
images and trusts his dreams to convey an "uncommon unconscious," Anger works predominantly in archetypal symbol. As the
magus, he is the juggler of these symbols, just as in the Tarot,
where the Magician is represented by the Juggler and is given the
attribution of Mercury, the messenger.

As a visionary Anger creates his own frame of reference which
is an extension of the vision and teachings of Aleister Crowley.
Crowley has been called "the Oscar Wilde of Magic" and called
himself "The Beast 666." An English magus born in 1875, he was a
contemporary and enemy of both Freud and Yeats (he quarreled
with the latter over leadership in the Hermetic Order of the Golden
Dawn). Although he claimed, in critiquing Freud, "I cannot do
evil that good may come. I abhor Jesuitry. I would rather lose than
win by strategem," [1] he is reputed to have jumped official rank in
The Order, illegitimately claiming the title of Ipsissimus. "There
was yet another order within the Great White Brotherhood, the top
order; it bore the name of the Silver Star . . . (Astrum Argen-
tinium). This contained the three exalted grades—Master of the
Temple, Magus, and Ipsissimus—they lay on the other side of the
Abyss."[2]

Entering unto this ultimate enlightenment as Master of the Temple and exiting as self-ordained god, Crowley and his discovery of
supreme apotheosis of the self produced his "do as thou wilt" philosophy. In his *Book of the Law* (the means by which he bridged
the Abyss to Masterhood) he proclaimed: "Bind Nothing. Let there
be no difference made between any one thing and another . . .
The word of Sin is Restriction . . . there is no law beyond 'Do What
Thou Wilt'."

Crowley's self-deification is reflected in the "joyful humanism"
of the Age of Horus or the Aquarian Age. The Cosmology of his
Book of the Law introduces the Third Aeon: after Isis's aeon of ma-
triarchy and Osiris's aeon of patriarchy follows the aeon of Horus,
the Child or true self independent of priests or gods. In his 777—

Book of Correspondences, Crowley cross-indexes Greek, Egyptian, and Hindu mythologies. Venus is found in Isis and corresponding goddesses. Lucifer is the Roman name for the planet Venus which was worshipped as both Aurora (the morning star) and Vesper (the evening star). Until these myths were suppressed by the Catholic Church the Gnostics worshipped Aurora/Lucifer as the Herald of the Dawn, the light preceding the sun. The Crowleyan/ Anger doctrine exchanges Lucifer with Horus as well: "It all began with a child playing with a chemistry set that exploded. An inno- cent, pure child prodigy, creating for the joy of it, just as Lucifer created his own light shows in heaven . . . Eventually he was ex- pelled for playing the stereo too loud."[3]

Like Cervantes's *mas bello que Díos,* Lucifer's sin lies in out- doing God. He is seen not as a leader but as the totally independent, original rebel; the Luciferian spirit manifests itself in the spirit of the artist, not as a Hell's Angel. "He is also Puck [the name of Anger's production company], the spirit of mischief, mortals are the toys in his playpen, the world belongs to Lucifer."[4]

But Crowley's major contribution to Anger's vision was his inven- tion of "magick," the performance of ritual which seeks to invoke the Holy Guardian Angel (the aspirant's higher self), an idea adapted from the medieval magus Abra-Melin.[5] The method of in- vocation relies on talismanic magic: the vitalization of talismans. Originally these were drawn vellum patterns, sort of a shadow- graph print of the demon one sought to "capture." Anger equates this with the photograph's ability to steal the soul of the subject. Medieval talismanic signatures were considered to be autographs by demons and Anger refers to them as "printed circuits" between physical and spiritual (or alternative) reality. He sees glyphs, hiero- glyphs, sigils, pictographs, billboards, and especially tattoos as "magical marks on the wall." In *Lucifer* he uses the Abra-Melin "Keys" or trademarks of the basic elements as overlaid inscriptions which interact with the visual energies of earth, air, fire, and water so that the symbols "call forth" variations in their visual counter- parts. Magickal insignias are an integral system at work in all of Anger's films. They are duly consecrated by optical isolation through special effects: the triangular "trademark" matted into a shot of Isis, the mirrored superimposition of magickal tattoos on Anger's arms in *Invocation of my Demon Brother* (1969), a door within Crowley's face which opens onto a superimposed zodiac in *The Inauguration of the Pleasure Dome,* the hand-tinted chartreuse fan ("the magickal weapon") in the otherwise blue-toned *Eaux d'Artifice* (1953), and, most recently, the addition of hand-tinting in *Lucifer* which unites the flying falcon-of-Horus and the live Kephra scarab with their respective carved hieroglyphs.

To conjure a successful transformation Anger-as-Magus-Artist mixes his palette according to Crowley's color system from the *Golden Dawn* (a Rosicrucian order), a codified alchemical scale

wherein planets are related to colors, sacred alphabets, drugs, per-
fumes, jewels, plants, magical weapons, the elements, the Tarot,
etc., etc. In the Royal Color Tables of 777—*The Book of Correspondences* the "Princess Scale" denotes the "pure, pastel colors of
idealism." This is the scale which Anger applies to his brief-but-
beautiful *Kustom Kar Kommandos* (1965). In *KKK* he makes his
invocation through his use of color, attempting the transposition of
the sign of Cancer (seashell blue and pink) onto the Machine. The
pastels of reflected flesh and the hard gleam of the dream buggy
(every inch a Tom Wolfe "tangerine-flake baby," from the knight
on the hood to the tires) are edited together to resemble the languid
movements of a boa constrictor. Dedicated to the Charioteer of the
Tarot, the "dream lover" owner of the car, is Anger's "silver knight
in shining armor." Like the car, he is a machine built for transmit-
ting energy; the blond boy is seated in a mirrored chamber with
velvet seats designed to resemble a vulva or giant twin lips, forming a red plush vertical smile. Anger feels that *KKK* closely resembles Dali's painting "Mae West's Living Room" in the portrayal of
a material universe wherein power is a poetic extension of personality, "an accessible means of wish-fulfillment." The lyrics "I want
a dream lover so I don't have to dream alone . . ." enrich the romanticism within the phallocentric vision of narcissistic-identifica-
tion-as-virility. A dream lover is a double, a "demon brother" and
mirror-reflection; *KKK* is an invocation of the ideal, not human elements, and is dedicated to an idealization of reality.

Romantic idealization, poetic irony, lush exoticism and the evolution of anti-classicist montage wherein the whole is subordinate to
the parts all reflect Anger's affinity with *fin de siècle* French literature (in 1951 he attempted to film Lautréamont's *Les Chants de
Maldoror*). His most profuse use of decadent symbolist imagery
occurs in *The Inauguration of the Pleasure Dome*. But the development of a montage-syntax which closely resembles the elaborate
syntactical constructions of Huysmans and the ambiguities of Du-
cassian mixed metaphor are nowhere more evident than in *Scorpio
Rising*.

Scorpio Rising is an extension of self-gratification into self-
immolation. The Machine (now a motorcycle) is totemized into a
tool for power; the "charioteer" is Death (the ultimate "dream
lover" by romantic standards). Violence replaces the poetic extension of personality and violent eroticism is combined with the tragic
death of the highway hero ("the last cowboys"): "*Scorpio Rising*
is a machine and Kenneth Anger keeps his spark plug burning on
AC (Aleister Crowley) current . . . Guess which one I was in love
with ten years ago? . . . Was it the chromium or was it the guy?"[6]

Sado-masochism, death and sensuality, sex and angst—*Scorpio*
is America's buried collective adolescence manifested in the isolated pop-art visions of decayed dreams. It reflects the last gasp of
the dying Age of Pisces (Christianity) as a motorcycle race roaring

toward oblivion. The big butch bikers encase themselves in leather; slung with chains they move indolently, like huge cats. Scorpio and his brothers/lovers ("Taurus" and "Leo"—both ruled by Venus) worship their machines. But people as well as objects denote fetishism, are transformed through mass adulation into becoming idols. James Dean is shown as the Aquarian Rebel Son, Brando, Christ, Hitler, all are objects of worship, "humans idolized by idiots . . . The different degree of impact each had was dependent on the degree of advertising between pop stars and Christ."[7] A grade-C Christ film, *The Road to Jerusalem*, produced by Family Films, was delivered to Anger's doorstep by mistake while he was in the process of editing *Scorpio Rising;* he accepted it as "a gift from the gods," toned it blue and intercut it (as the second major montage element within the film) with the bikers' Hallowe'en party. Christ is introduced walking with his disciples on Palm Sunday, two of the "theme songs" ("I Will Follow Him" and "He's a Rebel") link the Christ scenes to Brando and Dean; "Torture" (Gene MacDaniels) and "Wipeout" (The Surfaries) link Him to the biker's initiation and Hitler. The purpose of "following Him" is to race after the trophy, dying to be first, just as the sperm is racing toward oblivion in its desperate need to unite with the egg. The "egg" may well be the new aeon and the longed-for oblivion: the destruction necessitated by change. The new aeon is reached by moving from *Scorpio*'s "night" toward *Lucifer*'s "dawn." The skull-and-crossbones fluttering in superimposition over the cycle rally signifies the death of sensuality in much the same way as the death's head on the Masonic or Rosicrucian flags represents the philosophical death of man's sensuous personality—a transition considered essential in the process of liberating man's spiritual nature. The final shot of the film is the dead Scorpio's outstretched arm, lit by the red strobe of a patrol car, on it the tattoo "Blessed, Blessed Oblivion."

Anger's myths address mass-erotic-consciousness through a barrage of notorious symbols. These often war with one another in Reichian power-trips of rape, will-power, fascism, and revolution. "I find ridiculous the idea of anyone being the leader," Anger has said. Pentagrams war with swastikas in *Invocation of my Demon Brother*. Brando tortures Christ in *Scorpio,* Shiva asserts absolute power over his guests in *Pleasure Dome*. Historical heroes are reduced to pop-idols and history is demythified by comic book codes. "When earths collide, gods die."

Considering that Anger takes an anti-nostalgia stance and deplores the fact that "yesterday's heroes are still with us" (Brando), it is ironic that at the time *Scorpio* was released it enjoyed popularity as a dirty Hallowe'en party or as a celebration of the contemporary decadence it displayed. But today the pop-*Liebestod* lyrics of the sixties ("He's a rebel and he'll never be free . . . ," or "I still can see blue velvet through my tears") have strong nostalgic

resonances and, revived in the vacuous seventies, have audiences
stomping and clapping to the very songs which originally served as
a critique against idolatry and romanticism "turned in on itself and
beginning to rot." The value of Anger's strategic use of pop songs
transcends their being "structural units within a collage film"; [8]
they often act as a complicated running commentary in lyric form,
performing a narrative as well as structural function. In *Rabbit's
Moon, Puce Moment,* and *Kustom Kar Kommandos* the result is
that the naive poetry of the song replaces the temporality of spoken
dialogue in a timeless, mythic way. In *Rabbit's Moon* "There's a
Moon Out Tonight" and "I Only Have Eyes for You" underscore the
futility of "reaching for the moon"—a message visually expressed
in the repetition of shots of a *commedia*-style Pierrot supplicating a
Méliès-style moon which remains just out of reach. *Puce Moment*
takes on a spicier meaning when "I'm a Hermit" and "Leaving My
Old Life Behind" on the track are combined with the visuals of
shimmering antique dresses and a languishing Hollywood star. The
obvious suggestion here is a renunciation of drag-dressing, an escape from the fetishization of costume and a climb "out of the
closet." Anger's most complex and intriguing use of music occurs in
Eaux d'Artifice, where light, color, movement, and textures are
combined in baroque counterpoint with Vivaldi. With *Invocation*
and *Lucifer* he has begun to move toward an exclusive use of original musical scores.

Transubstantiation is one of Anger's favorite themes. Frequently
this takes the form of a reverse Eucharist where essence is con-
verted into substance, and this process can be discovered in *Fireworks* (1947—his first major film), *Puce Moment, Rabbit's Moon,
Scorpio,* and now *Lucifer.* These films summon personifications of
forces and spirits whose dynamic powers appear to "break through"
and turn against the character and/or structure. *Scorpio's* icono-
clasm is effected by the critique which the film conducts on itself,
demythifying the very myths it propounds by interchanging them
with one another and integrating them into a metamyth. Christ/
Satan (religion), Brando/Dean (popular culture), and Hitler (political history) are reduced to sets of systems which destroy one another through internarrative montage-of-attraction. Thus, the
film itself is the metamyth of the films which constitute it. Different
dogmas are equalized (and subsumed by) their structural and
ideological parallels. *Scorpio's* auto-destruction stems from the
center, "core" invocation and triumph of Satan over Christ. Machine
over Man, and Death over Life.

A somewhat less nihilistic subsumation of substance by essence
is the conventional Eucharist ritual performed in *Inauguration of
The Pleasure Dome* and *Eaux d'Artifice.* In the former, Lord Shiva
transforms his guests into spirits of pure energy which he absorbs
and recycles into a frenzied, operatic orgy. The pyrotechnics of
this celebration build to such visual intensity that *Pleasure Dome*

"destroys" itself by growing too large for the very confines of the screen. In the original (pre-Sacred Mushroom Edition—1958) the screen grows Gance-like "wings," and, for the final 20 minutes, each panel of the tryptich is loaded with up to six simultaneous surfaces of superimposition (eighteen separate planes). The visual material seeks to transform itself into pure energy. In *Eaux d'Artifice* ". . . The Lady enters the 'nite-time labyrinth' of cascades, ballustrades, grottoes and fountains and tries to lure out the monsters with her fan; she's trying to invoke the water gods . . . She fails, being weak and frivolous, and melts into the water (surrenders her identity) so that she can play on." [9] *Eaux* turns its hermaphrodite hero(ine) into a waterfall. Nature wins over artifice. Human confusion is subsumed by the larger order of things.

Lucifer Rising attempts to transcend the passive-active dialectics of power and the sexual preoccupations of adolescence, "the blue of eternal longing." Its theme (so far) is that of man's reunion with his lost gods: the dawning of a new morality. The cult of arrested adolescence is replaced by the fulfillment of its longing: reaffirmation of identity through spiritual communion between man, gods and nature. Fantasy and reality are no longer distinguished but are parts of a larger, more complete universe. Black Magick goes White, the hero is the "bringer of light," Lucifer, portrayed as a demon of great beauty. This "fire-light trip"[10] begins with the first frames of *Fireworks* (1947) (an invocation to Thor) when a fire-brand is extinguished in water. At the film's outrageous finale a sailor's penis is lit and explodes as a roman candle; this is followed by a denouement where a wax candle atop a Christmas tree dips into a fireplace, igniting the scattered stills from the film's opening dream sequence. *Invocation* (resuscitated from the leftover out-takes of the original *Lucifer*, "A fragment made in fury . . . the last blast of Haight consciousness" [11]) opens with an albino demon brother kissing a glass wand; later Mick Jagger's black cat goes up in flames and the film culminates with Bobby Beausoleil short-circuiting into Lucifer. Anger calls *Invocation* "a burn."

There is more light and less fire in *Lucifer Rising* (what the neo-Platonists would refer to as the "spiritual lux"). Assertion-of-will has matured into communication between anthropomorphic gods; glamorous Egyptian Deities within a universe which is established by an uncreated precondition for order—pagan spirits at play in a universe where God does not yet exist. These man-gods exist organically, as part of nature, they grow out of the shadow of cliffs and temples like living sculptures. We first see Isis as long legs disembodied by stone-shadows. Isis and Osiris, glistening with health and confidence, authentically costumed, perform their nearly static ritual from the cliffs overlooking a space-like sea (Crowley's "vast abyss between man and god"). Where it was the nature of the stone water gods to overwhelm man in *Eaux*, the "new" gods in Lucifer embody the "best" in man: pure, free forces, calling on

Lucifer Rising

nature to aid mankind, summoning the elements in preparation for
the Second Coming.

Lucifer is also a radical departure in visual form from Anger's
previous works. No longer does the power of any given image depend on the ritualistic repetition and recombination which essentially shapes the overall form of films like *Scorpio* or *Invocation*.
Invocation's structure is jumbled and dissonant, "an attack on the
sensorium" (Anger); the entire piece is edited for abrasiveness,
any residual visual flow is destroyed by the spasms of electronic
shockwaves from Jagger's sound track. *Scorpio*'s structure works
from the inside out: from image to montage to montage-of-attrac-
tions to the whole as one entire montage system. The whole is
purely a system of inter-relationships and no attempt is made to impose an external order on this network. Image-layers mount in
density, implications, and velocity toward the climactic "rebel
rouser" sequence when Scorpio, performing a black sabbath, transforms himself into his own demon brother and casts his death hex
on the cycle rally which, through the montage, seems a swirling
continuation of his ceremony of destruction.[12] This use of montage-
as-forcefield reappears in *Lucifer*'s invocation sequence; the aggressive vitality of tracking camera racing with the sorcerer's movements as he widdershins around a magic circle. These shots are
intercut with an exterior long-shot of baby gorilla and tiger cub
chasing about the base of a tree, the movements of nature coinciding
with the "unnatural" counter-sun-wise dance of the magus film-

maker. But in this case the sequence is imbedded in a less frenetic organization which makes up the majority of the film.

In *Lucifer,* the camera at last liberates its subject matter from its usual medium-close-up iconography through a long-shot/long-take *mise en scène.* A series of landscapes, seascapes, skyscapes gain mythical proportions through long-take montage; the longshots establish the vastness of this universe. Lingering takes of the broken pharaoh faces of the Colossus of Memnon have a quality of temporal displacement; they exist outside time and distance as defined by motion by either camera or subject. The impassive statues assume an ancient decadence, exhausted idols compared to the flesh of the living gods. This static vastness which the long-take/long-shot montage effects operates around a vortex or "core" of the film: the invocation sequence which gradually and erratically builds to a spinning forcefield of compressed energy. This disturbs and changes the natural universe of the film's structure: the exteriors are broken into by collage-inserts, then the external world reasserts itself with long, vertically dynamic takes and vertical wipes; nature rights herself and Lucifer is born.

The piece, as it stands, can either be seen as a complete work in itself or as a chapter with an appropriate ending to a forties science fiction serial. At this time Anger's originals for the remainder of *Lucifer* are tied up with his producer. A soundtrack is being prepared by Jimmy Page of the Led Zeppelin; at recent showings Anger plays a Pink Floyd symphony: *Atom Heart Mother* which syncs perfectly with the visual rhythms. The fragment presents a whole vision in itself. With *Lucifer,* Anger breaks through his previous nihilism to a "happy ending" (the Crowleyan assertion of love and joy over sorrow and sin), dealing with larger, exterior concerns rather than dramas of occult exoticism and decadent ideology. The sun breaks through the clouds.

NOTES

1. *The Confessions of Aleister Crowley: An Autohagiography,* edited by John Symonds and Kenneth Grant. (New York: Bantam Books, 1971.)
2. *Ibid.*
3. Kenneth Anger at a presentation of his films, San Francisco Art Institute, April, 1974.
4. *Ibid.*
5. *The Book of the Sacred Magic of Abra-Melin, The Mage*—As Delivered by Abraham the Jew Unto His Son Lamech—a grimoire of the fifteenth century, translated by S. L. MacGregor-Mathews (former Secret Chief of the Golden Dawn and Head of the Second Order in the Great White Brotherhood, Rosicrucians), edited by L. W. de Laurence. (Chicago: The de Laurence Co., Inc.)
6. Anger at presentation of his films, Wheeler Auditorium, Berkeley, April 10, 1974.
7. *Ibid.*
8. *Visionary Film,* P. Adams Sitney (New York: Oxford Press, 1974.)
9. *A Kenneth Anger Kompendium,* Tony Rayns, *Cinema* Magazine #4.
10. *Ibid.*
11. Interview with the author, April 25, 1974.
12. Raynes, *Ibid.*

(*Film Quarterly,* Summer, 1974)

STAN BRAKHAGE:

From *Metaphors on Vision*

Imagine an eye unruled by man-made laws of perspective, an eye unprejudiced by compositional logic, an eye which does not respond to the name of everything but which must know each object encountered in life through an adventure of perception. How many colors are there in a field of grass to the crawling baby unaware of "Green?" How many rainbows can light create for the untutored eye? How aware of variations in heat waves can that eye be? Imagine a world alive with incomprehensible objects and shimmering with an endless variety of movement and innumerable gradations of color. Imagine a world before the "beginning was the word."

To see is to retain—to behold. Elimination of all fear is in sight—which must be aimed for. Once vision may have been given—that which seems inherent in the infant's eye, an eye which reflects the loss of innocence more eloquently than any other human feature, an eye which soon learns to classify sights, an eye which mirrors the movement of the individual toward death by its increasing inability to see.

But one can never go back, not even in imagination. After the loss of innocence, only the ultimate of knowledge can balance the wobbling pivot. Yet I suggest that there is a pursuit of knowledge foreign to language and founded upon visual communication, demanding a development of the optical mind, and dependent upon perception in the original and deepest sense of the word.

Suppose the Vision of the saint and the artist to be an increased ability to see—vision. Allow so-called hallucination to enter the realm of perception, allowing that mankind always finds derogatory terminology for that which doesn't appear to be readily usable, accept dream visions, day-dreams or night-dreams, as you would so-called real scenes, even allowing that the abstractions which move so dynamically when closed eyelids are pressed are actually perceived. Become aware of the fact that you are not only influenced by the visual phenomenon which you are focused upon and attempt to sound the depths of all visual influence. There is no need for the mind's eye to be deadened after infancy, yet in these times the development of visual understanding is almost universally forsaken.

This is an age which has no symbol for death other than the skull and bones of one stage of decomposition . . . and it is an age which lives in fear of total annihilation. It is a time haunted by sexual sterility yet almost universally incapable of perceiving the phallic nature of every destructive manifestation of itself. It is an age which artificially seeks to project itself materialistically into abstract space and to fulfill itself mechanically because it has blinded itself to almost all external reality within eyesight and to the organic awareness of even the physical movement properties of its own perceptibility. The earliest cave paintings discovered demonstrate that primitive man had a greater understanding than we do that the object of fear must be objectified. The entire history of erotic magic is one of possession of fear thru the beholding of it. The ultimate searching visualization has been directed toward God out of the deepest possible human understanding that there can be no ultimate love where there is fear. Yet in this contemporary time how many of us even struggle to deeply perceive our own children?

The artist has carried the tradition of vision and visualization down through the ages. In the present time a very few have continued the process of visual perception in its deepest sense and transformed their inspirations into cinematic experiences. They create a new language made possible by the moving picture image. They create where fear before them has created the greatest necessity. They are essentially preoccupied by and deal imagistically with—birth, sex, death, and the search for God.

CAMERA EYE

Oh transparent hallucination, superimposition of image on image, mirage of movement, heroine of a thousand and one nights (Scheherazade must surely be the muse of this art), you obstruct the light, muddie the pure white beaded screen (it perspires) with your shuffling patterns. Only the spectators (the unbelievers who attend the carpeted temples where coffee and paintings are served) think your spirit is in the illuminated occasion (mistaking your sweaty, flaring, rectangular body for more than it is). The devout, who break popcorn together in your humblest double-feature services, know that you are still being born, search for your spirit in their dreams, and dare only dream when in contact with your electrical reflection. Unknowingly, as innocent, they await the priests of this new religion, those who can stir cinematic entrails divinely. They await the prophets who can cast (with the precision of Confucian sticks) the characters of this new order across filmic mud. Being innocent, they do not consciously know that this church too is corrupt;

but they react with counter hallucinations, believing in the stars, and cast themselves among these Los Angelic orders. Of themselves, they will never recognize what they are awaiting. Their footsteps, the dumb drum which destroys cinema. They are having the dream piped into their homes, the destruction of the romance thru marriage, etc.

So the money vendors have been at it again. To the catacombs then, or rather plant this seed deeper in the undergrounds beyond false nourishing of sewage waters. Let it draw nourishment from hidden uprising springs channeled by gods. Let there be no cavernous congregation but only the network of individual channels, that narrowed vision which splits beams beyond rainbow and into the unknown dimensions. (To those who think this is waxing poetic, squint, give the visual objects at hand their freedom, and allow the distant to come to you; and when mountains are moving, you will find no fat in this prose). Forget ideology, for film unborn as it is has no language and speaks like an aborigine—monotonous rhetoric. Abandon aesthetics—the moving picture image without religious foundations, let alone the cathedral, the art form, starts its search for God with only the danger of accepting an architectural inheritance from the categorized "seven," other arts its sins, and closing its circle, stylistic circle, therefore zero. Negate technique, for film, like America, has not been discovered yet, and mechanization, in the deepest possible sense of the word, traps both beyond measuring even chances—chances are these twined searches may someday orbit about the same central negation. Let film be. It is something . . . becoming. (The above being for creator and spectator alike in searching, an ideal of anarchic religion where all are priests both giving and receiving, or rather witch doctors, or better witches, or . . . O, for the unnamable).

And here, somewhere, we have an eye (I'll speak for myself) capable of any imagining (the only reality). And there (right there) we have the camera eye (the limitation the original liar); yet lyre sings to the mind so immediately (the exalted selectivity) one wants to forget that its strings can so easily make puppetry of human motivation (for form as finality) dependent upon attunation, what it's turned to (ultimately death) or turned from (birth) or the way to get out of it (transformation). I'm not just speaking of that bird on fire (not thinking of circles) or of Spengler (spirals neither) or of any known progression (nor straight lines) logical formation (charted levels) or ideological formation (mapped for scenic points of interest); but I am speaking for possibilities (myself), infinite possibilities (preferring chaos).

And here, somewhere, we have an eye capable of any imagining. And then we have the camera eye, its lenses grounded to achieve 19th century Western compositional perspective (as best exemplified by the 19th century architectural conglomeration of details of the "classic" ruin) in bending the light and limiting the frame of the image just so, its standard camera and projector speed for recording movement geared to the feeling of the ideal slow Viennese waltz, and even its tripod head, being the neck it swings on, balled with bearings to permit it that Les Sylphides motion (ideal to the contemplative romantic) and virtually restricted to horizontal and vertical movements (pillars and horizon lines) a diagonal requiring a major adjustment, its lenses coated or provided with filters, its light meters balanced, and its color film manufactured, to produce that picture post card effect (salon painting) exemplified by those oh so blue skies and peachy skins.

By deliberately spitting on the lens or wrecking its focal intention, one can achieve the early stages of impressionism. One can make this prima donna heavy in performance of image movement by speeding up the motor, or one can break up movement, in a way that approaches a more direct inspiration of contemporary human eye perceptibility of movement, by slowing the motion while recording the image. One may hand hold the camera and inherit worlds of space. One may over- or under-expose the film. One may use the filters of the world, fog, downpours, unbalanced lights, neons with neurotic color temperatures, glass which was never designed for a camera, or even glass which was but which can be used against specifications, or one may photograph an hour after sunrise or an hour before sunset, those marvelous taboo hours when the film labs will guarantee nothing, or one may go into the night with a specified daylight film or vice versa. One may become the supreme trickster, with hatfuls of all the rabbits listed above breeding madly. One may, out of incredible courage, become Méliès, that marvelous man who gave even the "art of the film" its beginning in magic. Yet Méliès was not witch, witch doctor, priest, or even sorcerer. He was a 19th-century stage magician. His films *are* rabbits.

What about the hat? the camera? or if you will, the stage, the page, the ink, the hieroglyphic itself, the pigment shaping that original drawing, the musical and/or all other instruments for copula-and-then-procreation? Kurt Sachs talks sex (which fits the hat neatly) in originating musical instruments, and Freud's revitalization of symbol charges all contemporary content in art. Yet possession thru visualization speaks for fear-of-death as motivating force—the tomb art of the Egyptian, etc. And then there's "In the beginning," "Once upon a time," or the very concept of a work of art being a "Creation." Religious motivation only reaches us thru the anthropologist these days—viz., Frazer on a golden bough. And so it goes—ring around the rosary, beating about the bush, describing. One thread runs clean thru the entire fabric of expression—the trick-and-effect. And between those two words, somewhere, magic . . . the brush of angel wings, even rabbits leaping heavenwards and, given some direction, language corresponding. Dante looks upon the face of God and Rilke is heard among the angelic orders. Still the Night Watch was tricked by Rembrandt and Pollack was out to produce an effect. The original word was a trick, and so were all the rules of the game that followed in its wake. Whether the instrument be musical or otherwise, it's still a hat with more rabbits yet inside the head wearing it—i.e., thought's a trick, etc. Even The Brains for whom thought's the world, and the word and visi-or-audibility of it, eventually end with a ferris wheel of a solar system in the middle of the amusement park of the universe. They know it without experiencing it, screw it lovelessly, find "trick" or "effect" derogatory terminology, too close for comfort, are utterly unable to comprehend "magic." We are either experiencing (copulating) or conceiving (procreating) or very rarely both are balancing in that moment of living, loving, and creating, giving and receiving, which is so close to the imagined divine as to be more unmentionable than "magic."

In the event you didn't know, "magic" is realmed in "the imaginable," the moment of it being when that which is imagined dies, is penetrated by mind and known rather than believed in. Thus "reality" extends its picketing fence and each is encouraged to sharpen his wits. The artist is one who leaps that fence at night, scatters his seeds among the cabbages, hybrid seeds inspired by both the garden and wits-end forest where only fools and madmen wander, seeds needing several generations to be . . . finally proven edible. Until then they remain invisible, to those with both feet on the ground, yet prominent enough to be tripped over. Yes, those unsightly bulges between those oh so even rows will find their flowering moment . . . and then be farmed. Are you really thrilled at the sight of a critic tentatively munching artichokes? Wouldn't you rather throw overalls in the eventual collegic chowder? Realize the garden as you will— the growing is mostly underground. Whatever daily care you may give it—all is planted only by moonlight. However you remember it—everything in it originates elsewhere. As for the unquotable magic—it's as indescribable as the unbound woods it comes from.

(A foot-on-the-ground-note: The sketches of T. E. Lawrence's "realist" artist companion were scratches to Lawrence's Arab friends. Flaherty's motion picture projection of NANOOK OF THE NORTH was only a play of lights and silhouettes to the Aleutian Islander Nanook himself. The schizophrenic does see symmetrically, does believe in the reality of Rorschach, yet he will not yield to the suggestion that a pin-point light in a darkened room will move, being the only one capable of perceiving its stasis correctly. Question any child as to his drawing and he will defend the "reality" of what you claim "scribbles." Answer any child's question and he will shun whatever quest he'd been beginning.)

Light, lens concentrated, either burns negative film to a chemical crisp which, when lab washed, exhibits the blackened pattern of its ruin or, reversal film, scratches the emulsion to eventually bleed it white. Light, again lens concentrated, pierces white and casts its shadow patterned self to reflect upon the spectator. When light strikes a color emulsion, multiple chemical layers restrict its various wave lengths, restrain its bruises to eventually produce a phenomenon unknown to dogs. Don't think of creatures of uncolored vision as restricted, but wonder, rather, and marvel at the known internal mirrors of the cat which catch each spark of light in the darkness and reflect it to an intensification. Speculate as to insect vision, such as the bee's sense of scent thru ultraviolet perceptibility. To search for human visual realities, man must, as in all other homo motivation, transcend the original physical restrictions and inherit worlds of eyes. The very narrow contemporary moving visual reality is exhausted. The belief in the sacredness of any man-achievement sets concrete about it, statues becoming statutes, needing both explosives, and earthquakes for disruption. As to the permanency of the present or any established reality, consider in this light and thru most individual eyes that without either illumination or photographic lens, any ideal animal might claw the black off a strip of film or walk ink-footed across transparent celluloid and produce an effect for projection identical to a photographed image. As to color, the earliest color films were entirely hand painted a frame at a time. The "absolute realism" of the motion picture image is a human invention.

What reflects from the screen is shadow play. Look, there's no real rabbit. Those ears are index fingers and the nose a knuckle interfering with the light. If the eye were more perceptive it would see the sleight of 24 individual pictures and an equal number of utter blacknesses every second of the show. What incredible films might ultimately be made for such an eye. But the machine has already been fashioned to outwit even that perceptibility, a projector which flashes advertisement at subliminal speed to up the sale of popcorn. Oh, slow-eyed spectator, this machine is grinding you out of existence. Its electrical storms are manufactured by pure white frames interrupting the flow of the photographed images, its real tensions are a dynamic interplay of two-dimensional shapes and lines, the horizon line and background shapes battering the form of the horseback rider as the camera moves with it, the curves of the tunnel exploding away from the pursued, camera following, and tunnel perspective converging on the pursuer, camera preceding, the dream of the close-up kiss being due to the linear purity of facial features after cluttersome background, the entire film's soothing syrup being the depressant of imagistic repetition, a feeling akin to counting sheep to sleep. Believe in it blindly, and it will fool you—mind wise, instead of sequins on cheesecloth or max-manu-factured make-up, you'll see stars. Believe in it eye-wise, and the very comet of its overhead throw from projector to screen will intrigue you so deeply that its fingering play will move integrally with what's reflected, a comet-tail integrity which would lead back finally to the film's creator. I am meaning, simply, that the rhythms

of change in the beam of illumination which now goes entirely over
the heads of the audience would, in the work of art, contain in
itself some quality of a spiritual experience. As is, and at best, that
hand spreading its touch toward the screen taps a neurotic chaos
comparable to the doodles it produces for reflection. The "absolute
realism" of the motion picture image is a 20th-century, essentially
Western, illusion.

Nowhere in its mechanical process does the camera hold either
mirror or candle to nature. Consider its history. Being machine, it
has always been manufacturer of the medium, mass-producer of
stilled abstract images, its virtue—related variance, the result—
movement. Essentially, it remains fabricator of a visual language,
no less a linguist than the typewriter. Yet in the beginning, each of
an audience thought himself the camera, attending a play or,
toward the end of the purely camera career, being run over by the
unedited filmic image of a locomotive which had once rushed
straight at the lens, screaming when a revolver seemed fired straight
out of the screen, motion of picture being the original magic of the
medium. Méliès is credited with the first splice. Since then, the
strip of celluloid has increasingly revealed itself suited to transformations beyond those conditioned by the camera. Originally
Méliès' trickery was dependent upon starting and stopping the
photographic mechanism and between-times creating, adding objects to its field of vision, transformations, substituting one object
for another, and disappearances, removing the objectionable. Once
the celluloid could be cut, the editing of filmic images began its
development toward Eisensteinian montage, the principle of 1 plus
2 making 3 in moving imagery as anywhere else. Meantime labs
came into the picture, playing with the illumination of original
film, balancing color temperature, juggling double imagery in superimposition, adding all the acrobatic grammar of the film inspired by D. W. Griffith's dance; fades to mark the montage sen-
tenced motion picture paragraph, dissolves to indicate lapse of
time between interrelated subject matter, variations in the framing
for the epic horizontal composition, origin of Cinemascope, and
vertical picture delineating character, or the circle exclamating a
pictorial detail, etc. The camera itself taken off the pedestal, began
to move, threading its way, in and around its source of material for
the eventual intricately patterned fabric of the edited film. Yet
editing is still in its 1, 2, 3 infancy, and the labs are essentially still
just developing film, no less trapped by the standards they're bearing than the camera by its original mechanical determination. No
very great effort has ever been made to interrelate these two or
three processes, and already another is appearing possible, the projector as creative instrument with the film show a kind of performance, celluloid or tape merely source of material to the projection-
ing interpreter, this expression finding its origins in the color, or the
scent, or even the musical organ, its most recent manifestations—

the increased programming potential of the IBM and other electronic machines now capable of inventing imagery from scratch.
Considering then the camera eye as almost obsolete, it can at last
be viewed objectively and, perhaps, view-pointed with subjective
depth as never before. Its life is truly all before it. The future fab-
ricating machine in performance will invent images as patterned
after cliché vision as those of the camera, and its results will suffer
a similar claim to "realism," IBM being no more God nor even a
"Thinking machine" than the camera eye all-seeing or capable of
creative selectivity, both essentially restricted to "yes-no," "stop-
go," "on-off," and instrumentally dedicated to communication of
the simplest sort. Yet increased human intervention and control
renders any process more capable of a balance between sub-and-
objective expression, and between those two concepts, somewhere,
soul . . . The second stage of transformation of image editing revealed the magic of the movement. Even though each in the audience then proceeded to believe himself part of the screen reflection,
taking two-dimension visual characters as his being within the drama,
he could not become every celluloid sight running thru the projector,
therefore allowance of another viewpoint, and no attempt to make
him believe his eye to be where the camera eye once was has ever
since proven successful—excepting the novelty of three-dimension,
audiences jumping when rocks seemed to avalanche out of the
screen and into the theatre. Most still imagine, however, the camera
a recording mechanism, a lunatic mirroring, now full of sound and
fury presenting its half of a symmetrical pattern, a kaleidoscope
with the original pieces of glass missing and their movement removed in time. And the instrument is still capable of winning
Stanford's bet about horse-hooves never all leaving the ground in
galloping, though Stanford significantly enough used a number of
still cameras with strings across the track and thus inaugurated the
flip-pic of the penny arcade, Hollywood still racing after the horse.
Only when the fans move on to another track can the course be
cleared for this eye to interpret the very ground, perhaps to discover its non-solidity, to create a contemporary Pegasus, without
wings, to fly with its hooves, beyond any imagining, to become
gallop, a creation. It can then inherit the freedom to agree or dis-
agree with 2000 years of Western equine painting and attain some
comparable aesthetic stature. As is, the "absolute realism" of the
motion picture image is a contemporary mechanical myth. Consider
this prodigy for its virtually untapped talents, viewpoints it possesses more readily recognizable as visually non-human yet within
the realm of the humanly imaginable. I am speaking of its speed
for receptivity which can slow the fastest motion for detailed
study, or its ability to create a continuity for time compression, increasing the slowest motion to a comprehensibility. I am praising
its cyclopean penetration of haze, its infra-red visual ability in
darkness, its just-developed 360-degree view, its prismatic revela-

tion of rainbows, its zooming potential for exploding space and its telephotic compression of same to flatten perspective, its micro- and macroscopic revelations. I am marvelling at its Schlaeran self capable of representing heat waves and the most invisible air pressures, and appraising its other still camera developments which may grow into motion, its rendering visible the illumination of bodily heat, its transformation of ultra-violets to human cognizance, its penetrating X-ray. I am dreaming of the mystery camera capable of graphically representing the form of an object after it's been removed from the photographic scene, etc. The "absolute realism" of the motion picture is unrealized, therefore potential, magic.

(Written 1960, published in *Film Culture*, No. 30, 1963)

STAN BRAKHAGE:

Letter to Yves Kovacs
(On Surrealism)

Near mid-Sept. 1964

Dear Yves KOVACS,

I must admit I'm finding it difficult to either fulfull your request
or reject it. You see, I simply do NOT write "On Subject," as it's
termed, nor work film-or-write-wise "Under Commission"; but then
your letters are either turning my mind to Surrealistic considerations
and/or are arriving at the opportune time when these considerations
are arising within me again in a form where they might loosely be
clustered under the term "Surrealism." I have, as you know, been
corresponding with poet Kelly about what we term "The Dream
Work." But then, I feel especiálly hampered in my writing to/for
you/your magazine in that whatever is to be of use to you must be
translated into French which restricts my sense of pun—as, for
instance, my thoughts turn to the phrase: "Sir Real & The Drag". . .
ah, well, if you'll forgive me that one & two pun, I'll try to be
gracious enough to give you a couple paragraphs of straight
thoughts on the subject specified without becoming too school-boyish
about it, viz:

Max Ernst, on the subject WHAT IS SURREALISM (from
Ausstellungskatalog Kunsthaus Zurich, 1934) says: " 'The accidental
encounter of a sewing machine and an umbrella on a dissecting
table' (Lautréamont) is today a universally known, almost classic
example for the phenomenon discovered by the Surrealists that the
juxtaposition of two (or more) apparently alien elements on an
alien plane promotes the most potent poetic combustion." With this
I would juxtapose some sense of William Carlos Williams' "No
ideas but in things" (from "A Sort of a Song"); and I might even
underline the "in" therein. Then I would direct you to the accidental
appearance of whatever page you're reading this off OF, and make
"OF" here signify SOURCE of/and/or/in this encounter. I would

deepen this experience with Robert Duncan's take-off ON a quote:
"The physical world is a light world. The real world, Thomas
Vaughan wrote, is invisible. Thus, in the physical or spiritual or
light world all forms or beings—stones, trees, stars, streams, men,
flames and turds—are really facts of invisible presence. Mineral,
wood, fire, water, flesh are terms of dense soul-full sense." And I
would re-direct the reader "Whomsoever" to specifics such as the
metal of a sewing machine, the wood handle of a remembered umbrella, this page as imagined dissected by flames, the thought-full
struggle of imagining a water-thing (without recourse to word-
sense "body of water" and/or imagined container) and the flesh of
the eye reading this. Then I'd take Jack Spicer's command (from
"A Textbook of Poetry") "See through into" and dissect that, as he
does, with his: "like it is not possible with flesh only by beginning
not to be a human being. Only by beginning not to be a soul" (Both
Duncan & Spicer quotes are from Duncan's "Properties And Our
REAL Estate" from "Journal For The Protection of all Beings—
No. 1").

Taking the above quotes as axiomatic in inter-action of the trace
from France (1) to Germany (E) to East Coast U. S. (W) and
thru filter of American continent to West Coast (D & S) of consideration's change from OF things to ON things to THRU INTO (the
eye of the reader taking place of "things"), that is: taking the above
as international law (of Surreal manifestation) and conditioning
sub-laws pertaining finally to properties of thingness, I find the fore-
most FORce of Surrealism TO BE a directing OF itself (History)
ON object ("object" replacing "things" in this light) rather than on
position of things ("juxta" or otherwise) for a going THRU INTO
("IN": The Present) in celebration of (Future: Imaged) sense of
Being; but, having come full circle (to: ". . . of . . . of") following
a thread of paper thru the things words are to the needle in the eye
of the imagined-future reader, let us (as imagined) celebrate
(rather than consider) the Surrealism created (originated) on the
thread between things; and let us remember (piece together) the
ashes of it, FOR (if we remember correctly) it was a burning
thread; and then let us wonder if we have (with/in all these considerations) but put out the fire (perhaps to prevent it from con-
suming the things.)

An Alexander (such as Burroughs or Byron Gyson) would at this
point simply cut the things (as Alexander did the Gordion Knot
when it was of prime consideration); but I do find *that* a killing of
the goose that lays the golden egg. We can deepen our considerations of this matter by a Western faith in the eternity of the thread
and/or an Eastern Zen resignation: sense of the burning of the page
this is printed upon, all print evaporating in a slow smoke; but I will
leave those processes, thankfully, to the whomEVER (theologian
and academician) reader and pass, gratefully, on to my sense of eye

as visible brain matter, as surface sense of brain; and I will continue, thereby, in consideration, viz:

A careful re-reading of the first paragraph, taking quotes as Law and conditioning sub-laws, gives sense that it was the light of the "combustion" which was most permanent in the course of our following from BETWEEN to THRU INTO things ("BETWEEN" now standing for OF -((SOURCE))-ON); but "things resist the light, reflect it, to block our seeing THRU INTO, yielding us only a surface-tension. But if we begin "not to be a soul," give up the drama of perception, and all other adventure-senses easily prefaced with "self," do we not ourselves become reflective OF the light? and can we not think ON the surface as beginning? as a gain; and have we not thereIN ignited the fire of the thread of imagination? (our double "of" telling us where we are again: Present to these past considerations). The things, as these words are things, will now put forth threads OF illumination entangling viewer, reader, and eachother. None will seem "alien" to eachother or on an alien plane either; but neither can they engender an INTERnational Surrealism, as each word hereIN must transform TO French word-clusters for the imagined-future reader. At the point where a relationship between things includes the imagined viewer-reader-etceterer, all communication becomes imaginary. But all communication IS imaginary in any given PRESENT. Even the Kinesics (such as Ray L. Birdwhistell) are scientifically informing us: "We do not communicate. We participate in communication." And I would again, underlie the "in." Or, as poet Charles Olson says: "Landscape is what you see from where you are standing." Or, as Gertrude Stein put it (in "Four In America"): "Now what we know is formed in our head by thousands of small occasions in the daily life. By 'what we know' I do not mean, of course, what we learn from books, because that is of no importance at all. I mean what we really know, like our assurance about how we know anything, and what we know about the validity of the sentiments, and things like that. All the thousands of occasions in the daily life go into our head to form our ideas about these things." I would, of course, underline "things." I include these last two quotes to make it clear that if I sent you objects, other than words, or pictures, moving or otherwise, it would in no sense alter the individuality of the gesture other than as I re-considered the imaginary viewer (as of "rather than reader") and made "re" otherwise referential in my considerations. Thus, Surrealism has become an individual matter, as it was at beginning, as was all-ways in consideration.

But then, what do we share (under title of "Surrealism" or other, such as "Nation," etcetera) in these exchanges? It is, of course, The Light (which I now capitalize to signify its signification). Surrealism (a capitalization signifying several seemingly related combustions which, occurring at a time, or The Time, made many men aware of the light, simultaneously aware, did engender a dance thereby, which has now become The Dance), takes its shape there *by:* "Who shall most advance the light—call it what you may," as William Carlos Williams wrote (in "Asphodel"), and as it would, as a Thing, search THRU INTO does depend upon past tensions such as outlined by Olson (in "Pieces of Time"—"1. Proprioception"):

> "Physiology: the surface (senses—the 'skin': of 'Human Universe') the body itself—proper—one's own 'corpus': PROPRIOCEPTION the cavity of the body, in which the organs are slung: the viscera, or interoceptive, the old 'psychology' of feeling, the heart; of desire, the liver; of sympathy, the 'bowels'; of courage—kidney etc.—gall. (Stasis—or as in Chaucer only, spoofed)":

does take its directive ON, as Olson continues:

> "Today: movement, at any cost. Kinesthesia: beat (nik) the sense whose end organs lie in the muscles, tendons, joints, and are stimulated by bodily tensions (—or relaxations of same.) Violence: knives/anything, to get the body in.":

THRU INTO you, WHOMever. But, for example, if the word-thing "Surrealism" sees thru into you as you see thru into it; the "it" being an other word-thing will disperse the vision (except, for instance, as you "read-into" Surrealism—for in-stance read "it" into "Surrealism") unless you participate in SEEING THRU INTO, in the sense of participating in communication. Such participation resists a reading-into, or any other form of Projection, resists your imposing upon a thing, and/or Super-imposition, as the surface of a thing resists light for reflection. Thus the individual surreal encounter (uncapitalized surrealism, original of Surrealism) is created as an imagined you (or as I imagine myself) imagines a thing seeing thru into you which you see thru into seeing thru into you seeing thru into, etcetera. Olson suggests this with:

> "The gain: to have a third term, so that *movement* or *action* is 'home.' Neither the Unconscious nor Projection (here used to remove the false opposition of 'Conscious'; 'consciousness' is self) have a home unless the DEPTH implicit in physical being—built-in space-time specifics, and moving (by movement of 'its own')—is asserted, or found-out as such. Thus the advantage of the value 'proprioception.' As such."

The dream-work of Surrealism seems to me to formulate itself (historically) thus: "I see thru into myself seeing thru into you seeing thru into yourself seeing thru into me seeing me see you seeing you see me." Poet Robert Kelly (in "THE DREAM WORK/2," in "matter/2") strings names along a line, thus:

> "Europe) Gilgamesh Aristotle Cicero Chaucer Colonna . . . Freud Jung":

and, in earlier writing confined to "dream as psychic event in the life of the dreamer," writes: "My premise is that the dreamworld in us is (like our lives, Q. E. D.) a complex solid of such a nature that 'crystalline structure' is a more useful analogy than 'line,' chemistry a better ancilla than history." ("THE DREAM WORK," "matter/1") This is a strong *prime* envisionment; but as I imagine myself crystalline in my seeing thru anything seeing thru into me, I am blocked from seeing thru into me seeing thru into anything seeing thru into me seeing thru into . . . the "I" cut off from secondary exchanges. Thus I am inclined to string "myself" along a line of terms like "I" and "me"—a dream becomes a thing, again, to be told-OF or to be visually represented as, say, picture OF crystal OF, etcetera. In following these considerations I would soon find myself as dependent ON three-dimensional perspective and sense of immobility as most Surrealistic painting; and words would become as specifically referential, immobile as symbol, as in most Surrealistic poetry; and my film work would soon restrict the "motion" of "motion pictures," as Surrealistic films have never shown themselves in complexities of movement, have rather tended to "slow motion"; and the sense of seeing would reduce to scenes referential to drama, as Surrealistic dramas, in films or even improvizations, present themselves primarily as staged events.

I cannot, at this time, suggest a more useful analogy than 'crystalline structure,' turn Kelly's crystal around and around in my head, letting it dissolve like snow "settling crystals locking and unlocking with crystals" as he suggests, re-freezing it again and again. It took the Zen masters time to come from "Dust is misplaced matter" to "The dust is in the mind." I feel sure it is The Time in which we are related THRU reflection, rather than combustion, IN small "s" rather than capped surrealism TO SEEING THRU INTO.

(Written for *Etudes Cinématographiques*, where only a few sentences were excerpted for translation.)

Letter to Ronna Page
(On Music)

mid-April 1966

Dear Ronna Page,

Jonas Mekas will have whatever material has been salvaged on and/or by me—old clips, "stills", etcetera—as I make a practice of sending them all to him for Film-Makers' Cooperative files.

As to quotes out of my past, I imagine you have ample material in FILM CULTURE issues and my book METAPHORS ON VISION. I am presently working on a long film (16mm) to be called: SCENES FROM UNDER CHILDHOOD. It would probably be of particular interest to your Parisian readers to know that this work-in-progress is to some extent inspired by the music of Olivier Messiaen and, to some lesser extent, Jean Barraque, Pierre Boulez, Henri Pousseur, and Karlheinz Stockhausen (all, I believe, former pupils of Messiaen).

Fifteen years ago I began working with the film medium as primarily shaped by the influence of stage drama. Since that time, both poetry and painting have alternately proved more growth-engendering sources of inspiration than either the trappings of the stage or the specific continuity limitations of any "making up a story", novelistic tendencies, etcetera: and the first departures in my working-orders from "fiction" sources gave rise to an integral involvement with musical notation as a key to film editing aesthetics. Some ten years ago I studied informally with both John Cage and Edgar Varese, at first with the idea of searching out a new relationship between image and sound and of, thus, creating a new dimension for the sound track, as Jean Isidore Isou's VENOM AND ETERNITY had created in me a complete dissatisfaction with the conventional usages of music for "mood" and so-called "realistic sounds" as mere referendum to image in movies, and Jean Cocteau's poetic film

plays, for all their dramatic limitations, had demonstrated beautifully to me that *only* non-descriptive language could co-exist with
moving image (in any but a poor operatic sense), that words,
whether spoken or printed, could only finally relate to visuals in
motion thru a necessity of means and/or an integrity as severely
visual as that demonstrated by the masterpieces of collage. The
more informed I became with aesthetics of sound, the less I began
to feel any need for an audio accompaniment to the visuals I was
making. I think it was seven/eight years ago I began making *inten-
tionally* silent films. Although I have always kept myself open to the
possibilities of sound while creating any film, and have in fact made
a number of sound films these last several years, I now see/feel no
more absolute necessity for a sound track than a painter feels the
need to exhibit a painting with a recorded musical background.
Ironically, the more silently-oriented my creative philosophies have
become, the more inspired-by-music have my photographic aesthetics and my actual editing orders become, both engendering a
coming-into-being of the physiological relationship between seeing
and hearing in the making of a work of art in film.

I find, with Cassius Keyser, that "the structure of mathematics is
similar to that of the human nervous system" and have for years
been studying the relationship between physiology and mathematics via such books as Sir D'Arcy Thompson's ON GROWTH AND
FORM: and following those "leads" along a line of music, I've come
to the following thoughts (which I'll quote from an article of mine
which appeared in the magazine WILD DOG):

"I'm somehow now wanting to get deeper into my concept of
music as sound equivalent of the mind's moving, which is becoming
so real to me that I'm coming to believe the study of the history of
music would reveal more of the changing thought processes of a
given culture than perhaps any other means—not of thought shaped
and/or Thoughts but of the *Taking shape,* physiology of thought or
some such . . . I mean, is there anything that will illustrate the feel of
chains of thought gripping and ungripping, rattling slowly around,
a block-concept, an Ideal, as Gregorian Chant, for instance? . . .
And doesn't The Break occur in Western Musical thought in terms
of melody, story, carrying blocks, making them events, along a line?
(Or, as poet Robert Kelly put it to me recently: '& event is the
greatness of story, i.e., where story and history & myth & mind &
physiology *all* at once interact'—and is not THAT the greatness of
Bach, the interaction of blocks becoming events as they inter eachother in the act, in the course, of the line of melody? (I'm reminded
here that Gregorian notes WERE blocks in manuscript, stems attached later to make flowers of 'em, and then, still later, strung along
lined paper, etcetera. And sometime later, when the notes were well
rounded, flowering right-and-upside-down, sporting flags, holes, etc.,
and all planted in the neat gardens of the page, all in rows, it was
possible for Mozart to play Supreme Gardener; but there lurked
Wagner who would, did, make of each line of melody a block, spe-

cifically referential, so that the French could image melody as a landscape, all thought referential to picture, i.e. to something OUTside the musical frame of reference. But then Webern made of it a cube, all lines of melody converging on some center to form a cluster or what composer James Tenney, writing about Varese, does call 'a Klang'. And it does seem to me that with John Cage we are, thru chance operations, to some approximation of Gregorian Chant again—not held to links, as of a chain-of-thought, but rather to the even more rigid mathematical bell-shaped curve."

J. S. Bach has been called "the greatest composer of the 20th century": and his current popularity is probably due to the facts that (1) he was the greatest composer of his own time and (2) most of the western world has, in the meantime, come to think *easily* in a baroque fashion—come to think *naturally* baroquely, one might say were it not that this process of thought is the result of these several centuries of cultural training. The most modern baroqueists in music were, of course, the twelve-tonists: and my ANTICIPATION OF THE NIGHT was specifically inspired by the relationships I heard between the music of J. S. Bach and Anton Webern. The crisis of Western Man's historical thought processes struggling with the needs of contemporary living (technological as against mechanistic) has never been more clearly expressed than in Webern's adaptation of Bach's MUSICAL OFFERING (which piece has inspired several films of mine, most dramatically the sound film BLUE MOSES): but the most essentially optimistic (if I may use so psychological a word) force of musical thought has come from Debussy, Faure, Ravel, Roussel, Satie, and even Lili Boulanger, etcetera—all moving along a line of hearing into the inner ear (the sphere of "music of the spheres" being now *consciously* the human head) . . . just as all visual masters of this century who've promised more than a past-tension of The Illustrative have centered the occasions of their inspiration in the mind's eye (so-called "Abstract Painting" having a very *concrete* physiological basis in "closed eye vision").

I seek to hear color just as Messiaen seeks to see sounds. As he writes (in notes for the record of CHRONOCHROMIE):

Colour: the sounds *colour* the durations because they are, for me, bound to colour by unseen ties.

I find these "ties" to be sense impulses of the nervous system and find them to have exact physiological limitations but unlimited psychological growth potential thru the act of seeing and hearing, and/or otherwise sensing, them. Messiaen goes on:

When I listen to music, and even when I read it, I have an inward vision of marvellous colours—colours which blend like combinations of notes, and which shift and revolve with the sounds.

I recall first hearing shifting chords of sound that corresponded in meaningful interplay with what I was seeing when I was a child in a Kansas cornfield at mid-night. That was the first time I was in an environment *silent* enough to permit me to hear "the music of the spheres", as it's called, and visually specific enough for me to be aware of the eye's pulse of receiving image. John Cage once, in a sound-proof chamber, picked out a dominant fifth and was told later that he was hearing his nervous system and blood circulation: but the matter is a great deal more complicated than that—at least as much more complicated as the whole range of musical chord possibilities is to the, any, dominant fifth . . . for instance, any tone of the inner-ear seems to be hearable as a pulse, or wave of that tone, of *irregular* rhythm and tempo, "waveringness" one might say: and yet these hearable pulse-patterns *repeat*, at intervals, and reverse, and etcetera, in a way analogous to the "theme and variation" patterns of some western musical forms. . . External sounds heard seem to affect these inner-ear pulses *more* by way of the emotions engendered than by specific tonal and/or rythmic correspondences: whereas the external pulse perceived by the eye does seem to more directly affect ear's in-pulse. But then that's a much more complicated matter, too, because the eye has its own in-pulse—the color red, for instance, will be held, with the eyes closed, as a retention-color with a much different vibrancy, or pulse, than red seen with eyes open, and so on—and the rythm-pattern-flashes of the eye's-nerve-ends, making up the grainy shapes of closed-eye vision, are quite distinct from inner-ear's "theme and variations" . . . so much so that no familiar counter-point is recognizable. Well, just SO—for these fields of the mind feeling out its own physiology via eyes and ears turned inward, so to speak, are prime centers of inspiration for both musical and visual composers of this century who take Sense- as Muse (as do all who recognize the move from Technological to Electrical Era of 20th century living) . . . and there is very little historical precedence in the working orders, or the achievements, of these artists.

Well, all of the above essaying (which grew way beyond any intended length) should at least serve to distinguish my intentions and processes, and whatever films of mine arise there-thru, from most of the rest of the so-called Underground Film Movement: and (as you asked specifically about this in your letter) I'll take the opportunity to emphasize that I feel at polar odds and ends therefrom whatever usually arises from that "movement" into public print, especially when journalists and critics are presuming to write about myself and my work. I'm certainly nothing BUT uneasy about the any/everybody's too facile sense of mixed-media, which seems by report to be dominating the New York Scene, at the present. Whether the "mix" is per chance (operations) or per romance (opera) or per some scientific stance (Op) or just plain folksy, Grand 'Ol Opry, dance (Pop), I've very little actual interest in it, nor in The Old Doc-(umentary) school, with its "spoon full of sugar helps the medicine go down" either—all these socio-oriented effect-films being related to "The Cause" rather than Aesthetics . . . and some of them, naturally, working beautifully in that context; but most of them, these days, causing sensibility-crippling confusions in the long run, because all are sailing into import under the flag of "Art", leaving that term bereft of meaning and those films which are simply "beautiful works" (which will "do no work" but will "live forever", as Ezra Pound says of his songs) lacking the distinction that there IS that possibility for cinema, as established in all other arts, of works that *can* and *must* be seen many times, *will* last, *have* qualities of integrality to be shored against the dis-continuities of fashionable time. I do not ever like to see a "Cause" *made* of, or around, a work of art; and I strive to make films integrally cohesive enough to be impregnable to the rape of facile usage (shudder at the thought of Hitler shoveling eight million Jews into the furnace off the pages of "Thus Spake Zarathustra", etcetera, for instance). To be clear about it (and to answer another of your questions about my attitude toward increasing censorship): I've many times risked jail sentences for showing films of mine which were, at the time, subject to sexual censorship laws, and will do so again if the occasion arises: but I have never, and *will never*, force said works upon an unprepared or antagonistic audience, have never made than party-to/subject-of (and/or)/illustration-for "The Cause of Sexual Freedom" or some-such. I made those films, as all my films, out of *personal* necessity taking shape thru means available to me of *historical* aesthetics. I risked imprisonment showing them in order to meet the, as requested, needs of others. To have *forced* these works upon others, because of my presumption of the good-for-them in such occasion, would have been to blaspheme against the process out of which the works arise and to have eventually destroyed myself as instrument of that process . . . freedom, of expression-or-other, can only exist meaningfully out of full respect to the means of its becoming: and a work of art does never impress, in the usual sense of the word, but rather is free-express always—and it does, therefore, require some free space, some fragile atmosphere of attenuated sensibility, in which to be received . . . the social strength of the arts is rooted in human need to freely attend, which demonstrates itself over and over again in that people finally DO create such an UNlikely (free of all likenesses) space wherein aesthetics (shaped with respect to his/somebody-else's and history's means) can be received. Let society's sex-pendulum swing "anti" again, if it will (tho' I hope it won't), the works of art of sex impulse will continue to be made as surely as babies and to have an eventual public life as surely as babies grow up.

Blessings, Stan Brakhage

PETER KUBELKA:

The Theory of
Metrical Film

(From Lectures on *Adebar, Schwechater,*
and *Arnulf Rainer*)

[Peter Kubelka has become one of the most influential theoreticians
of the cinema in America since his initial visit in 1966. However
the only readily available text of his position has been an interview
with Jonas Mekas, published in *Film Culture* in 1967. Since then his
theoretical discourse has been refined, amplified, and developed. Its
form has been a series of public or academic lectures entitled "The
Essence of Cinema." Kubelka has been reluctant to allow verbal
transcriptions of the dramatic seminars to be printed; for they lack
not only the gestures but the excerpts and loops of his films which
illustrate his points. The following text is a series of excerpts from
his lectures at New York University, transcribed by several of his
students from tapes, selected and edited by the editor of this volume,
who has tried to preserve the fundamental features of Kubelka's
language and style of presentation while rendering a readable and
coherent prose.

In an interview with Jonas Mekas in 1966 Kubelka made the following statements which will serve as a preface to his lectures of
1974-5.]

I heard this expression yesterday,
"to hit the screen," that's fantastic, in English. Hit the screen—this
is really what the frames do. The projected frames hit the screen.
For example, when you let the projector run empty, you hear the
rhythm. There is a basic rhythm in cinema. I think very few film
makers—if there ever was one, I don't know—have departed from

making films from this feeling of the basic rhythm, these twenty-four impulses on the screen—brrhumm—it's a very metric rhythm. I thought, the other day, that I am the only one who ever made metric films, with metric elements. These three films, Adebar, Schwechater, and Arnulf Rainer, are metric films. You know what I mean by metric? It's the German expression "Metrisches System." The classic music, for instance, has whole notes, and half notes, and quarter notes. Not frames as notes, but the time sections that I have in my films. I mean, I have no seventeenths and no thirteenths, but I have sixteen frames, and eight frames, and four frames, and six frames—it's a metric rhythm. For example, people always feel that my films are very even and have no edges and do not break apart and are equally heavy at the beginning and at the end. This is because the harmony spreads out of the unit of the frame, of the $\frac{1}{24}$th of the second, and I depart from this ground rhythm, from the twenty-four frames, which you feel, which you always feel. Even when you see a film by DeMille, you feel it prrrrr as it goes on the screen.

Cinema is not movement. This is the first thing. Cinema is not movement. Cinema is a projection of stills—which means images which do not move—in a very quick rhythm. And you can give the illusion of movement, of course, but this is a special case, and the film was invented originally for this special case. But, as often happens, people invent something, and, then, they create quite a different thing. They have created something else. Cinema is not movement. It can give the illusion of movement. Cinema is the quick projection of light impulses. These light impulses can be shaped when you put the film before the lamp—on the screen you can shape it. I am talking now about silent film. You have the possibility to give light a dimension in time. This is the first time since mankind exists that you can really do that. To talk about the essence of cinema, it's a very complex thing. Of course, when you ask what's the essence of music, you can say one thing, and another, and another—there are many things in cinema. One is this great fascination that light has for man. Of course, cinema is still very flimsy, a pale thing, and it passes quickly, and so on—but still, as weak as it is, it is a very strong thing, and it has a great fascination just because you can do something with the light. Then, it's in time. It can be conserved, preserved. You can work for years and years and produce—as I do—one minute of a concentrate in time, and, ever since mankind existed, you never could do such a thing. And then—sound. The meeting of sound and image. And we come to this problem: Where does film become articulate? When does a language become articulate? Language becomes articulation when you put one word and another word. One word alone is one word alone, but, when you put two words, it's between the two words, so to speak, that is your articulation. And, when you put three words, it's between one and

two, and between two and three, and then there is also relation between one and three, but two is in between.

It can be a collision, or it could be a very weak succession. There
are many many possibilities. It's just that Eisenstein wanted to have
collision—that's what he liked. But what I wanted to say is: Where
is, then, the articulation of cinema? Eisenstein, for example, said it's
the collision of two shots. But it's very strange that nobody ever said
that *it's not between shots but between frames*. It's between frames
where cinema speaks. And then, when you have a roll of very weak
collisions between frames—this is what I would call a shot, when
one frame is very similar to the next frame, and the next frame, and
the next frame, and the next frame, and the next frame—the result
that you get when you have just a natural scene and you film it . . .
this would be a shot. But, in reality, you can work with every frame.

1. *Adebar*

Today we will be again trying to work out a concept of reality,
documents of reality, personal reality and non-personal reality or
outside reality. Let me immediately say what I want to show—that
for each of you there's only one reality, and this is your personal
reality. Each of you, as you sit here, lives a different life, so to say:
the same time: a different consciousness, a different mood, different
observations, different evaluations of the observations. These things
or courses of interest come out from practically the past of humanity
—come out from your age, your experience, your education, your
state of health, your parents, your parents' parents and where they
have been and so on. It goes back to the beginning of time.

I want to follow this up. I will now give you this [hand points
to a tree] . . . . So what was this, what did you make out of what I
just did? What did you look at? You? [Asks class and most answer
'the tree.'] Those who looked at the tree, why did you look at the
tree? So, those that looked at this tree, looked at this tree, why?
Because my hand was pointing in that direction. Now, I said, "I
give you this," which could be anything. Now you are watching me
and you had another articulation, namely my hand. You figured out
the direction in which my hand was pointing because you knew I
normally would stand still. If I gesture, there is a reason for it. I do
this—synchronous, sync events at the same time when I say, "this".
So, "I give you this" and the gesture have to do with each other. You
conclude: since he wants me to see something, apparently, he wants
me to see this. Now you figured out where I was really pointing. As
you can all see when you think back, even the apparent simplicity
of what I did (I said, "I give you this") already was received differently by everybody. I don't want to go into longer examples of this.
Let me just make statements. As you live your life, it is clear that
every one of you always lives in the way he alone can live it. I say
your personal reality—yours, yours, yours . . . for your reality, you

say *the* reality—because it's yours. You have only this one and you cannot imagine how another one would look. If at the same point of time two people stand at the top of Rockefeller Center and one jumps down and the other not, each cannot imagine why the one does not jump and the other jumps. Everybody is confined to his reality. There's nothing wrong about it, but that is the case. When I want to communicate something about life or something about reality—*the* reality—when I want to make a film, I think I want to document something about life, about reality, about what is going on. And I want, let's say, to make a picture of nature. Now from your point of view this is my reality, my special nature, as I see it. And, now again, if I say, "I give you this", what will happen? Nobody will know what I actually wanted to give you, because everybody will look at the tree, maybe 2/3 of you will look at the tree, and those that look at the tree will all stay within their own reality. So when I want to say something about nature, I must really understand that this is my nature, and that I have to articulate that for you, so that you clearly see what I was thinking about. Because nature, in itself, is completely shapeless. It is open to any kind of vision, action, interpretation. It will do something different to anybody; it's therefore useless. If I want to give you my tree, I have to articulate my tree. Now, let us articulate my tree for you with this Polaroid camera. [Kubelka and a student photograph tree.] We have two trees, my tree, his tree. What's the difference? Is there a difference? And where is the difference? Yes, there is a difference. I wanted the whole tree on it. I managed one side of it, but only where it comes out of the earth. I know that half of the tree is inside. So the trees are like when you screw together two things. The trees screw together the sky and the earth. But you can't see that here of course. Every time when I see a tree, I know that it's half in the earth and that's a very important point for me. My tree feeling is that this is a part where heaven and earth are held together by this being. Half here, half there. It's between the two elements. A tree has a fantastic double existence. But this didn't come out in the photograph. That fact came out a little bit when I talked about it. It comes to decision making. . . . You can make two or three decisions. You can choose to stay here, stay there, hold the camera higher, lower. You might have chosen to open the lens more, or close it more, and then the tree would have become darker still and you would have had more outline.

Now let's compare what's on this photograph with the real tree. Everybody will agree that the green is in no case the green of the tree. Where have these two photographs a real value? They have a value in that they distinguish a little bit him (the student photographer) from me. So, they say something, not about the tree, but about him and me. So, again, the value of one picture is almost nil. The value of two pictures already says something about us. We took different pictures whatever small decisions we made.

Where a medium is really mirroring nature, it is valueless. Where it absolutely follows nature, it cannot be manipulated, it cannot be worked upon, it cannot be used for articulation. It cannot be used for building my reality, which I want to give you. You have to see everything as your reality. The world which you see, nobody else sees. So you can see my world doesn't exist for you, if I cannot build an image of my world. Then my world may become your world or your world may change after seeing my world. And my world may change after seeing your world. Again, everything is interpretation. Everything is documentation and articulation. The real thing is without interest and value.

This whole argument is directed against the belief in photography and the value of reporting the real world. What I say that you must do in cinema is not try to report or bring the real world—to use the qualities of the cinematographic camera to mirror the real world, but that you have to articulate as you do when you talk or draw. The danger in filmmaking lies in that people think that bringing nature to somebody else is useful. It brings my world. Of course when you draw it's very evident that no two drawings are ever the same. But when you make photographs, and you stand where I stand and you also shoot the tree from the same angle, then the photographs are practically alike. This factor is rather strong in photography because this machine has a strong articulation of its own, which is not desirable, which we have to remove.

Every artist tries to mirror the world, because what he thinks of as the world is his own world. You see I don't say "I want to mirror my world"—what is my world? I say "I want to mirror the world" and then it's my world anyway. There is no painting which is mirroring the world. Every painting talks. And every painting mirrors the world of the man who painted it. You see, of course you say, "I want to mirror the world"—it's a formula to help you understand that you have to get a little bit of distance to yourselves, and that you acknowledge that there are other beings who each have their own reality and think that this reality is the world.

Every painter tries to discover objective reality. But what is for me, objective, may not be for you. My *Arnulf Rainer* film is a documentary; it *is* an objective film; it is a world where there is lightning and thunder twenty-four times a second, let's say. And when you read President Nixon's new tapes, you see that his world. . . . I mean this is a known fact—he lives in a ballgame world, and he uses always these ballgame references. And there are always rules of ballgames, and he thinks of events as ballgames, when he says, "This is a new ballgame" and "This is an old ballgame," and then crises are the ninth inning or something. When they make comparisons, everyone always takes paradigms from his own world, from your world! In the old times it was from the *métier*, what you did. So the shoemaker may have always said, "Well, this is like a new pair of shoes, this is like an old pair of shoes, and it's like when you drive a nail through the sole," and so on. And the butcher would compare things with his *métier*. I had talks with peasants. I talked with a peasant who had a son in America, and he went to visit him. And then he came back and talked about what he had seen. And it was just fantastic. He had seen everything in terms of sowing and harvesting and of weather conditions, of plant size and of differences in plants; and, I mean, there was not one emotional, romantic observation in the whole story. He looked like I look. But what was in his head bore no similarity to what was in mine. He didn't even see the towns. He saw grass and he would immediately compare this grass with the grasses he had seen. His whole past comes in.

✿   ✿   ✿

The invention of photography was a very strong upcoming. Immediately many people started this belief in photography which is still rampant now: believing photography can bring you the real reality, which is a philosophical error.

✿   ✿   ✿

Adebar was my second film. Until then I had only seen, outside my own personal vision, the normal, commercial cinema, low-key cinema; and I had a very deep dissatisfaction with what cinema was about. I was lacking a satisfactory form. At that time I already had the feeling that cinema could give me the qualities and beauties which the other arts had been able to achieve. I saw how beautiful classic buildings were; I saw Greek temples and architecture of the Renaissance. I had studied music and I knew about the rhythmic structures in music and I knew about the fantastic enjoyment of time with which music grips you. But in cinema there was nothing! When you regard the time in which films take place (a normal, storytelling film, good or bad), it is a time which has no form; it's very very amorphous. So I wished to create a thing which would establish for my eyes a harmonic time as music establishes a harmonic, rhythmic, a measured time for the ears. In all the arts where time is flowing, you have a concern with rhythm. What is rhythm? Why is mankind so concerned with rhythm? And why does it give us ecstasy? That is a question which has never really been answered. Let us observe for a little while how rhythms are found. There is one rhythm or one beat which is the most important, one of which all the others are then variations, or complements: the one beat repetition. One, one, one, one, one, one. It's the regular repetition of one event. The regular repetition of the same element is something on which the whole universe seems to be based. Practically everything is a multiple of equal elements which repeat. Consider your body. You have the heartbeat, breathing, walking; one two, one two. You then come to the rhythm of the day: the sun goes up, goes down, up and down. The years repeat: and then when you swing your bell, it goes bing-bong-bing-bong. Then you have repetition of elements, such as a pear tree, there's one pear tree, then there's two, three,

four, five: and they are all alike. There are people, all people with a
nose, two eyes, a mouth. You always see a single element and multiplication of it. Why this is so remains beyond us.

It has always been a fascination of mankind to imitate the structures which we find in the world. In what we call classic European
music you have the most simple divisions of a single beat: it can
be divided in half. Then you have fourths, eighths, sixteenths; it's a
simple division in two. I'm trying to convey the step from the amorphous rendition of natural events to *Adebar*.

This film was made in 1957. I had never seen anything like that.
I just had the wish to create something which would have a rhythmic
harmony for the eyes, distill out of the amorphous, visual, outside
world something harmonic.

✿   ✿   ✿

Here is another example of the synthesis of motives of the film-
maker and outward pressure. The outward pressure was that there
was absolutely no money and no possibility of working with any
technical help. I could only buy a piece of negative, develop it, and
then, maybe, make some prints. I had no editing table, no projector.
It was made in 35mm because there was no 16mm in those days.
So I was forced to make the film with my hands, without having an
editing table. This outward difficulty brought me into contact with
the material which then led to a whole new development; namely, I
took the film strip, I looked at it, and saw the slight changes between
images, and then some series of images which I liked. Then I realized
what is now a very clear fact: that film in itself is already divided
into a one beat rhythm. It is one image after the other image; it is
already there when you make the film strip. The projector has a
regular speed. Thus they are projected at a completely regular
speed, which makes it fantastic, since it calls for a rhythmic treatment. Cinema is already rhythmic in its basic appearance. I decided
I would introduce measure in time, which had been in music for
hundreds of thousands of years: architecture had it for many thousands of years. Equal elements in time. It was such a simple thing,
but for me it was a change of a world! It was like being born into a
completely new visual world, to see things happen at the same
rhythm. In my film every element is the same length, or a double
length, or a half a length. The basic length of the elements is 26
frames, and half the length is 13 frames, double 52 frames. The main
thing that is achieved is that the visual element is in regular elements. In a Greek temple there are pillars which are all equally
long, equally thick, and at equal distances from each other. You get
the feeling of harmony. In a piece of music there also is the repetition of form. I took a very old, very primitive and ecstatic piece of
music for the film. It was pygmy music with one motif, exactly 26
frames long. I made a recording, cut it, edited it. I recorded it many
times and then I chose visual elements, that had to have the length

of either 26 or 52 frames. They also had to fit my theme of meeting and departing, or attempts at meeting and not reaching. All these forms are about that, or about the melting of two people into one form. Then I started to analyze the change of frames, always by hand. One important point was the initial image where the whole theme started. I came upon three types. I realized that three points were important.

For example, I had two dancers standing together in silhouette. Then they make a dance movement; the woman goes out and the man remains alone. In ending, I had these three stages: the departure, a development, and the arrival. I printed the first frame 26 times to create a static element of the departure. The next element was a whole chain of events (the going-under of the one figure) and the last element was a multiplication of the last frame, also to the length of 26 frames. The next special case, by the way, was a little bit different. The movement element was 52 frames, a double element, and the end 26 frames.

In painting there is the incredible struggle of the painter to arrive at the harmonic purpose. He has a certain space to fill. There was an incredible amount of energy expended to find the laws of harmony and of measure for a visual space. The painter is much superior to the film-maker in this one respect: when he feels that the earth should be a little bit bigger he can make it bigger: and if the face should be bigger in respect to the body, he makes it bigger. All this I could not do. My event had taken place. I had filmed it somehow and there was not very much harmony in that. So how did the visual harmony come about? I came upon static laws. I was interested in the movement and in the form, not in the details. I realized that I had to extract this sensation, that is, just these forms. I had to articulate these filmed elements more strongly through relation between black and white. How could I go about achieving this equal intensity and harmony which would make up my cinematographic building?

I always envisaged it like an architecture. The building is equally high at all times. So, I said, I have to do the following: I will make a sandwich which would be one second of light overall. I would get one second of the whole light, every square inch or millimeter receives one second of light and every square inch of the screen receives one second of darkness. Why is this so? Because the first second, one part of the screen receives white, in the second second the other part of the screen receives white, but in the whole time I practically fill the whole screen with equal amounts of light. Here I suddenly found harmony, measurement, measure; I had my pillars. I decided to have all the elements which I use in positive and negative. Of course, seeing the film the first time, or the second time, few people may be able to discern that. But they feel that there is harmony in light; they feel evenness. This film becomes then, suddenly, as indivisible as a Greek temple. I mean if a Greek temple has nine

 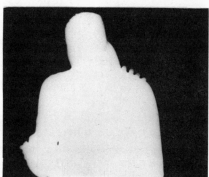

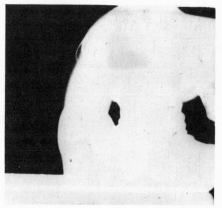 

Adebar

pillars here and nine pillars there, when you cut out one pillar of one side the temple falls down. You have to have nine pillars here and you have to have nine pillars on the other side. I wanted to make myself an ecstatic time, to take me out of the amorphousness of daily life.

I decided that I would have every one of the chosen elements meet every other one. I have elements one, two, three, four, and element five. I want to bring these five into an order which would not make one of the meetings heavier than the other. One meets two: two meets three, three meets four, and four meets five. Five meets one and we start again with one. One has already met two, so one meets three; three has met four; three meets five; five has already met one, so five meets two; two has already met three, so two meets four. See, I have my second strophe, or second stanza. My second repetition contains again all the elements, each just once, and each meeting with a different one than the first time. All these articulations come into being by the meeting of two elements. I established another law which says two positives never meet. When a positive appears I want it to be succeeded by a negative. Positive can never meet positive, negative can never meet negative.

In cinema one establishes such rules, regulatory rules, balancing rules, which you have in music when, for example, the musician wants the whole length of his piece divided in 4/4 measures. With this he establishes an overall structure within which he will then compose. All of these compositions will have an overall character like an overall smell, a taste, which is the four beat. This is what cinema has been lacking. Law and order is the basis of creating. In music, you establish your overall rhythmic structure: then you establish your character in pitch: you say it will be C major, which means the piece starts with C major and ends with C major. Composition is just a multitude of such rules and laws which are put there and which relate to each other in a way they have to relate, following again laws which are derived from the medium. We have the intervals also. We have no 3/4 tone, no 1/4 tone, we have either a whole tone or a half tone in between, and then after twelve half tones the scale repeats. Fantastic reduction! Reduction of all the possibilities in the sound world to these twelve intervals. The fifth is the basic interval. So people made music having fifths and then maybe a fourth, and maybe a second, and that was that. They ruled off everything else, and they functioned under this law until very late when the half tone emerged. This 1/2 tone is something very tasty and very specifically musical. There are many systems of composition which ruled out this harmony. If you used the half tone in some religious societies you would be killed.

What I want to achieve for cinema is a sensual sensitivity as refined as it is in music. Music for the eye. With this film, began my concept of making things which are repeated and repeated and repeated. You can see *Adebar* five hundred times and it will never resolve. There is no one movement, no one meeting, which would start to edge out, which would be alone. It is too balanced. You can live in a Greek temple or you can go there everyday and it will never look like a house.

2. *Schwechater*

I will again try to get you into *Schwechater* from both sides; from the side of the motive of the maker, and from the side of the outward pressure, which may mark the strongest contrast of all my work. This film was for me, the real discovery of the fact that cinema is not movies, which means, the discovery of the strong side of the medium, which lies in the fact that you can use these light impulses one by one.

Schwechater lasts one minute. The content is practically zero. Or it is a negative content. There are elements of people drinking beer. That content came out of the outward pressure. I was forced to film that. The content is not at all a source of energy in this film. Yet there is an incredible visual energy. In fact there's more visual energy in this minute than in any other filmic minute I have ever seen. Where does it come from? It comes from the fact that here I *broke* the old aesthetic, the old laws of cinema, which say that cinema is movement. There is never ever a movement on the screen. Cinema is nothing but a rapid slide projection. A slide projection which goes in a steady rhythm: twenty-four slides per second, you could call it.

When you see something on the screen which you accept as movement, it is an illusion, a magician's trick. It is very interesting that the second important user of this medium after Lumière and his cameramen, was George Méliès. He was a magician. Originally he used cinema as an addition to his magic shows. He started the whole tradition of film tricks. He invented most of the film tricks which are known today. When you see movement on the screen, it's a trick, a special case and not the original situation. The original situation, as you find it all over the world, in every cinema, and with every projector is *a rapid projection of still, non-moving images.* Only if you program the projector so that the form of these images which are projected are very similar, will movement appear. If you film me walking, then project it, you will also see me walking up and down here in the same way. Now compare the two things: me walking up and down, and the film image of me walking up and down. There is *only* a loss with the film. What do you lose? When you see me really walking up and down you have real colors. You see me plastically. You have the authentic feeling of presence. I mean, it's real. I'm there. The film walking up and down has false colors, has false proportions because the optics of the camera change things. The gross reproduction only slightly resembles me walking up and down. What have you *gained* against reality?

There is an old struggle: medium against reality. The reality is too complex and inarticulate, and it has been overcome. Our articulatory medium has to overcome the laws of reality. When you just film what is happening in time, and then project it, you have only a loss. Filmed reality is inferior to real reality. You can reproduce reality in a very faint way. Film is a lousy substitute. It's ugly. It would *not* be a medium of its own right which can speak its own language, if this were its function.

Where then is the powerful side of the medium? It is that in this medium I do *not* have to respect the movements as they occur in reality. I can start a movement when I want, and I can stop a movement when I want. Or, I can not have a movement at all. The strength of cinema is that I can give you visual information each 24th of a second. You will readily admit after seeing *Schwechater*, that you will never have seen anything like this in reality, to make the most modest claim.

Here we are again at a definition of all art. Art is not a faithful imitation of reality. Art is *about* reality. Isn't it articulation *about* reality?

After *Adebar* I had lost all my possibilities again. The film had been a scandal and was never shown anywhere. Then the factor of uniformedness in Austria came to my aid. I went to people seeking grants or things like that. I ended up with some recommendations to one of the most important, wealthy persons in Vienna, who owns a huge brewery, called Schwechater. Schwechater is a little town. The beer which they make there is called Schwechater. There I went. I made a very well-prepared speech about what I wanted to do in cinema, that cinema was an art of its own, and all that. Like these lectures. Not as articulate maybe, I had the same purpose. What I wanted was to make cinema. These people listened, and said, all right, all right. In fact, they had not listened. Then they said, "Go to my son, he has a publicity company and he will order a film. Then you can show your talent, and you'll see what we'll do." So, they ordered the beer film. They ordered two films, one about a beer, and one about a wash cleanser. In my despair, I said okay. Why don't I try to make a beer film and then I can do what I want.

It started when I went there to present my ideas. I worked out theories on publicity films. They never listened. Anyway, one of the ideas which evolved at that time, which I had even had before, involved the preciousness of time for publicity; because you pay for each second, or split-second. The more you pack into it the more economical it is. I elaborated on that. Our relations became more and more strained, because every project I presented they refused. I made the film, they saw rushes, and it was fixed. They cancelled one of the films. I had already worked on both films and spent the money I had received as an advance. So, I was moneyless. They said, "We cancelled one film, and the other one you have to re-do." I was completely out, because there was no money left to make a new film.

They found out that I liked to stay up at night, that I didn't get up early; so, they made an appointment with me every day at 7:00 in the morning. They started a real brainwashing system. There were always three of them and I had to sit in front of them. I said something, or one asked me something, I answered him, and then the others spoke. It was incredible. I became sick, quite sick, and I was completely down. In the end I started to do what they suggested. It was the only way to get out. I just wanted to get out of this torture system.

They said, "We have here a lady, she was Miss Bosom last year. We want you to have her in your film." I said okay. They had hundreds of photos of all their girlfriends, of course, and they had to give them parts. Then they came up with ideas, such as, "Why don't we rent the most expensive restaurant in Vienna, give them champagne coolers with the beer in them. That would make it more fashionable. Then, maybe they can say, 'Oh, Schwechater.'" I said okay, very good. Then, they became suspicious, and they asked, "Why do you suddenly agree so much? You see, this will be artistic. You want to be an Avant-Gardist as you said, and this will be a new thing. We want to send it abroad." So, I said, "Let's be honest. Nothing is mine anymore. I'll do what you say, it's your thing, and I just want to get out." So they said, "Oh, oh, no, you are a young talent and we want to help you. You just have to learn, you have to adjust. I, myself, was a lawyer. But now . . . I work for this publicity agency and I can't afford French lessons for my children. You have to learn that's what life is." So, I got these lessons. So, they said, "Off you go. You go home, have new ideas, then you come back with your new ideas. We'll have patience." So I went home, and I came back, and the same thing happened again. They said, "Shouldn't we have them say, 'Cheers!'" I said yes. Then they said, "Schwec . . ., this is your idea." Then I said yes, *my idea!* I was really crushed. Not only had I to accept whatever shit they were imposing on me, I also had to declare that that was what I wanted. That that was my artistic idea, and this was what my talent dictated to me.

They rented the most expensive restaurant in Vienna. They hired twenty-five models, and they had huge trays with food and drinks. I was supposed to film it. Now, at that time, I was really without enough money to rent a camera. A friend of mine had found an old scientific camera on the roof of the university, from the twenties. It weighed about one hundred pounds, or more. It was very big, and had no viewer. We could not see through it. It only functioned with a magazine, a very heavy magazine, which nobody knew how to fill. I took the magazine, found out how to thread the film. (I had to spend the whole night in darkness, of course.) I bought one box of film, that's all I could still afford. Furthermore, see, my order was for a color film. But, I had no money for color anymore, so I bought a black and white film. I had sixty meters, black and white film, which is exactly two minutes worth of shooting time.

With every movement I made, every thought, there was defeat. But I still wanted to win. I still wanted to beat them. Of course you can imagine the aggression I had, against a whole civilization in which I lived anyway. But I believed in my cinema. I had a hunch that I would do it. The showdown came when I had to film this stuff. My friend was ready to act as my assistant. I dressed in a black suit, the only one I had. It was like a funeral, wedding, or something. It was a ceremonial suit. My friend came with this old car, and he brought the loaded camera. I walked through the town with my black suit. When I arrived there, there were twenty-four models waiting. There was the special envoy of the publicity agency, who had to make sure that I did film what they wanted. I had beer casks. So I put these beer casks there, and I put the camera on them symbolically: beer film—camera on the beer. The publicity man said, "Well, how about now having a little beer poured." I said "Okay, let's do it." The waiter came and poured beer.

It was a hand-cranked camera, of course, and had several speeds because it was made for scientific purposes. You could go at two frames a second with one gear, or you would stick it into another gear and it would go up to three hundred frames, and make a ZZZZZZ. It also had a speedometer where you could read how fast it was going. It was a very interesting instrument. I started cranking, and this man came and said, "Oh, what is this camera?" I said, "This is a special camera only for your film; I have to control the speed so exactly that I have a speedometer as you can see." The speedometer was going, so he was very pleased with this thing. Then they directed all that was to go on, and I was always cranking. I ran out of film, of course, after two minutes, we worked the whole day, and I was always cranking. They were bringing things out and drinking beer. It was, in a way, somewhat to my liking. Over the years the funny effect has, of course, grown. At the time it wasn't so funny. It was mad: they had all the power, and I was really dancing on a tightrope. I did it *regardless* of what would happen. I became very hungry, and there were all these trays with food. But I could not find an excuse to get some of it, because it was decoration. Then, it occurred to me that I could order some drinks by pretending that the models were not in the right mood.

Anyway, the day ended and everybody went home very content. And I had a roll of film. I developed it, and then I saw this incredible mess. It was absolutely nothing. I said, I will make the greatest film ever made. Now let's get back to the formal side. Since childhood I desired visual speed. In my first film there is a sequence of very short shots where I attempt to speed. I cannot account for this wish. But, I was dreaming of works of art which I could make, which would last half a second, or a second, like lightning signals. I wanted to make a film with the most visual speed. What I really wanted to make at this time, and what I also asked the beer people at the beginning to pay for, were nature studies. At the time my

Schwechater

model was running water. It was not running water as the painter
sees it. When you go to a little brook and sit down and you look in
front of yourself, you see a certain field of water. This is something
which has been done perhaps since mankind has existed. The shep-
herds do it; they sit and they look, or the lovers do it. There is this
fascination which comes from the incredible variation which is in
these forms.

When you watch, you see the bubbles, little beams of light, and
little waves; and it changes, and changes, and seemingly it never
comes back. Then, in this variation, you dream. Then you start to
dream up something which is helped by this form. A similiar model
is the changing of clouds in the sky. Here cloud-dreaming occurs. I
see a big horse, then it becomes a tree, then a castle. Another model
would be fire. When you look in the fire, it repeats. Or wind in a
tree. The leaves always change, and the branches change. This is
what I wanted to bring into my film. I wanted to make a film which
would act like such a structure.

A brook is *exactly* ruled. When suddenly a bubble appears and
then makes its way, what factors are involved? One is the general
speed of water. But is this speed always the same? It is not the
same. The speed of water is determined by the input of other sources
from other brooks. When there is more water there is more speed.
Why does the bubble not move straight down? Before the water
comes here it is influenced in many ways from the rivulet on the
bottom which comes to form the bubble. Next is wind. The wind
comes always steadily from one side. The wind comes, in different
speeds, and in different directions. It changes its direction. Why so?
Because for the formation of the wind, again, there are rules which
form the wind.

✿   ✿   ✿

I wanted to make such a film, which has not one of the simple
forms which can be composed. I wanted to make something which
looks like burning fire, or changing clouds, (which practically depicts the way the universe is functioning) out of these two minutes
of stupid, beer-drinking material. I established predominate rules
which override each other. I had as my basic material a two minute
film. Then I broke it up into several elements. One minute was the
length which they wanted. It is exactly 1,440 frames. There are two
sounds, a high sound and a low sound. On the sound-track you see
two kinds of exactly regular waves, sine waves.

The overriding rule is alternation of image and non-image: one
black frame, one frame image; two black frames, two frames image;
four black frames four frames image, etc.; one-one, two-two, four-
four, eight-eight, sixteen-sixteen, thirty-two-thirty-two, etc. When
you have thirty-two blacks, there is rather a resting point.

Let me say some words on how the image functions. From the
two minutes of material I took some image elements. For example,

one is a close-up of the bottle pouring beer. This element lasts sixteen frames. I had a negative of this one element. Then I made a positive. I printed this positive many many times to get enough repetitions of the sixteen frames to cover the whole 1,440 frames. One length of the film was a repetition of this one element. Then I had another, slower element, when a lady would start to drink beer. It is over fifty frames long.

All the elements exist in formal groups and they exist in the following way: in the mind, and also of first recorded reality [writes on the blackboard], exist all these other elements. I had twelve layers of different loops all of 1,440 frames. The actual film would receive frames from each of these layers according to the rules imposed. Whenever I decided that the actual film to have an image of, let's say, layer A, this frame would have to have the exact position which it would have from the repetition of the sixteen frames. This system guaranteed that all rhythms of these various elements are going on undisturbed throughout the whole film. When, at the end of the film, the bottle appears, it is exactly a repetition of this movement which goes on all over the film. When you have at frame 1,320 an image of the layer A you can figure out exactly which one it is. These visual rhythms are practically interspersed with each other. They are all imposed on your mind.

I used red, because the color of the beer is red. Schwechater is that color. The other reason was that I had been commissioned to make a color film, so I had to get some color into it.

3. *Arnulf Rainer*

After *Schwechater* had been shot I was totally wiped out. I really felt nothing at the time, and had only a few friends, one of which was Arnulf Rainer. He's a painter, and was quite rich at that time. In fact he always seemed to have a little more money than everyone else. I wanted to make a film about him, and he agreed to pay for everything if it should be in color, and reveal him doing his work. So I decided to make a film for him. I went out and bought the color film and shot the footage. I think that's about all of the outside story that I can give you.

I looked at the footage I had made of Arnulf Rainer, which was a bit like *Schwechater* and . . . about the same time in Brussels I had seen Brakhage's *Anticipation of the Night* and noticed the similarities. I had also shown my films there and Stan had seen them. This was our first contact; it was also the first contact I had had with American independent films. I was very impressed with what Stan did with his camera . . . so the movie I subsequently made of Rainer was inspired by Stan's handling of the camera, but I didn't really like the film and didn't want to do anything with it. I couldn't see what I should do . . . you see, at times I was completely isolated and extremely aggressive. I wanted to fight for my medium to the utmost, and I wanted to become the strongest. I wanted to be not less than Michelangelo; so in order to meet people on their level you must be very careful. It's like boxing against the world champion; you cannot afford to give even a little bit of fighting power away. When I looked at these images and I saw the paintings of Goya, of Rembrandt, of Vermeer, I said that I had to stand up against them.

I wanted to put cinema where it can stand with every musician and every painter. I wanted to be able to count the cinema as a force which competes with these arts. Also, I wanted to get to the absolute basis of my medium, and to handle it as purely as was possible.

When languages came about, before you had the word "red", you had the word "rose", that is, you had things that contained red. To understand the word "red" is a very analytical achievement—it's already dividing things and taking components of the whole, and this is a very difficult thing to do. I tried to do this with cinema. Cinema is feeling in time, of rhythmic and harmonic being. Cinema can use the simple components of light and sound, and for the first time cinema can blend pure sound with light in time. It is possible to handle both carefully and get a result. It is all done by the machine.

What is the wish people have for visual harmony? What is this thing with harmony and pleasure anyway? In our classic music you have those established intervals—the 5th, 4th, 2nd, and 3rd, and you have the octave. Certain of these intervals give you a feeling of harmony. When I say harmony, you probably think of it in the sense of the normal everyday language. For example, the 5th gives you a feeling of purity and beauty, more so than say the 2nd or the minor 2nd. Why is that so? It's very easy, very discernible. The incredible thing is that our music and architecture operate out of the same principles of harmony, which is the Pythagorean harmony. When you take the string and hang it between two points, you get one sound. When you divide this string in half—what do you get? You get a sound that is exactly one octave higher than the first note. This is the point where architecture, painting, geometry, and music come together—eye and ear come together at the same point, the octave. If you would double this string relationship, that is an octave deeper. To go with this when you divide the distance of a chord 2 to 3, you get a 5th, 3 to 4 would be a 4th, 15 to 16 would be a 2nd which tells you something about a 2nd—it is a grinding relationship. Now when you go into a building by Palladio, the ground space would be 5 parts long, 3 parts wide and 2 parts high, which would give you a 2 to 3 to 5 relationship. When you would look at a wall, you would have a 2 to 3 relationship—very musical and very harmonic.

Now, of course, you can go further and say such relationships are harmonic to human beings, but there analysis stops because you don't know why. It's analogous to the structure of the universe. We are built symmetrically as an animal—nose, mouth, eyes, ears . . . but why it is really good for us, no one knows.

Just as we have to accept that we are born, live, die, eat, and sleep, we have to accept the possibilities of human expression and all the activities of human thought linked to this system.

Now we come back to my film. The cinematographic machine allows me to introduce this harmonic measurement in time and light. I can give you a visual signal which lasts half time, double time, fourth, third, as I choose. Cinema allows me to introduce exact measurement in time. Cinema can sense the other previous mediums and add a new achievement—to produce happiness, harmony, and ecstasy. Let me talk again about another thing cinema gives: it allows me to make a contemporaneous event for both senses, eyes and ears. I can exactly place these events up to 24 times per second. A meeting of light and sound, thunder and lightning, if you like. Comparing cinema with nature, that is, my light and sound event with the real thing, cinema is pale. There are technical problems: the loudest we can get is just painful; the image appears not nice enough. So cinema compared with real lightning and thunder is just ridiculous, but I can do it faster, make thunder and lightning 24 times a second. I can place it in time exactly where I want to, up to a 24th of a second. I can give you a visual signal that lasts exactly half time, double time, of anything you want, as I choose. I can have lightning with or without sound. The greatness of cinema is not that you can repeat natural light with natural sound, but that you can separate it. In nature no lightning can occur without thunder, no thunder without lightning, but I can separate it.

The motive for the sync event between light and sound is as old as mankind. In *Unsere Afrikareise* it was the prime method of analyzing nature. We know its wholenesses. We know the lion and what consequences it has for us. And how does the lion exist? It exists by sync events. When the lion attacks he roars, or when you hear him coming, each step he takes makes a sound. Sound and image sync events always link up in nature, and these clusters of sound and image make up the outside world. We are very used to these things. Art is always imitating systems in the universe, and people have tried to create sync events out of sound and image. One of the main arts is dance. One establishes a beat 1-2-3, and then one jumps up and down. That is one of the most beautiful of the ancient dances; the drummer drums, and, given the rhythm, people jump up and down. Of course you can start evolving and make it more complex.

The nature of man is to meet exactly visual and acoustical rhythms. You have a beat or a melody, and the dance meets the melody. When a dancer is out of rhythm, immediately everyone cringes, because not meeting step with sound is the worst thing a dancer can do. So this establishment of sync events, one of the oldest wishes of mankind, fantastically becomes possible for the first time in cinema. In the laws of nature if I want to get a dancer from here to there, I have to get the dancer to walk, run, or jump over there, but there is an in between which I can never get out. In cinema he can be here, and in the next 24th of a second he can be there. I am not dependent on the natural flow of events in cinema. All these ancient attempts at establishing sync events are very clumsy.

There is one fantastic adventure which I had in Africa. I came into this stone age village, and the people there were just able to make their spear heads, a very old civilization. They were having a feast, preparing a building for an ecstasy which would last all night. The main element there was sync events—dancing, singing, stomping, all sync events. Then it became evening, and I noticed all attention was focused on the open plain. There was nothing to see but the people gathered to watch the plain and the horizon. There were no drummers up to that time, but then suddenly the drummers came and the excitement started to grow. Then the sun started to set, very fast, you know the closer you come to the equator the faster the sun sets. The more the sun neared the horizon the more the tension grew. Then exactly when the sun reached the horizon the chief made one bang on his drum. I was moved to tears because I saw my own motive right there, as old as mankind. What I wanted to do with sound and light, they did too. This was a fantastic, beautiful sound sync event. Against them I was ridiculous with this thing here. This comparison of their sync event and mine exactly describes the situation of our civilization. Much less sensual substance and beauty, more speed. They had one day. I had every 24th of a second. That doesn't make mine better, but it's faster. It may be that the interior reality is more important. When you are not used to the sun and the drum, you may accept my little sync event as sufficient to live with.

Now to come to ecstasy, which comes from the Greek, and it means being situated out of it, and it's a means to beat the laws of nature, not to be slaves of nature. It means to get out of the prison of nature—in English you have this great expression "to serve time" in prison, and that really is what normal life is—you serve time. This cycle of life, being born, youth, age which is so idealized by so many civilizations and philosophers, is rejected by some, and I am one of them. I don't want to die, but I have to. I don't want to age either, but I must serve under it. There is a possibility to get out of all of it, even if it is just for my interior reality. I want to cease to be the noble beast obeying the laws of nature. I want out, I want other laws, I want ecstasy. There have been many ways to achieve ecstasy; subtle ways, not so subtle ways; consequential, not so consequential ways. The dance ecstasy, the drinking ecstasies, the drug ecstasies, the art ecstasies; then of course the cooler ecstasies—the philosophical, the religious, and the sport ecstasies. There are innumerable ones. With this film I was after the cinematographic ecstasy.

Let me emphasize that I use the word primitive or old with nothing but envy. I have given you a description of stone age ecstasy that needs no explanation. They ate and drank until they were completely exhausted, which was all provided for in their civilization.

Now, how will one get ecstasy in the cinema? Well, what I can do in the cinema is to make a rhythmic building between light and sound which is complex, exact, fast and has a certain strength. Also, it must have exact measure, harmony and beat. That is one of the possibilities of cinema.

＊　　＊　　＊

Arnulf Rainer consisted of four strips—one composed of completely transparent film leader, then a strip of completely black film, and then two strips of magnetic sound, one completely empty, no signal, and the other continuous sound. The continuous sound is called white sound and it consists of all oscillations . . . I mean all frequencies, that is 10, 20, 30, 20,000 or whatever comes out of the speaker. It is in a way parallel to white light; it is the acoustic equivalent of the color band of white light. It is in a way two things which correspond to each other. So I had these four strips, and like the tailor with the scissors, I made the film. No camera, no editing tables, just right into a core. This core was made after two years of preliminary work, finding out what I was to do. When I talked about music, I said that it was not that the 12 octaves were always there and always played. Sometimes the 5th and 4th come in more often, out of rule. The rules are there; you find them; you do not decree them. The system of feeling harmony in a 2nd to 3rd, or 3rd to 4th is there, it's not decreed. So I found during the making of this film certain laws, laws of nature that were there. I did not just do something. There was a sensual elaboration of the material, which means I made some elements, made loops of these elements, then looked at them, tasted them. When you have black-white-black-white and you make a loop of it, that is an unforgettable taste. That is the strongest of elements. Then you could have 3 black-3 white, or 2 black-2 white, or 1 black-2 white, 1 black-2 white, a wave like that. I cannot go into that too much, but there are other rules like a positive-negative form in time, time and light, which, if you know all about positive and negative in a black and white image, you have the possibility of everything black, or vice-versa.

With this film I have done something which will survive the whole film history because it is repeatable by anyone. It is written down in a script, it is beyond decay. It can be made exactly after my script without any faults. Someday I will put the script in stone, granite, then it will last 200,000 years, if it is not destroyed. You see the normal age of black & white film is 50 years. Now it is only 15 years, since the chemicals and materials are much worse than they were in 1905. A color film rots in about 10 years and then the colors fade and decay. In the entire world there is no way to preserve a color film. But *Arnulf Rainer* will last forever.

STEPHEN KOCH:

Andy Warhol's Silence

Warhol has passed through a series of phases as a film-maker, and the latest—if it is indeed *his* phase—is still running strong. It is the epoch of Warhol's "success" as a film-maker, success that accumulates grosses bankers listen to, that rates listings in *Variety*, that lights up Warhol's name on marquees across the land. But the success is not Warhol's; the present laughing era of commercial sex farces like *Flesh*, *Trash*, *Women in Revolt*, *Amour*, and *Heat* has been pulled together almost entirely by his collaborator, Paul Morrissey—their factual director, their creator, their energy. And—though Morrissey is a man who despises the ego that lives on risk, a true businessman—their success has increasingly made the disciple feel free to slip out from behind the shield of the more famous name and let the world learn the simple facts about his real role. These are the "Warhol" films most moviegoers have seen, vaguely knowing that they are not "really" Warhol films. A typical Warhol dilemma, that word "really." One can just hear the word crawling from the mouths of the Factory denizens: she didn't *really* say *that*, we didn't *really* do *that*, they don't *really* believe *that*. And so, *Heat* isn't *really* a Warhol film— they're puttin' you *on*. The Vivaesque whine announcing these small revelations against the real resonates in one's ears; the boredom of it, *who* could tell the truth? People put down their three dollars and file into Cinema II, vaguely sensing that this isn't the *real* thing. Yet the coy aggression in that offense has no sting. They also vaguely sense that the real thing—Warhol's own films—are unattractive, painful, esoteric, unwatchable: They have a reputation surrounded by rumors of joyless perversity and killing tedium. What a relief! These movies are fun.

All of them were made after Valerie Solanis tried to murder him. And the brash, hyped, slick, yuk-it-up sensibility most of them purvey saved him from a dilemma in which he had been splashing around in the months just before. Warhol had begun to "experiment"—experiment very unsuccessfully—with new (to him) narrative forms, with pornography, with nudity in films such as *Nude Restaurant, Lonesome Cowboys,* and *Blue Movie,* a phase which had begun in early 1967, immediately after he made *The Chelsea Girls.* He was no longer painting, Viva and Joe Dallesandro had become the central superstars, the films were being made exclusively in color. Prior to that, in phase two, there were the black-and-white sound films, the portrait films, the works scripted by Ronald Tavel, and the epoch of the first superstars: a period which begins in 1964 with Warhol's first sound film, *Harlot,* and ends with *The Chelsea Girls* in 1966.

But the first age was silent. Marked by the films that were later most indelibly associated with everything outrageous in the Warhol name. *Eat*—forty-five minutes of a man nibbling a mushroom. *Kiss*—one close-up after another of people kissing. And then *Sleep.* The infamous *Sleep.* Dear God in heaven, six hours of some guy asleep with a towel draped across his groin. *Six hours!* And at last the triumph, put-on of put-ons, the final delight of all *avant-garde* delights. Eight uninterrupted hours of the Empire State Building. *Eight Hours of the Empire State Building!*

These are the films—I myself think they're among Warhol's most brilliantly successful and important—that people still associate with Warhol so strongly that they are surprised to discover that *Trash* and *Women in Revolt* are so different. When the silents were made, they were accompanied by a brush fire of word-of-mouth report, throughout New York. But that word-of-mouth was sufficient unto itself. They seemed plainly films to be talked about. True, since people were talking about them, they must, for some obscure reason, have some obscure value. But it was *very* obscure. Nobody had to go.

Unfortunately, another case of Warhol's genius for publicity obscuring his work. He is pegged in the public's mind as the maker of the Campbell's Soup cans, but how much more immediately exciting, more swiftly and disturbingly ingratiating, are the complex configurations of the grieving Jacqueline Kennedy, the bizarre disaster series, the self-portraits, the series—portraits of some horrible celebrity—made from the electric chair. It often seems that the least interesting aspect of Warhol's theatrical gift was exercised in the Dada gestures that made him so famous. Likewise, the Dada gesture, the put-on, in these early works has obscured their sumptuous beauty.

❖   ❖   ❖

1963 was a year of enormous activity, not only for Warhol, but for the entire independent film movement in New York. Much of it centered on the Film-Makers' Cinematheque then located at the Gramercy Arts Theater on 27th Street, as well as at the Film-Makers' Co-Operative at 414 Park Avenue South. Impromptu screenings had begun to take place each night at the Co-Operative, not so much of completed work but of rushes just back from the lab. As the screenings began to be known, an audience developed, made up mainly of film-makers and their friends, stars of the films, friends of friends. At some point, Andy Warhol became an inconspicuous member of this select audience, slipping in every night to watch the work-in-progress of the American Independent Film. Jonas Mekas remembers that, early in 1963, somebody came up to him after one such screening to say, "Pretty soon Andy is going to start making films. He's sitting here every night, he's seeing all these films, I think he's going to make his own." The imperturbable Mekas, utterly absorbed as ever in his quadruple role as film-poet, philosopher, Diaghilev, and one-man ambience, had somehow never noticed the famous man with the silver hair quietly arriving before each screening.

"Andy? Who's Andy? Which one is Andy?"

Who's *Andy?* Even then, the question must have provoked a double take. But, sure enough, Warhol shortly began to come in with his films—segments of *Kiss*, which Mekas promptly began to screen "as a serial," a new segment each week.

The response was immediate, and, by November of 1963—the month *Eat* was made—Warhol was, so far as Mekas was concerned, a major film-maker whose every new work was to be anticipated with excitement. *Sleep* and *Kiss* were given their public screenings and the controversy had begun, especially over the six-hour marathon of the former. At the second screening of *Sleep* at the Cinematheque, Warhol himself was present. Mekas greeted him with a rope, led him to a seat in the second row from the back, and tied him down. Somewhere halfway through the film, Mekas decided to check that seat and see if the master had lingered with his disciples. "I found the rope," he recalls.

Actually, Warhol had begun to make *Sleep* before *Kiss*, even though the segments of *Kiss* were the first screened. People who have never seen *Sleep* (in other words, almost everybody) are sometimes under the impression that Warhol's notoriously immobile camera remains rigidly fixed for the full six hours, a mere mindless sentry perpetually at attention, gazing at a sleeping man. As a matter of fact, if not properly speaking edited, *Sleep* was assembled and constructed from several different shots of the somnolent nude. There were numerous shooting sessions; over a period of several weeks, the *avant-garde* poet John Giorno (who did the sleeping) returned repeatedly to slip off his clothes and resume his easeful task on the couch.

A man who is familiar with the corpus of *avant-garde* film as few critics have ever been, P. Adams Sitney, describes the particular visual effects of *Sleep* in his monumental scholarly study, *Visionary Film:*

[Warhol] made famous the fixed frame in *Sleep,* in which half a dozen shots are seen for over six hours. In order to attain that elongation he used both loopprinting of whole one hundred foot takes

(2¾ minutes) and, in the end, the freezing of a still image of the sleeper's head. The freeze process emphasizes the grain and flattens the image precisely as rephotography off the screen does.

But the fundamental way of using film in *Sleep* is very much the same in *Kiss, Eat, The Thirteen Most Beautiful Women,* and innumerable other silent films. A motorized Bolex would be set up, loaded with approximately three-minute, one-hundred-foot magazines. Shooting consisted simply in turning on a key lamp, starting the camera, and letting the magazine run out. There was never a camera movement and only a very occasional zoom (I can think of precisely one in *Kiss;* two or three perhaps in *Sleep*). Editing consisted of gluing together each 100-foot take on leader, invariably leaving in the weakening and whitening emulsion and the perforated tags at the end of the roll. It was in this way that the "serial" of *Kiss* (a new segment shown every week at the Cinematheque as a short subject, like *Merrie Melodies*) was transformed into a "feature." And it is how the portraits in *The Thirteen Most Beautiful Women, The Thirteen Most Beautiful Boys,* and *Fifty Fantastics and Fifty Personalities* were strung together.

The technique with the refinements Sitney mentions is the same in *Sleep,* but the effect of *Sleep* is slightly different. With each new episode-magazine, *Kiss* and the portrait films introduce new "stars"; *Sleep* simply changes its angle on the same subject. More than a series, it is a serial construction. In a tape recording made in 1965, Warhol recalled that "it started with somebody sleeping and it just got longer and longer and longer. Actually, I did shoot all the hours of the movie, but I faked [faked?] the final film to get a better design." With each new cartridge of *Sleep,* Warhol chose a new camera position: a close-up of the breathing abdomen, a long shot taken laterally from the knee (the extended body swimming back into deep space), a near close-up of the face, slowly withdrawing in a very slow zoom from above, and the like. When the film was assembled, each take was used twice and made part of a cinematic structure conceived, as Warhol puts it, "for design."

Each of the several shots in *Sleep* is an arresting example of Warhol's most indelible pictorial style, and assembled together they invest the work with an architectural richness not found elsewhere in his films. *Sleep* is a serial composition in the tradition of Duchamp —a tradition that consolidates its quiet, implosive strengths by numbing itself in paradoxes of movement and stillness. That numbness is central to his art. One can seek to understand movement *as* stillness, stillness *as* movement. It was Duchamp's innovation to level a critique against virtually all art by shaming it as the dupe, the fool, of this paradox. Art is usually attacked from the perspective of reality, as the betrayer and corrupter of the sense of the real. But Duchamp's famous polemic (exercising itself with its mute, mocking economy across far more of the intellectual and artistic terrain than

I could possibly sketch here) was hardly mounted from outside art in the name of the full-blooded and actual. On the contrary. Duchamp's mockery speaks from within the very paradoxes he wishes to challenge, from within a very perverse, extraordinarily indulgent engagement with them. Above all, the whole polemic seems dominated by a wry, tightly controlled, but very deep thirst for silence. For stillness. The polemic is no crusade; it is the exercise of yearning need. The joke turns out to be not a critique but a means of dealing with the problem of being alive; the rejection of "art" no disburdening, but a means of enlisting that same "art" as a prime device for dealing with the unmanageable. The ethic of cool is born, but cool's critique of art's inadequacies, far from being dismissive, seeks to expand art—with a sneer, if necessary—to the stability and usefulness of an ethic. Nothing so uncool, of course, as a religion of the aesthetic. But some means must be found to protect the poor, battered, overwhelmed perceptions from the inchoate, violent surrounding ocean of Fact and interaction, from the demanding and merciless Real. Some means must be found for protecting the existential solitude and quiet of the self caught in the despairing trap of simultaneously desiring absolute action and absolute stillness. A means, that is, other than suicide or murder.

The simultaneously indulged and mocked paradox of stillness and motion so essential to Duchamp's early career (I'd also argue, essentially the metaphoric paradigm for all of it) has this peculiarity from whatever perspective it is approached, and, in the end, invariably favors stillness. In the fusion of this immaculate conception, stillness is the dominant gene, motion recessive. A passive force invariably finally controls the work and our perception of it. "An explosion in a shingle factory," some pundit called *Nude Descending a Staircase,* and the insult has remained in the vocabulary as an ironic image. But the image misleads—the pundit could not have really *seen* the picture—because it speaks of an explosive energy. No. The energy of *Nude Descending a Staircase,* like a filmed explosion run in reverse, implodes toward stillness and an original order, not that of the nude's stillness, but that of the surface of the canvas itself. Duchamp's dissociative paradox of movement and stillness invariably—though always metaphorically—moves toward *stasis*—toward hypostasis, to be precise. And that hypostasis speaks to the sensibility of our time—both through Duchamp, and through his most celebrated living inheritor—in a manner that is not marginal, but central to this book.

The *Nude Descending a Staircase* is a serial meditation on movement, conjugated and arrayed as quietude within the abstracted irreality of paint. *Sleep,* on the other hand, is a serial meditation on stillness, run through its variations and protracted within the irreal, yet temporal and concrete medium of film. Thinking of the *Nude,* I look for descriptive language, and the word "retinal"—hardly original, to be sure—leaps to mind. The painting recalls the crisis on the surface of the eye provoked by a strobe light, recalls the way the strobe shatters time's visual continuity and pins the autonomous action of the eye under an overmastering disjunction. Yet, no, the recollection misleads. The *Nude* is still. We look at it in the guarded, discreet silence of a museum. It does not move. The eye is not overwhelmed; it chooses its involvement in the painting as one might pick up a candy. And, though the *Nude* passes through space, her passage—surely she is female—is, through the dissociative analysis of that space, subdued within the peculiar timeless time that the surface of painting invariably presents.

Now, the proper medium of film is that same real time that Duchamp reduces to the condition of a surface. In *Sleep*, Warhol inverts the Duchampian paradox into a moving picture. Throughout, time remains itself, steadily flowing past at the speed of the clock, in the rhythm of the breath, of the heartbeat. And yet, every movement made by Warhol's nude carries us deeper into his accentuated meditation on the stillness of sleep.

Turning on a single paradox, both works share a single theme; it is the dissociation of time in the name of a hypostatized quietude. The cocktail party's "Jesus God! Six hours!" is the clue to the film's innovation, its absolutely trenchant redefinition of what filmic time is and can be. For it is exactly in the arena of time—of speed, if you will—that *Sleep* is so radical. The film entirely modifies the very nature of film viewing. Obviously, very few people are able to sit through all the film and give it the kind of attention ordinarily given to a movie. At the early screenings, audiences came forewarned, intending to make an evening of it. People would chat during the screening, leave for a hamburger and return, greet friends and talk over old times. All the while, the film serenely devolved up there on the screen of the Film-Makers' Cinematheque. The Sleeper breathed, stirred sometimes on the couch.

One can imagine that hall of 1963. It is small and narrow. Though the tickets have been sold out, there are people in only half the seats. In the lobby, clusters of people stand chatting, smoking, somebody abstractedly tearing the rim of a paper take-out coffee cup he's using as an ashtray. A man and a woman step to the door of the screening room and stand there a few minutes staring. Then they return for more conversation. Somebody douses a cigarette, cracks a joke, and returns to his seat in the hall. He will be there for another half-an-hour. People come and go.

The film remains on the screen always. Its time is utterly dissociated from that of the audience: The Image glows up there, stately and independent. Its cinematic isolation on the screen exerts a bizarre fascination beyond its immediate pictorial allure. Even if one only glances at the image from time to time, it plunges one into a cinematic profundity; in a single stroke, that image effects a complete transformation of all the temporal modes ordinarily associated with looking at a movie. The knot of attention is untied, and its strands are laid out before us anew. We've been told that film records literal time; but the literal time of *Sleep* is undermined, rendered hallucinatory and other, by the use of silent speed (all Warhol's silents were shot at 24 frames per second, but they should be projected at 16 frames per second; the effect is an unchanging but barely perceptible slow motion). And yet as the minutes tick on, the work seems to insist upon its hallucinated literal time as few other films ever do. Meanwhile, the audience's participation in the image is never allowed to fall into the slot of that *other* temporal reality—that acceleration and deceleration of the audience's temporal sense created by narrative fantasy or conventionally edited structure, as in almost any other film one can think of.

Warhol is perhaps the first film-maker ever to concede that his audience might not wish to see every minute of his work. At the very least, he is the first to be content with that disinterest, to use it. *Sleep* has its own temporal pace, of course, and a very different one from our own. But we slip in and out of that time at will. It is a meditative time, erotic, almost necrophilic, while ours is—well, our time is our own, and perhaps the clock's. The movement—and it is our *own* movement—from one temporal realm to the other is among the major sources of interest, and incident, in this masterpiece of quiescence. It is the meditative pleasures of dissociation that the film proposes to us. Its time and ours are not melded but irresolvably contrasted, and the operation of that contrast from minute to minute gives the film its life.

But there is a final trope in that contrast that is the film's stroke of genius: its subject, *Sleep*. What is sleep, after all, but the metabolic transformation of the entire experience of time, our nightly release from the clock's prison, filled and flashing with the dreaming motions of the mind and yet an immobility, a quietude in which seconds and hours are confounded. *That* is what we gaze at so voyeuristically in *Sleep*, bound to the unchanging clock of the camera's mechanical eye.

The film is obsessed with the quiescence of the flesh. The lovingly voyeuristic camera meditates on that quiescence, creating, by its very attention, a series of perceptual paradoxes within the realm of stillness. I have described the opening frames in another chapter, but I can't refrain from speaking of them again. The screen is bright with a brilliant, almost blistering light playing over the sleeper's moving, breathing abdomen. The effect is a kind of fleshly abstraction; one senses life before grasping what is being seen. Pictorially, the shots are often close to being abstractions on the body, and under the haunting slowness of silent speed and the stillness of the body, they convey the sense of the Person divested of anything but the essentials of life itself. In sleep, as in the orgasm, the personality veers toward the impersonality of a universally shared experience. The life one sees in this film is abstraction on the vitalism of the personality.

That abstraction is erotic. It may be that all sexual absorption has some of this abstract element within it. Certainly, a familiar paradox of sexual excitement is the union of very particular sensations with a universalizing instinct: The way this woman, this man I'm touching becomes somehow all women, all men. And the concentrated intensity of particular sexual acts, like the kiss, is a kind of abstraction as its pleasure invades the sensibility and the details of personhood are replaced by sexual openness. And then, of course, there is the orgasm itself.

But the orgasm is an event.

✻   ✻   ✻

Time is, of all modes of existence, the most obsequious of the imagination.—*Samuel Johnson*

I know what you mean by saying that Warhol's central metaphor is voyeurism, and it was an inescapable conclusion on my part, just from watching him watch the films, like the twenty-four hour film *Couch,* which is just twenty-four hours of people coming in and having sex in all different ways on this couch. He would sit and watch it with such contentment that I felt I was in the presence of a Buddhist who had achieved the desired transcendent state. Total satisfaction and total calm. Though in his case it struck me as being a necrophilia too; because what he was trying to move toward in the films was a stillness.—*Ronald Tavel,* in conversation.

Sex is always just on the verge of any Warhol film, one can feel it; but his early silent films are not really sexual in the way his later films became, all shimmering with crevices and organs and groins. (*Couch,* of 1965, is a conspicuous pornographic exception.) But the early works are erotic in a less obvious sense. They are the creations of a profoundly voyeuristic mind.

Now, the voyeur is a strange kind of person. *He is a man who absents himself.* He is a man who keeps his distance; and remoteness from the sexual scene is integral to his excitement. His passion and patience stand in a murderous equipoise. He is one who waits, waits with fanatical scrutiny, not missing the smallest detail. He is not a sentry, because he attempts to hide himself rather than give an alarm. Instead, his is a vigil in which the impulse to conceal himself becomes more and more intense as more and more is revealed. And, by thus extinguishing himself in his own excitement, the voyeur achieves a profoundly effaced impersonality, perhaps that impersonality that tends to dominate all compulsiveness. In the voyeuristic situation, his personality becomes radically diminished; the man who cracks jokes in the office and likes malted milks becomes merely someone watching, and all the energy of his personality is for a time diverted into that watchful persona. Since his is a sexuality in which nothing is shared, the voyeur's desire is peculiarly abstract—it is abstracted, usually faintly pornographic desire—and the woman or man is only all women or men, while the voyeur himself is merely

One Who Sees. And, by defining himself as someone whose presence must remain unknown, as one who is not there—*there* at that point across the distance where all interest resides—his depersonalization is complete.

Viewed psychoanalytically, the voyeur might seem to be somebody who feels excluded from human contact, and for that reason a figure of pathos. But he has not been excluded; he has absented himself. In doing so, he is solving a problem. Presence is threatening to him: Distance is essential, itself a source of gratification. Distance gratifies because it resolves, and the voyeur's claim (if made) to be frustrated at that distance is almost invariably phony with half-truth: However ambivalently, he wants and needs it, and will defend it. What is his problem? He can find no wedge of entry into the primal scene: He cannot present himself where the love is. But he clings to his exclusion and protects it; unlike most people suffering from the sting of exclusion, he has no interest in at last breaking in. For the menace of some terrible threat hangs over the voyeur's impulse to present himself. One cannot speak generally about what this menace might be, except to say that it is very dire. Never underestimate its power; an entire personality and its most profound energies have been reconstructed, redefined to avoid what most people call gratification, to create what most call frustration. Somewhere in this is what the unconscious mistakenly understands to be the threat of death. Like all compulsives, the voyeur is trying to save his own life by refusing to live.

Even more than it does most movies, voyeurism dominates all Warhol's early films and defines their aesthetic.* Obviously, almost any important film-maker is likely to be a highly scopophilic individual, and, of course, film has always been the voyeur's delight, has always extended delicious appeal to the voyeuristic dimensions of us all. But works like *Kiss* and *Sleep* and *Eat* reconstruct in their eventless essentials a kind of paradigm, a structured filmic model of the voyeur's relation to the world. One could almost diagram it. And that paradigmatic structure, with its absented, depersonalized voyeur, and its uncaring, ungiving, self-enclosed spectacle embodies a kind of artistic and human drama felt moment by moment as the work reels through the projector, a vision of remoteness.

Everything in this paradigm follows from the situation of the camera in place of the absented voyeur. Before its witnessing and recording eye, the spectacle—the kiss; the sleeping, breathing torso; the man carelessly eating—is brought into the interplay of presence and absence that is central to Warhol's entire work at its best. Most important, in the hypertension between the spectacle and the camera, Warhol discovers a new dimension of the unreal.

---

* Voyeurism, the discovery of the height of sexual intensity in watching, should not be confused with scopophilia, the love of gazing endemic to all human sexuality. Technically speaking, voyeurism is a transfixed and compulsive diversion of scopophilic energy. In practice, the distinction between them can sometimes be rather vague.

Several peripheral elements impinge on the central effect. The first is silence, that silence to which Warhol was condemned, out of technical ignorance, at the beginning of his career. It is an endistancing silence, a mutism of otherness spread over the reality that the camera so patiently records. It forces the spectacle into some region behind the transparencies of film itself, a region from which no sound can reach us, in which a past made present is silenced, and a minutely recorded photographic reality made to seem, in its silence, remote and unreal. These are surely among the most interesting silent films made since it has been possible to choose silence.

In conjunction with that effect, there is the matter of the projection speed. Almost all 16-millimeter film, including Warhol's, is shot at 24 frames per second. Warhol insists—it is strange to think of Warhol insisting—that all his silent films be projected at what is called the "silent speed" of 16 frames per second, with which most projectors are equipped. The result is a *ritardando* exerted over all movement and an effect that is extraordinarily alluring. Yet that allure is faintly paradoxical, since the Warhol silents are famous for their supposed placement within literal clock time. Indeed, literal time has sometimes been pointed to as their chief contribution, proposed as evidence that Warhol has renounced any of those transformations of reality required by a romantic vision. But Warhol is, in fact, a romantic aesthete of a peculiarly modern kind. Needless to say, anybody watching *Sleep* is going to sense the slow, murderous crawl of literal time passing him by moment by moment, but that sense of literal time is also retarded by the subtle undertow of the most immediately alluring, the most decorative of all cinematic techniques—the visual hush of slow motion.

It is a technique that faintly dislocates the pressure of real time, extends it, and makes it just slightly Other, in a lush, subtle experience of movement and time possible only in film.

All these effects combine to create the fixated distance of the Warhol stare. Watching *Sleep* and *Kiss*, watching even the portrait films—remote from the sexualized quiescence of the sleeper, remote from the kiss, from the grinding of flesh on flesh, we find ourselves voyeurs at both a proximity and a distance no voyeur could ever know, both near and far away as only the camera can be, unreal with its minutely recorded literal reality.

Flesh becomes filmic. The lovers are close-up on the screen, but we in the audience sit at a distance from the screen. This *doubling* of our witnessing proximity transforms the felt presence of the camera—and all the while we hear the projector chattering behind us—into a metaphor for alienated consciousness. And the filmic art as well.

This metaphor is a prism, with its facets both in consciousness and the real space of the hall in which we see the film. Implicit in the close-up on the screen is a certain space: the distance between the camera and the real lovers under the circumstances in which they were filmed, the distance of the camera's focal length. Meanwhile, the audience sits in the hall, and, excluded from any narrative fantasy of immediate identification, feels peculiarly conscious of its somewhat impatient location there in real space, looking on.

Sexual and filmic fascination meld. Though we watch with the voyeur's gaze, there is a central difference between our experience and his. We are held back from the sexual spectacle not by the voyeur's impulse to hide and withdraw, but by the fact that what we see is unreal, is film. The doubled experience of remoteness—the consequence of a brilliantly diffracted experience of film watching—becomes a criss-crossed metaphor for the interplay of the real and the unreal, in conjunction with a basic trope of language and perception installed in the nerves as part of the language and the experience of interchange and gratification. It is the notion of desire and frustration understood in terms of a distance in space. (The language is filled with the image: "You seem remote"; "Mr. X is withdrawn"; "We are very close"; "He was distant"; a figure of speech with images of heat and cold to describe human relations.) This metaphor for love as a distance in space is plainly a voyeur's ideal metaphor, and, in Warhol's films, a filmic metaphor for the real and the unreal melds and identifies a metaphor of human nearness and distance to shock us with a double truth—pitched on a *tao* of frustration—just at the moment that the perforated, torn piece of film end flashes by on the screen.

The most powerful of the silent Warhol films are dominated by the same voyeuristic aesthetic, but their immediate look modulates considerably from case to case. In *Sleep,* the languid, immobile frame changes from one sleek pictorial voluptuity to another; from the image of the breathing abdomen, to a long shot of the nearly nude body (shot from the knee at an angle just high enough to reveal the sleeper's entire body stretching back into space), to a close-up of the sleeper's expressionless face—frontally, in profile—and then back again, the pattern recapitulated. But, in *Kiss,* almost every shot is framed in exactly the same way: It is the standard close-up of the kiss and fade-out. In both *Sleep* and *Kiss,* light is used to concentrate the voyeuristic scrutiny on movement—or, rather, on stillness— as the moments slip by. In *Eat,* an entirely different photographic style appears. Eating his self-renewing mushroom—like the food in the palace of *Beauty and the Beast,* regenerating itself on its glistening platters after being consumed—Robert Indiana is shot with light values suggesting still photography, and a classically conventional usage at that; richly contrasted, graded blacks and whites seemingly bathed in the photographic luminescence of sunlight flooding in from a source at a window—very like the fashionable French portraiture of the 1940's and 1950's, calling to mind Cartier-Bresson, for example. However striking, the image suggests again a classic aestheticism, terribly "good taste," a kind of photographic decorativeness.

Indiana sits in a high-backed wooden chair: He is wearing a hat; his face is bland, open, indifferent. At times, he seems to silently respond to what must be people out of frame, speaking to him; other times, nibbling on his mushroom, he gazes with meditative, wistful boredom out the window, the source of all that pretty sunlight. The camera makes a few listless movements: There is a zoom to his hand—without, however, revealing the precise identity of the shapeless substance he's munching—then withdrawing for a while to a three-quarter shot until deciding (one senses the decision being made) to move in, just a hair, on the profile. That studied profile with its sad, outward gaze.

Eat was the first released Warhol film portrait,* followed seven months later by *Henry Geldzahler,* a portrait of the museum curator puffing on a cigar. The temperature of the film is extremely cool—not that its immediate predecessors are hot with bristling, grinding passion. In *Eat,* the meditative disjunction between subject, camera, and spectator is simple, uncomplicated by any of the fleshly, sensual paradoxes informing the earlier films. Compared to them, *Eat* is a less demanding and finally less exciting work. It *is* a portrait, and as a portrait it gathers a kind of slow power on its own momentum. Indiana's meditative self-containment—his being, his very flesh seem to feed on that self-containment—is itself the subject of a meditation. But, filmically, the work adds nothing to what has been done before, seems even to provide less. *Eat* is the image of a man simply allowing himself to be. I confess that I am very near a merely personal judgment here: One would have to find the purely meditative mode more exciting than I do (exciting is perhaps not the word) not to suspect that perhaps *Eat* comes near a rather clever preciosity.

Still, it does accomplish in its own terms what is so exciting in *Kiss.* Within the voyeuristic structure I have proposed, the endistancing accuracy of the camera is allowed to record the tropisms of life and response, sensitive to the smallest revelation of the Person within the face. Yet this, too, is wrapped in a paradox: The sleeper's deep distance from us, the lovers' absorption in one another, Indiana's placid contentment—all find themselves in the distances of silence, in a decorative disjunction of time, in the nearness and remoteness of film mingling in an experience of the Person revealed and withheld at once.

(From *Stargazer: Andy Warhol's World and his Films*)

---

* But certainly not the first portrait film Warhol made. The film portrait dominated all Warhol's early film activity, and vast amounts have never been released. In those early days of 1963, Jonas Mekas reports that a Bolex had been installed on a fixed tripod in the Factory, a huge pile of film rolls beside it, and that it was never taken down. Any new guest—remember that in 1963 Warhol was entering the most conspicuous era of his fame; there were *hundreds* of guests—was put into a chair before the camera as soon as he or she arrived. They would sit through the roll, their film portrait being made. When Warhol wasn't there, Billy Linich or Malanga operated the camera: it became a standard and inescapable tradition of the place. Wherever those films may be now—lost, stolen, stashed in Warhol's basement for a rainy day—hundreds of them were made.

ANNETTE MICHELSON:

Toward Snow

The working of his thought is thus concerned with that slow trans-
formation of the notion of space which, beginning as a vacuum
chamber, as an isotropic volume, gradually became a system in-
separable from the matter it contains and from time.
　　—Paul Valéry, *Introduction to the Method of Leonardo da Vinci*

My eye, tuning towards the imaginary, will go to any wavelengths
for its sights.
　　　　　　　　　　　　　—Stan Brakhage, *Metaphors on Vision*

There is a metaphor recurrent in
contemporary discourse on the nature of consciousness: that of
cinema. And there are cinematic works which present themselves as
analogues of consciousness in its constitutive and reflexive modes,
as though inquiry into the nature and processes of experience had
found in this century's art form, a striking, a uniquely direct presen-
tational mode. The illusionism of the new, temporal art reflects and
occasions reflection upon, the conditions of knowledge; it facilitates
a critical focus upon the immediacy of experience in the flow of
time. Thus Aron Gurwitsch, on the origins of this inquiry: "Hume
expressly likens consciousness to a theater, but it is, so to speak, a
theater without a stage. In modern terminology one could compare
consciousness with a perpetual succession of kinematographic pictures . . . a unidimensional sphere of being, whose fundamental
structure consists only and exclusively in temporality." [1] And Gérard
Granel, discussing its modern developments: "Phenomenology is an
attempt to film, in slow motion, that which has been, owing to the
manner in which it is seen in natural speed, not absolutely unseen,
but missed, subject to oversight. It attempts, slowly and calmly, to

draw closer to that original intensity which is not given in appearance, but from which things and processes do, nevertheless, in turn proceed." [2] Epistemological inquiry and cinematic experience converge, as it were, in reciprocal mimesis.

There are, in the history of film, a very few artists whose work, in its radical purity and incisiveness, strikes one as paradigmatic in this respect. Among them is Michael Snow, whose *Wavelength*, some four years old, is now a celebrated film, a turning point for many in the history of the medium as in the maker's own development. It was once described in this review by Manny Farber, distinguished for the accuracy of his insights, the vigor of his style and the firmness of his allegiance to the tradition of American action film, as "a pure, tough forty-five minutes that may become *The Birth of a Nation* in Underground films . . . a straightforward document of a room in which a dozen businesses have lived and gone bankrupt." [3] And indeed, the film does seem to be, among other things, just that—which is to say "that" observation strikes one as "just" and accurate—conveying, however, an insight which, in some fifteen successive viewings and considerable reflection on the film, had never at any time occurred to me. I will wish to examine briefly and to account for both the accuracy and the surprise of that remark. But here, to begin with, is Snow's description of his film, prepared for the 1967 International Experimental Film Festival of Knokke-le-Zoute in which it took first prize.

> *Wavelength* was shot in one week Dec. '66 preceded by a year of notes, shots, mutterings. It was edited and first print seen in May '67. I wanted to make a summation of my nervous system, religious inklings and esthetic ideas. I was thinking of, planning for, a time monument in which the beauty and sadness of equivalence would be celebrated, thinking of trying to make a definitive statement of pure film space and time, a balancing of "illusion" and "fact," all about seeing. The space starts at the camera's (spectator's) eye, is in the air, then is on the screen, then is within the screen (the mind).
>
> The film is a continuous zoom which takes 45 minutes to go from its widest field to its smallest and final field. It was shot with a fixed camera from one end of an 80 foot loft, shooting the other end, a row of windows and the street. This, the setting and the action which takes place there are cosmically equivalent. The room (and the zoom) are interrupted by 4 human events including a death. The sound on these occasions is sync sound, music and speech, occurring simultaneously with an electronic sound, a sine wave, which goes from its lowest (50 cycles per second) note to its highest (12000 c.p.s.) in 40 minutes. It is a total glissando and a dispersed spectrum which attempts to utilize the gifts of both prophecy and memory which only film and music have to offer.

Among details one would want to add to that description would be the quality of the "human events," their somewhat scattered, random aspect. They take place abruptly, are discrete with respect to one another, are played in a range which runs from the strongly distanced and flat to the conventionally mimetic, linked in some suggestion of causality by only a few lines of dialogue. Secondly, there is the occurrence, through the film, of color flashes in a range of extraordinary intensity, of sudden changes of the field from positive to negative, of superimposition of fixed images over the progressive zoom, itself by no means absolutely steady, but proceeding in a slight visible stammer. The superimpositions and stammer function as a sort of visual obbligato, as does the evidence of splice marks, the use of varying film stocks, creating within the movement forward, a succession of fixed or still moments. Then there is the precise nature of the visual field in focus: it is, as we have said, the far end of a loft, opening through windows onto a street whose signs, sounds, traffic and traffic lights are perceptible to us beyond the tall, rectangular windows which are each in turn composed of eight small rectangular panes. The perception of wall, of window, of street will be modified in clarity by color, by superimposition, as the crescendo of the sine wave will modify our perception of the sound within and beyond the loft. The camera's movement is, of course, beginning to slowly reduce and re-define the visual field, and as we ever so slowly move closer to the wall, we begin to perceive—or rather to sense—two things: first, the presence of some other, rectangular objects on the central panel of the wall (they are as yet only perceptible as small rectangular surfaces) and then, as well (though the temporal threshold of this perception will vary with the viewer), the destination of the camera. Or rather, we sense the fact that it *has* a destination, that its movement will terminate inexorably in a focussing upon a particular area not yet known to us. The camera, in the movement of its zoom, installs within the viewer a threshold of tension, of expectation; within one the feeling forms that this area will be coincident with a given section of the wall, with a pane of the window, or perhaps—in fact, most probably—with one of the rectangular surfaces punctuating the wall's central panel and which seems at this distance to bear images, as yet undecipherable.

Now the effect of these perceptions is to present the movement forward as a flow which bears in its wake, contains, discrete events: their discreteness articulates an allusion to the separate frames out of which persistence of vision organizes cinematic illusion. Above all, however, they create, through the slow focussing in time, through relentless directionality, that regard for the future which forms an horizon of expectation. We are proceeding from uncertainty to certainty, as our camera narrows its field, arousing and then resolving our tension of puzzlement as to its ultimate destination, describing, in the splendid purity of its one, slow movement, the notion of the "horizon" characteristic of every subjective process and fundamental as a trait of intentionality. That steady movement forward, with its superimposition, its events passing into the field from behind the camera and back again beyond it, figures the view that "to every

perception there always belongs a horizon of the past, as a potentiality of recollections that can be awakened; and to every recollection there belongs as an horizon, the continuous intervening intentionality of possible recollections (to be actualized on my initiative,
actively), up to the actual Now of perception." [4] And as the camera
continues to move steadily forward, building a tension that grows in
direct ratio to the reduction of the field, we recognize, with some
surprise, those horizons as defining the contours of narrative, of that
narrative form animated by distended temporality, turning upon
cognition, towards revelation. Waiting for an issue, we are "suspended" towards resolution. And it is as if by emptying the space of
his film (dramatically, through extreme distancing, visually by presenting it as mere volume, the "scene" of pure movement in time),
Snow has re-defined filmic space as that of action. The eye investi-
gates the length of the loft, moves towards that conclusion which is
a fixed point; in its movement toward that point, alternative conclusions and false "clues" have been eliminated, as street signs and
movement and certain objects pass from view. The camera reaches
the object of its trajectory. That object is indeed another surface, a
photograph of the sea. The view is held, as the sound mounts to its
highest intensity, splitting off from itself, doubling, sliding up and
down the range of cycles as the photograph is re-projected in superimposition upon itself. The eye is projected through a photograph
out beyond the wall and screen into a limitless space. The film is the
projection of a grand reduction; its "plot" is the tracing of spatio-
temporal *données,* its "action" the movement of the camera as the
movement of consciousness.

The film is a masterwork, a claim hardly to be seriously contested
at this point in film history, and though we have strayed some distance from Farber's observations, we are now in a position to consider them more clearly and to see their very real interest. Indeed,
for someone so deeply and exclusively committed to the film of tight
narrative structure, *Wavelength* could, above all other films from the
American avant-garde, present something both new and familiar,
welcome, in any case—*if* one understands the continuity of the
zoom action to stand as a kind of quintessential instance of that
spatio-temporal continuity subtending the narrative integrity of
those comedies, westerns, gangster films which formed the substance
of the Hollywood tradition, and the object of Farber's delight and
lifelong critical attention. Or to put it another way: Snow's work
came at a time in the history of the American avant-garde when the
assertive editing, super-imposition, the insistence on the presence of
the film maker behind the moving, hand-held instrument, the resulting disjunctive, gestural *facture* had conduced to destroy that spatio-
temporal continuity which had sustained narrative convention.

The entire tradition of the independently made film, from Deren
and Anger through Brakhage, had been developed as an extension,
in American terms, of an avant-gardist position of the twenties in

Europe, distending the continuity, negating the tension of narrative. Grounded in the experience of Surrealism and of Expressionism, its will to destroy narrative was an attempt to situate film in a kind of perpetual Present, one image or sequence succeeding another in rapid disjunction, tending, ultimately in the furious pace of single-frame construction, to devour or eliminate expectation as a dimension of cinematic experience. The disjunctiveness of that perpetual Now can be seen, at its most intense, in both the work and the theoretical writings of Stan Brakhage. As film maker and theoretician, Brakhage is concerned with the primacy of a kind of quintessential vision, innocent, uncorrupted by the conventions of a perspective inherited from the Renaissance and built into the very lens of the camera. With that Platonically inflected terminology characteristic of the Expressionist sensibility, this vision is described in the writings as truer, finer, higher, in that it is the direct visible projection of inner or "inward sight"; it is, in fact, presented as a "closed eye" vision, the inner vision projected through the eye. Reading Brakhage, and especially when watching the films, one recognizes the images in question as tending towards both the intimacy and elusiveness of those we know as "hypnagogic," those experienced in the half-waking state. Like the hypnagogic image, the Brakhage image, "truer than nature," does seem situated inside the eye. It aspires to present itself perceptually, all at once, to resist observation and cognition.

Alain, in the *Système des Beaux-Arts*, defies anyone entertaining an hypnagogic image of the Pantheon to count the number of columns of the facade in the image. For the hypnagogic is immediate, appears all at once, disappears all at once, does not fade into appearance or out of view; it is not subject to the laws of perception— to those of perspective for instance. It has the property of exciting attention and perception. "I see something but what I see *is* nothing." [5]

Such indeed is the state toward which the style, the rhythm, the cutting and lighting of Brakhage's films tended. In the great works of his maturity, in the *Songs, The Art of Vision, Anticipation of the Night, Fire of Waters,* among others, there is no time, nor room, as it were, for expectation; the spatial *données* are obscured or fractured by spasmodic movement, by painting upon film, by speed; continuity is rhythmic, postulated on the metaphoric syntheses elicited in the viewer by cutting from one image to the next. *Wavelength*, then, in a very special sense was an "eye-opener," as distinguished from both the hypnagogic vision of Brakhage and the stare of Warhol. Snow, in re-introducing expectation as the core of film form, redefines space as being what Klee, in fact, had claimed it was: essentially "a temporal notion." *Voiding the film of the metaphoric proclivity of montage, Snow created a grand metaphor for narrative form.* The consequences are still incalculable; Snow's example and influence, intensified through subsequent work, in film as in other media, acknowledged and unacknowledged, are among the strongest factors in a current situation of the most extraordinary interest. Together with the films of Frampton, Jacobs, Gehr, Wieland, Landow, and largely influential upon them, Snow's work defined a new level of cinematic endeavor, opened a new era in the evolution of cinematic style. This, I do believe, explains the manner in which it could unite, in attention and fascination, critical opinion of a great many kinds and normally divergent. Snow, in restoring the space of "action" through a sustained, firm and relentless investigation of the modes of filmic presentation, created a paradigm, transcended the *a priori* distinctions between the "linear" and the "vertical," the "prose" and "poetic" forms, the "realist" and "mythopoeic," the "vertical" and "horizontal," the styles of continuity and of montage which had animated the film theory and polemics of the past forty years or so.

The paradox which turns upon the creation of a grand metaphor from the elimination of the metaphoric function of montage is by no means unique in Snow's work. One might say that all of the films of the mature period are animated by a central visual or perceptual paradox. *One Second in Montreal* is a cinematic construction which plays upon the seriality of film images. A succession of still photographs, representing park sites for a projected monument in the city of Montreal under winter snow, is the film. Each unit is held progressively longer as we approach the center, and the pace speeds up again as the film comes to its end, forcing upon the spectator the consciousness of time as duration—precise but unmeasurable, expanding and contracting in the act of attention to detail, the acceleration producing a curious effect of structural contraction. But the central paradox involves the presentation of still photographs in film and the still more curious impression that, despite the fixity and discreteness of each image, we are involved in a filmic experience, rather than a slide projection. Classical experiments in cinematic perception do instruct us that the projection of a photograph of a place or object and that of the place or object as filmed do not produce the same visual effect. The flow of time is somehow inscribed in the filmic image, immediately given, perceptible in our experience of it. That inscription remained to be articulated. Snow seizes upon it, projecting the photographic still cinematically, so that the flow of time is superimposed, inscribed upon the projection of the photograph's fixity—as the discrete images of the loft had been superimposed upon its traversal by the zoom.

In ←⎯⎯⎯⎯→ he isolates the panning movement of the camera and in acceleration of that movement carves out a kind of sculptural segment of its projected space (that of a classroom, as against a loft), producing the impression of a flatness and pure directionality which negate its visual depth and incident. The film, proceeding, as in *Wavelength* and *One Second in Montreal*, through temporal acceleration, does, as it speeds up, convert a haptically defined space

into an optical one, returning, in a *ritardando,* from the projection
of a space flattened by that speed into a plane parallel to the screen's
surface, back to the projection of room space. The film holds in
balance those two degrees of visual illusion. As in *Wavelength,* the
"human events" (a class in session, a sweeping, a cop peering
through a window, men sparring with one another) are, so to speak,
contained, as discrete units within the rhythmic structure of the film,
at variance with it, and though these events (the passing of a ball
back and forth, the sweeping, etc., the appearance of the title sign
upon the blackboard) echo the panning movement of the camera,
they punctuate rather than structure the action of the film. In general, the effect is one of succumbing to the grip of the moment;
compelled to follow it, we are unable to focus, to settle upon a given
object or point within the field. The effect, then, is of rhythmic
compulsion and relaxation. The notion of limitation is transposed
from the gradual reduction of the size of field to the gradual imposition of insistent directionality, intensified by the metronomic click
which seems sometimes to lead, sometimes to accompany, the action.

In these three filmic works, the artist has seized upon a strategy
proper to the medium and carried it to ultimate consequences, exploring its resonances, re-inforcing it with parallel strategies, insisting on the isomorphism of part and whole. These strategies, and the
persistence of a certain speculative quality in Snow's art, a preoccupation with the manner in which a statement generates counter-
statement, variation and extension can be seen as constant in his
evolution as film maker and as painter, sculptor.

Snow's early work is that of an extremely talented young painter
passing quickly from the rhythmic articulation of the figure to very
sophisticated strategies of abstraction articulated in a somewhat
geometric mode. *Lac Clair* and *The Drumbook,* both of 1960, explore the modalities of a figure-ground relationship. In *Lac Clair*
(oil on paper on canvas), the central area is a kind of *bleu canard,*
painted in very free but light strokes, intercepted at each corner by
a strip of paper superimposed on the canvas side. It is an altogether
simple and elegant work, very much involved with a kind of single-
image later to become quite popular in New York in the '60s. And
The Drumbook is a series of rectangles, dark blue upon yellow
ground, of slightly varying sizes, setting up discrete and contiguous
framing areas which seem, nevertheless, to form a continuous
ground. *White Trash* of that year is a collage of "soiled and folded
paper," managing in its pleated elegance to convert its soiled aspect
into subtle color, like that of a worn tennis shoe. There are a number of works in folded paper, pencilled and "expanded" or expan-
sible, which in their modesty, casualness and subtle variety testify
to a kind of constant playfulness, later to flower in the major series,
implementing metaphors grown central to Snow's investigations.

The central, pivotal series of works, executed during the sixties, is
the *Walking Woman* series, and I shall, in this introductory essay,

largely concentrate upon it. They are pursued during a critical time in his development. Accompanying his move from Canada to New York, they constitute one of the largest, most obsessively pursued themes and give rise to a countless series of variations, which are pursued parallel to his major film works. They are also highly controversial, and, I believe, little understood.

The basic image of the *Walking Woman* is a very simple, minimally articulated silhouette, a series of summary curves describing a figure truncated at wrists and ankles. The curves of hair, breast and thighs describe a mesomorph in striding position, tilted slightly, one arm extended forward a bit and the other somewhat further to the rear. The series consists in a vast number of encyclopedic variations upon a given silhouette of simple, almost caricatural contours. Conceived and executed largely during the years of Pop, these works neither offer the polish nor the sensuousness of the work of the major American Pop artists. The irony and sensuousness of media images and plastic materials to be found in Lichtenstein and Warhol are absent from these works. Lushness of surface, intensity of color are also lacking, as are the kinds of irony available in the use of consecrated images—familiar labels, packages and such. The series does, on the other hand, explore in a fashion that parallels the Americans, the possibilities of a single basic figure, of its serial organization or variational play effected by change of context. They explore much more radically and extensively, however, the contrast between pictorial and sculptural space, modes and degree of representation and variety of materials.

Walking Woman, then, came to exist as painting, as depiction of painting, as series of interrelated drawings, as focal point for mixed media pieces, for distributional pieces. She was used as emblem, as decoration, as decalcomania, exhibited, carried about, deposited in subway corridors, streets. She was made of wood, twisted out of stiffened canvas, blotted into a double Rorschach-like image, painted, drawn, printed. Finally, she was filmed, then amplified into a series of immense steel pieces, exorcised, as it were, in the 11-part dispersed composition commissioned for EXPO '67. The inquiry for which she served as point of departure was relentless. I select, without regard for chronology, a few major pieces. In *Gone* (1963), one confronts, head-on, a length of painted and plasticized canvas projecting, on its left side from the wall, proceeding in diagonal to the right-hand frame, its left-hand side flaring stiffly and irregularly, like a banner in a wind. Moving to the side, we see the irregularity as the contour of the posterior half of the silhouette. *Torso* (1964), also of wood and painted canvas is, typically, a form created by "torsion" of canvas stretched between the anterior and posterior sides of the silhouette which has been cut into flat, wooden panels, painted white and set perpendicularly to each other at a distance of about 24 inches. The painted canvas is stretched and twisted between them. This soft, stiffened sculpture is rather strange, result-

ing, as in a number of others, in the conversion of a flat figure into
an abstract, sculptural form. Here is the single, obsessive, animating
impulse behind this enormous series, which projects the figure into
every conceivable material, spatial situation and degree of illusionism
in an attempt to exhaust it, plot the limits of its transformational potential. They are aimed at a balancing of figure and abstraction, as
Wavelength was to constitute a "balancing of 'illusion' and 'fact.'"

Five Girl Panels (1964) consists of five of the figures adapted to
format (from horizontal to nearly square to vertical) at varying degrees of tilt, as in a suite of distorting mirror images.

Among the variational highlights, however, is *Hawaii* (1964),
crucial in that it seems to provide a point of transition between the
Walking Woman series and the concentration upon the themes essential to Snow's recent work. *Hawaii* is composed of three panels
of varying size. The largest, central one is a picture executed with
the somewhat unctuous simplicity of a cartoon. Its play of rectangular forms seen in three-quarter view composes an interior. Upon a
table is an open record player, its case and lid echoed by the rectangular shapes, both flat and implicitly solid, of the frames and sub-
divisions of window on the left—and even by the tiny rectangle
framing the socket into which the record player is plugged. The central point of focus is the framed image, set over the table, drawn as
in slight projection, of the *Walking Woman's* profile. The triptych's
two other panels involve an image of the profile depicted directly,
its size somewhat larger than the one seen within the composition
of the central panel. And to the left of that panel stands another portrait, still smaller, the shape of the support reifying the optical effect
of perspective depicted in the central composition. We pass, thus,
from an image to the depiction of an image to the literal rendering
of a depiction. With this work, Snow is involved in a complex reflection on the modes of illusionism. *Walking Woman* is ready to
cross the threshold of illusion into film, and she does so. Snow projects her into the space of film, extending the notion of the cut-out as
framing. In *New York Eye and Ear Control, Walking Woman*, tra-
versing a landscape and its changing light, introduces, through her
own fixity and flatness, an emphasis upon depth, volume and change,
the illusionistic modes of their articulation. In the series of monumental pieces referred to as her final exorcism, the experiments of
Torso, Gone, Estrus, and others, are developed and intensified and
the *Walking Woman* ends by absorbing, through the placing of its
highly polished surfaces in an outside environment, the reflection of
the volumes and changing light about her. We will encounter her
no more unless—as one continually encounters forms in Snow's work
—in recollection of the past, as the sublimated material of present
formal occupations.

The series completed, Snow has turned his attention to the articulation which stimulated and emerged from his immersion in the
processes of filming and recording, turning back, as well, from time

to time, upon past work (as the past is visualized in the space and movement of *Wavelength*), upon its materials and processes. For Snow everything is usable, including old work.

Thus *Atlantic*, a structure which holds thirty-six photographs of the sea, placed in deep metal frames. The frames, sides projecting at a slight angle to the back surface constituted by the photograph, reproduce the conical visual field of film. These frames, moreover, reflect the image contained within them. One sees, then, a surface of water in photograph, continuous, contained within the larger frame of its reflection, a rendering of the penultimate superimpositions of *Wavelength*, with the images held flat as the zoom image within the depth of a conical field, described by that of the camera.

Snow's recent screenings have also given us *A Casing Shelved;* it is, to begin with, a redefinition of the notion of film through sound. One colored slide shows us a series of shelves in the artist's studio; they bear a very disordered load of materials, objects, photographs, implements. The film then starts as the artist's voice, taped, begins cataloging the objects, bringing them into our view, directing the spectator's eye in a reading of the image, thereby making of that still image, a movie—and, once again, a narrative movie. For the contents of the shelves, framed by the twelve or so box-like structures composing it, are mostly materials that have been used in the making of film or sculpture, and the describing, the telling of their origin and function, composes the narrative of the maker's past as he directs the viewer's eye.

If, for Snow, everything is usable, it is also re-usable—at least once. Thus *Untitled*, shown recently at the Bykert Gallery, is a sumptuous "slide show" which alludes largely to the making of *Wavelength*, using stills from the film, the filters, the plastic colored sheets employed in its making, emphasizing, in a very painterly manner, the ambiguity of spatial relationships created by superimpositions, juxtapositions of filters, alterations of perspective and of angle of vision. Red and purple filters are seen over and against each other on white. A plastic sheet, seen in three-quarter view, is read alternately as flat or in perspective. Hands hold up, press down upon, flat sheets of color, hold up a still from *Wavelength*, are seen under purple plastic, seen still closer through red. A still is seen again at night. A strip of Kodak film, superimposed against the daytime blue beyond the loft window, creates a strangely elusive and purely optical distance between the blue of the windowpane and the blue to be seen through the clear interstices of the strip. In a characteristic gesture, the camera has apparently been trained back upon the projector itself, so that we see its lens through color. Or the window of the loft is seen against a flat white surface whose distance from the wall on which it is projected is, again, purely optical. Filters, used as windows, held over the windows of the loft, gorgeously stain the white radiance of daylight. Strenuous reading efforts induce ambivalence in the spectator: planar differences are cued by color

values, but the cues can be misleading. A hand peeling red plastic
from a white surface is succeeded by a field of pure color, an optical
magenta, made probably of two superimposed filters, but we no
longer can be sure. Within the succession of the slides are tiny re-
capitulations of fragments of the film. We see a hand holding a small
photograph of *Wavelength*, all under plastic. We look out the window, we draw closer in another slide, still closer in another, and a
sunny yellow patch appears in the lower left-hand corner . . . The
succession of slides in the carrousel composes these projections of
film making, slide making, projection into a loop of coloristic variations which stands somewhere between *Wavelength* and *One Second
in Montreal.*

It is indeed that circularity one would want to stress as characterizing Snow's work. Operating on two levels, it involves, first, a
movement of revolution about the formal object, the multiplicity of
approaches through variety of materials, the freely variational form,
the manner in which language itself is pressed into service—with
playful and witty results that strain at the limits of meaning. The
solution of sculptural or filmic or painterly problems is often returned
to again, used as material, transposed into other contexts, or hy-
postasized [6] from film into object or sculpture. Secondly, there is the
manner, shared with other artists, in which the individual work
tends toward the circular structure, the tautological form, the perception of the work necessitating the recognition or recapitulation
of the process involved. Thus, to cite only recent examples: *Crouch,
Leap, Land*—a series of three photographs taken of a woman in
these actions and photographed, presumably through glass, from
below—is suspended, face down from the ceiling, obliging the spectator, in bending, to peer up from a position approximating that of
the photographer. Or *Tap*, a complex work, a kind of "still sound
movie" composed of black and white photographic print, typewritten text, enclosed speaker, black wire and tape recorder which, distributed over several rooms of the Art Gallery of Toronto, made for
a work experienced in circuit, and whose circular structure was
heightened by its own discursiveness (in the typewritten text) on
the process of composition. *8 x 10*, first shown in the Toronto retrospective and more recently in New York, presents 80 photographs of
a rectangle, their dimensions a standard eight by ten inches, separated by intervals of identical dimensions, marked out, framed in
tape. The variables within the photographs—distance, angle, lighting—produce an immense range of spatial articulations, distending
and contracting space in the circular play upon the notions of framing as photography and of photography as framing. And both *A
Wooden Look* and *Of A Ladder* oblige one, in the perception of the
curious optical bend produced by successive photographs of a single
object, to re-situate the object in the photographic field of vision,
reconstruct the progressive process of its recording in relation to
one's own perception of that record.

The charting, then, of Snow's course, produces a shifting constellation of epicyclic figures, whose complex and firm geometry is sustained by the breadth and probing consistency of an inquiry into the modes of seeing, recording, reflecting, composing, remembering and projecting. Those shifting, interlocking cyclical movements might describe as well the architecture of the work just now in progress: "a film in which what the camera eye did in space would be completely appropriate to what it saw, but at the same time equal to it. . . . You see, the camera moves around an invisible center point completely in 360 degrees, not only horizontally, but in every direction, and in every plane of a sphere. Not only does it move in predirected orbits but it itself also turns, rolls and spins. So that there are circles within circles and cycles within cycles. Eventually there's no gravity . . ." This work will be known as *La Région Centrale*.

(*Artforum*, June, 1971)

NOTES

1. Aron Gurwitsch, "On the Intentionality of *Consciousness*," in *Phenomenology: The Philosophy of Edmund Husserl and its Interpretation*, p. 125.
2. Gérard Granel, *Le Sens du temps et de la perception chez Husserl*, (Paris: Editions Gallimard, 1968), p. 108. The translation is my own. For other instances of this increasingly frequent metaphor, I refer the reader to pages XXI and XXII of Peter Koestenbaum's Introductory Essay on Husserl's *Paris Lectures*, translated by Koestenbaum and published in 1967 by Martinus Nijhoff, The Hague. The view sustaining these observations is also adumbrated in an essay of my own, *Bodies in Space: Film as Carnal Knowledge*, (*Artform, February*, 1969), written, however, before the present essay had presented the occasion for this sort of anthologizing. The earliest text known to me, bearing upon these considerations in Hugo Munsterberg's *The Film: A Psychological Study*, originally published in 1916 and reissued in 1970 by Dover Publications, Inc. It is an early and remarkable attempt at a phenomenological analysis of the cinematic experience.
3. Reprinted in *Negative Space: Manny Farber on the Movies* (New York: Praeger Publishers, 1971), p. 250.
4. Edmund Husserl, *Cartesian Meditations* (The Hague: Martinus Nijhoff, 1960), p. 44.
5. For the discussion of the hypnagogic image, I have relied heavily on Jean-Paul Sartre's *L'Imaginaire* (Paris: Librarie Gallimard, 1948), pp. 58-76.
6. As Dennis Young has remarked in his introduction to *Michael Snow, A Survey*, published at Toronto by the Art Gallery of Ontario in collaboration with the Isaacs Gallery on the occasion of the exhibition, "Michael Snow/ A Survey," February 14 to March 15, 1970. This volume contains as well P. Adams Sitney's discussion of Snow's cinema, by far the finest and the most comprehensive published to date.

MICHAEL SNOW:

Two Letters and Notes on Films

LETTER FROM MICHAEL SNOW

21 August 1968

Dear P. Adams (and Jonas)
Reminding. Feel our/my esp. remarks (taped) to have been kind of dumb. Attempting to be less in this letter.

OK. Some ramblings occasioned by things unsaid: feel there to be some submerged issue about my work in other media and wish that we had a couple of days to go into their connections. If I were a "mixed media" artist perhaps it would be easier. Have been, not opposed but the general won't cancel the specific. Sculpture: I know a lot about objects, how they get to be what and where they are. Painting: surfaces and colours of things. What I'm fussing about is EG. (and not EGO but just to be clear) Jonas "knows" a *lot* about light but I don't think he knows about sound except as "support" for light, maybe. Music has to be acknowledged equal value. Not that it can't be "used" supportively or any way at all but it's (music) a world too. Anyway I've been to, have lived in the worlds of objects, surfaces, static-colour-images, sound and light. WAVELENGTH is, as I said in the note for the Knokke catalogue: ". . . a summation of my nervous system, religious inklings and aesthetic ideas" and "A definite statement of pure film space and time" and "A time monument." All my activities have been partly an effort of self-clarification and before the Knokke prize had happened I knew that WAVELENGTH was crucial in my life and work. The note for Knokke was originally written for the N.Y. Coop Catalogue, when I expected the film (I knew it was great) to disappear like NEW YORK EYE AND EAR CONTROL. The friendship of Ken Jacobs and the love of Joyce Wieland had been steering me a little (it's complicated) but while still an Artist (capital A) the effect the film had on other people has been helping me to realize myself as perhaps essentially time-light-sound poet. The other activities not given up but in order of weight.

From 1961 to 66-67 all my work used the same images, the Walking Woman. I worked in every material and method I could think of. It was a huge theme and variations composition. In painting, for example, I used watercolour, ink, tempera, oil, enamels, spray enamels, acrylics, etc. on various grounds. I stenciled ties, sweatshirts, match books, made rubber stamp compositions; had things printed, mass made; used printed stickers and rubber stamp to make dispersed and lost compositions. Some of these had a time aspect: that one might see a part (printed sticker) in the Sheridan Square subway stop, find another on the stairs, then find another in the 8th Street Bookstore (1962). Unfinished film made with Ben Park. Hope to finish someday. Spring, summer '64 shot NEW YORK EYE AND EAR CONTROL. Think it's great too and was happy that Richard Foreman, Ken Jacobs, and Andy Warhol thot so too when it was first shown at Cinematheque. This film is a true determinate simultaneity. It is all (about/is) polarities, opposites, supposed opposites. If WAVELENGTH is metaphysics, EYE AND EAR CONTROL is philosophy and ←————→ will be physics.

I think now it was a bit unfair to show you and Jonas ←————→ in its raw state. Quite a lot of it is still in my mind although all the material exists. As a move from the implications of WAVELENGTH it attempts to transcend through motion more than light. There will be less paradox and in a way less drama than in the other films. It is more "concrete" and more objective. EYE AND EAR is analytical, all the parts, are dealt with, inspected separately. You are given backgrounds then later foregrounds for example. It is perhaps more linear than the others. ←————→ is sculptural. It is also a kind of demonstration or lesson in perception and in concepts of law and order and their transcendence. It is in/of/depicts a classroom. When it is finished I think it will be seen to present a different, possibly new, spectator-image relationship. My films are (to me) attempts to suggest the mind to a certain state or certain states of consciousness. They are drug relatives in that respect. ←————→ will be less comment and dream than the others. You aren't within it, it isn't within you, you're beside it. ←————→ is sculptural because the depicted light is to be outside, around the solid (wall) which becomes transcended/spiritualized by motion-time whereas in WAVELENGTH it is more transcended by light-time. However ←————→ involves one's neck as well as one's mind-eyes. Sound yet to come. During our conversation I wanted to talk more about the issue of "story" that came up in Jonas' column referring to Ernie Gehr's films and to WAVELENGTH. Now: one of the subjects of or one of the things WAVELENGTH attempts to be is a "balancing" of different orders, classes of events and protagonists. The image of the yellow chair has as much "value" in its own world as the girl closing the window. The film events are not hierarchical but are chosen from a kind of scale of mobility that runs from pure light events, the various perceptions of the room, to the images of moving human beings. The inert: the bookcase that gets carried in, the corpse, as seen, dying being a passage from activity to object. Inertia. It is precise that "events *take place.*" The various kinds of events imply or demonstrate links which are, more or less, "stories." We tend to make a strong human event link between the death and the phone call. It is the beginning of what we conventionally call a "story." Before the man dies to after he dies the "story" changes levels and one "reads" relationships. His entry (He is not seen. Behind you?) is announced/preceeded by breaking glass etc. sounds as well as image-colour fluctuations. The sound is "representational," "realistic" as he is seen, walks in, dies. This is *against* the "abstract" sine-wave glissando. When he dies the "realistic" sound stops and is now *seen.* The colour-image waves which on other occasions are sensed as light events tied to what-is-happening-to-the-room (?!) belief are now sensed as ripples of life-heart struggles or the reverberations of hitting the floor. It is a very involved subject to try to write about. The "story" is on different levels of belief and identification.

I mentioned Cezanne in a comment about the illusion/reality balancing act in painting. Tho many many other painters have worked out their own beautiful solutions to this "problem," I think his was the greatest and is relevant because his work was representational. The complicated involvement of *his* perception of exterior reality, his creation of a work which both *represents* and *is* something, thus his balancing of mind and matter, his respect for a lot of levels are exemplary to me. My work is representational. It is not very Cezannesque tho. WAVELENGTH and ←———→ are much more Vermeer (I hope).

I sensed the existence of that dull subject: knowledge, skill, preconception as opposed (?) to the random, luck, etc. during our conversation.

Planning doesn't make anything better or worse and there are millions of ways to plan. WAVELENGTH involved many worried-over decisions. I put the camera high on a platform so that one could see more of the street, tops of the sides of the trucks. It's all planes, no perspectival space. Discovered the high angle to have lyric God-like above-it-all quality. ←———→ camera is 5' above the floor. The colour and light value changes were given their tendency by arranging of the different kinds of film stock which was done before shooting. Within that I played/improvised with plastics and filters while shooting, feeling it out but bearing in mind certain prior considerations: their relationships to the human events (announcing, echoing etc.), when they should perhaps be most pure, their phrasing/timing and that though there are passages of complementaries as a general form thru the film they go from warm colours to cool (spectrum). Oppositions are drama. I didn't always make a "choice." Just felt like it or less just did it. I was surprised and I wanted to be. However I set up a system or container which could both shape the fortuitous and give it a place . . . who knows?

Waves are the visible registrars of invisible forces.

(*Film Culture* No. 46, 1967)

LETTER FROM MICHAEL SNOW TO PETER GIDAL ON THE FILM *Back and Forth*

8 March 1972

Thanks for yr. letters and the article on ←——————→ which I found very interesting. In the light of what the film *is* the violence of your reaction to the 'coda' attests to a kind of success for it I'd say. Still its ill-mannered, snotty, total condemnation doesn't seem like 'criticism'.

←——————→ *is* action reaction or to put it another way: oscillation which implies 'opposites'. It is also a kind of educational film.

I can't claim to be 'right' about it but as far as depiction goes I feel the relativity view is as 'correct' as the $E=MC^2$ one. In other words the depicted solid (mass) is transformed into energy (light) by velocity. But it isn't totally transformed even as depiction because it gets as far as it might, it (disappointingly?) turns into its 'opposite', i.e. in reaction to ←——————→ there is $\updownarrow$. Now as you say seeing the film is a very physical experience. (I can't understand why you didn't also say 'hearing' it because the sound, its qualities, relationship to the image, effect, are *so* important to the whole thing.) That is: the 'body' of the film is very physical but *it itself* has *its* reaction which is the unstructured 'mental' superimpositions of the 'coda'.

This is 'recollection', 'reminiscence'. Superimpositions are 'dreamy'. The 'coda' lacks 'body' and 'direction' especially by contrast to what went before. Being forced to use my own mind as an example of a mind at work I didn't wouldn't don't remember the order things happen in the a film in the order they happen. One muses at first. Remembering them, unless there's a specific effort (and even then it only goes so far), is a seemingly random selection. The 'coda' is on the other side of the 'credits' which are of course part of the film, i.e. ←——————→, and are also obviously pedagogical which might also lead one to interpret the 'coda' as a 'review' of what went before. It has some beauties of its own visually, too.

On the screen the space of the room is asymmetrical. The move is from parallel to the picture plane to perspectival. Speeding up 'flattens' it, almost 'fuses' opposites. The total shape of the film is asymmetrical pivoting on the greenboard credits (the only hold, but there one's eyes are ←——————→ing) . . .

I thought your article was powerful . . . but there are several points that I don't understand: to say that the film deals with 'nothingness' seems peculiar. I think it deals with 'somethingness' with 'nothingness' as its (mental) shadow.

The people actions in ←————→ have some resemblance to those in *Wavelength* but mostly they have very different qualities and functions. They 'people' the space, they 'real' the space like in *Wavelength* but there are so many other things to them, migawd! They embody, by what they do, what the film is, they partake of what the film is.

All my films are attempts to control the type or quality of belief in the 'realistic' image. For example think about the beginning. First the 'outside' naturalistic shots. Green. Then the indoor sequence which is just long enough (to me) to become very 'abstract'. This 'abstractness' is broken in a (to me again) thrilling way when one first sees the person outside working on the windows. This *kind* of thing happens in all the sequences with people. There's a lot to them and their function. How they appear and disappear is beautiful (I think).

←————→ is percussion and *Wavelength* is song and the people parts in each case have qualities proper to those 'idioms'.

←————→ naturally consists of pros and cons and so totally experiencing it (to repeat, I think) calls for a kind of attitude which there seems to be too little of. I think ←————→ is the way things are. Yes the 'Marxist' (humanism?) is balanced by a cosmic so what . . . I'm glad the film matters to you . . . And you have an interesting advantage on me (one I'd like to have had) in considering it: I've never seen ←————→ for the first time.

Yours
Michael Snow

(*Structural Film Anthology*, ed. Gidal, British Film Institute 1976)

La Région Centrale (1970-71)

"If you become completely involved in the reality of these circular movements, it's you who is spinning surrounded by everything, or conversely, you are a stationary centre and it's all revolving around you. But on the screen it's the centre which is never seen, which is mysterious. One of the titles I considered using was !?432101234?! [an adaptation of a sculpture title] by which I meant that as you move down in dimensions you approach zero and in this film, LA REGION CENTRALE that zero point is the absolute centre, Nirvanic zero, being the ecstatic centre of a complete sphere. You see, the camera moves around an invisible point completely in 360 degrees, not only horizontally but in every direction and on every plane of a sphere. Not only does it move in predirected orbits and spirals but it itself also turns, rolls and spins. So that there are circles within circles and cycles within cycles. Eventually there's no gravity. The film is a cosmic strip.

I'd wanted to use another non-verbal title like ←————→ but hadn't settled on one when Joyce saw the words "La Région Centrale" in a book on physics in a bookstore in Quebec City and suggested it. I think it's fine, very appropriate.

(From a conversation with Charlotte Townsend, *Artscanada* #152-153, Feb.-March 1971)

Rameau's Nephew, By Diderot (Thanx to Dennis Young) By Wilma Schoen (1974)

To me it's a true 'talking picture'. It delves into the implications of that description and derives structures that can generate contents that are proper to the mode. It derives its form and the nature of its possible effects from its being built from the inside, as it were, with the actual units of such a film, i.e. the frame and the recorded syllable. Thus its 'dramatic' development derives not only from a representation of what may involve us generally in life but from considerations of the nature of recorded speech in relation to moving light-images of people. Thus it can become an event in life, not just a report of it.

Echoes reverberate to 'language', to 'representation' in general, to 'representation' in the sound cinema, to 'culture', to 'civilization'.

Via the eyes and ears it is a composition aimed at exciting the two halves of the brain into recognition.

JONAS MEKAS:

The Diary Film

*(A Lecture on Reminiscences of a
Journey to Lithuania)*

Reminiscences falls into the form
of a notebook, or a diary, a form into which most of my later work
seems to fall. I did not come to this form by calculation but from
desperation. During the last fifteen years I got so entangled with the
independently made film that I didn't have any time left for myself,
for my own film-making—between Film-Makers' Cooperative, Film-
Makers Cinematheque, *Film Culture* magazine, and now Anthology
Film Archives. I mean, I didn't have any long stretches of time to
prepare a script, then to take months to shoot, then to edit, etc. I
had only bits of time which allowed me to shoot only bits of film.
All my personal work became like notes. I thought I should do
whatever I can today, because if I don't, I may not find any other
free time for weeks. If I can film one minute—I film one minute. If I
can film ten seconds—I film ten seconds. I take what I can, from
desperation. But for a long time I didn't look at the footage I was
collecting that way. I thought what I was actually doing was practising. I was preparing myself, or trying to keep in touch with my
camera, so that when the day would come when I'll have time, then
I would make a "real" film.

The second week after I arrived here in 1949, I borrowed some
money from people I knew who came before me, and I bought my
first Bolex. I started practising, filming, and I thought I was learning.
Around 1961 or 1962 I looked for the first time at all the footage
that I had collected during all that time. As I was looking at that old
footage, I noticed that there were various connections in it. The
footage that I thought was totally disconnected suddenly began to

look like a notebook with many uniting threads, even in that unorganized shape. One thing that struck me was that there were things in this footage that kept coming back again and again. I thought that each time I filmed something different, I filmed completely something else. But it wasn't so. It wasn't always "something else." I kept coming back to the same subjects, the same images or image sources. Like, for example, the snow. There is practically no snow in New York; all my New York notebooks are filled with snow. Or trees. How many trees do you see in the streets of New York? As I was studying this footage and thinking about it, I became conscious of the form of a diary film and, of course, this began to affect my way of filming, my style. And in a sense it helped me to gain some peace of mind. I said to myself: "Fine, very fine—if I don't have time to devote six or seven months to making a film, I won't break my heart about it; I'll film short notes, from day to day, every day."

I have thought about other forms of *diary*, in other arts. When you write a diary, for example, you sit down, in the evening, by yourself, and you reflect upon your day, you look back. But in the filming, in keeping a notebook with the camera, the main challenge became how to react with the camera right now, as it's happening; how to react to it in such a way that the footage would reflect what I feel that very moment. If I choose to film a certain detail, as I go through my life, there must be good reasons why I single out this specific detail from thousands of other details. Be it in the park, or in the street, or in a gathering of friends—there are reasons why I choose to film a certain detail. I thought that I was keeping a quite objective diary of my life in New York. But my friends who saw the first edition of *Diaries, Notes, & Sketches* (*Walden*), said to me: "But this is not *my* New York! My New York is different. In your New York I'd like to live. But my New York is bleak, depressing . . ." It's then that I began to see that, really, I was not keeping an *objective* notebook. When I started looking at my film diaries again, I noticed that they contained everything that New York *didn't have* . . . It was the opposite from what I originally thought I was doing . . . In truth, I am filming my childhood, not New York. It's a fantasy New York—fiction.

I realized something else. At first I thought that there was a basic difference between the written diary which one writes in the evening, and which is a reflective process, and the filmed diary. In my film diary, I thought, I was doing something different: I was capturing life, bits of it, as it happens. But I realized very soon that it wasn't that different at all. When I am filming, I am also reflecting. I was thinking that I was only reacting to the actual reality. I do not have much control over reality at all, and everything is determined by my memory, my past. So that this "direct" filming becomes also a mode of reflection. Same way, I came to realize, that writing a diary is not merely reflecting, looking back. Your day, as it comes back to you during the moment of writing, is measured, sorted out, accepted, refused, and re-evaluated by what and how one is at the moment when one writes it all down. It's all happening again, and what one writes down is more true to what one is when one writes than to the events and emotions of the day that are past and gone. Therefore, I no longer see such big differences between a written diary and the filmed diary, as far as the processes go.

By the time I decided to look at my ten years of early footage, I had used up three Bolexes. That was a time when the liberation of the independent film-maker was taking place, when the attitudes to filming were changing radically. Like many others, during the years 1950-1960, I wanted to be a "real" film-maker and make "real" films, and be a "professional" film-maker. I was very much caught in the inherited film-making conventions. I was always carrying a tripod . . . But then I looked through all my footage, and I said: "The park scene, and the city scene, and the tree—it's all there, on film—but it's not what I saw the moment I was filming it! The image is there, but there is something very essential missing." I got the surface, but I missed the essence.

At that time I began to understand that what was missing from my footage was *myself:* my attitude, my thoughts, my feelings the moment I was looking at the reality that I was filming. That reality, that specific detail, in the first place, attracted my attention because of my memories, my past. I singled out that specific detail with my total being, with my total past. The challenge now is to capture that reality, that detail, that very objective physical fragment of reality as closely as possible to how my Self is seeing it. Of course, what I faced was the old problem of all artists: to merge Reality and Self, to come up with the third thing. I had to liberate the camera from the tripod, and to embrace all the subjective film-making techniques and procedures that were either already available, or were just coming into existence. It was an acceptance and recognition of the achievements of the avant-garde film of the last fifty years. It affected my exposures, movements, the pacing, everything. I had to throw out the academic notions of "normal" exposure, "normal" movement, or normal and proper this and normal and proper that. I had to put myself into it, to merge myself with the reality I was filming, to put myself into it indirectly, by means of pacing, lighting, exposures, movements.

Before we go further, I'd like to say something about this thing of "reality". Reality . . . New York is there, it's "real". The street is there. The snow is falling. I don't know how, but it's there. It leads its own life, of course. Same with Lithuania. So, now, I come into the picture. And with the camera. As I walk with my camera, something falls into my eyes. When I walk through the city, I don't lead my eyes consciously from that to that or that. Rather, I walk and my eyes are like open windows, and I see things, the things fall in. If I hear a sound, of course, I look towards the direction of the sound. The ear becomes active, and it directs the eye; the eye is searching for that thing that makes that noise. But most of the time things keep falling in—images, smells, sounds, and they are being sorted out in my head. Some things that fall in strike some notes maybe with their color, with what they represent, and I begin to look at them, I begin to respond to this or that detail. Of course, the mind is not a computer. But still, it works something like a computer, and everything that falls in, is measured, corresponds to the memories, to the realities that have been registered in the brain, or wherever, and it's all very real.

The tree in the street is reality. But here, I singled it out, I eliminated all the other reality surrounding it, and I picked up only that specific tree. And I filmed it. And if I now begin to look through my footage, that I have collected, I have a collection of many such singled-out details, and in each case they fell in, I didn't seek them out, they chose me, and I reacted to them, for very personal reasons, and that's why they all tie in together, for me, for one or another reason. They all mean something to me, even if I don't understand why. My film is a reality that is sorted out through me by way of this very complex process, and, of course, to one who can "read" it, this footage tells a lot about me—actually, more about me than about the city in which I film this footage: you don't see the city, you see only these singled-out details. Therefore, if one knows how to "read" them, even if one doesn't see me speaking or walking, one can tell everything about me. As far as the city goes, of course, you could say something also about the city, from my *Diaries*—but only indirectly. Still, I walk through this actual, representational reality, and these images are all records of actual reality, even if only in fragments. No matter how I film, fast or slow, how I expose, the film represents a certain actual, historical period. But as a group of images, it tells more about my own subjective reality, or you can call it my objective reality, than any other reality.

I used the process of elimination, cutting out parts that didn't work, the badly "written" parts, and leaving in those parts that worked, practically without any changes. Which means I was not editing the individual sequences. I left in those parts which, I felt, captured something, meant something to me, and didn't offend me technically and formally. Even if some parts caught something of essence but bothered me formally, I threw them out. I have this joke, that Rimbaud had *Illuminations,* and I have only eliminations.

I spend much time figuring out, trying out how this detail or that one, this note or this sketch works in the totality of the reel. It was a lesser problem in *Reminiscences,* but with *Diaries, Notes, & Sketches* (*Walden*) I really had to work hard and long. After you sit for two hours, watching a movie, it's important what comes during the third hour. The question of repetition comes in. Sometimes I have to eliminate even parts which I like, because too much of something is too much. In this case, in the case of *Reminiscences,* the editing was very fast. Hans Brecht of Norddeutscher Television helped me to pay for the film stock and Bolex in return for the rights to show it on German television. But then I came back, and I completely forgot about Hans Brecht. And he forgot about me. But then, on Christmas day he called me. "Is it ready? I need it on January twentieth." "January twentieth? Why didn't you tell me this earlier?" I went to my editing table and I stared at it. After I came back from Lithuania, I kept thinking: "How am I going to edit it?" This footage was very very close to me. I had no perspective to it of any kind. And even now, today, I have little perspective to it. I had about twice as much footage as you see in the film. So now I stood there and I said to myself: "Fine, very fine. This emergency will help me to make decisions." For two or three days I didn't touch the footage, I thought about the form, the structure of the film. Once I decided upon the structure, I just spliced it, very fast, in one day. I knew that this was the only way I could come to grips with this footage: by working with it totally mechanically. Another way would have been to work very very long on it, and either to come up with a completely different film, or destroy the footage in the process.

I have shifted the time sequence only on a few occasions. In *Reminiscences* I kept the time sequence. In *Diaries, Notes, & Sketches (Walden)* in a few places, when I had two long sketches side by side, I pushed one of them further in time, or back in time, for structural reasons.

Those of you who have seen the first edition of *Diaries, Notes, & Sketches (Walden)*, and now *Reminiscences*, will see the difference between the two. The basis of *Walden* is the single frame. There is a lot of density there. And when I was going to Lithuania I thought I would bring back material in the same style. But, somehow, when I was there, I just couldn't work in the style of *Walden*, there. The longer I stayed in Lithuania the more it changed me, and it pulled me into a completely different style. There were feelings, states, faces that I couldn't treat too abstractly. Certain realities can be presented in cinema only through certain durations of images. Each subject, each reality, each emotion affects the style in which you film. The style that I used in *Reminiscences* wasn't the most perfect style for it. It is a compromise style. I'll explain why. For instance, I made one bad mistake which I'll never make again. My third Bolex died just before I had to go on this trip. I had fixed it several times, but this time I just couldn't fix it any more. So I bought a new Bolex. The Lithuanian footage was the first footage that I shot with this new Bolex. But even if two Bolexes were totally identical, just the very fact that you never held the new one in your hands effects you. You have to get used to every new camera so that during the filming it responds to you, and you know its weaknesses and its caprices. Because, later, when I started filming, I discovered that my new Bolex wasn't identical with the old one at all. It was, actually, defective, never kept a constant speed. I set it on 24 frames, and after three or four shots it's on 32 frames. You have constantly to look at the speed meter, because the speeds of frames-per-second affect the lighting, exposure. And when I finally realized that there was no way of fixing it or locking it—I decided to accept it and incorporate the defect as one of the stylistic devices, to use the changes of light as structural means.

As soon as I noticed that the speeds were changing constantly (especially when I filmed in short takes, brief spurts) I knew that I wouldn't be able to control the exposures. I don't exactly mean that I wanted to have "normal," "balanced" lighting. No, I don't believe in that. But I can work within my irregularities, within my style of clashing light values, only when I have complete control, or at least "normal" control over my tools. But here that control was slipping. The only way to control it was to embrace it and use it as part of my way of filming. To use the over-exposures as punctuations; to use them in order to reveal reality in, literally, a different light; to use them in order to imbue reality with a certain distance; to compound reality.

When I went to Lithuania, I was offered a team of cameramen, and cameras, and I could have used them. But I didn't. I knew that although the images recorded by these technicians, following my instructions, would have been "better" professionally, they would have destroyed the very subject I was going after. When you go home, for the first time in twenty-five years, you know, somehow, that the official film crews just do not belong there. Thus I chose my Bolex. My filming had to remain totally private, personal, and "unprofessional." For instance, I never checked my lens opening before taking a shot. I took my chances. I knew that the truth will have to hang on and around all those "imperfections." The truth which I caught, whatever I caught, had to hang on me and my Bolex. When you shoot with a Bolex, you hold it somewhere, not exactly where your brain is, a little bit lower, and not exactly where your heart is—it's slightly higher. . . . And then, you wind the spring up, you give it an artificial life. . . . You live continuously, within the situation, in one time continuum, but you shoot only in spurts, as much as the spring allows. . . . You interrupt your filmed reality constantly. . . . You resume it again. . . .

I dislike any kind of mystery. The more I can tell about the people in my films the happier I am. In all my later films, I use titles to tell what you see. I like to tell in advance what it is, what's coming, as much as I can. Of course, there is no need to tell everything; there are limits.

My friends have been asking me: "What are your brothers doing there? Where do you come from? How does it look there?" I put all that information into the titles. Kostas has been in charge of the granary for ten years and it may be his life for another ten years. The other one is an agronomist, and he has been one ever since he came out of school.

I decide later, after the filming, whatever sounds I use. I collect the sounds whenever I can. Usually I end up with certain footage, and certain sounds surrounding the same situation. I look at my footage as memories and notes, the same way I look at my sounds, collected during the same period. In the case of the music for the Lithuania part of *Reminiscences*, it's just a coincidence that I received a record that I had admired very much. It's music written around 1910 by a young Lithuanian composer-painter, Ciurlionis, who died very young in the insane asylum. I recorded certain passages over and over, some parts of it. There may be influences of Scriabin in it (that's what some have said) but essentially it is Lithuanian music. There are certain notes in it that speak to me and I used to listen to it all the time until the record was stolen from me together with the phonograph about ten years ago. So that this music means something to me, is very close to me, and that's why I used it. I used it like a loop, in a sense. I thought it will help me to join all the disparate pieces together, by means of this sound loop. I used Bruckner for the Kubelka sequence in Vienna because Bruckner happened to be one of Kubelka's favorite composers. The madrigal I used in the Kremsmuenster library was one of Kubelka's favorite madrigals. So it's all very personal.

I found a little black square in my early footage. I was experimenting, in 1950, trying to work out divisions in a film, like chapter marks in a book, and I thought I'd use a square to indicate the different film chapters. But I never came to using it, until I discovered it again, while working on *Reminiscences*. You will notice that I use the numbers from 1 to 100 only in the Lithuanian part. Everywhere else I use the black square for chapter separations. Or maybe it's only paragraphs. I couldn't think, under the time pressure, what else I could do about it. I did not want to use black leader.

I say it in the film: "The time in Lithuania remained suspended for me, for twenty-five years, and now it's beginning to move again." So that when people ask me how is life there now, I am beginning to try to answer it. But till now I have been avoiding it. I usually say: "Oh, go and see my film, everything's there, I have nothing more to say, I know nothing about it." Because, the truth is, I didn't see the *real life* there. I was always looking for what was left of the memories of what *was*, what *has been* long ago. I missed the reality of *today*, or I saw it as through a veil. There are two kinds of travellers, people who go away from home. One category is those who leave their home, their country on their own. You decide, "Oh, I hate it all, I'll make more money somewhere else; people are better somewhere else; the grass is greener there . . ." You go, and you settle down somewhere. And, of course, occasionally, then, you think about your old home, your old folks; but eventually you grow new roots, and you forget all about it. You may occasionally think that maybe it was more beautiful there, in the old country. But you don't break your heart about it.

Then, there is the other group of people who are uprooted from

their homes by force—be it the force of other people or the force
of circumstances. When you are uprooted like this, you always want
to go back home, and it stays there, and it doesn't disappear. You
think about your old home, you romanticize it, it swells and swells.
You have to see it again, to actually go back there and start it all
from the beginning. You have to leave your home for the second
time. Then it begins to change. That's why in the *Diaries* (*Walden*)
I was shooting New York, but it was always like shooting my old
home. So, now, after I went back, all this, very probably, will begin
to change.

Ken Jacobs told me that *Reminiscences* interested him in the first
place because it represented the experience of a Displaced Person,
an experience which he never had but to which he is attracted,
because of his own childhood in Williamsburg, Brooklyn, which
practically is no longer there. So that we have, in America, a third
category of the Traveller: one whose home is constantly wiped out
from under the feet by the modern building code.

I have been doing a lot of reading, lately. I picked up Goethe's
Wilhelm Meisters Wanderjahre, his travelling years. I had read it
years and years ago. But now, I started reading it, and it had a
completely different meaning to me. As Wilhelm travels and meets
different people, and sees different places, I started thinking about
my film diaries. I began seeing interesting connections. He also visits
places and meets people, goes to monasteries, like myself in Austria. But he travels by his own choice. He decided to leave his
home and see the world, to meet different varieties of people, to
learn. Goethe's Wanderer is from a different century. My travels
represent one typical Wanderer of the mid-twentieth century—and
you will find this Traveller in every continent and every country,
today: a Displaced Person. The Displaced Person, the Exile, as
Traveller. There is such a thing, and it's not an abstract concept. A
Displaced Person, a D.P., is a reality of today. Because of the levels
and complexities of the present-day civilizations, we have a Displaced Person. And I happened to be one. And a Displaced Person
is not identical with Goethe's Wilhelm. A Displaced Person cannot
choose, hasn't chosen to leave the home. A Displaced Person has
been thrown out into the world, into the Travel, forced into it.

Reminiscences is not dominated by sadness. There is much joy, or
playfulness in the film. It's balanced, I think. What it is, really, is
that in most cases, in art, sadness is eliminated as part of human
experience, as if there were something wrong with it. But there is
nothing wrong with sadness. It's a necessary, essential experience.
Sadness is a state that is very real. We need it. And, of course, since
sadness is usually censored, then, when one sees it in a film, then
they think it's *too* sad.

The real difference between these two travellers is only in the
beginnings of their journeys. In the first case, one is consciously
seeking, looking for something; in the second case, one takes what

comes. People keep telling me: "Don't you want to go there, and there, and there," and I keep telling them: "No, I don't want to go anywhere! I never wanted to travel. I am very happy where I am." "Yes," they say, "but you have been there, and there, and there." "But no, I never wanted to go to any of those countries; I was always taken there either by force or by a necessity, when there was no other choice left for me." Wilhelm goes, and searches, and looks after certain things; he wants to educate himself, to find out about the world, to see the world. But I never wanted to see the world. I was very happy right there, in the small world, and I didn't have any need or wish to go anywhere. But here I am . . . And it's a slightly different situation from that of Wilhelm.

But, sometimes, these two fates come together . . .

When a Displaced Person becomes conscious of the Travel, then the two, Wilhelm Meister and the Displaced Person, begin to come together. At least in my case this is becoming so. Wilhelm Meister and a Displaced Person meet in a new home, and they discover that they both have the same home: Culture.

But there will be very few cases where the fates of Wilhelm Meister and that of a Displaced Person will meet in Culture. Most of the time they'll die, the first generation of Displaced Persons will die with all the memories of their old homes in their eyes.

(International Film Seminar, August 26, 1972)

P. ADAMS SITNEY:

Autobiography in Avant-Garde Film

For Robert Haller; much of the material in this essay was developed in lectures he invited me to give at Pittsburgh Film-makers. I also gratefully acknowledge a grant from the National Endowment for the Arts which supported the writing of this text.

Preface

For twenty years the word "personal" has been attributed to a majority of independently made avant-garde films. One can presume that some meaningfulness, within a range that includes both the hermetic and the spontaneously intimate, sustains this longevity. Elsewhere I have attempted to specify generic distinctions within the same range of works. Those distinctions, based upon attitudes the films reflect toward the camera, the protagonist, or the scene of action, tend also to constitute, not so innocently, a history. In some way the epithet "personal" is repeated as a mute polemic against such histories. Yet again a coincidence of structural patterns within the films of several major artists in the span of less than a decade calls forth a generic and historical analysis. This time I follow more comfortably the declarations of several film-makers and critics, and even a large conference at the State University of New York at Buffalo: the development of the filmic autobiography is my topic.

A literary autobiography is a diachronic narrative whose author is its subject and which makes claims to extra-textual veracity. The central tradition within literary autobiography, including St. Augustine, Rousseau, and Wordsworth, gives a privileged status to the moment at which the author realized his vocation as a writer. Metaphors involving reading and writing play central roles in the fabric of these autobiographies. The film-maker finds himself in a very different position as autobiographer. Whereas the writer has a language fully developed for the substitution of sentences for past events, the film-maker is at a loss to find veracious film images for the foci of his memory. He can, of course, invent an autobiographical fiction, as Truffaut is said to have done in *Les 400 Coups* or Fellini in *Amarcord*, but the ontological status of these films is fundamentally different from that of autobiography: they are fictions made under the same rules which operate in all novelistic films. The true cinematic autobiography must identify itself as different from the fictional film.

One can go further: the very quest for a cinematic strategy which relates the moments of shooting and editing to the diachronic continuity of the film-maker's life is the true theme of our contemporary avant-garde film autobiographies. The nature of this *relating* is certainly not the same in any of the films to be discussed here. In this respect the film-makers resemble the literary autobiographers who dwell upon, and find their most powerful and enigmatic metaphors for the very aporias, the contradictions, the gaps, the failures involved in trying to make language (or film) substitute for experience and memory.

Consider the following paragraph from J.J. Rousseau's *Confessions*. The young composer and music-copiest is on his way to visit Diderot in prison. As he walks he reads in his newspaper that the Academy of Dijon is offering a prize for the best essay on whether the arts and sciences have led to the elevation or degeneration of man. At this point he decides to become a writer:

> The moment I read this I beheld another universe and became another man. Although I have a lively recollection of the effect they produced upon me, the details have escaped me since I recorded them in one of my four letters to M. de Malesherbes. This is one of the peculiarities of my memory, which is worth noting down. It only serves me for so long as I need to rely on it; as soon as I commit its burden to paper it deserts me; and once I have written a thing down, I entirely cease to remember it. This peculiarity extends also to the matter of music. Before I studied it I knew great numbers of songs by heart; but since I learned to sing from written music, I have been unable to remember any of them, and I doubt whether to-day I could repeat a single one of all my favourites right through.[1]

If we believe the author, then the very act of writing the *Confessions* constitutes a monumental erasure, the obliteration of his memory, virtually the end of himself. Even if we turn to the letter to M. de Malesherbes, the moment of loss, the gap, reappears, this time in psychological rather than linguistic terms:

If there ever was something like a sudden inspiration, it was the movement which happened within me when I read this; all of a sudden I felt my mind dazzled by a thousand lights; throngs of living ideas presented themselves there all at once with a force and a confusion which threw me into an inexpressible turmoil; I felt my head seized by a dizziness resembling drunkenness. A violent palpitation hurt me and swelled my breast; I could not breathe any longer as I walked, so I let myself fall under one of the trees of the avenue, and I passed a half an hour in such an agitation that when I got up I noticed that the whole front of my jacket was soaked with my tears without my having felt that I was shedding them.[2]

Rousseau set out to tell the truth, to write the very book he would bring before Peter and upon which he would be eternally judged. Wordsworth quite differently agreed to his friend Coleridge's request that he write an autobiographical poem to record "the growth of a poet's mind." That request, he confesses in the first book, got him going again, broke a writing block, and was to stand as *The Prelude* to a giant poem he never got to write. Just as Rousseau claims that he found the advertisement for the prize by accident, so Wordsworth casually comes upon a blind begger in the streets of London:

> And once, far-travelled in such mood, beyond
> The reach of common indications, lost
> Amid the moving pageant, 'twas my chance
> Abruptly to be smitten with the view
> Of a blind Beggar, who, with upright face,
> Stood, propped against a wall, upon his chest
> Wearing a written paper, to explain
> The story of the man, and who he was.
> My mind did at this spectacle turn round
> As with the might of waters, and it seemed
> To me that in this label was a type,
> Or emblem, of the utmost that we know,
> Both of ourselves and of the universe;
> And, on the shape of the unmoving man,
> His fixed face and sightless eyes, I looked,
> As if admonished from another world.[3]

The vertiginous flooding of the poet's mind comes from the recognition that the sightless beggar is the very metaphor for the autobiographer, unseeing but seen, holding up the words which constitute the narrative of his life.

        *   *   *

One strategy of the film-maker is to assemble all of the filmed images of his past, by and large home movies, and use them as the foundation-blocks of his film. Between them he invents double-edged figures which obliquely represent the unfilmed past while proclaiming the loss in continuity they would repair. If any single figure could be isolated as the major sign of *absence* in the filmed autobiography it is the use of the still photograph. Most Americans of this century preserve random images of their past in collections of snapshots; many have organized them diachronically into photo albums. Yet when the filmmaker turns his camera upon the still, the opposition of the frozen moment and the illusion of continuity comes into play. Artists like Hollis Frampton, Jerome Hill, Stan Brakhage, James Broughton, who have repeatedly questioned the status of the filmic image in their nonautobiographical films, do not let the pathos and the irony of the encounter of camera and still go unexplored.

Often the photographic album, diachronically arranged, has a rudimentary commentary, the scholia of names and dates written below or on back of the snapshots. Not just the temporal ordering, but an act of naming anchors the images. In many of the new auto-biographies the conjunction of language, often of the film-maker's voice, and images provides a second (problematic) moment. At the point at which film seems to recover the full rhetorical range of the literary autobiography (for the film-maker can, of course, write such a text and read it to us) and even to supplement it, illustrate it with images, these film-makers locate another chain of enigmas where the traditional problematics of the literary autobiography meshes with those of the visual record. Here what is important and what makes autobiography one of the most vital developments in the cinema of the late Sixties and early Seventies is that the very making of an autobiography constitutes a reflection on the nature of cinema, and often on its ambiguous association with language. Let us inquire then of the recent film autobiographies: what is the news about cinema?

1

Jerome Hill's *Film Portrait* establishes the perimeters of the diffi-cult congruence of linguistic and cinematic time-structures at its opening. Hill, standing before his shaving mirror, tells us "this is the me that am." The morphological rupture indicates the inadequacy of language to name the cinematic present. He continues: "Or, rather, that was the ME that was at that moment and never will be again. The ME that am, alas! lasts no longer than a single cinemato-graphic frame." Several revelations are impacted here. In the first place, there is always an indeterminate temporal difference between the time of photographic recording and the moment of projection. Thus every speaker naming himself in a film is past in respect to the viewing of the film. The great literary biographers, too, often called attention to this fact: Chateaubriand called his massive auto-biography *Memoirs d'outre tombe*. More specific to cinema is the fact that all continuous images on film are illusions. If being, or presence, is no longer than the atomistic division of filmic continuity, one twenty-fourth of a second, then it has the ontological status of a single still photograph. The rapid succession of such images, in any film, would constitute, then, not a representation of something present in the present tense, a testimony to the real, but a voluntary illusion, a deliberate invention of a pseudo-continuity to persuade us of the veracity of the author's version of chronology. I would contend that this nexus of theoretical insights, of which Hill demonstrates he is conscious at the beginning of the film, permeates the structure of the film on all levels; in fact, his "autobiography" is not so much the intimate chronicle of his behaviour, as the structured representation of how he came to have those very insights and their consequences in his art.

While still speaking to the mirror, he whimsically envisions his possible penultimate or ultimate moments: images of Hill as a senile cripple, a bum, a horse-carriage driver, Pope, President, patriarch, sunning with Brigitte Bardot, walking in space, conducting an orchestra, receiving an Oscar; as an acrobat, rock star, convict, eaten by a shark, the victim of automobile and skiing accidents, mugged. The catalogue of fates mixes different modes of representation, several of them deliberately unconvincing, such as the cut-out collage of Hill and Bardot on a beach speaking to each other in handwritten cartoon balloons or the photograph of the immense patriarchal family with the same image of Hill's face pasted over the shoulders and under the hairline of each man, woman, and child. Costume alone represents him as Pope, a simulated oval office with the seal shows him as President. One of the fates is imagined as a repetition: "It would be nice if this could take place again." We see and hear him receiving an Oscar for his film *Albert Schweitzer*. The moment which refers to film-making itself holds a special place; it is the only point at which he is not overtly mocking himself. The sequence as a whole gently criticizes its maker's unwillingness to commit himself fully to a single art form; for Hill was a composer, painter, and poet, as well as a maker of fictional, comic, documentary, and animated films. Yet even the Academy Award presentation is not without its ironic reverberations. Repeating it seems hardly probable and certainly not for *Film Portrait*, Hill's most original film.

Within the sequence before the mirror he employs yet another technique for questioning the status of the present image: he switches between color positive and color negative film stock. By intercutting the swirls of shaving lather in the water of the sink, in color negative, so that the forward and reversed motion of the same strip of film can evoke both clockwise and counterclockwise spirals, he invents another metaphor for the reversal of time. ("Enough of these speculations on the future! Let's try to reverse time. Movies can do this very well. Let's look at the Me that was.") Before we examine the validity of this claim for the movies, according to the evidence of the film, let us dwell upon the opening sequence. The fiction of the film seems to claim that the complex chain of autobiographical reflections occur to the maker as he is

shaving. This familiar daily act, then, is raised to a special significance. What is involved in shaving? Obviously the presence of the
mirror is a determining factor. The myth of Narcissus has often
been construed as an allegory of autobiography, sometimes as a
model for metaphor itself (as in a passage from Dante to which
I shall refer later). In the mirror the self confronts itself as an image.
Within the dynamics of the spatial organization of cinema this
allows for the possibility of the doubled image (figure and reflection) and, more importantly, for the substitution of the camera for
the mirror, in which the frontal stare of the figure can represent his
self-scrutiny of the mirror. The opposition of self to self in the mirror
becomes a vehicle for the affirmation of a present tense, the interlocked stare being the extension or duration of a moment. There is
a long history of this figure in the avant-garde cinema, going back to
Cocteau's *Le sang d'un poète*. Insofar as a mirror reflects only what
is present to it, and does not retain the trace of its previous image
making, it can be used as a metaphor for the continuing present. The
most wonderful cinematic elaboration of this principle comes not
from the avant-garde cinema but from the Marx Brothers and Leo
McCarey: in *Duck Soup* Groucho encounters Chico who, disguised
as Groucho, tricks him into believing a doorway is a mirror by
precisely imitating all of his very sudden gestures.

The constitutive moment of *Film Portrait* is the confrontation with
the mirror. Yet Hill adds to this the act of shaving. As a daily
ritual it suggests that the autobiographical reflex is not a peculiar
moment but a regular pattern, sustained and grounded by the
diurnal repetition of the same act. Somehow the fact that we respond
to the cyclical time of the solar day reinforces our commitment to the
cumulative chain of those days over years. Shaving itself is a renewal, an uncovering, a discarding of the previous day's growth.
The change of the face from day to day is so small that the illusion
of continuity, of no change at all, confronts the man in the mirror.
Here the problem of repetition and continuity would be shifted from
the physiological plane of persistence of vision in the flashing film
frame to the psychological plane of aging. That is why in the sequence immediately following, Hill presents us with a series of
photographs taken three years apart.

Just before showing the photographs Hill spoke of reversing time.
He assured us: "Movies can do this very well." However what we
see are still pictures, arranged in reverse chronology from adulthood
to infancy. The strategy is simple and brilliant, so that the movement
toward birth appears as divesting of contingent features and a quest
for essence. What movies are doing very well at this point is not
reversing time, but rhythmically presenting a series of snapshots
(non-movies, *stills*) so as to undo a cliché of growth.

The psycho-history that Hill gives us is almost exclusively geared
to explain why he became a film-maker: his earliest sense impressions (chimes, oil smell, copper taste, enamel feel, and a play of

Film Portrait: *a negative image of Jerome Hill shaving.*

colors) found their synthetic unity in a clock by his bed. "The fact that it told time interested me only later," he concludes. Autobiography as the telling of time always demands that aspect of "later" as its organizational focus.

A story of the family's isolation from the world and from its news concludes with a memory of the sinking of the Titanic. Yet this is all a prelude to a flipping of the family dictionary, on the edges of which the child Jerome had animated the disaster. "A stroke of the thumb in the other direction and the boat came up again!" The film shows us both movements.

In a Proustian cartoon the film-maker draws images of himself being tucked in for a nap by his mother. A hole in the shade converts his room into a camera obscura with an inverted image of his grandfather's house (next door) on the wall. This constitutes the most explicit association of an Oedipal fantasy with the occupation of film-making.

His first encounter with movies gets the emphasis one would expect. We see the bits of films made of his very wealthy and prestigious family, and learn that they had their own private film theater and collection of prints. This event coincides with a shift in the materials of the *Film Portrait;* instead of still photographs and animations, we see primarily film clips from this point on.

The sequence of movies, made by professionals, of the Hill children, climaxes in a moment of error and leads to the strongest psychological declaration of the film: "Yes—these people to whom I belonged curiously enough did *not* belong to Me! Of everything they did, and did so well—I was incapable! More and more I realized I was leading a life apart—a life which for many years I shared with no-one." These remarks conclude a series of comments on images of his siblings. While we see his sister playing with birds, we are told she was terrified of the aviary, but entered to please the cameraman. His older brother pretended to read a newspaper for the film, and Jerome himself was forced to mime the painting of a picture which someone else had executed. This negative moment, at which film is caught lying, marks the inaccessibility of cinema to the self and its natural preference for simulation. The tropes for Hill's isolation are formulated as aberrations of perspective: the view through a Tiffany stained glass window, the exotic vegetation evoked by putting the camera at ground level, the conviction of a mystical numerology of colors, derived unconsciously, from pool balls. The accumulation and superimposition of these patterns of fancy and error constitutes Hill's definition of his solitude.

A division in the film occurs after the boy's ceremonial initiation as a Blackfoot Indian. Here an epistemological model is sketched out: "The beauty of this aboriginal world could not fail to influence my imagination—and the games we all played. We tried to learn their songs and their dances. My brother and I even succeeded in catching on to their complicated sign language." The movement from fascination through imitation to the acquisition of a language takes on significance when contrasted with the following sequence, a repeated alternation of two photographs, one of Hill at twenty-three, the other at thirteen. The juggling of these two images stands for a decade of schooling, he tells us, which was not only an empty detour in his history, but of which he retains "only the vaguest memories." The encounter with the Indians is the paradigm for his independent learning. And he learns more than their sign language. Inscribed within the narrative of this episode is another aspect of his solitude: his hostility to his family. On the screen we see Hill's father posing with Indians in a newsreel, apparently on the occasion of his moving the tribe off of property he owned in order to create a national park. Hill refers to the unscrupulousness of this move. After the initiation he was given an Indian name. "I was proud to have a name which I didn't share with anyone else!" This crucial sequence represents his need to dissociate himself from his father, whom he represents here in morally ambiguous terms. He achieves this by identifying with the tribe his father displaced and by concentrating his imagination on the aboriginal aspects of Indian life. In the subsequent passage of the film he recognizes this reduction to fancy and play as a state near death. Serious illness ensues. As a student "interested only in the past," he "hadn't begun to live."

His birth, as an artist, coincides with his acquisition of a film camera. The next several passages of *Film Portrait* constitute an anthology of Hill's early cinematic works, then a rapid summary of his mature films. This central portion of the film is essentially unproblematical. The chronology of the life is represented by excerpts and whole short films, over which the narrating voice describes the vicissitudes of their production.

In the last part of the film, Hill returns to the theoretical issues with which he began. Now we can see him costumed as Vermeer's astronomer, poised over an editing table. He describes the unedited footage to his left as the future, the finished material on his right as the past. "How about the present? Might the synchronizer in the center be compared to the present? . . . What is this ephemeral present about which one cannot speak? Does it exist? For me the only real, valid present is the eternal moment, seized and set down once and for all—that is the creation of the artist. Through cinema, time is annihilated." He cuts from the stairway of his home in Cassis, France in 1930, to 1950, and then to 1970. But in what sense is time annihilated? If anything, this brief sequence of three shots impresses us first with the changes of time, and then with the idea that a man has filmed the same spot for forty years. The annihilation is not of time: it is the imminence of death, for which he is seeking an image.

Earlier he had quoted one of the very first films, the Lumières' *Arrival of the Train at La Ciotat,* and told us "In 1932 I often saw those two delightful old men (Louis and Auguste Lumière) lunching on the terrace of my hotel, and they must have witnessed my first experiments with my new camera." After the sequence of the stairway he shows an electric train rushing through the modern station in the same town. It is the final shot in his film. "And the trains still go through the station at La Ciotat," he concludes. The nature of this "still" is highly problematic; for everything looks changed. That speeding train, apparently selected casually, becomes the metaphor for Hill's death. This final image of a recurring event, whose regularity seems not to be disturbed by the total physical change visible in the contrast between the films of 1895 and 1970, tells us that the trains will continue after the film-maker's death. What dies is the consciousness as an organism for establishing the diachrony of a life, an organism which finds its simile in the film synchronizer; for "the creation of the artist" is both the work he makes and his self-invention as artist. Similarly *Film Portrait* is a self-portrait on film, and a portrait of the self of film. The pattern here is one which we will find throughout the avant-garde film autobiography, and I suppose in large measure through the influence of *Film Portrait:* a chronology is constructed in a context in which the authority of chronology and the truth of imagery is denied; consequently the categories of memory and causal sequence cease to be the founding forces of the film and enter an indeterminate arena where they might well be seen as illusions derived from, or at least reinforced by, the very conditions of film production and its apparatuses.

2

Stan Brakhage was explicit on this issue in an interview about *Scenes From Under Childhood:*

It would be very autobiographical in one sense but some other things besides. Autobiographical in a Proustian sense, rather than in the usual sense of autobiographical.

Proust is very appropriate here, because the work is very involved

with the memory process. The first, simple, daily impulse to make
it was to see my children—to see them as something much more
than mine, much freer than that possessive word "mine" would
imply, to share with each and every one of them (and I have five)
various parts of their life more directly than I felt I was being able
to. Photographing them was one way (I'm most intensive and excited
when I'm doing that) to begin a relationship of better seeing, or
entering their world. But I felt that I had to do something much
more than that, which was to remember *my* childhood, to relate in
that way.

I immediately was mistrusting my own memory process, and
rightfully so. I could prove that the mistrust was justified, inasmuch
as my memories tended to give me the sense that the childhood
realm is a more innocent, more pure, more happy state than . . .
and so on. And I could see that that wasn't so, that in fact the various
hells and heavens and purgatories of each of my children's struggling
with what was confronting them—the emotions they felt—were
certainly no less intensive than mine. The agonies they suffered over
trying to master the tying of shoelaces, for instance, were certainly
no happier a state for them than any economic or terrible complexity that would seem to be thwarting me.

So I really had to push into that sense, to the point of remembering so I could defeat the "editor" in the head (an editor who is
determined to make sure certain spans of life have a happy ending,
others not, that one period of life is a tragedy and that another is a
comedy, and so on) and get into a more "daily living" sense of
working with thought processes . . . and of *living*. So an attempt
just to understand the children became involved in memory process,
and through that, becoming specific about what it is that a person—
say, that I do most of each day, and how I do it.

So the film evolves into being very involved in particularities of
daily living. The kitchen table, and the bathroom, and the sunlight
moving across certain plants in one way at one time of year and a
different way in another, and so forth. Slight movements—movements that would be regarded as boring were it not for the intensity
of the need to see them as adventuresome, as being really the major
center of any living. Just how one rests one's elbow on the table
and shifts it slightly, and changes that, and what that has to do with
the way someone across the table then does that. The screwing of a
lid on a jar, but not in any euphoria or play.

That's the other mistake: when people start concentrating on daily
living they tend to start sentimentalizing that in the way of saying
either that it's a dreadful bore and a catastrophe (which is, I take
it, Beckett's too-easy-for-me solution) or that it's lovely and wonderful (which would be Shirley Temple's sentimentality). I think Shirley
Temple as an image of a child did more damage to consciousness
in children—I mean she did more damage to the world in that role
than she would if she became President of the United States.[4]

Scenes From Under Childhood, a four part film, is itself the first
chapter of a projected giant work, *The Book of the Film*. Another
chapter in three parts, *The Weir-Falcon Saga*, has also been completed. When Brakhage calls this work an autobiography in the

Proustian sense, he means that the film makes no claims to represent the facts of his life; instead it reproduces the structures of his experience as he remembers them. The distinction Brakhage makes is between classical autobiography and the autobiographical novel. The Proustian model confuses more than it clarifies, unfortunately, since Brakhage seems to be referring to *A la recherche du temps perdu* naively, as if the novel were not poised over the void of its own cognitive structure. A more useful distinction can be drawn within the strict autobiographical tradition: Augustine in his *Confessions* presents himself as a *typical* man, in all else but the very fact that he writes. Rousseau, in his *Confessions*, portrays the *extraordinary* individual, an absolutely unique case. Brakhage has operated in both autobiographical modes. *Scenes From Under Childhood* and *The Weir-Falcon Saga* participate in the Augustinian manner. Their "fictional" principle is that the film-maker allows his observation of the events of his children's lives to stand for his own life. But insofar as this substitution is overtly declared as such, and the distance between the film-maker and the children is inscribed in the structure of the films, the fiction dissolves. In its place there emerges the suggestion that the activities of children can reveal a universal model for psycho-history. Brakhage's Rousseauistic confession, *Sincerity,* of which only the first reel had been released at this writing, describes the events leading from his own childhood to the making of his first film.

Brakhage was an adopted child, filled with fantasies about his natural origins. He had no siblings. The intersubjective reactions of the Brakhage children in *Scenes* constitute the negative moment of his dialectical reflection on growing up. In one sense the children form a synchronous order of the stages of the father's diachrony. The problem of representing one with five, or two with five (since the autobiographical subject seems at times to be both Brakhage and his wife Jane) is linked to the opposition of the synchronous to the chronological in all autobiographies. The autobiographical gesture, for Brakhage, is the invention of a meaningful chronological model which has to be imposed upon the random synchronous order called memory.

The opening section of *Scenes* describes two contradictory movements: on the one hand we witness the emergence of consciousness from a red "prenatal" field. Images of the child gradually come into focus; perspectives eventually stabilize into the synthetic unity of objects. Much of the film is a prolonged and wonderfully precise dramatization of the origins of sense certainty, something that Hill had rapidly described in his memory of his bedside clock but did not illustrate. The forward movement of the film can be understood as the quest of memory: out of the red haze of the autobiographer's closed eyes, memories come to the fore and slip away. The entire section, then, would describe the difficult attempt to establish a cinematic transcription of memory.

Memory itself comes into question through the metaphor of the photograph. The earliest images of the film-maker are still photographs. In a letter to Sidney Peterson Brakhage wrote:

> I am working on a long color and sound film called SCENES FROM UNDER CHILDHOOD: and your exposition on "Blanks" in my work (black/white leader in "Dog Star Man," etc.) and your statement that "there are essentially two kinds of sound, mood-music and lip-sync" are still sharp cutting tools in the endeavor . . . problem IS: the actual statics of childhood memory (the essential 'stillness' of childhood scenes remembered—all movement, true to the *act* of memory,—very limited, as if a set of scrapbook pics. were seen thru heat waves) does condition the editing in such a way as to throw all film aesthetics back on painting, aesthetics of painting . . . something like: slightly moving pictures emerging from and dissolving into "blanks" of colored 'leader'. Then there are, in concentrated memory act, interruptive flashes of various colors that seem to come in rhythmic 'blocks' which seem to denote specific emotion responses. To be general about it—red/anger, blue/sadness (blue-grey/nostalgic-sadness), green/jealousy, yellow/cowardice, etc. . . . the degrees of color, color-mixture etc., shifting these emotions into their subtleties while the rythms of their flashings seem to qualify their means (meanings) in relation to each other and to the image being invoked (envisioned): all of which throws film aesthetics back on music, aesthetics of music. As I begin to into-it, there's a felt-*trap*, for film, in all such deep-*end*ency upon t'other arts: but I can't seem to intellect it nor quite (physiologically speaking) put my finger upon it!

Therein lies a phenomenological justification for the use of the stills in the film. Brakhage has in mind some version of the distinction Proust made, following his cousin Henri Bergson, between automatic and induced memories. But the significant point for *Scenes* is that since memory is not committed to chronology, association occurs between memories and fantasies from very different periods of life. How is the autobiographer to organize his memories into a narrative? The literary autobiographer often depends upon an implicit calendar to give narrative form to his memory: "This happened when I was four . . . this when I was five . . ." In *Scenes,* and even more explicitly in *Sincerity,* Brakhage uses the photograph album as the external scaffolding of memory. In one way the film represents the impossible effort of the autobiographer to use the photographs he finds in the snapshot albums of his and his wife's childhood to evoke memories. The simultaneity of these several lines of development (the birth of consciousness, the will to remember, the reading of the album) determines the film's skepticism. For Brakhage any genealogy of the mind must be a fiction; the autobiographer interprets the sequence of his coming to remember as the sequence of his life; and even that ordering needs the support of a conventional model, the snapshot album.

3

Scenes From Under Childhood had a curious genesis. As early as 1963 Brakhage's father-in-law provided him with film and developing expenses to make a film about his children. He started to make a fantasy film, inspired by the novels of L. Frank Baum and George MacDonald, to which he is quite attached. The title was originally invented for this work which was never completed as such. He did film some scenes of his children in costume, opening the door to a stairwell, in which, at one point an artificial window "magically" appears. These fragments are dispersed through the first two parts of the final film; they are associated with childrens' dreams. This project began while the Brakhages were living in considerable poverty in a house, lent to them for free, in Denver. In the fall of 1963 they moved to Custer, South Dakota, when Brakhage accepted a commercial job for a small company, Nauman Films. There he found the most comfortable working conditions he had ever encountered in his several attempts to survive by doing commercial cinematography. In the year that he remained in Custer he had access to finer cameras than had ever been at his disposal before. He shot much of *Dog Star Man: Part Four* there, and began the elaborate anamorphic photography that characterizes the beginning of *Scenes from Under Childhood.* Subsequently his economics improved slightly; since 1965 he has lived from teaching, lectures, grants, and his film rentals. With some of his first grant money, from the Avon and Rockefeller Foundations, he made the intricate dissolves and fades in *Scenes.* The shift from amateur to professional tools and the support for laboratory technology contributed to the textural difference easily visible between *Scenes* and his earlier films.

Brakhage tends to avoid structural pre-determination in most of his film-making. "The Book of the Film" however seems to be an extreme case; for aside from the vague notion of a very long autobiographical collection of composite films he has little sense of what it will be; he has even been uncertain whether or not one film (*The Trip to Door*) will be part of it. Apparently *Sincerity*, the strictly autobiographical film-in-progress will also be part of "The Book of the Film." *Sincerity*, with its complex and persistent use of still photographs, recalls the function of the snapshot album in the structure of the earlier *Scenes*, where the still images are interspersed, rarely and with sudden precision, among the first, second, and fourth parts. The letter to Sidney Peterson, which I quoted and which illuminates the theoretical perspective of the stills, was written when only the first section of *Scenes* was edited.

In that initial section a single moment is elaborated. A male baby is sitting on the floor eating. Amid flickers of pure color, his image very gradually comes into focus in an anamorphically distorted space. Other children walk past him; only their legs are recorded by the camera. This image recurs several times, as if the author were trying to grasp and extend a tatter of memory. At one point two photographs of Brakhage come into focus: one is as an infant, the other as a young boy. The alternation of these photographs indicates both a gap in the memory and the inability to *will* a first memory to consciousness. The boyhood image cannot be censored out in favor of the infantile. As a whole this section moves from visual obscurity to clarity. A seemingly final and totalizing moment occurs near the end when, in a clear and undistorted view a very young girl feeds the sitting baby honey from a spoon. As she feeds him, she begins to train him not to push the spoon from his mouth or block its passage with his hand.

Although there are glimpses of the parents, they play next to no role in this section, which is a quest for a memory from the period of sensory-motor development. A brief allusion to the "magical" fantasy episode occurs during a sequence of twilight or night landscapes. The central and most striking part of the film, however, is a visual exploration of the texture of the floor on which the child sits. (It may even be a rough-hewn table.) It dissolves between negative and positive, color and black and white. The rough boards, their irregular natural lines, the crevices between them, are the subject of an exploration, principally through fades and dissolves on the same image in different film stocks, which is both fascinating and mysterious. It constitutes of course one of the many self-conscious attempts in Brakhage's cinema to represent the optical adventure of an emerging consciousness.

In *Film Portrait* there is a sequence where Jerome Hill tells of his mystical association of pure colors with numbers. On the screen several numbers, in different colors, float through an empty space. "What a disappointment much later to find that it all came from *this!*" he says as he shows pool balls, racking themselves up in reverse motion. The color theory which Brakhage outlined to Sidney Peterson, and apparently practiced in the editing of *Scenes from Under Childhood* has a much more ambiguous status than Hill's self irony. The cautious allusion to a relationship between color flashes and music in Brakhage's letter may provide us with a clue for unpacking some of the intricacies of this thought here.

In the second and third sections the work of the color flicker is replaced by colored fields of swarming, flashing dots, representing the phosphenes that can be seen when the eyelids are closed. The color flicker returns for an extended phase near the end of the fourth part. I believe that the question of color cannot be separated from the general question of representation as Brakhage conceived it while making the film. For this purpose I would like to cite long passages from two letters to the poet Michael McClure. The first goes back to the beginning of October, 1964. Brakhage had been considering making a film, *Nolight,* of McClure's play *The Feast.* Here he writes of the imagery inspired by McClure's lines (in quotes). The letter is prolix and obscure, but nevertheless it is a valuable and rare instance of Brakhage's speculation on imagery. It is also all the more useful in that it does not directly refer to anything in *Scenes from Under Childhood*.

A move "from shadow to light" *in negative* means the swallowing up of shape so that a bringing into shape can ONLY occur in the mind of the imagination extending itself upon the given possibility. If the change occurs at the instant of taking shape and the change be visually from positive to negative, only the sense of shape will ever occur (and that only in the transformation); and thus shape will only occur in the extending of the imagination of the viewer feeding upon what was sensed (in transformation.)

"What is carved in air is blank as the finger touching it." Give me a finger moving in air; and it will be picture of finger for *one frame only* (1/40th of a second), will become a carve of solid shape in air, thus: each frame is exposed full-time length needed for the movement (say: 20 seconds), and first frame finger is still at starting point, second frame finger has retained its position and then moved fraction of an inch during the exposure, third frame finger returns to starting position and moves two fractions of an inch during exposure, and so on for 480 frames—finger carves solid shape OF itself in space of picture area . . . is finger-picture ONLY at time-source of itself, thus only in the referential mind of the viewer.

THUS: Illustration, MOVING illustration, which, taking language as source *only,* cannot possibly interfere with the images language engenders in the mind of the viewer but only encourage that activity further by being TOUCH—(upon the optic nerves)—TONE upon the eyes of the viewer.

The second text, also to McClure, was included in a letter Brakhage sent to Jerome Hill dated late March 1966:

A few more words about "Scenes From Under Childhood"—

Viz, say, the sense of some particular power remembered, I'm after the rythm of blinking of:

> "A black rainbow in 3D
> curved and solid blinking
> black neon
> in a chrome box":

and after the particular colors this black pulse takes upon itself—for the colors are INdrawn, one color always more than another at each pulse, while all of such a mix as to engender the sense of black OR white (why you call the box "chrome", natch); and in this working, I have had black & white positive and negative prints made of much of the color film so that these can mix in exact superimpositions, pulsing according to need, in the editing.

It is that the work itself, the finished film, should be source only for what occurs in the mind of the viewer . . . as is always the case, natch, but never before (or hardly ever) premised so clearly in the making, taken as such exact assumption in the creative process. But, to be clearer yet, this process is actually opposite of the PREsumptions of Op Art (where I find the intention is to affect the viewer, his affectation necessary to pull off, so to speak, the effect the work is—that he must be optically bugged, as it were, for the work to exist) because I am simply here involved with a process so naturally always existent its workings have been over-looked: that the light take shape in the nerve endings and IS shaped, in some accordance we call communication, thru physiological relationship.

Central here is the relationship of the concept "shape" to "the mind of the viewer." He published a letter on the influence of music on his work:

> I'm somehow now wanting to get deeper into my concept of music as sound equivalent of the mind's moving, which is becoming so real to me that I'm coming to believe the study of the history of music would reveal more of the changing thought processes of a given culture than perhaps any other means—not of thought shaped and/or Thoughts but of the *Taking shape,* physiology of thought or some such . . .[5]

Here "taking shape" becomes a fundamental mental category. All three texts reveal the mixture of idealism and associational psychology in Brakhage's thought. In the early text the moment of perception ("the instant of taking shape") coincides with an act of the imagination, where the sheer sense intuition, ("the given possibility") is synthetically apprehended in flux ("transformation"). Here the classical distinction between sensation and perception remains intact. The rhetoric of flux and metamorphosis that he uses to draw this distinction shows that Brakhage wishes to extend and divide these two moments of cognition as much as he can. The traditional discourse of such an extension is developmental psychology. For Brakhage the autobiographical genre constitutes an aesthetic equivalent of that discourse.

The example he gives, of a finger gesture, emphasizes the instability of things and the primacy of processes within the temporal structure of cinema's illusion of motion. Marey called this process of extended exposure "chronophotography." Brakhage's version, it would seem, uses the atomism of cinema to analyze the stages between the still image of the finger and the chronophotograph of the completed gesture in an effort to translate the force of the word "blank" in McClure's poem into the epistemological context of film. I know of no place in Brakhage's oeuvre where such an image is attained. The heuristic force of this "illustration" would have been to demonstrate the ideational status of the representation ("only in the referential mind of the viewer"). This Brakhage has often achieved; in *Scenes from Under Childhood* especially.

As the later text states, the use of color and black and white, negative and positive, plays a congruent role. The disparity between the phenomenological orientation of the letter to Peterson and the performative argument in the later letter to McClure is revealing. As autobiography, *Scenes from Under Childhood* recognizes, and builds upon, a series of representational failures; principally of the adequation of observation, while filming, to memory. The letter to Peterson would disguise a substitutive strategy ("scrapbook pics . . . seen thru heat waves") as an innocent simile for an experiential process of the subject. In the second letter to McClure, Brakhage, somewhat defensively, indicates that the color would induce a free play of memory on the part of a viewer. The expression "taking shape" indicates in one place a representational strategy and in the other an automatic "physiological" response. Rhythm and music mediate between these very different senses.

4

Brakhage is not a practicing psychologist but a film-maker, and although he may sometimes deny it, considerations of the ontology of cinema consistently take precedence over the observation of phenomena in his work. At the time he made *Scenes from Under Childhood* a new development within the theory of the avant-garde film did not escape his attention. The dominant model of film as a metaphor for cognition was put into question. The theoretical work of Peter Kubelka was an influence in reconsidering this issue. Paul Sharits' films and theories certainly engaged Brakhage at this time. The color flicker film, as Sharits practiced it, attempted a synthesis of the animated, graphic film tradition and the more subjective psychopoetic cinema of which Brakhage had been a champion. Up to this point all discussions of "the viewer" had been banished from Brakhage's theoretical discourse. An element in Brakhage's earlier theory had been a polemical insistence on the priority of the present tense (which he supported with frequent quotations from the writings of Gertrude Stein). Insofar as *Scenes from Under Childhood* thematically undertook a consideration of developmental schemata, over time, some corresponding theoretical realignment was called for. The complex double structure of the film, as reconstructed chronology and as an analysis of the synchrony of the moment of reconstruction, was one response; the introduction of "the mind of the viewer" was another.

Both Brakhage's art and his theory continually verge upon solipsism. Periodically he makes works or takes positions which resist the excesses of that solipsism. For example, shortly after completing *Scenes*, he made his so-called "Pittsburgh trilogy," three films, shot from a police car, in a hospital, and in a morgue. All three themes were chosen to provide a powerful exterior situation as a counterweight to the engulfing interiority of his cinema. Insofar as *Scenes from Under Childhood* shifts the problem of autobiography from the personal to the formal level and seeks a range of schemata where observation and introspection converge, it constitutes one of the adjustments by which Brakhage tried to mitigate his solipsism. It should not be surprising then that Brakhage tends to elevate those moments of convergence into a universal color theory or a model for the viewer's mind. In the end, we may be able to get no closer to an understanding of his color theory than he himself achieves when he writes to McClure of "the rythm [*sic*] of blinking."

Although the repeating, wobbling finger gesture imagined for *Nolight* does not appear in any Brakhage film, it does suggest some important elements in *Scenes*. In the Second Part there is a long held shot of the parents' bedroom, still and clearly in focus, but filmed so that the figures within the film are almost dissolved into speeding translucent ghosts. We can tell from their movements that they are undressing and going to bed, but not much more. When this sequence occurs in the context of children's perspectives, it becomes the first of several intimations of the primal scene (the child's uncertain, obscure blend of observing and imagining his parents' lovemaking). The images which follow, of the mother's pregnant belly, and of the empty double bed itself, confirm the interpretation.

For the most part, the second section of the film explores the nature of play and imitation in the children and introduces an analysis of their affections. An opening montage of rhythmic physical games, such as swinging and whirling, is soon superseded by a cluster of shots of the different children, at widely different ages, crying. Throughout this part the montage is exceptionally fluid, with the superimposition of the phosphene imagery and the regular fading and dissolving reinforcing the elisions. This imparts to the thematic components (games, toys, imitations, emotions, and the parents' sexuality) a sense of interlocking association. He cuts in an image from the photograph album only once here: the image of a boy, perhaps Brakhage, on a bicycle, appears over the children riding their various vehicles. Perhaps more significantly there is a shot of Jane looking through the album itself in a context that suggests that her nostalgic attraction to these past images itself constitutes a form of, or an outgrowth of, play.

In the broad movement of the section there is a shift from physical-rhythmic games (the swing) to the use of vehicles and ultimately to mimetic toys. A transition that links the images of the primal scene to the toys occurs when shots of the mother's nude body and of the father urinating precede the image of an unclothed doll. Doll-house play follows, and even the dressing of one doll in a wedding gown.

However the crucial moment in the analysis of mimesis had taken place earlier in the section. Brakhage established a metaphor for cinema, its framing process and illusory depth and movement, by superimposing very quickly several shots of a large window, shot at varying distances. The frame rapidly diminishes and expands, recedes and emerges, as the short views of the same "thing" are manipulated. This self-conscious figure of a film within the film, is immediately followed by a clip from a Shirley Temple movie on television. The antithesis of the myth of happy childhood and the cinematic analysis of children could not be more bluntly articulated. Brakhage also shows us the enthralled and nervous expressions of his children as they watch the movie on the t.v. screen. He wants to underline the way in which mimetic representations of childhood help to form the children's affective patterns and inculcate the mythology of childhood in them. This mimetic closed circuit is an important moment in *Scenes,* and reflects *its* circularity, which is indeed the basic circularity of serious autobiographical enterprises.

Many of Brakhage's earlier films, and especially *Dog Star Man,* were eschatologically structured, moving from a pristine moment of origin to a totalizing end. All of his autobiographical works deny this eschatology, and, as I shall try to show, the theory of metaphor which attends it. In his autobiographical reflections, there can be no true beginning, no immanent structure, no totalizing end. As an autobiographer, he discovers that even his memory has been influenced by the scrapbook his mother structured, his emotional patterns trained by movies which would pass on absurd myths of childhood.

In the fourth and final section of the film this repetitive, circular geneology of the psyche is rearticulated from a different perspective. Brakhage may be taking the liberty Gertrude Stein, one of his central sources, took when she wrote *The Autobiography of Alice B. Toklas* and *Everybody's Autobiography:* for this part is centered on Jane. As she cries, apparently in prolonged grief, photographs of her mother and of herself as a child appear. These in turn are superimposed over her daughters. For the first time in the film a continuity is suggested in which the children repeat the patterns which they learn from their parents while the parents can see their own patterns only as reflected in the children. Early in the film a cheerful snapshot of two children, presumably Jane and her brother, is superimposed over a fight among her children. Much later in the film her eldest daughter is isolated in tears, corresponding to the opening grief of the mother.

Near the end of the film we can catch the reflection of Brakhage filming the eyes of Jane and the children, his "eye" being the mechanical viewfinder with its three lens sights. After this, he makes a disturbing appearance. Obviously in a foul humor he growls, "I'm hungry" (the phrase is easily read from his lips) and angrily shakes his finger at the camera. This dramatic finger gesture is *not* transformed into a chronophotograph, as in the early McClure letter, but a juxtaposition underlines it. At the end of a sequence in which adolescent boys fly a remote-control model airplane, one of the boys twice describes the arc of the plane's flight with a graceful arm and wrist gesture. Brakhage's finger and the boy's arm both "carve the air" at the point in the film, the end, at which Brakhage's aggression is associated with a montage of youthful sports events. These events, intercut with a photograph of some institution, possibly a high school, represent a stage at which gesture and play become social aggregates.

5

Two letters provide Brakhage's synopsis of the three films of *The Weir-Falcon Saga:*

The term "The Weir-Falcon Saga" appeared to me, night after night, at the end of each of a series of dreams: I was 'true' to the feeling, tho' not the images, of those dreams in the editing of this and the following two films. The three films 'go' very directly to-gether, in the (above) order of their making: yet each seems to be a clear film in itself. At this time, I tend to think they constitute a 'Chapter #2' of "The Book of Film" I've had in mind these last five years (considering "Scenes From Under Childhood" as Chapter #1): and yet these 'Weir-Falcon' films occur to me as distinct from any film-making I have done before. They engender, in me, entirely 'new' considerations. I cannot describe them: but there is an excerpt from "The Spoils", by Basil Bunting, which raises hair on the back of my neck similarly:

> "Have you seen a falcon stoop
> accurate, unforseen
> and absolute, between
> wind-ripples over harvest? Dread
> of what's to be, is and has been—
> were we not better dead?
> His wings churn air
> to flight.
> Feathers alight
> with sun, he rises where
> dazzle rebuts our stare,
> wonder our fright."

I might add that "The Machine (of Eden)" *operates* via 'spots'—from sun's disks (of the camera lens) thru emulsion grains (within which, each, a universe might be found) and snow's flakes (echoing technical abberations on film's surface) blots (upon the lens itself) and the circles of sun and moon etcetera: these 'mis-takes' give birth to 'shape' (which, in this work, is 'matter', subject and otherwise) amidst a weave of thought: (I add these technicalities, here, to help viewers defeat the habits of classical symbolism so that this work may be *immediately* seen, in its own light): the 'dream' of Eden will speak for itself.

(To Sally Dixon, July 2, 1970)

Chapter 2 of "The Book of Film" is composed of three works ending on an image of the moon: "The Weir-Falcon Saga", "The Machine of Eden" and "The Animals of Eden and After." This Chapter, then, takes the concept of Dream (remembered Dream, note!) head-on. The childhood dreams most readily remembered are usually those which spring out of illness and (for me at least) premise themselves around some confrontation with possible Death—thus usually draw-ing on specifically religious arch-types, etc. "The Weir-Falcon Saga" exists as that first stage of illness wherein a fevered-waking-state and simple-dreams mix. "The Machine of Eden" seeks to work-out a clear Biblical story (the first story!) using only the particular objects and environs available to the patient-child. "The Animals of Eden and After" reclaims 'health' as 'sights' "common to all men" but *charged* by the completed (in "Machine") synthesis of dream-and-waking vision. "The Animals . . ." develops a whole myth (even religion, complete with morality) with these charged particles of normal daily living. There is, of course, very much more going on in all three of these films; and I am only tracking the most technically optic development of these works. . .

(To Annette Michelson, November 8, 1971)

As Brakhage's comment indicates, *The Animals of Eden and After* portrays the process of convalescence as a normalization or accommodation to socially dictated patterns of perception and thought. According to the implicit scheme of the three films, fever and illness so jar the perceptual patterns that a reexperiencing and a re-mythologizing of the world has to occur. The phenomenal level at which this happens, according to Brakhage, is the dream and the liminal states between dreaming and waking. Actual dreaming is beyond the access of cinema, obviously. So Brakhage introduces a further distinction when he emphasizes the relationship of his film to the *memory* of a dream. The status of this distinction is cinematically null, but the phenomenon to which it alludes, the censor mechanism, is the paradigmatic case of experiential loss. The way in which this entire theoretical formulation interacts with the possibilities and structures of cinema determines the actual makeup of the film.

The opening shot introduces both the notion of metaphor and that of the filmic image. The camera looks into Brakhage's house through a window on which is imprinted the outline of the child's hands. This shot indirectly refers to one of the most famous images in the history of the American independent cinema, in which Maya Deren looks dreamily out of a window, her hands pressed to the pane, while the shadows of the trees outside blend with the waves of her hair within (from *Meshes of the Afternoon*). The recurrence and alternation of the window and the mirror as metaphors for cinema might be said to define the avant-garde cinema's image of itself. In this shot from *The Animals* we are reminded that the film itself, like the window, is a translucent surface upon which the vestiges of something now absent are imprinted. C. S. Peirce called this kind of image an index, a sign that witnesses the existence of that to which it refers (a bullet-hole, a footprint, and a photograph would be other examples). Indexicality is a problematic assumption in cinema; yet even though films continually unveil the ontological ambiguity of their images, the testimony of the index remains a continual seduction.

The emphasis on illness is not unusual in autobiographies. Whereas a biographer might note in passing any number of common childhood afflictions which his subject survived without damage, the autobiographer tends to present the illness less as a medical problem than as a crisis in consciousness. The attention of the parents, the puzzling effects of fever, the experiences of pain and fear, the restrictions of convalescence, etc. mark the period of sickness as a special moment in the memory. In the first of the three films, Brakhage represents the hospitalization of his youngest son, suffering, it appears, from pneumonia. Color negative visions of his siblings playing attempt a representation of his fever, but for the most part the film depicts the anxieties of the parents during the drive to the hospital and while waiting there.

I shall confine my analysis to the final part, *The Animals of Eden and After*, where Brakhage's theory of metaphor is developed more elaborately and more thoroughly than anywhere else in his films. I only wish to point out the irony of the title, *The Machine of Eden*. The machine which attracts the sick boy's attention is a loom! Adam and Eve had little use for such a thing as long as they lived in the Garden. "Machine" could also refer to the cognitive activity of the film, the mythopoetic mechanism. In either case this title is another of Brakhage's indications of the significance of metalepsis in the autobiographical films he has made: the end term of the mythic narrative—the loom—becomes the source of the myth. I would also draw the reader's attention to a further use of the concept "shape" in the letter to Sally Dixon, where the phenomenology of the myth-making tendency is collapsed upon an acknowledgement of the material conditions of film-making.

The most elaborate formulation of the paradox of imagery may occur in the third canto of Dante's *Paradiso*, where the *ad hoc* status of the entire vision of heaven the poet is about to witness is demonstrated:

> Quali per vetri trasparenti e tersi,
>   o ver per acque nitide e tranquille,
>   non sì profonde che i fondi sien persi,
> tornon di sì nostri visi le postille
>   debili sì, che perla in bianca fronte
>   non vien men tosto alle nostre pupille;
> tali vid' io più facce a parlar pronte;
>   per ch' io dentro all'error contrario corsi
>   a quel ch'accese amor tra l'omo e 'l fonte.
> Subito sì com' io di lor m'accorsi,
>   quelle stimando specchiati sembianti,
>   per veder di cui fosser, li occhi torsi;
> e nulla vidi, e ritorsili avanti
>   dritti nel lume della dolce guida,
>   che, sorridendo, ardea nelli occhi santi.

As through smooth and transparent glass, or through limpid and still water not so deep that the bottom is lost, the outlines of our faces return so faint that a pearl on a white brow does not come less quickly to our eyes, many such faces I saw, eager to speak; at which

I ran into the opposite error to that which kindled love between the man and the spring. The moment I was aware of them, taking them for reflected semblances, I turned my eyes to see whose they were, and saw nothing, and turned them forward again straight into the light of my sweet guide, whose holy eyes were glowing with a smile.[6]

I do not know if this crucial passage in Dante ever attracted Brakhage's attention; certainly some aspect of Dante has. The *Divine Comedy* is one of the few book titles the camera scans, as if by accident, in *The Animals of Eden and After*. Ezra Pound's observation that the *Paradiso* was literature's fullest example of a sustained single image came to Brakhage's attention when he was making *Dog Star Man: Part One* and lecturing on his version of Pound's theory of the sustained image. Furthermore Brakhage was reading the *Inferno* and studying Rauschenberg's collage illustrations for it when he made *The Horseman, The Woman, and The Moth*. He often repeated at that time his feeling that it was almost impossible for a modern artist to achieve a Paradiso in any form, or even a Purgatorio; Parker Tyler's biography of Pavel Tchelichew was one source for this pessimistic notion, but it was clear that Brakhage was referring to a problem in his own work when he brought this up in his lectures of the late 1960s.

To a certain extent the error of Narcissus and its opposite are demonstrated in *The Animals*. Yet Brakhage is not supported by the metaphysical certainty of a Dante. His theory of metaphor does not lead the mind to an ultimate source, to God. Rather like Rousseau and Nietzsche, he concludes that metaphoric thinking is the basis of language and, to use their common example, the invention of the word "tree" means the reduction of a visual particularity to a generalized type. The recognition of a similarity (metaphor) in a number of sights gives rise to the word and concept. Thereafter the particularity of those sights disappears. Instead one sees "a tree." This loss of sensual immediacy is compensated by an increase in power. This argument which Rousseau and Nietzsche share might be the scenario for *The Animals of Eden and After*.

The first part of the film is a metonymic series of shots of Brakhage's home, interior and exterior, apparently from the point of view of the child. The surrounding landscape during different seasons, details of furniture, hearthfire, children playing, and above all the numerous animals of the menage (goats, birds, dogs, an ass) appear in a montage of wanton lushness. The motive for joining one shot to another is primarily optical, not conceptual; something in the texture, color, saturation, or rhythm of one shot calls for a complement in the next. Among the most characteristic images of this first part is one of the mother sunbathing with a child at one side and a goat at the other. For Brakhage this metonymic sensual vision represents Edenic consciousness. He recognizes it not as an aboriginal state but as a moment situated between the fevered aberrations of intense illness and the conceptual and socially determined vision of the fully "recovered" child.

The turning point of the film follows the birth of a goat. Brakhage cuts from the color image of the animal's labor to a black and white image of a crying baby. The shift in film stocks emphasizes the decisiveness of this moment. Within the narrative of the film, this is the point at which the child, witnessing the birth of the animal, imagines his own birth. Since animals are so born, he must once have been. The actual birth is of course not within his conscious memory. Thus metaphor enters the scheme. It is an act of interpretation which brings the self of the observer into a regulatory relationship with what he sees. Metaphor is an act of identification, yet the act is predicated upon the difference of the elements which are to be equated. Every metaphor postulates a coherence where it first recognizes a disparity. The error of Narcissus was to take the image for reality, and to assume that the reality was other than himself; the opposite error would be to take the object of sight for the reflection of something unseen. The theory of metaphor is suspended between these two options.

The child in Brakhage's film takes the newborn goat as a type for his own invisible past; through metaphor he enters into the first and simplest autobiographical reflection; for it is with the introduction of this metaphoric montage that a linear operation of time enters the film. His recovery begins. He can play outside. There we see him recapitulating the primitive history of the species. He points his toy rifle at the dog, miming the primeval hunter. Mime itself is a further aspect of metaphor. The mother shoos away an annoying goat. The child feeds goats with a nippled baby's bottle. Many other shots distinguish the animals from the humans. At the moment when the child realized he was *like* the goat, he realized he was not the very same. Through metaphor he invented himself as human and reduced goats, dogs, etc. to the role of animals. Then they could be hunted, domesticated, even bottle-fed with a metaphoric rubber nipple. The sequence of feeding the goats is followed by an image of the hearth-fire and then the child eating. Here the montage schematizes the role of animals in the human universe.

The subsequent development of the film traces the amplifications of metaphor through play. With the initial recognition of the difference between animals and men comes a large increase in human power and authority, culminating in the eating of the animals who were born and raised for that purpose. At the same time the animals are seen to have something which is lacking in man. To recover this loss the human resorts to sympathetic magic. In the context of the film we now see the child wearing various halloween masks and aping animal gestures. Shortly afterwards the canary we had seen before in closeup, reappears now clearly imprisoned in a cage. Two different metaphoric developments of the bird follow. First, continuing the postulation of the film-maker that the games of children recapitulate the origins of human religion, the canary is followed by the image of the child wearing a dime store "Indian" headdress, which reminds us that these feathered chapelets gave their wearers the attributes of birds. Another sequence intercuts the caged bird with the crying child. Here is an elaboration of the initial man/animal comparison. The trapped bird now stands for the feeling of the weeping child. Metaphor comes to be the exterior representation of an invisible interiority. (In the portrait of his daughter Crystal in *15 Song Traits* Brakhage had earlier explored the cliché of representing a child's sadness with a caged bird.)

The curtain of a stage and the edge of an American flag appear in the penultimate montage. The very fragmentation, the effectiveness of synecdoche at this point, is a formal demonstration of the triumph of conceptual montage as the film ends. The curtain alludes to the prehistorical transition from sympathetic magic to religious, ritual theatre. The flag is the incarnation of the inflated symbol. Since the landscapes of the film represent the immediate environs of the Brakhage house in all the seasons, the immediate vision of home is determined by the horizon. The idea of a nation is a succession of horizons which can only be symbolically or metaphorically represented. The flag is the nation, visually. It is the largest and the most powerful of the metaphorical movements away from the immediate and the optical.

All three films in *The Weir-Falcon Saga* end with a shot of the moon. In *The Animals of Eden and After* that shot is immediately preceded by a Christmas-like decoration, a gilded tinsel in the shape of a five-pointed star. Here the difference between the popularized and secularized vestige of a religious ornament and a visible heavenly body (of which it is an abstracted, formalized representation) is cumulatively illustrated. Not only is the difference perceptual; it is also historical; for the ornament not only represents a star, but also Christmas and the more ancient fertility festivals of which it is a survival.

Brakhage's point is that we are always surrounded by a world of metaphors, overlaid like a palimpsest, conventionalized traces of once powerful perceptions, which induce us to see the world as reflections of ourselves. The child of his film, and the film-maker himself, for whom the son stands as an autobiographical metaphor, was born into and is part of such a world. His illness created a temporary disengagement from this world of symbolical meanings. His readjustment to the normal world takes the form of a myth of creation (*The Machine of Eden*) followed by a myth of evolution. The key word in the title of the last film is "After." Eden comes into existence only *after* it disappears. Any version of innocence is a negative metaphor, something unlike the present. Metaphoric thought defines human consciousness. Although it cannot be avoided, it can be suspended and explored. Within cinematic terms, metaphor is the aftering of one shot by another. We see a kid being born; *after* that the human "kid" cries. The process Eisenstein called intellectual montage (which he considered the summit of cinematic representation) is the *after*ing of images such that the later image controls and makes more precise the meaning of the earlier. The most famous example in Eisenstein's work is the "God and Country" sequence in *October*, where he uses the iconology of comparative religion to deflate the idea of God and the overabundance of military medals to diffuse the idea of country. This *after*ing is a fundamentally retrospective process, which becomes a model for all temporal thought. Perceptual abstraction, then, is the superimposition of some past upon the sensual present, in which consciousness invents history, the self, the principles of identity and difference, and by compounding these metaphors, God and Country.

6

If *The Animals of Eden and After* explores the fact of cinematic succession as a model for autobiography, *Sincerity* (*reel one*) treats the autobiographical moment in terms of the encounter of camera and object. Just as the *after*ing of frames and shots is an a priori condition of all films, the stare of the camera at something is not the only, but certainly the overwhelmingly dominant way of producing images on those frames. The theme of *Sincerity* (*reel one*) is Brakhage's incarnation as an artist. Here he quests impossibly to represent the moment he became a film-maker. The time span runs from his birth to the making of his first film, *Interim*.

Wordsworth having been given the task of writing an autobiography that would record "the growth of a poet's mind" gives us the following exchange of glances as the earliest moment of his *Prelude*:

> Blest the infant Babe,
> (For with my best conjectures I would trace
> The progress of our being,) blest the Babe,
> Nursed in his Mother's arms, the Babe who sleeps
> Upon his Mother's breast; who, when his soul
> Claims manifest kindered with an earthly soul,
> Doth gather passion from his Mother's eye!
> Such feelings pass into his torpid life
> Like an awakening breeze, and hence his mind
> Even [in the first trial of its powers]
> Is prompt and watchful, eager to combine
> In one appearance, all the elements
> And parts of the same object, else detached
> And loth to coalesce. Thus, day by day,
> Subjected to the discipline of love,
> His organs and recipient faculties
> Are quickened, are more vigorous, his mind spreads,
> Tenacious of the forms which it receives.[7]
>
> (Book II, 237-254, 1805-6 version)

I doubt that Brakhage has paid too much attention to Wordsworth;

he is too thoroughly excluded from the Poundian paideuma to which the film-maker largely subscribes. Yet something of what he would have found in the *Prelude* he encountered in an essay of Ray L. Birdwhistell, of which I can find no copy or even a reference:

> We work together in the sense that I'm very concerned to get woman's vision into it. I mean that every woman in the world for instance has a certain specific, different visual possibility than any man: one of them is that women are trained (as has been proved by Ray L. Birdwhistle [*sic*] the kinesiologist) to move their eyes while the eyes are closed: and all of boy babies (and therefore—men) are trained by the same mothers to never move the pupils of their eyes during a blink or while the eyes are closed: and no one knows why mothers all over the world train babies this way. Certainly it's mysterious when you consider that a woman for the first time in her life, confronting her son, begins to hold her eyes steady while blinking and closing them (which she has never before done in her entire history as a woman—or certainly never easily or often): she does this specifically with her son without knowing why, or even knowing that she does it, so that he'll have that specificity of sight, as distinct from any daughter. This is just one thing we know. There's an infinite number of differences in what all women share very closely as distinct from any man, in sight: and I'm concerned to get simply the woman's view into the work. And so Jane (in an incredible number of mysterious ways, leading from conversation, to frowns, to smiles, to the whole mysterious complex of our life) makes this possible.[8]

The grandmother's eyes and the mother's face are the first images in *Sincerity*. The entire film might be seen as an elaboration on that moment, as if all that passed, between the opening encounter of the camera and an old photograph and the final scene of the mature Brakhage staring into the camera, took place during the moment of the film-maker's meditation on the static image of his mother.

In *Sincerity* the photograph album is extensively exploited. The opening shots follow a pattern. The camera shifts from the young Brakhage in the pictures to some detail, e.g. a trellis, part of a roof, in the background. Then in color, and with a moving camera, the film-maker seeks out that site today. The autobiographical dilemma of this film is the failure of a site to recover the plenitude of past experience. That is why so much of the film is a study of the campus of Dartmouth College, where he went for a semester and quit while "faking" a nervous breakdown. The quitting of college coincided with a decision to make films.

The college site is particularly fitting to the film-maker's enterprise. Colleges, especially in the Ivy League, are unusually conservative environments. Architectural change is shunned. Thus Brakhage can wander with his camera through the same rooms, across the same lawns, into the same cafeterias that he ate in, twenty years earlier, without encountering much physical change. The look of

Sincerity: *two sequential images; the first shows Brakhage in the 1950s (in black and white), the second shows a view of Dartmouth (in color)*

the students certainly has changed, but Brakhage only shows them from a far distance, or as shadows. The token of the failure of place to stand for memory, however, is the painted sign of the Dartmouth Inn, with its 18th Century banqueters, which recurs several times in this passage. It plays the same double role of the still photographs; it demarcates the area of representation for which it suggests irrecoverable pastness.

Isolated images which had been used metaphorically earlier in the film, such as some broken glass, or a distorted reflecting surface, are encountered in the college episode as metonymic details of the environment. This strategy diffuses the earlier metaphors and puts into question the temporal organization of the whole film. However, the crucial metaphoric substitution is of a different order in this film than the comparable moment in the *Animals of Eden and After*. Brakhage is filming the view from the window of a college room when the scene cuts to an expressionistic avant-garde film of the 1950s. He throws a cup of water against the wall of his room and, in frustration, moves to the window. This sequence is matched with the position of the window in the color sequence of the college. Here the implication is that the emotional tone which he cannot recover at present day Dartmouth is preserved in the "fictional" film in which he acted soon after leaving the college.

Soon after this turn the film shifts to the site of his own first film, *Interim*. Fortunately for *Sincerity*, Stan Phillips, Brakhage's cameraman for that initial venture, would take shots of the crew with the bits of film left near the ends of the reels. The young Brakhage seems to have deplored this playfulness; for he appears in many of these clips furiously ordering the cameraman to stop. In any case, one has for the moment of making *Interim* what was lacking in the other moments of the autobiography, a filmic record. At least apparently so.

It is remarkable that none of the crew, nor the actors when they are not performing, can stand the gaze of the camera. They clown, grimace, turn away, blush, or order the shot stopped. The entire film is directed toward this scene of recovered representation which turns out to be camera shy.

Among the production clips is a long shot of eyes. He quickly intercuts that youthful stare of the protagonist of *Interim* with another shot of his own eyes at the time of making *Sincerity*. In this case, the alternating montage creates an impossible mutual stare over more than twenty years. Of course, the temporal displacement is not the only one. Any encounter represented by the intercutting of two sets of eyes or two faces in cinema is mediated by the unseen presence of the camera. In this case, the actor looked into a camera in 1953 and Brakhage looked into one sometime in the 1970s. The alternating montage fictionally erased the presence of the camera and aligned the eyes. This substitution of another image for the presence of the camera is as important in defining the cinematic

limitation of autobiography as is the more dramatic and obvious
trope of the stare across time. For the one demarcation of the
present here is presence to the camera, which is always a past, or an
absent moment at the time of editing. The alternations of montage
are tropes to recover the presence of the moment of filming. Again
the encounter of self with self as dramatized in *Sincerity* becomes
a study of the artificial temporality of all cinema. The moment of
artistic incarnation is represented not as a moment within the film,
but as a recognition of the status of cinema as demonstrated by the
form of the film.

7

I spent some paragraphs analyzing the dilemma Brakhage encountered when he began *Scenes From Under Childhood* in formulating theoretically a performative model for an essentially representational film. The unarticulated principle behind Brakhage's theory
could be expressed thus: the mnemonics of watching the flicker
effect is universal; so a sufficiently schematic representation of the
mnemonic response will induce a personal and proportional reaction in every viewer.

At approximately the same time the performative autobiography,
par excellence, was being made by Hollis Frampton. It is entitled
(*nostalgia*), and is part of an elaborate, nonautobiographical series
Hapax Legomena. In (*nostalgia*) Frampton presents his incarnation as a film-maker as the terminus of his work as a still photographer. While metaphor is the figure that continually fascinates
Brakhage, irony holds a comparable lure for Frampton. The subjective is not a primary dimension of Frampton's cinema, and the subjectivity of (*nostalgia*) is ironized after the manner of one of his
literary masters, Borges. The specific nature of this irony consists
in clarifying the difference between the maker's stimulus and the
viewer's response. For Frampton the sympathetic congruence between the self of the film-maker and the self of the viewer (Brakhage's equation) is an absurdity.

The structure of his film is a series of systematic displacements
between language and image, between flatness and depth, between
stillness and motion. The most striking of these displacements is the
linguistic, which very obviously undermines the indexical unity of
picture and sound. Such a unity manifested in Hill's *Film Portrait*
every time he would use the word "this." ("It would be nice if *this*
would happen again," he tells us, and we take the "this" to refer
unproblematically to what we see, the presentation of an Academy
Award.) Frampton does not respect this form of unity. He shows us a
still photograph and while we are looking at it, he tells us about the
next one we will see. Yet he does so without letting us in on the
displacement. The present tense and the demonstrative pronouns
are deliberately deceptive. In this way the correspondence between
picture and description is postponed until the viewer makes the

adjustment, which can be after several of the stills have gone by. This simple technique effectively unpacks the temporal category of the present in the film; the words anticipate the pictures, the pictures recall the words, so that as we look at the film we are induced to perform simultaneous acts: to imagine a photograph which would correspond to the description (and thereby to repeat again and again the recognition of the limitations of the pictorial imagination), to remember the earlier description and appreciate the irony with which it describes what we are seeing, and finally to experience, in the present, the disjunctive synchronicity.

But that is not all. The photographs rest, one at a time, on a hotplate. After some minutes the shape of the electric coils begins to burn its way through. The new, pristine photograph comes on only after the previous one has been reduced to a crisp. The metaphor of the consumption of memory turns into an ironic joke. Yet at the same time, without any visible cause, the still image has turned into a moving (burning) one; each time the fire comes as if from within the still. In this transformation we repeatedly recognize our disorientation; for we are looking *down* upon the horizontal hotplate although our tendency is to interpret the internal orientation of the photographic image as a vertical camera setup. Finally, the patently flat space of the still's surface, with its illusionary mapping of depth, turns into the shallow depth of the space between the hotplate and the camera, or at least the illusionary mapping of that depth on the flatness of the film screen.

The anticipatory descriptions leave one image unaccounted for: the first, of the darkroom itself; and one only left to the imagination: the last, which is said to be so horrifying that it terminated the artist's will to be a still photographer. The temptation is set for us to interpret the film's time as circular. This temptation is even greater the first time one sees the film when the image of the darkroom has so faded in the memory that it is all the more susceptible to the paranoid rhetoric of the final description, which I will quote in full:

> Since 1966 I have made a few photographs. This has been partly through design, and partly through laziness. I think I expose fewer than fifty negatives a year now. Of course I work more deliberately than I once did, and that counts for something. But I must confess that I have largely given up still photography.
>
> So it is all the more surprising that I felt again, a few weeks ago, a vagrant urge that would have seemed familiar a few years ago: the urge to take my camera out of doors and make a photograph. It was a quite simple, obtrusive need. So I obeyed it.
>
> I wandered around for hours, unsatisfied, and finally turned towards home in the afternoon. Half a block from my front door, the receding perspective of an alley caught my eye . . . a dark tunnel with the cross-street beyond brightly lit. As I focused and composed the image, a truck turned into the alley. The driver stopped it, got out and walked away. He left his cab door open.

My composition was spoiled, but I felt a perverse impulse to make the exposure anyway. I did so, and then went home to develop my single negative.

When I came to print the negative, an odd thing struck my eye. *Something,* standing in the cross-street and invisible to me, was reflected in a factory window, and then reflected once more in the rear-view mirror attached to the truck door. It was only a tiny detail.

Since then, I have enlarged this small section of my negative enormously. The grain of the film all but obliterates the features of the image. It is obscure; by any possible reckoning, it is hopelessly ambiguous.

Nevertheless, what I *believe* I see recorded, in that speck of film, fills me with such fear, such utter dread and loathing, that I think I shall never dare to make another photograph again.

Here it is!

Look at it!

Do you see what I see? [9]

If the film describes a circle, then the horror is the terror of solipsism, of finding only the metonomies of one's origins in the accidents of exterior vision. This may only be a deliberate attempt to make us consider the seductions of the myth of cyclical time, and again be confounded. There is still another obscure option. The one thing one does see after the question "Do you see what I see?" is the film-maker's monograph, the HF with which he signs his films. Yet this holds even less satisfaction than the circular form. The simple, unbearably ironic answer to the final question must be: "No. I do not see what you see." The narrator is no longer listening, of course. But that seems to be much of the point—the fruitlessness of the entire subjectivist quest, so complexly articulated by Brakhage, of establishing a correspondence, or even a calculus of the limits of a correspondence, between the film-maker's vision and his films. Frampton is having his cake and eating it too; but that indeed may be his definition of all autobiographical madness. The very wantonness of the pronoun "I" does not escape him. In "A Pentagram for Conjuring the Narrative," he wrote:

"I" is the English familiar name by which an unspeakably intricate network of colloidal circuits—or, as some reason, the garrulous temporary inhabitant of the nexus—addresses itself; occasionally, etiquette permitting, it even calls itself that in public. How it came to be there (together with some odd bits of phantasmal rubbish) is a subject for virtually endless speculation: it is certainly alone; and in time it convinces itself, somewhat reluctantly, that it is waiting to die.[10]

In the film Michael Snow reads the text Frampton wrote. As a result there is a comically touching passage in which Snow apologizes to himself for an unsatisfactory job Frampton did in making a photographic announcement for his (Snow's) show of sculpture.

The language of the various descriptions freely mixes a great number of deliberately veiled personal references to events unrelated to images on the screen, often of an erotic nature, with parodies of

(nostalgia): *self-portrait of Frampton at 23 years old.*

several kinds of art-historical discourse. There is an hilarious Panof-skian interpretation of the religious iconography of two toilets. The formalistic language associated with the followers of Clement Greenberg is finely misappropriated for a found-object image of a forlorn planter among his flooded grapefruits. Vassarian biography, technical shoptalk, and art gossip have their chances as well. We are left, especially after the quasi-apocalyptic tone of the final text, with a thorough suspicion of the relationship of word to image, which corresponds apparently for Frampton with the moment of his incarnation as a film-maker.

The second description (and the third photograph) of (*nostalgia*) reflects the autobiographical paradox. The text promises a self-portrait of the artist at twenty-three years old and exults in the complete physical renewal of his cells since that time. There is considerable humor in hearing Snow delighting in not being Frampton, or Frampton not being himself, depending upon where one locates the narrative voice. If we believe this witty text there is hardly anything which connects either Snow *or* Frampton with the picture of the young man of a dozen years earlier.

INTERLUDE

The film of artistic incarnation is one of the primary forms of the avant-garde film autobiography. Frampton's ironic treatment of this topos extends to a note he published along with the text:

The narrative art of most young men is autobiographical. Since I have had little narrative experience, it seemed reasonable to accept *biography* as a convention, rather, however little information was available to me.

My subject, hoping abjectly to be taken for a man of his time, had practiced rigorous self-effacement for a decade or more. So I was forced into examining his leavings and middens, like an archaeologist sifting for ostracising pot shards.

Since he had once been myself, I knew exactly where to look. Random debts and documents aside, he had left behind some thousands of still photographs made during his apprenticeship to the art I expound. Because my results were to be made public, I chose a mere dozen of these specimens to examine, leaving the rest for later investigators who would be doubly fortunate: first in their sentiment for their antagonist, and again in their intimacy with his work.

Since I still shared some of his aspirations, I found the photographs I chose (as distinct from those I discarded) fairly embarrassing. So I decided, humanely, to destroy them (retaining the negatives, of course, against unpredictable future needs) by *burning*. My biographical film would be a document of this compassionate act! [11]

(*nostalgia*) is the object of a brilliant parody by George Landow in his film *Wide Angle Saxon*. There it is a typical avant-garde film by the imaginary film-maker Al Rutcurts, whose name is an anagram for "structural," a term I used to characterize what was held in common by film-makers such as Frampton, Snow, and Landow in the late 1960s, and to which Landow (and most of the others) thoroughly objected. The subject of *Wide Angle Saxon* experiences a religious conversion while watching "Regrettable Redding Condescension," the Al Rutcurts film whose title parodies Landow's own *Remedial Reading Comprehension*. The very boredom with which he experiences the film allows his mind to wander to a Biblical passage which converts him. In the parody of (*nostalgia*) we see red paint poured over a hot plate which eventually makes it bubble, while we hear Michael Snow's voice describing this "art" and asking "Do you see what I see?"

Although there is obviously hostility in Landow's parody of Frampton, Landow himself incorporates a number of perceptual and linguistic ironies in his own three versions of the film of artistic incarnation. He has referred to *Institutional Quality* and *Remedial Reading Comprehension*, in conversation and in interviews, as autobiographical films. They are actually hardly autobiographical in the sense I have been elaborating here: they do not represent diachronical reflection in any manner. They are elaborately witty films about the moment of artistic vocation. Both ironically situate that moment as an aberrant response to institutionalized testing situations.

Institutional Quality is "a test to see how well you can follow instructions," in the words of the female examiner, a schoolmarm type, who appears at the opening of the film. Landow has a great love for instructional films; this is the first of several "facsimiles" he has made of that genre. In this test, the audience is told to look at a "picture" of a room. The only thing moving in the room, which distinguishes it from being a still, is the banding on the television. We are told to put numbers on objects to which the examiner refers. Following the first instruction, a hand appears, carrying out the order. This image has two functions: it suddenly interrupts the fictive rapport between the film and the viewer by shifting the "you" of the examiner's instructions from being any viewer, to a specific unidentified hand; and at the same time the scale of the room shifts as a pencil as big as the couch puts a number on the lamp. Thus the "I" of the film-maker is ambiguously introduced as the examinee. The tone of the instructor evokes those standardized examinations administered in public elementary schools, not so much to determine individual achievement as to test native intelligence (the I.Q. of the title) or to provide broad statistics on education. Those tests typically constituted special, sometimes fearful, interruptions of the normal academic schedule. The film suggests such a privileged moment in the history of a developing mind.

The hand performs three tasks: numbers the lamp, the mirror, and the television. All three have been employed within avant-garde films as metaphors for cinema. The numbering of the television alludes to still another instructional moment in the past of the film-maker. During his childhood a didactic television program for children, Winky Dink and You, "taught" drawing by having the child-viewer cover his television with a "Winky Dink screen" and follow the hand of an artist who traced a simple figure before the camera.

The jargon of television reappears in the final part of the film when we see the term "a re-enactment" superimposed over the threading of a projector by a very self-conscious young woman. In the language of advertising a reenactment is the theatrical representation of the testing or demonstration of a product, which is reputed to have occurred at some originary moment in the past. By ending his film in this way, Landow comments upon the fictional status of any authorative representation of the past while he shows with perverse literalism the restaging of an act essential to the experience of his own film, the threading of the projector sometime in the past.

Between these two points most of the film consists of questions and demonstrations of film equipment, while the examiner drones on, unheeded, about numbering the now unseen bed, towel, etc. If we follow the subjective presence alluded to by the numbering hand, and consider the entire work as situated within his consciousness, then the shift from the "picture" to the meditation on film equipment comes to represent the wandering attention of the incipient film-maker. He defies the instructions, or he listens to another set of "instructions" which are his vocation.

Remedial Reading Comprehension is a very similar film in structure. Its central element is a found object, a filmed test, in which phrases flash into focus in very quick succession either to test or to improve the viewer's reading speed. The test itself happens to concern the abuses of the classical academic situation and the god-like authority of the teacher over pupils. This test shares the center of the film with a "facsimile" advertisement for preprocessed rice (which Landow abhors), and these two foci are framed by the image of the film-maker running. As he runs he is superimposed over his own shadow in an image rephotographed from a screen with deliberate crudity, so that the flatness and the cinematic thinness of the double self-image is apparent. Over the first of these framing images the words appear: "This is a film about you." And over the repetition the sentence concludes: "Not about its maker." If we understand by "you" the address of Landow to his own image as it appears on the screen, the text refers simply to the impossibility of autobiography. However the determinations of "you" become very ambiguous. Right after the first phrase appears on the screen the advertising announcer repeats and extends it: "This is a film about you. Imagine your name is Madge and you have just cooked some rice." With the name, a woman's face appears. Our instinctive reaction is to assume she is Madge. But, no, she too addresses the viewer: "This rice is delicious, Madge." The very instability of the shifter "you" (or by implication "I") thus is fundamental to the structure of the film, which has at least one more twist. The opening image is of a young woman sleeping; a tiny movie appears above her head, like the cartoon of a dream. It eventually expands to fill the whole screen, covering the sleeper's image. Her negative silhouette comes back during the reading test, as if to remind us of the oneiric framework of this elaborately framed film. The dream is of a classroom auditorium, much like the rooms in which *Remedial Reading Comprehension* is usually projected. So proceeding along the sequence of structural qualifications this would be a film about a dream about a class seeing a film about "You . . . not its maker" which is interrupted by a fraudulent rice advertisement and a reading test.

Here is a note the film-maker wrote about it:

> *Remedial Reading Comprehension:* The important thing to see is that the film contains visual metaphors. The first image is a female head, horizontal and more or less suggestive of three-dimensional space. The next to last image is the same head which becomes a white silhouette in a shallow white (not black) space. Compare the two grains of rice—whole grain (brown) and processed (white). The white rice grain has lost its "essence" (the germ), just as the silhouette has lost its three dimensionality. One thing this suggests is the process of removing substance, which is done to food, art, environment, religion, etc. An art that becomes personal removes some of the substance to get a "purer" product. The film-maker himself appears in the film, yet he tells us it is about us and "not about its maker." Certain images—the rice, "Madge's" friend—are impersonal. They might be images from TV Commercials or industrial promotional films. There is a relationship between the personal and non-personal images which is roughly the same as the relationship between the first image and the next-to-last image. Before the

female becomes a silhouette there is a transition period in which a struggle seems to take place between the three dimensional form and the flat one. The rhythm of the sound track is the rhythm of this alteration. When the struggle is over, the three dimensional form disappears and a new rhythm is heard—the rhythm of the abstract symbols—words—which have been moving across the field of struggle.[12]

The deliberate plan of the film situates the moment of vocation in a compound experience of academic, oneiric, linguistic, and advertising instruction. The shifter "you" stands as the formal model for the necessarily negative power derived from these instructions. He becomes a film-maker by displacing their meaning. He turns against his schools, against the dominantly subjective and oneiric cinema of Deren, Brakhage, and Markopoulos, against the rhetoric of the commercial, but he nevertheless draws formal inspiration from all of them. In attending to the grammar of the art, not to its themes and polemics, he comprehends his vocation, which is to be remedial.

On April 2, 1974 Landow projected several of his films for the New York Film Council using two projectors at a time. On that occasion he spoke of making one long feature film by incorporating and if necessary revising his earlier works. "I'm looking back over my life and trying to find some consistency," he told them. Two years later, I confronted him directly on the issue of autobiography in his work (June 4, 1976, Arts Forum Program WNYC-FM). He answered: "I do not mean autobiography in the sense of actual events that really happened to me, but an attempt in a formal way to reenact or restage the kind of events that have happened and are happening to me." In this context his reaction to a malicious arts-school prank becomes interesting. Two students, inspired by Landow's performances as part of a theoretical course he was giving, staged a performance of their own. They hired thugs to kidnap the teacher for some hours. Landow's description of his frightened reaction before he knew what the prank was about was, "I thought the characters of my films had come to attack me." The sudden encounter with the figures of his own imagination is the subject of his third film of incarnation. Here is how he described *New Improved Institutional Quality* in the Canyon Cinema News:

A reworking of an earlier film, INSTITUTIONAL QUALITY, in which the same test was given. In the earlier film the person taking the test was not seen, and the film viewer in effect became test taker. The newer version concerns itself with the effects of the test on the test taker. An attempt is made to escape from the oppressive environment of the test—a test containing meaningless, contradictory, and impossible-to-follow directions—by entering into the imagination. In this case it is specifically the imagination of the filmmaker, in which the test taker encounters images from previous Landow films: the blinking test pattern girl from FILM IN WHICH THERE APPEAR EDGE LETTERING, DIRT PARTICLES, SPROCKET HOLES, ETC., and the running alien from REMEDIAL READING COMPREHENSION (where the "alienated" filmmaker himself appeared). The test taker is "initiated" into this world by passing through a shoe (the shoe of "the woman who has dropped something") which has lost its normal spatial proportions, just as taking the test has caused the test taker to lose his sense of proportion. As he moves through the images in the filmmaker's mind, the test taker is in a trance like state, and is carried along by some unseen force. This is an allusion to the "trance film" and the "triumph of the imagination" described in P. Adams Sitney's *Visionary Film*. At the end of the film the test taker is back at his desk, still following directions. His "escape" was only temporary, and thus not a true escape at all.[13]

One of the basic strategies of literary autobiography is for the author to narrate his life by reviewing his writings. Kierkegaard's *My Point of View as an Author: Report to History* is such an account of what the autobiographer deems important in his life; much of Nietzsche's *Ecce Homo* addresses itself to the rubric "why I write such good books." The *New Improved Institutional Quality* is Landow's examination of the power and status of his cinematic imagination. In an interview with P. G. Springer, Landow said: "The biggest question that keeps coming back, haunting you, wherever you go, in various forms is 'Why did you make that film?'" And that's impossible to answer. You might as well be asked why you even make films, why you are an artist. And there are so many factors that go into determining that: heredity, early childhood experiences, prenatal experiences . . ." Landow is talking about the questions posed by naive audiences, but he is also touching upon the haunting questions that the autobiographer asks himself. If the question "Why do you even make films?" is too complicated to answer, as he implies, he brings it under control by shifting it from the genetic form to a study of the imagination as demonstrated by his own previous films.

The first film that the 1976 *New Improved Institutional Quality* looks back upon is, of course, the *Institutional Quality* of 1968. In repeating most of the sound track of the first film, he shifts the "person," which had been a second-person address to the camera as viewer (with the insertion of the first-person hand as both the filmmaker and the mediator of the viewer). Naturally the synecdoche of the hand leaves the respondent's age, sex, and characteristics empty. The tone of the questions, and the way they are repeated, suggests that the test is for a group of school children. There is comic irony therefore, in seeing a man with grey hair looking into the camera, as if at a teacher, and grimacing as he tries to follow directions, when the later film opens. Like many of the characters in Landow's films, he is a middle class, undistinguished type who behaves slightly out of place; at times he is somewhat grotesque. Even more so is the large "woman who dropped something" who appears in the middle of the film as if she were an object. The choice of such figures entails a desire to cut off any act of identification on the viewer's part or to stall any assumption that the film-maker is representing himself through these characters. Without being particularly distinguished, figures like these, or Earl Greaves in *Wide Angle Saxon,* are socially defined, non-artistic types, not shadowy universals.

The man obeys when he is told to look at the picture in front of him. "Picture" is a crucially ambiguous word for Landow. He has made two films in a series *What's Wrong With This Picture?.* Something is depicted in a picture; and the status of this something cannot be rigorously determined through the depiction. In *Institutional Quality* the attention wandered from the "picture" at the point where two things happened: first, the instructions ceased to generate metaphors for cinema; and second, the instructions no longer referred to objects we had seen in the "picture" or at least the portion of it filmed. In the *New Improved* version, the examinee attempts to answer all the questions even after he has been warned "You will not be able to answer some of the questions." But before he has a chance to respond to even the first one, Landow introduces a doubt into the picture/sound relationship. While the unseen voice continues a sentence uninterrrupted, the image of the man dissolves into another of him in the same position as if an indeterminate amount of time has passed. Here the "picture" that we are looking at does not exactly correspond to the situation implied by the sound.

His responses at first resemble the earlier film: a large hand with a pen writes a number on the image of the television. But after that another dissolve occurs. This one readjusts the scale in the opposite direction: the actor is suddenly in the actual room of the "picture" and he repeats his task by putting a number on the actual television. From this point until almost the end of the film, the man moves with the world of the "picture" numbering things, not their depictions, and, in general, looking quizzically back at the camera as he tries to take the figurative instructions literally.

The form of the instructions always involves imagining an event in the actual world, e.g., "Turn on the television," then numbering the corresponding image in the world of the picture. The examinee, having entered the "picture", does not perform the hypothetical action, but numbers "the thing he would touch." At times the resistance of the object to being written upon intensifies the comedy. For example, among the more intricate directions ignored in the original film is, "If the bed is made up, put a number 15 on the bed; if the bed is not made up put a number 16 on the bed." In the 1976 version we seen an expanse of flowery bedspread for the first time. It was not in the first "picture" the man looked at. On to it crawls the examinee, filmed from above. He pulls down the bedspread and writes a 16 on the now unmade bed, apparently because it is easier to write on the white sheet than on the yellow flower pattern.

In the initial version there was an association implied between the numbering of images and the number-grid that the film-maker superimposed over the projector to identify its parts. In the middle of the new version this association is made explicit. The number 18 appears over the umbrella when that is called for by the instructing voice. The film-maker is thus complying with the exigencies of the test in the way he makes his images. This superimposed number also scrambles the temporal illusions of the film, since the film-maker's act of following the instructions is not simultaneous with the examinee's. A later superimposition of the phrase "Insert close-up" compounds the temporal vertigo by implying that the film is not yet finished, and that a reminder of a task to be done later remains on the surface of the film-in-progress.

These two superimpositions are the first two steps by which Landow begins to integrate his image-making with the act of imagination depicted from the moment when the test-taker entered the "picture." The next step involves the referentiality of the objects to be numbered. In the first version, there was a framed picture sitting on the television which was the object of an instruction. That it was a "picture" was enough; we could not make out the image within the frame. In the later film it is a color photograph of a woman, herself "framed" by a three-dimensional pattern of color bands. The image is a "facsimile" with some displacement of the single image of Landow's *Film In Which There Appear Sprocket Holes, Edge Lettering, Dirt Particles, Etc.*, where a woman in a found bit of a commercial color test pattern blinks repeatedly in a loop. The examinee dutifully numbers this photograph (or pseudo-still) from the film-maker's earlier work.

The most striking sequence in *New Improved Institutional Quality* begins when the man tries to number the shoe of "the woman who dropped something." As he crawls toward her foot, the scale shifts once more. He is suddenly crawling within an enormous replica of her shoe. It seems to be about twelve feet long and seven high. As he examines the shoe a telephone rings and the instructor says, "Answer the telephone, answer the telephone, put a number 4 on what you would touch." This is the only correspondence between sound and instruction in the test; the telephone never enters the "picture." As the examinee tries to respond he floats off as if in a trance, past two images from Landow films. The girl of the photograph, her image filling the whole screen, has come alive and blinks at the camera, and another actor, running in place, wears the sign "This is a film about you," which is a displaced facsimile from *Remedial Reading Comprehension*. He never reaches the telephone. The film ends with a shot of him at his desk as he was in the beginning.

The two facsimiles by which Landow chooses to represent his cinematic imagination are very interesting. In the case of the blinking woman, the image Landow used in *Film In Which* was something he found, not something he made up, imagined. So here he reimagines her twice. First, as a still photograph, a parody of a graduation portrait that might be found in the type of middle class home represented in the "picture." Second, the mechanical illusion of loop printing, her blink, becomes a physical attribute. The jogging figure too is no longer an image born of the film laboratory when words were superimposed over an already doubled image. He carries this sign like an obsessed preacher. Or, recalling the metaphor for the autobiographer Wordsworth "found" when he encountered the blind beggar who wore the story of how he came to be so on his chest, we can contrast Landow's paradox of subjectivity: the film-maker is most himself, truest to his style, when he either finds his shot, or when he is denying his centrality to his own film. For in reimagining the sequence from *Remedial Reading Comprehension* he has chosen to objectify the most ambiguous moment in his works.

As in several other Landow films there is a linguistic reference in the full title *New Improved Institutional Quality: In the Environment Of Liquids and Nasals A Parastic Vowel Sometimes Develops.* Landow has said that this phrase which he found in a book on language struck him because of the ambiguities of the words "liquids", "environment", and "parasitic." According to the theme of the film, in certain environments the imagination temporarily manifests itself. It is parasitic to the extent that it cannot invent its images whole-cloth, but shifts scale, takes the figurative literally, alters materials, condenses and displaces elements from its past experience. An example of the formation of a parasitic vowel between a liquid and a nasal would be the common mispronunciation *filum* for *film.*

The two earlier films of artistic incarnation postulated the moment of becoming a film-maker as the moment of recognizing the ontological instability of filmic representation. The converse moment would occur when the film-maker considers his images as if they had a life of their own; their status would be "improved." That is what momentarily happens in the version of 1976.

Landow emphasizes the temporary, and therefore illusionary, quality of the imaginative environment. In this respect, with characteristically ambiguous irony, he has some fun with my book *Visionary Film.* In order fully to situate the temporality that the three films of incarnation reveal, we must briefly consider the other films that Landow has made since 1968. The title, *Thank You Jesus For The Eternal Present,* which puns on "present" as gift and as time, is the most explicit reference to the film-maker's conversion to Christianity, or more specifically to Messianic Judaism, in 1968. The theme of conversion as such does not occur in any of the three films of artistic incarnation, but in the nonautobiographical *Wide Angle Saxon.* Christian autobiography focuses on the moment of conversion. Conversion is the turn which makes it possible for the author to make sense of his earlier life, which he subsequently narrates as the stages leading to conversion. Landow however has decided to deal with his incarnation as an artist in the most secular of his recent films. I believe this is because he recognizes that the problematics of time in cinema are at odds with both the eschatology and the temporal/eternal distinction in his Christian films. As a Christian, Landow acknowledges a rational historical order which takes its meaning from the historical drama of Christ as the fulfillment of ancient prophecies and the definition of the future of time. All this is quite explicit in *Wide Angle Saxon.*

The films of artistic incarnation, however, are all investigations of repetition. In *Institutional Quality* the very repetition of threading and projecting the film appears at almost the last moment to confound the pseudo-decisions about how to *start* to make films. The point of origin in *Remedial Reading Comprehension* is itself repeated and varied: a dream, a class, a film, an advertisement, the reading of a text. It is re-medial, or a new origin and a new artist, to undo the patterns of aberration already inscribed in dreams, schools, films, advertisements, tests, and texts. The *New Improved Institutional Quality* locates the moment of imagination in the momentary illusion that images are "things you would touch." This is not an eternal realm; and unlike some of his fellow avant-garde film-makers Landow does not seem to believe that the artist has a privileged relationship with God. The realm depicted here is parasitic, continually shifting and displacing images taken from all that has already been made, including art, even the art of the "same" film-maker.

8

Autobiographical cinema is complex in essence. In the examples from Brakhage it is hyperbolically complex. The complexity of the autobiographical films is linked to the prevalence of ironic structures these films require. Perhaps it is the avoidance, or at least the attempt to contain irony, that leads to the intellectual complexities of Brakhage's *Book of the Film.* Of all the films I have been analyzing here, it is the least humorous. The others are all very funny.

I come lastly to the autobiography of the greatest ironist of the avant-garde cinema: James Broughton's *Testament* is the purest and to my mind the most powerful of the recent film autobiographies. In style and in technique it is quite eclectic; its most moving sequence comes right out of *Film Portrait,* a sequence of photographs moving backward in chronology. Yet an extreme and profound transformation of the strategies of autobiography is the result of Broughton's art.

The opening trope brings together an allusion to Maya Deren (the reversed sea from *At Land*), who was one of the major inspirations of Broughton's early cinema, and a recollection of "the aging balletomane" (the rocking chair), the icon of retrospective fancy in Broughton's *Four in the Afternoon.* In this shot, the film-maker himself sits in a rocking chair on a beach. His rocking movement indicates a sympathetic union with the sea he contemplates. This image, with its several variations, including reverse photography (where Broughton walks backwards out of the backwards rolling waves to reoccupy the empty chair) presents the constitutive moment of the film: everything occurs as if recalled from the extended rhythmic figure. The empty chair is one of the strong substitutions for the moment of death in *Testament.* When the film-maker comes back into it, he acknowledges the ad hoc cinematic illusion of autobiographical continuity. This metaphorical use of reverse motion also occurred in *Film Portrait*. Broughton's choice of imagery, his superb timing, and the quality of the verbal text which accompanies the images raise this figure to a power unanticipated by the self-irony of Hill's shaving scene.

The other intimation of death, juxtaposed in the editing to the sequence of the empty chair, is the montage of photographs to which I referred. There are several interludes of still photographs, showing Broughton's parents, his collaborators on the sets of his various films, and his home life. The most dramatic however occurs at the end of a processional march, in which the poet, in an elaborate feathered costume, is carried on a litter through the streets of Modesto, California, his birthplace, on a day when he was publicly honored by the town's library. Parading with him, under the banner "In memory of James Broughton" are many of his students costumed as totemic animals. Perhaps the most remarkable aspect of this procession is the inclusion of the faces of the puzzled and amused bystanders. Where Hill had told of his family, "These people to whom I belonged, did not belong to me," Broughton vividly demonstrates the isolation and the strangeness of his poetic vocation in this marvelous parade. The procession brings him to a graveyard. A shot of his fascinating wrinkled face dissolves into the sequence of photographs in anti-chronological order. As the images rush toward infancy one sees the unmasking of the mature features as a movement towards an essence. It is as if after the earliest picture we should expect some image of primal nonexistence. Instead the montage cuts powerfully from the baby's face to a still image of the aged poet under a weblike veil, which emphasizes both the lines of his face and the birdlike nature of his costume. In his text for the Twelfth Independent Film Award, Ken Kelman described *Testament* as "a ritual mask with sardonic bite which opens to giddy depths and lets out the roar of good old animal spirits." The whole processional sequence is the giddiest of those depths and one of the sublime moments of the cinema in this decade.

The text of the film is an anthology of passages from *A Long Undressing*,[14] Broughton's collected poems, carefully excerpted and intoned as if they constituted a single autobiographical poem. Early in the film when a voice (presumably of one of the townspeople watching the procession which is seen much later) asks "Who is James Broughton?" the citation is in fact from the poem "I Am A Medium", the autobiographical forward to the collection:

> I am third generation Californian . . .
> My grandfathers were bankers, and so was my father.
> By my mother wanted me to become a surgeon.
> However, one night when I was 3 years old
> I was awakened by a glittering stranger
> who told me I was a poet and always would be
> and never to fear being alone or being laughed at.

That was my first meeting with my angel
Who was the most interesting poet I ever met.

The indifference to being alone or being laughed at is illustrated by
the outrageous procession through Modesto, later in the film. But
the moment of poetic incarnation is illustrated at this point by the
dance of a nearly naked youth, in silver body paint, with a long
goat-like phallus, which he rubs against an immense egg, representing the poet. A motherly figure hovers over it too. Even Christ makes
a brief appearance, to bless it.

The issue of artistic incarnation is fundamentally different in *Testament* from the variations we have observed in the other film-
makers. There is no question of psychological development, dramatic
reorientation, or the patterning of aberrant responses. The story that
Broughton tells us is of a calling, pure and simple. Perhaps not so
simple. For it is a fusion of erotic and religious origins. The mythic
representation of the angel poet, as well as the Great Mother and
Christ in this Orphic trinity, looks forward to another scene of incarnation, that as a film-maker *per se* a little later in the film. But
before we can come to that point, a more detailed look at the modes
of representation throughout the film must be had.

Early in *Testament* there is a sequence of color photographs or
slides interrupted by flashes of a mildly comic couple in bed. This
passage accompanies a reading of the poem "The Girl With The
Beady Black Eyes" from *An Almanac for Amorists*. Although it has
no direct function in the autobiographical narrative, it forms the
moment of transition from the allusions to early life in Modesto to
the history of the poet's "education" which he introduces by saying
"At an early age I arrived in San Francisco. There I spent the rest
of my life growing up." Each of the stanzas of this short poem ends
with the line "when the old hotel burned down." In the final stanza,
it is hyperbolically repeated, "when the whole town burned to hell."
This image of conflagration constitutes the autobiographer's demarcation of the threshold of cinematic recovery, the point before which
there can be no pretense to a cinematic continuity.

On the near side of this limit, Broughton represents his film-able
life in terms of his actual films. Starting with a parody of the compositions and foreshortening of *Mother's Day*, with his son, Orion,
standing in for the young poet, the sequence proceeds through a
remontage of *The Adventures of Jimmy* in which Broughton played
the main role, *Loony Tom, The Golden Positions, Nuptiae, This is It*
and *The Bed*. Autobiography becomes, then, for Broughton, a particular (linear) mode of interpreting his works, both cinematic and
verbal. Appropriately then, he recites three songs from his book
Musical Chairs, out of the "Nursery Problems" section: "Papa Has
A Pig", "Mama Is Gone" and "Junior's Prayer." Together they de-
lineate an Oedipal conflict and the formation of the autonomy of the
child. The poems themselves appear in this context as if they were
the utterance, or the inner monologue of the child. Their nursery-

rhyme quality implies that the mature poet is drawing upon his childhood experiences and moods to write these ironic lyrics. Thus some form of temporal continuity, or repetition, links early childhood, and the first experiences of reading, with early maturity, or the first serious writing. This would be part of what he means when he says he spent the rest of his life growing up.

Into this matrix of poetic origins, as an interlude in the parody of *Mother's Day*, Broughton inserts the fictitious projection, by the boy for himself, of *The Follies of Dr. Magic*. He introduces the film by saying, "To amuse myself I made my first movie," and concludes bitterly, "I thought it showed *great* promise. Unfortunately no one else thought so." The context would seduce us into assuming that the two sentences refer to *The Follies of Dr. Magic*, itself a parody of very early fantasy films, as Pathé or even Méliès made them. The title is an allusion to Gance's early anamorphic film, *The Folly of Dr. Tube*, which is conventionally chronicled as the first avant-garde film. The statement, "To amuse myself I made my first movie," however would be literally true of either *The Potted Psalm* which Broughton made with Sidney Peterson, or of *Mother's Day*, his first solo film. The latter reference is more likely, although the negative critical reception would be true of both. (Here the film-maker is taking some license; for all of his early films were well received, but only within the very narrow circle of people who knew and cared about advanced cinema.)

It is significant that the film-maker locates the making of his first film in an ambiguous space between two parodies: one of his first solo films and one of what must be a mélange of some of his earliest memories of films; for *The Follies of Dr. Magic* includes scenes of devils appearing, unrequited love, a snake charmer, and Orpheus playing his lyre. It can even be seen as a charmingly vulgar version of the rite of incarnation which Broughton filmed with his silver "angel." In both cases, cinema is manifested at this crucial moment as a re-imagining of something earlier and distant, a re-imagining newly channeled into the categories relevant to the mature maker and his particular mode of thought at the moment of making.

It would seem that Broughton is not very interested in isolating the moment or the process of artistic incarnation, but in defining the way it sustains itself. The long hiatus in his film-making, from *The Pleasure Garden* to *The Bed*, 1953-1968, does not become an issue in this cinematic autobiography. The poems of those fifteen years represent the continuity which is dominant here. In fact, "I Asked The Sea," the opening poem of *Tidings* (1964) provides the text for the opening and closing of the film:

I asked the Sea how deep things are.

O, said She, that depends upon
how far you want to go.

Well, I have a sea in me, said I,
do you have a me in you?

As he rocks sympathetically by the shore Broughton is able to ven-triloquize the ocean. But their "dialogue" gently touches upon the disharmony between the mortal self and the endlessly repeating sea. The initial appearance of the empty chair suggests that indeed the "me" of the film has entered the sea forever. But after the autobiog-rapher returns, backwards, to his seat, the sea in the final passage wants to open up the theme of death:

> Let's talk of my dead,
>   the Sea said.
> Let's not, said I
>   I'm dry on my dune . . .
>   Then, said the Sea,
> When I wash up the dead
>   will you wade in?
> I'll swim, I said.

Broughton rocking by the sea recalls a commonplace in American poetry initiated by the great poems of poetic incarnation of Walt Whitman: "A Word out of the Sea" (first titled "A Child's Reminis-cence" and from which the image of the ocean as "Out of the rocked cradle" comes), and "As I ebbed with an ebb of the ocean of life." The Pacific is gentler to Broughton than the Atlantic was to the suf-fering Whitman in delivering the same deadly message. "I'll swim," is an heroic taunt at the limitation of this metaphoric ocean, and it touches us precisely because it evokes the temporal advantage of the sea over the swimmer.

Just before the processional scene there is a superimposition of the film-maker reading his Tarot at a stump in the woods under the image of the dancing angel, a cinematic representation of the simul-taneity of the moment of reflection and of incarnation. At this mo-ment the poet reads the conclusion of his exquisite "True and False Unicorn." Here the poem of 1957 is called up to comment on the authority of autobiographical cinema in the film of 1976. It articu-lates the ambiguity inherent in the relationship of the authorial self to his own representation, as accurate for cinema as it is for words:

> This is my only, this is my fate.
> This is my godhead grown from doubt.
> I am my unicorn, and he is I.
>
> I am myself my own true and false.
> I am myself my real unreal.
> He is my unicorn, and I am he.
>
> This is my I, my one, my me.
> This is my own, my two, my we.
> I am my unicorn, and so is he.

CODA

This essay should not end without a note on the diary film, a vastly important genre today, and one so close to my topic that some might think it indistinguishable. The film diary differs from the autobiography in this: it does not choose a fictive vantage point to reflect upon the past; in fact, it has next to no reference to the past. It would offer, instead, a series of discontinuous presents. The most important cinematic diarist, Jonas Mekas, does not set for himself the most extreme self-limitations in filming his diary. He is often very close indeed to an autobiographer; for he allows himself the second, or doubling, movement of verbal commentary, which very often smuggled the ironic perspective back into a genre that is sealed against irony.

Howard Guttenplan, perhaps the most rigorous inventor of self-imposed constraints for his diary films, tells us that he will not film anything out of his normal path. He does not go out of his way to get a particular shot. He films from where he is at the very moment of inspiration, and he does not edit aside from eliminating weak, or false elements.

Harry Smith did not edit his New York and Oklahoma diary, *Late Superimpositions*, but he did allow himself the freedom of organizing the completed rolls of film, leader and all, so that they move from maximal density and saturation of images to the thinnest point in the middle of the film, and then back to deeper colors and more complex layering. The curve also describes the shift from short and animated bits to longer and longer takes of live photography, and then back.

Editing is by no means banned from all the diaries. Andrew Noren has released many versions of his closely edited *Kodak Ghost Poems*, but he has not indicated the movement of his changing attitudes to the film within it. Each version appears as the definitive totality and each remains rigidly achronological.

Most of the diarists show an ambiguous attitude, a hesitation toward their fundamental metaphors. They offer them as if they were the most casual encounters with the phenomenal world. So in the center of *Late Superimpositions* an Indian boy reacts to the manipulations of the cameraman by trying to twist his head around to keep his image straight in the turning camera. This sequence is the most touching of several demonstrations of the formative power of the camera and the film-maker in the film which pretends to be purely passive in relation to its imagery. Mekas, too, saves an image of conflagration (the burning of the Vienna fruit market) for the climax of *Reminiscences of a Journay to Lithuania*, in which it is an apocalyptic metaphor for his distance from his origins. However he makes every effort to emphasize, on the soundtrack, his random stumbling upon this fire scene. Also in *Lost, Lost, Lost,* the diaries of his early years in America, he keeps saying, "I was there, recording it all with my camera." Yet one cannot but be struck by the elliptical, personal, fragmented recording of this supposed totality. If that claim refers to the life of the Lithuanian exiles in his film, as it seems to, it must be ironic, for he records next to nothing of it. We see above all his own nostalgia and isolation.

Noren is quite interesting in this respect. One remarkable aspect of the *Kodak Ghost Poems* is its sexual explicitness. After seeing this film, the other diaries and autobiographies look a little strange in their modesty. Yet in this film even the sexuality becomes a metaphor for the film-maker's relationship to his genre; for when we watch fellatio or intercourse from the point of view of the cameraman in the sexual act, we are again made aware of the impossibility of the representation through the limitation to the visual and the exclusion of the tactile. Noren seems to make this limitation a central theme in his film. It opens with shots of himself on a roof. We see his face in a reflective surface. As the camera explores this "mirror" it blurs and the face of a woman appears in it. The relationship of the self to another, especially dramatized in sexual encounters, is the theme of Noren's diary. But the metaphors for it are sewn into the fabric of the film as if they were simple accidents.

The diary film draws upon the pure lyric, and often becomes indistinguishable from it. It arises out of the film-maker's self-consciousness about the temporality of filming and editing. It explores that temporality as if it were the time of living. Often it suppresses the compounding of editing or sound in order to press home that equation. However it is the autobiographical cinema *per se* that confronts fully the rupture between the time of cinema and the time of experience and invents forms to contain what it finds there.

(*Millennium Film Journal,* Winter 1977-78)

NOTES

1. Jean-Jacques Rousseau, *Confessions,* trans. J.M. Cohen (Baltimore: Penguin-Books, 1975), p. 327-8.
2. Jean-Jacques Rousseau, *Oeuvres Complètes* I (Paris: Bibliotèque de la Pleiade, 1959), p. 1135.
3. William Wordsworth, *The Prelude* (1805-06 version) ed. J.C. Maxwell (Baltimore: Penguin Books, 1972), Book VII, lines 607-622.
4. Stan Brakhage, "Some Remarks", *Take One.* Vol. 3. No. 1. Sept.-Oct. 1971, p. 8.
5. Stan Brakhage, "Film and Music", *Guerilla,* June 1967, p. 17.
6. *Dante's Paradiso,* trans. John D. Sinclair (New York: Oxford University Press, 1961), pp. 48-49.
7. Wordsworth, *The Prelude,* Book II, lines 237-254.
8. "Interview with Stan Brakhage", Esther Schwartz, *Paunch* No. 31, April 1968, p. 20.
9. Hollis Frampton, "(nostalgia): voice-over narration for a film of that name, dated 1/8/71", *Film Culture,* 53, 54, 55. Spring 1972, p. 111.
10. Hollis Frampton, "A Pentagram for Conjuring the Narrative" in *Form and Structure in Recent Film,* ed. Dennis Wheeler (Vancouver Art Gallery, 1972).
11. Hollis Frampton, "Notes on (nostalgia)", *Film Culture,* 53, 54, 55, Spring 1972, p. 114.
12. George Landow, "A Note on *Remedial Reading Comprehension*" in *Form and Structure in Recent Film.*
13. George Landow, "Notes on Film", *Canyon Cinema News* No. 2, 1977, pp. 8-9.
14. James Broughton, *A Long Undressing:* Collected Poems 1949-1969 (New York: Jargon Society, 1971).

ERNIE GEHR:

Program Notes for a Film Screening at the Museum of Modern Art

A still has to do with a particular intensity of light, an image, a composition frozen in time and space.

A shot has to do with a variable intensity of light, an internal balance of time dependent upon an intermittent movement and a movement within a given space dependent upon persistence of vision.

A shot can be a film, or a film may be composed of a number of shots.

A still as related to film is concerned with using and losing an image of something through time and space. In representational films sometimes the image affirms its own presence as image, graphic entity, but most often it serves as vehicle to a photo-recorded event. Most films teach film to be an image, a representing. But film is a real thing and as a real thing it is not imitation. It does not reflect on life, it embodies the life of the mind. It is not a vehicle for ideas or portrayals of emotion outside of its own existence as emoted idea. Film is a variable intensity of light, an internal balance of time, a movement within a given space.

When I began to make films I believed pictures of things must go into films if anything was to mean anything. This is what almost everybody who has done anything worthwhile with film has done and is still doing but this again has to do with everything a still is— a representing. And when I actually began filming I found this small difficulty: neither film, filming nor projecting had anything to do with emotions, objects, beings, or ideas. I began to think about this and what film really is and how I see and feel and experience film.

Morning and *Wait* were the first works in which I tried to break down the essential contradictions of still and shot by enormously emphasizing the still frame—each frame—as a particular intensity of light, a frozen composition in time and space and its difference and its relation to the shot/film. Out of this came a new balance in the shot and in the frame (now seen, rather than seen through). The film became an arrangement of stills.

Reverberation began as an attempt at a portrayal, a representing of a concept of a life situation by way of film, and turned in the making of it into a presentation of the physical movement of film itself, stranding the photo-memory of persons/objects/their relationships in a cinematic force-field wherein images are offered up and simultaneously swept away by conflicting energies.

Sound as it comes from a speaker has its own quality. No matter how close it comes in reproducing sound of living beings or objects this quality is always the sound of the projector, the wires, the tubes and the speakers. This is its actuality. And it can be heard and experienced as sound, a form of energy.

History. Motion on a non-perspective plane. In which we infer a struggle for space-form determined by inner necessities. Movement and countermovement. The step the eye-brain takes from a surface to a point of light and to a point of darkness. The whole process of seeing something in seeing. The process of seeing and perceiving film. What happens to film as it is exposed to light. As it is developed. How this becomes a form that is film. History. Film in its primordial state in which patterns of light and darkness—planes —are still undivided. Like the natural order of the universe, an unbroken flow in which movement and distribution of tension is infinitely subtle, in which a finite orientation seems impossible. ("At last, the first film!": Michael Snow.)

In *Serene Velocity* the optical and psychological factors—persistence of vision/reciprocal tension—that allow for the movie illusion of motion and space become the subject of the film itself.

Still. A pictorial orientation of a surface of light populated by opaque, semi-opaque and transparent shadows (light apparitions). Our experience of the film plane filtered (colored and pulled on) by the film image is determined by inner human conditioning and development of perception. (These introductory notes on *Still* were *not* written for the final 60 minute work. They were written specifically for a 10 minute excerpt of a then work-in-progress shown that evening at the Museum of Modern Art.)

(January, 1971; revised December 1977)

Reverberation

ANTHONY McCALL:

Two Statements

Line Describing a Cone

Line Describing a Cone is what I term a solid light film. It is dealing with the projected light-beam itself, rather than treating the light-beam as a mere carrier of coded information, which is decoded when it strikes a flat surface (the screen).

It is projected in the normal way, on a 16 mm film projector.

Though inevitably there will be a wall that limits the length of the beam, a screen is not necessary.

The viewer watches the film, by standing with his, or her, back towards what would normally be the screen, and looking along the beam towards the projector itself. The film begins as a coherent line of light, like a laser beam, and develops through the 30 minute duration, into a complete, hollow cone of light.

Line Describing a Cone deals with one of the irreducible, necessary conditions of film: projected light. It deals with this phenomenon directly, independent of any other consideration.

It is the first film to exist solely in real, three-dimensional, space.

This film exists only in the present: the moment of projection. It refers to nothing beyond this real time. (In contrast, most films allude to a past time).

It contains no illusion. It is a primary experience, not secondary: i.e. the space is real, not referential; the time is real, not referential.

The form of attention required on the part of the viewer, is unprecedented. No longer is one viewing position as good as any other. For this film, every viewing position presents a different aspect. The viewer therefore, has a participatory role in apprehending the event:

he or she can, indeed needs to, move around, relative to the emerging light-form. This is radically different from the traditional film
situation, which has as its props, row upon row of seats, a giant
screen and a hidden projection booth: here, the viewer sits passively
in one position, whilst the images of the film are "brought" to the
viewer; this viewer can only participate vicariously.

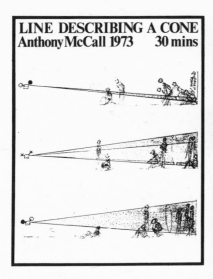

LINE DESCRIBING A CONE
Anthony McCall 1973   30 mins

photo Peter Moore

Important conditions for the projection.

A. That the projector be inside the viewing space, i.e. it should
not be inside a projection booth. As the focal point, and the source of
the light, it is an integral part of the film.

B. That the projection space be entirely empty of chairs or other
furniture.

C. That the space be absolutely pitch-dark. Owing to the delicate
nature of light, even a slight spillage of ambient light can seriously
affect the film's visibility.

D. The vertical height of the frame, at the wall (which stops the
beam), should be about 6 feet (1.75 to 2 metres). The base of the
frame should be about 1 foot (30 centimetres) from the floor. The
projector should stand at a height of about 3 feet (1 metre).

E. The light of the beam is visible through contact with particles
in the air, be they from dust, humidity or cigarette smoke. Smoking
should not be prohibited.

(*5th International Experimental Film Competition Catalogue*, 1973)

Long Film for Ambient Light

The work used no actual film nor film-projector. Three distinct elements combined to form the 'film', and no one of these was regarded as being prior to the other two:

1. A time-schema on the wall, covering fifty days. At the centre, the actual time-period of the presentation was indicated.

2. An altered space. A single electric light hung in the centre of the room at eye-level. The windows were covered with white paper, limiting them to being light-sources during the day and reflective surfaces during the night (screens).

3. A two-page statement, on the wall, 'Notes in Duration'.

Long Film for Ambient Light

Notes in Duration

This film sits deliberately on a threshold between being considered a work of movement and being considered a static condition. Formalist art criticism has continued to maintain a stern, emphatic distinction between these two states, a division that I consider absurd. Everything that occurs, including the (electrochemical) process of thinking, occurs in time. It is cultural habit that persuades us otherwise—perhaps a function of intelligence, that breaks up perception of continuous time into 'moments' in order to analyse them. Our insistence upon static, absolute lumps of experience, as opposed to continuous, overlapping, multiple durations, shows a warped epistemology, albeit a convenient one.

Art that does not show change within our time-span of attending to it we tend to regard as 'object'. Art that does show change within our time-span of attending to it we tend to regard as 'event'. Art that outlives us we tend to regard as 'eternal'. What is at issue is that we ourselves are the division that cuts across what is essentially a sliding scale of time-bases. A piece of paper on the wall is as much a duration as the projection of a film. Its only difference is in its immediate relationship to our perceptions.

A static thing, in terms of impulses to the brain, is a repetitive event. Whether the locus for consideration is 'static' or 'moving', we deal with time-spans of attention, the engagement of cognition and memory within the context of art behaviour. Neither objects nor events are for the most part accessible. They are rarely 'on show'. Since they are intentional, meaningful signs, this is of no consequence: once an idea is established 'in mind', it has entered the circuit of (art) ideas, and it won't go away, except through debate within the circuit. The apprehension of any artwork, static or moving, is a fleeting moment, as are all experiences. It is their mental residue that is important. One of the norms of film presentation has been 'limited, group access'. It has been necessary to assemble at a particular time to see the work, thus forming the social group, 'audience'. This group has specific behavioural characteristics.

With *Fire Cycle* (MOMA, Oxford, 9 June '74, duration 13 hours) and *Long Film for Four Projectors* (completed Nov '74, NYC), I established to my satisfaction that extending the duration could significantly alter the kind of concentration possible on the part of the spectator. Because the time-span of attention was not prescribed, the works being advertised as merely 'open' between certain hours, people came and went in their own time. The structure of each of them, though continually shifting, had a systematic evenness. No special viewing positions were dictated, and in each case the entire space was utilized so that there was no particular axis of attention (unlike earlier films like *Line Describing a Cone* where, though there was an infinite set of possible viewing positions, there was nevertheless a one-line axis running through space, which in terms of eye direction always ended at one point, the lens of the projector). When there were several people present at one moment, the scale was sufficient to provide spatial separation. These formal characteristics made possible a one-to-one relationship between spectator and work.

I am now interested in reducing the 'performance' aspect, in order to examine certain other fundamentals, *viz* temporality, light. I am presently assuming that it is possible to do this without using the customary photochemical and electro-mechanical processes (which have the disadvantage of being expensive, *i.e.* slow). I am aware of the dangers of back-tracking, that behind every 'first principle' lurks another, and I do not rule out the possibility of continuing to make 'films'. However, for the time being I intend to concentrate less on the physical process of production and more on the presuppositions behind film as an art activity.

(NY, June 1975)

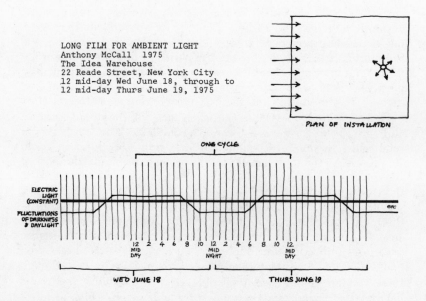

LONG FILM FOR AMBIENT LIGHT
Anthony McCall 1975
The Idea Warehouse
22 Reade Street, New York City
12 mid-day Wed June 18, through to
12 mid-day Thurs June 19, 1975

PLAN OF INSTALLATION

ONE CYCLE

ELECTRIC LIGHT (CONSTANT)
FLUCTUATIONS OF DARKNESS & DAYLIGHT

12 MID DAY   2   4   6   8   10   12 MID NIGHT   2   4   6   8   10   12 MID DAY

WED JUNE 18   THURS JUNE 19

PAUL SHARITS:

Hearing:Seeing

It is the middle of the year 1975,
ten years after I began work on the film "Ray Gun Virus", the first
segment of my project of deconstructing cinema from a very particular frame of reference, a frame which is still not wholly defined. I
had made films prior to 1965 but those works—sketches and several
"imagistic", haiku-like pieces involving actors/actresses and rather
fragmented narratives—while critical of "cinematic illusionism" at
a sort of Brechtian level, were not central to the more focused and
intensive analyses of film which characterize the current project; to
emphasize the irrelevancy of the early works, I destroyed them some
years ago. This is not to say that concerns with narrativity were immediately dispensed with; there is a formalization of narrative structures in *Ray Gun Virus* (1966), *Piece Mandala* (1966), *Razor Blades*
(1965-68), *N:O:T:H:I:N:G* (1968), *T,O,U,C,H,I,N,G* (1968) and,
to a certain extent, *S:TREAM:S:S:ECTION:S:ECTION:S:S:EC-
TIONED* (1971), but that formalization is not a primary feature
of these films in terms of the more radical "meaning-building" they
propose. I do not want to discuss these issues in this context because
many of them have been dealt with elsewhere [1] and because there
is one aspect of my involvement in film which has never been expressed, by others or by myself, upon which I would now like to
make a few comments.

Speaking rather generally, one could claim that much of the critical writing about a group of independent films made in the middle
1960's and early 1970's (including my work), in establishing the importance of the qualities of "wholeness" in these films, underempha-
sized the specific articulations of their internal parts, implying, perhaps unintentionally, that the filmmakers were constructing strictly
from the outside inwards. This emphasis on the works' macrostruc-
tures did help clarify what some of the more general aesthetic strategies were in the making of these films but it also led to an under-
estimation of the importance of their qualities of inner complexity.
My own published statements regarding my work also tend to be

overly general (or, more questionable, some of the statements are so diaristic and impressionistic that they confound theory with emotive mania and a kind of cartoon romanticism). At my most reasonable, I have at best suggested only certain concerns—analysis, information documentation, problems of filmic representation and signification—but have not indicated other concurrent involvements, such as the frame-by-frame ordering of images and sounds. I've approached this micromorphological level of construction from a number of perspectives, including the logical and mathematical, but what I want to focus through here is a perspective which, for lack of a better term, I will call the "musical".

While I was studying painting in the early 1960's—involved, naturally enough, with some of the prominent issues of "formalist" art —I was also making films, those which no longer exist. I stopped painting in the middle 1960's but became more and more engaged with film, attempting to isolate and essentialize aspects of its representationalism. I had also become most intrigued with the differences between reading and listening, or, more inclusively, the larger discontinuities between seeing and hearing; film, sound film, appeared to be the most natural medium for testing what thresholds of relatedness might exist between these perceptual modes. In making films, I have always been more interested in speech patterns, music and temporal pulses in nature than in the visual arts for exemplary models of composition (perhaps because I had studied music as a child and had internalized musical forms of structuring). I do not wish to suggest that I was or am captivated by the notion of "synesthesia" and I hope that what follows will be clearly distinguishable from such a notion. I am not proposing that there exist any direct correspondences between, say, a specific color and a specific sound but that operational analogues can be constructed between ways of seeing and ways of hearing (and sometimes, when such structural analogues are composed, one can thereby experience those levels of ultimate difference between the two systems).

My early "flicker" films—wherein clusters of differentiated single frames of solid color can appear to almost blend or, each frame insisting upon its discreteness, can appear to aggressively vibrate—are filled with attempts to allow vision to function in ways usually particular to hearing. In those films of 1965 to 1968, the matters of "psychological theme" and perceptual analysis of filmic information were part of a set which included regard for the way in which rapidly alternating color frames can generate, in vision, horizontal-temporal "chords" (as well as the more expected "melodic lines" and "tonal centers"). The fades and lap dissolves of these films function not only as theoretic metaphors of "motion" but also flow along with and into the more discretely differentiated frame sequences, acting as "active punctuation" for the "sentences" being visually enunciated.[2] The sprocket soundtrack of "Ray Gun Virus" works towards establishing an accurate representation of technological modularity, framing—and thereby noting—the ultimate matrix of 16 mm film's capability for visual re-presentation (there being one sprocket hole for each frame of image along the film strip). The even meter of sprocket sound is found mirrored in spoken word forms in some of my later films. In these word-soundtrack works, linguistic meaning levels, which form a sort of horizontal commentary to the streams of visual imagery they accompany, and phonemic sound qualities, which exist in a vertical-harmonic relationship with the flow of visual pulses, are both equally operable. Having brought sound(tracks) into this discussion, it is a good point to begin developing my basic thesis by posing a question: can there exist a visual analogy of that quality found in a complex aural tone, the mixture of a fundamental tone with its overtones? One can think of paintings which by various means—resonation between colors-shapes, echoing forms, etc.—create such a sense; Matisse went so far as to explain the curved lines emanating from-around his subject in his painting of 1914, "Mlle Yvonne Landsberg", as being overtonal.[3] But how can one film frame of one solid color possess such a quality? It cannot. Yet, a series of single frames of different colors, which creates "flicker", can, depending upon the order and frequency of the tones, suggest such a quality; but, it can only *suggest*, because to truly simulate the sense of overtones one must have several visual elements existing within the same space. This problem intrigued me from the days of my earliest studies with so-called "flicker", it continued as a concern throughout my work and is still an element of consideration in my works-in-progress, while it is not a primary, formative consideration, it is a kind of sub-text operating actively within the larger propositions I wish to make about cinema; the rest of this discussion will revolve around "overtonality".[4]

If painting can achieve effects of overtonality in the spatial frame, then why not just borrow from painting those methods and adapt them to the film frame? Aside from the comical hybridic result such an approach would constitute (music to painting, painting to film), there were, for me, other objections. It was obvious that it was necessary to somehow divide the frame into "parts", to introduce enough complexity into the instantaneous image so that overtones could be legibly generated. However, having taken certain "modernist" conventions rather seriously, I could not simply complicate the surface of my images in just any manner—I was convinced that any such complexity, to have its "integrity", would have to be generated through an attentiveness to the natural qualities-textures-images of film, in terms of the film material and filmic processes. It occurred to me that one alternative to surface division might be to multiply the single screen and, in the two-screen film "Razor Blades", I attempted to create various levels of dialogue between the side-by-side screens, color and shape dialogues and agreements and conflicts between meanings. In the final section of T,O,U,C,H,I,N,G I wanted to visualize "inverse pain" as a kind of imploding reverberation of the picture edge—the screen appears to collapse, in rhythmic pulses, into itself. This latter mode—of introducing shapes into the frame which were reflective of the film frame's perimeter-shape and which acted as a commentary on the state of consciousness of the film's protagonist at that point in the (backwards) "narrative"— struck me later as being somewhat too related to strategies of painting, as did other aspects of my films of that early period. After 1968 I wanted to remove from my work all influences of painting; also, I wanted to remove from the work literary structures and dramatic-psychological themes. In relation to the removals of painting and literary elements, color rhythms which evoked or produced senses of emotionality also would be eliminated; more sophisticated levels of "feeling", derived from intense contemplation of filmic realities, were to replace the earlier, less specifically filmic methods and images.

In *S:TREAM:S:S:ECTION:S:ECTION:S:S:ECTIONED* I finally came to use superimposition, as a way of attaining both "chordal depth" and the possibility of "counterpoint"; united with these "musical" motivations, there was the larger concern with the relationship of water's directionalities and the flow of film through a projector. (By stressing the "musical" model, I am running the risk of oversimplifying other, more theoretical factors in the making of the films being discussed; it is hoped that the reader will recognize this and not jump to the conclusion that "musicality" is the primary intention behind the films.) The (emulsion) scratch, a very natural surface-dividing actuality of cinema, became a prominent image-generating method in S:S:S:S:S:S, referring always back to the vertical movement of the film strip downwards through the projector as well as serving as countermovement to the currents of the water images. Planes of water imagery interact with (white) textural planes composed of groupings of individual scratches. The soundtrack, composed of superimposed layers of word loops—oscillating from high to low frequencies—functions on several levels in relation to the visual images, creating deeper "harmonic spaces".

In later works where flat fields of film grains are enlarged—in "Axiomatic Granularity", which is concerned with the fundamentals of image formation in/on emulsion, and in "Apparent Motion", which deals with the basis of the filmic illusion of movement— undivided coherent surfaces are maintained, as in the "flicker" works, but, since the surfaces are particlized and appear to be "moving", when they are superimposed over each other, harmonics, resonances and a sort of "overtonality" within the frame are possible.

Other works of the past few years are composed by rephotographing strips of "flicker" footage in a home-made system, wherein the projector element has no shutter blade or gripper arm and thereby allows the "subjects"—the "flicker" film strips—to be observed as continuous strips of film, with their sprocket holes visible; not only is there a natural horizontal and vertical division of the frame but there is also possible a layering of color planes (when the strips are projected at a rapid speed and rephotographed, their differently colored frames begin to blur into each other, forming whole ranges of shimmering color bars and planes, several appearing at a time within the frame, some assuming dominance—like fundamental tones—while others pulse around/behind the dominants, as if they were their overtones). The works which are made this way—such as the single-screen piece, "Color Sound Frames", and the three-screen piece, SYNCHRONOUSOUNDTRACKS—are certainly more complex than I have described them: because their images "move" at varieties of speeds, contain superimpositions, have sound elements (sync-soundtracks of the sprocket hole images' rates of passage), etc., these factors also contribute to the films' total "chordal fabrics".

Something else having to do with "musicality" should perhaps be noted: all of the single-screen films since S:S:S:S:S:S are made up of very definite and equally lengthed sections. ("Inferential Current" has three sections, "Axiomatic Granularity" and "Color Sound Frames" have four sections, "Apparent Motion" has two sections and each of the "Analytical Studies" series has from four to seven sections.) On one level, this sectioning has to do with a desire to create logical propositions and with an analytic desire to set up elements for comparison; on another level, this also indicates my interest in developing cinematic ideas in the form of "movements", as in the sonata and/or in other related musical forms.

The spatiality of music, the separation of instruments which determines the physical scale (width and depth) of a performed piece of music and which constitutes a compositional dimensionality beyond the simpler horizontal and vertical ordering of tones, is obviously something the single-screen film would have difficulty approximating, even if film could visually approximate all of music's devices. However, if one had several screens to work with, arranged properly, one might be able to begin composing in ways at least related to the ways a composer might approach, say, a quartet: one screen could state a theme and another could answer it, elaborate upon it; the other screens could respond to this dialogue, vary it, analyze it, recapitulate it, etc. There were numerous motivations for the work I began with multiple-screen, installation pieces ("locations"); one of those motives was to approach the complexities of music's spatial dimension. In the making of the first of these "locational" pieces, "Sound Strip/Film Strip", I had in mind some of the forms I had come to admire in Beethoven's late quartets. When several filmmaker friends previewed the piece with me, before its first public exhibition, one of them, Michael Snow, commented that the work had reminded him of the "Brandenburg Concertos". Beethoven or Bach, either way, it was gratifying to me that my sense of the work's "musicality" was not a singularly personal delusion.

I have only sketched out, rather briefly and generally, some of those factors in my work which have to do with their internal structures; I've pursued one of many possible models—the "musical"—in discussing this inner level of construction and have made a few comments on the general impact that musical form has had upon my work of the past ten years. A detailed account of what I have only mentioned would necessitate specific examples accompanied by color reproductions of the films' scores and clips from the films; the magnitude of such a task is clearly beyond the scope of this set of introductory remarks. I hope that I have at least given some access to a part of my work which has otherwise remained undiscussed.

(Written 1975; published in *Film Culture* No. 65-66, 1978)

NOTES

1. Chronologically: Regina Cornwell, "Paul Sharits: Illusion and Object", *Artforum* (September 1971); Rosalind Krauss, "Paul Sharits: Stop Time", *Artforum* (April 1973); P. Adams Sitney, *Visionary Film* (N.Y., Oxford Univ. Press, 1974), pp. 423-427; Annette Michelson, "Paul Sharits and the Critique of Illusionism: An Introduction", *Projected Images* (Minneapolis, Walker Art Center Exhibition Catalogue, 1974).
2. My notions concerning the relationships of film construction and signification to linguistics are not central to the present discussion but I do want to at least make some allusion to them in referring to a string of film frames as a "sentence".
3. Frank Trapp, "Form and Symbol in the Art of Matisse", *Arts Magazine*, Vol. 49, No. 9 (May 1975), p. 57.
4. In 1929 Sergei Eisenstein enthusiastically proposed a visual ("montage") model of the aural overtone. I am in general agreement with his concepts but have developed my model from an essentially different set of circumstances and suggest that interested readers who wish to make comparisons see "The Filmic Fourth Dimension", *Film Form and The Film Sense* (Cleveland, World Publishing Co., 1963), pp. 64-71 (*FF*).

PAUL SHARITS:

From "Words Per Page"

To begin getting a clear perspective on these complex questions, it would be valuable to regard cinema as an informational system, rather than starting with a priori metaphysical theories or with a fully developed aesthetic or with the kind of exclamatory presumptions that Vertov's "Kino Eye" concept typifies (the drawing of morphological analogies between the human body and the nonhuman instruments). Let us investigate the system as it exists in a descriptive, concrete modality of comprehension. It would be a mistake to be initially concerned with the *intentions* that formed the system, the naive pseudo-aesthetic that "caused" the technological development of photography ("capturing a likeness of the world") and cinematography ("capturing a likeness of the world in motion")—after all, the system exists today, with or without our "intention" that it do this or that. The system simply exists, and a taxonomy of its basic elements seems a more appropriate beginning for analysis than propounding rashly abstract, speculative "reasons" *for* its existence. This latter case, in its simple overgeneralizing, has led, from the very beginning, to premature, so-called "languages of the film," "grammars of the film." Such a beginning accounts for the normative postulate that "the shot" is one of cinema's irreducible particulars. As if their remarks were analytically suggestive, "informed cineastes" speak of "mise en scène." My hypothesis does not exclude the formation of higher abstraction classification; I only suggest that there is nothing to be gained by starting with highly abstract and highly questionable presuppositions. Lumière was so emphatic in his belief in "the shot" that he constructed both the internal structure and external boundaries of his films with one and the same shot.

* * *

Light and color are obviously primary aspects of cinema. However, even in fine cinema works color has not very convincingly realized its temporal potentialities. Some works use color as a "func-

tional/symbolic" tool, in an Eisensteinian sense, or for psychological
reference and physical effect, or for definition and clarification of
images in the picture. In a lot of lesser works, color is decorative
and ornamental or is used nonphilosophically merely for its stimula-
tory values; this latter use of color to produce essentially nonfilmic
"psychedelic effects" is conceptually uninteresting and is better
suited to video works where color more intense than cinema's reflected screen color can be obtained. This area has elicited very little
systematic concern from filmmakers and film critics. In many cases a
great deal of attention is paid to getting "proper color balance" for
no good *cinematic* purpose; this technical "attentiveness" is not
what I mean by "systematic concern." The vast problems of cinematic light and color structuring call for a separate discussion.

Perhaps the most engaging problem of cinema is the relationship
sound may have to visual image. Although Warhol and Snow have
used synchronous sound in convincing ways, an uncritical acceptance of this traditional mode of correlation usually leads to work
in which both sound and image are mutually weakened: this is true
in both the "lip synch" of anthropomorphic works and in the sim-
plistic paralleling of sound and image effects in non-narrative works.
Eisenstein's idea of "vertical montage" is a classical point from which
one can consider nonsynchronous uses of sound. It may be that
through a controlled continuous collision of sound and image an
emergent psychophysiological heterodyne effect could be generated.
Both light and sound occur in waves, and in optical sound composite
prints are both functions of interrupted light, that is, both are primarily vibratory experiences whose "continuous" qualities are illusional. The major difference, aside from obvious differences in
physical qualities between the two systems, is that the soundtrack
operates in terms of continuous passage over the projector sound-
head while the image intermittently jerks in discrete steps through
the film gate—there are no frame lines in the soundtrack. From this
angle, it is apparent that drawing direct relationships between
systems that have significant structural differences is an illusional
oversight. There is also no intrinsically filmic relational logic supportive of the use of "mood music," whether it be the electronic
music *background* for so-called "abstract movies" or Bergman's use
of Bach fragments to act as psychological *backups* to certain key
visual passages in his film *Through a Glass Darkly*. The variations on
sound systems that are basically supportive of visual images are
innumerable and vary widely in their levels of conceptual relationship to visual images. Whether or not the audio and visual systems
should be discrete and powerful enough in themselves so that they
achieve mutual autonomy is a serious question. What possibilities
are there for developing both sound and image from the same
structural principle and simply presenting them side-by-side as two
equal yet autonomous articulations of one conception? Of course,
sound need not be considered as a primary aspect of cinema; the

wealth of films that succeed on visual levels alone is enough to justify silence. Aside from a few eccentricities, the first projectors had no sound option; the sound variable could be regarded as an arbitrary addition to an already complete visual system. (If we regard works that have no sound tracks as "silent films," then why don't we regard listening to music without visual accompaniment as "blind music"?) Only a few types of sound can be regarded without doubt as cinematic: the case in which the sound of a synch sound camera might be recorded and projected in synch with the visual "recording"; the case in which the drone sound of a projector projecting a visual "projection" might be heard; and the case in which one hears the sound of sprockets acting as a commentary on the length each frame of visual image has in time.

In the end, the cinematic process as the "subject matter" of a new cinema, as in a work like Ken Jacobs' brilliant *Tom, Tom, the Piper's Son,* which is literally a film of a film, or as in more filmically concrete or conceptually filmic works, has already proven its viability. When a focus on highly general and prematurely fixed narrative or narrative-like forms is blurred in shifting perception to more distinctly contemporary focal lengths, then that "blur" measures wide angle lengths *from* "reality," telephoto lengths *to* micromorphological understandings of "cinema" and, lengths *of* temporal modulation in what is ultimately an omnidirectional grammar. Certainly an analysis of the focusing process itself is necessary; but "focusing" does not necessarily mean "reductiveness." It may be that by "limiting" oneself to a passionate definition of an elemental, primary cinema, one may find it necessary to construct systems involving either no projector at all or more than one projector and more than one flat screen, and more than one volumetric space between them. A focused film frame is not a "limit."

(This essay was originally presented in 1970 as an introduction to a course in film production at Antioch College. Reprinted from *Afterimage,* 4 [Autumn, 1972], by permission of the author, Copyright © by Paul Sharits.)

TONY CONRAD:

A Few Remarks
Before I Begin

A few remarks before I begin.

A year ago I published a statement which may be most singular in the objectives which it places at the motivational stratum of filmmaking.

This article is called "Non-Linguistic Extensions of Film and Video" [1], and it offers (as an aspiration) the idea that "thoughts", in some sense, may appear, may reach the point of articulation, may be expressed for the first time, at least some thoughts which would be new to consciousness, and that this could occur *within film*.

Well, I have mulled over my commitment to this evidently neo-classical posture ever since.

The greatest embarassment that the article offers me at present is that it suggests *HOW* to extend 'language' in a manner which I now find very ill-appointed.

I had suggested that language might be extended through the ability of film to model an *analytical* or artificial-language system; in particular a system of binary logic.

I have several friends and correspondents who have contributed their interests to the general mulling on the subject of *artificial* and *natural* languages, and the relationships between them.

The impression which now forces itself upon me is that the problem of bonding natural and artificial languages is unsolvable for unexpected reasons, but that it should afford consequential insight along wholly unexplored avenues of review.

The great effort that has been seen in mathematical logic to press the roots of both math and logic beyond the necessity of access through the natural (English) language has of course revealed a basic condition of unsolvability, which I interpret thus: There are in fact *no* artificial nor analytic languages, in *any* real sense of the words.

You cannot start a book on logic without words in English (or whatever natural language). In short, the "artificial language" is a bud sprouted on English, just as company brand names are.

To return to my article for a moment: I might propose to myself (for my own redemption) that *Film* may afford a system that *does* introduce a truly discrete "artificial" language, simply by being independent of the symbology of verbal discourse (or that it could, if used in a cagey way). The problem, of course, is that speech also contains the precursors for an "artificial" language, in the form of DATA which may support some kind of deliberate structure. A very close parallel is offered by SONG.

[Sing]   mmm
        1
        Acquainted as I am   mmm
        3   →4/3   1
        With the variables of attachment   mmm
        9   4/3→9 4/3 9→4/3→9   1
        To such objects as this one
        9   4/3 9
[Hold up a can of film]

The pattern of thought seems in these circumstances to fall back upon a relational substructure of understanding—to an underpinning of relational modality which we might call

          form   vs.   content

analysis; which could equally well be prodded out of a concept-structure deriving from

        thought   vs.   thought-about,
        word   vs.   object,

or individual association.

Music is almost always about TASTE, when it is most closely guarded from incursions of poetry, dance, and so forth.

Film, on the other hand, might be more characteristically thought of as having *syntax* as its subject matter. How conjunctions of component materials are used is the stuff which most commonly affects us in a film, whereas the composer more often traps us with the evocation of taste-association which proceeds as a mood or atmosphere directly from the choices which they have made.

What I begin to find important is the shelving of all of this clutter: let's wrap up a few things for the convenience of our discourse:

A. There are no artificial languages.

B. Some relational propensity in our thinking calls into being illusions of such impossible discriminations as

form	:	content
word	:	object
analytic	:	synthetic
data	:	association

C. Information about the problematic character of these false discriminations will derive only with difficulty from within the systematic approach which has served to produce our particular awareness of their inadequacies: in short, *some other thought strategy* is necessary to get further in the discussion.

Here are a few thought strategies:

1. I simulate what I like. If I like how someone speaks, I speak like them. If I like white, I dress in white.

2. I justify my thoughts with care, based upon a system of logic which is (one hopes) not so precise that it reveals that it is corrupted by its tie to my own speech.

3. I repeat and repeat whatever I am interested in.

4. I always consider lying, and being lied to.

Now what, as an activity, seems futile here, may be reviewed from a thoroughly different angle.

The film scholar has never been up to dealing efficaciously with the problem of *anticipation, suspense, temporal composition*. This is nothing out of the ordinary: nobody (film scholars *or* makers, or the corresponding commentators and artists in any of the fields of music, dance, theater, etc.) has been able to do much more than annotate the *decisions of taste* which underlie temporal composition strategies.

BUT: BUT: BUT: BUT:

Always, always, always, people. People respond with their attention in ways which can be *programmed*.

This is a program.

The program is perhaps the most difficult chunk for the serious film person to bite off and chew:

Program equals *Pap*.

There is gut emotion in the rejection or acceptance of programming schedules.

Why am I informed, as I write these notes, that the Tibetan lamas who

"We went yesterday to hear Tibetans chant—Kagya lamas of Gylwa

Kaiwapa doing Inahakala puja. (They watch TV the rest of the time.)" writes David Hykes.[2]

The patterns of anticipation and resolution which are incipient in the common practice *program* have something going for them. What?

There is a wave of interest presently in a discipline which (similarly) prods before us highly unresolved social *data*. I'm thinking of sociobiology, naturally.

Sociobiology is a curious structure, regarded purely as a thought-framework. Clearly the first question to ask of sociobiology is: Is it self-exemplifying?

I apologize immediately for this tangent, even though it is fitting as an introduction to the two sentences which I have selected to illustrate these comments:

THIS COMMENT IS
SELF-EXEMPLIFIED

THIS SLIDE IS
ALSO AN EXAMPLE
OF ITSELF

NON-SELF-ILLUS-
TRATIVE STATE-
MENTS, LIKE
THIS, ARE LESS
PARADOXICAL.

Typical of the job of the film theorist, in these circumstances, is to evaluate the relative values of the messages (on the one hand) and the fact that they are presented as slides (on the other hand) in shaping an impact upon "an audience". As you watch this slide, perhaps you can separate and evaluate these factors mentally. Surely you are aware of what stimulates your attention, but is there anything systematic to say about what does it, why, and how it works?

We know that *attention* is the key item in linking experience to thought: it stands to reason.

The *types of thought* and the *patterns of attention* must then be interactive, and the terms of this interaction must develop alongside of a new sort of logic or thought-systematization. Can this interaction be described? Maybe it is possible to describe the *description* at least: it would seem that self-observation must play a component role (relative to the data-constituent offered to us internally by our attentiveness variability). It must also seem that the new thought pattern characteristic of self-observation at this level (at the level of generalizing about different types of *thought* and *attentiveness* experiences and interactions) will have to be (metaphorically speaking) cloudlike, holistic; unsystematic to be sure; at any rate, it must pass muster as being *un*systematic, *un*repetitive, *un*imitative, *un*lying, and so forth.

Basically, this piece is a romance, with the real and transcendental components bonded in the brain of the sender/receiver: It is another in a series of calls for *thought*.

As a performer, I have come to value the site which is presently being made available for the playing out of these words, for the particular kind of game that occupies my attention today: the game of thinking inside of other people's heads.

It is conspiritorial rather than confessional of me to give you a knight in this way.

There is no objective of art or media clearer than the making of *money*, within the economic reality of our capitalist-socialist world. However, the intellectual community resists this reality to some slight degree thru a vestigial awareness of other valuational schemata. In principle, it is Pure Reason that could be called upon as a ground, as a reality for the cultural institutions which support our communication and inventiveness.

Pure reason, of course, is a notion. The varieties of thought itself are never a *subject matter;* how could they be such, when the invocation of *thought varieties* for discourse—for use as examples, for example—must be such a tenuous matter.

There may be two ways out of this boot-in-the-quagmire. One: to examine the varieties and structure of thoughts or systems of ideas, and to examine the mechanisms by which they may propagate themselves from brain to brain (or by which particular ideas may contrarywise prove ill-suited to such propagation). My contributions to this field shall be composed under the rubric: Ideology Engineering.

The other way to study communication is to study *attention*. I use the word "communication" in a considered way, as *communication* and *thought* have to be seen as bearing the same relationship to one another as *individual organism* bears to *gene*. I mean to say that there is no thought without communication. This is a crucial conceit to Route 2.

How long, actually, does any particular thought take? How often would you have to work on a good one, to get it really going? How long is our attention span?—Perhaps you could get an idea of this by seeing how long it takes not to hear insects chirping outside the window. How long did it take not to notice the page having been turned? We are very aware that we are made very aware by *changes* that occur in the environment.

Consequently, it is safe to say that very probably human thought requires constant renewal and alteration. In fact, the variety of thought available to humans is almost directly a function of the number of scales of attentiveness which are achieved within the individual.

It is possible to have one thought in mind for a certain limited time, so long as it fits into a particular thought-type. If you want to get a thought really going, you have to get attached to it; to prod it into position all the time, and to give it plenty of relief time.

Here's some relief time from that last thought:

Taste, I would hope, could serve as the *subject* of film, as well as of music.

In structuralist discourse the relation between word and thing/idea is privileged: In spite of a hundred years of philosophy spent in tight infighting about this relation, the structuralist ignores the outcome (which *must* be that word and object are in an ontologically unstable relationship), and in effect makes the *word* elemental to their work.

Another sort of understanding altogether must be brought to bear upon the whole nexus of issues which have been associated by the structuralist siege: the tactics which suggest the greatest excitement to me are those accessible through approaches of those such as Harry Jerison and David G. Hays. Jerison [3] makes as his starting point in relating to language the extremely sensible observation that our *use* of language is not at all linked (in terms of causal appearance in an evolutionary context) with interpersonal *communication*.

Notice I didn't say that *thought* and communication are unglued. The fact is, simply, that language contains traps for thought, and that varieties of linguistic thought may not even be *consistent*. For example, Henry Flynt [4] points out that you may *think* you could imagine not having language, but it is impossible to clarify this idea.

Most language traps seem to lie in wait around philosophical problems, rather than around practical problems.

When you dispose of a dead person's effects and papers, and thoughts and communications, you find yourself reduced to this

What use is it?

What use are ideas? Or communication? Or the intellectual community? Thoughts might best be categorized in these terms:
  1. What use are they?
  2. What are they worth in money?

What is A THOUGHT, exactly, anyway? This is an important ISSUE.

Clearly the cultural community depends upon being able to demonstrate that a body of thoughts or ideas has been communicated to its members. Otherwise, the jig is up. In practice, tho, a *forum* on the subject of education as communication is a rusty turkey to try to flush from academia.

This is a performance. Fortunately, as a practitioner of a discipline which nobody can describe (media study) I am protected from serious engagement with thoughts of any real consequence. What is this subject, media study, which I profess to elucidate? Is there, seriously, such an intellectual subject as making videotapes? Come on.

How about making it *more* serious by studying *communication* instead, and doing that by studying the *movies?* Are you joking?

Being in this position, it is necessary for me to invent the actual discipline which is requisite to the present performance, and to consecrate that performance to the passage of time.

Naturally, the advantage of being serious by not being serious is that it is impossible to communicate by being serious. That is, there is no thought, as a consequence of seriousness, any more than there could be thought as a consequence of this. How would you describe this?

Perhaps you would discriminate between serious style of presentation and the real serious stuff, which has to have solid thinking to back it up. I would not find such an attitude helpful, if you were in my field. Of course, it does depend also upon individual interests.

Jerison, by splitting apart the evolution of language from the use of language for communication, makes himself liable to suggest *another use or motivating function for language.* He suggests that language, like the senses, gives homo sapiens an ability to represent, record, and relate spatially and temporally to the environment. This environment was originally, of course, the competitive environment shared with the roving predators—the dogs, cats, etc.

Such speculation is not similar to sociobiology, which simply attempts to arm us with new DATA: namely DATA concerning our inbuilt dispositions as physical organisms. Jerison instead gives us the *mapping function* as an (in a sense) irreducible element of our linguistic structure: his contribution suggests that *the code* used to carry a message is non-elemental; associational thought must be derived not from the *code* but from the *conjugation* of codes, as elemental pairings.

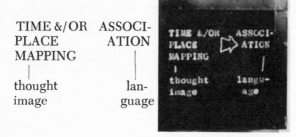

TIME &/OR   ASSOCI-
PLACE   ATION
MAPPING |
  |
thought   lan-
image   guage

As the ideas here flex in and out of unruliness, it becomes harder to invest the emotive mechanism in them that holds them under intense

ATTENTION

A conjugation of codes, though, is highly attention-getting.

There are simply more conjugations of codes than you can shake a stick at. The only reason to classify them, à la Rudolf Arnheim,[5] would be to use up the boring ones. Can life be continually thrilling forever?

Many who claim to find life thrilling also meditate.

We will all generally have *learned* thru being offered conjugative material; the offering of DATA is (tho not inimical to, at least) not very supportive of communication or thought as one might wish to find it.

Why is relational structure so troublesome, when it is pandemic to ratiocination? This is simply the wrong question. Failing relational structure is the most attention-directing principle of human thought. This attention-driving mechanism also powers the means by which attention rises to a new level of generality. In the present instance, for example, we can force tiresomeness into our recognition of common attitudinal systems operative within the following relations:

FORM   :CONTENT
WORD   : OBJECT
RELATION :   DATA

FORM : CONTENT

WORD : OBJECT

RELATION : DATA

Presently, we may discover generality with enough clarity to form a new relation:

PROBLE-   AT-
MATICAL   : TEN-
RELATIONS TION

Can the brain easily bridge this gap? The answer that has to be predicted is YES.

Hello out there? Are they still functioning?
Hello

ADDENDA

If one thing is sure, it is that none of this is consistent with the attitude that *association* is more or less "correct", as a principle for constructing art or literature.

By saying that mental activity is "associational", I would not like to be construed as saying that other thought structuring may be available or accessible to "us".

I write what comes to mind. We all do.

Attention needs guideposts for focus. Exploration of alternative attentiveness is a valuable cultural commodity.

(Buffalo, New York, August 27, 1977)

NOTES

1. Conrad, Tony. "Non-Linguistic Extensions of Film and Video." *Quarterly Review of Film Studies*, Vol. 1 No. 3, August 1976. Pp. 276-282.
2. Hykes, David. Personal Correspondence, unpublished.
3. Jerison, Harry J. "Discussion Paper: The Paleoneurology of Language". *Annals of the New York Academy of Sciences*, Vol. 280, October 1976. Pp. 370-382.
4. Flynt, Henry. *Blueprint for a Higher Civilization*. Multhipla Edizioni, Milan, 1975. Pp. 13-15.
5. Arnheim, Rudolf. *Film as Art*. Berkeley: University of California Press, 1957.

HOLLIS FRAMPTON:

Lecture

[*This lecture was given at Hunter College on the afternoon of 30 October 1968*. The written text was pre-recorded. Tape play-back equipment was placed on the forestage, beneath a large projection screen. An empty variable-speed projector was set up in the rear of the room, turned down to its slowest rate to produce a distinct flicker, the gate focussed to fill the screen. A red gelatin filter and a common pipe cleaner were at hand. On being introduced, the speaker simply switched on the recorder and retired to operate the projector. The following text was read, rather deliberately, with pauses of subjective length indicated by the breaks. *The lecture lasted about 25 minutes.*]

Please turn out the lights.

As long as we're going to talk about films, we might as well do it in the dark.

We have all been here before. By the time we are eighteen years old, say the statisticians, we have been here five hundred times.

No, not in this very room, but in this generic darkness, the only place left in our culture intended entirely for concentrated exercise of one, or at most two, of our senses.

We are, shall we say, comfortably seated. We may remove our shoes, if that will help us to remove our bodies. Failing that, the management permits us small oral distractions. The oral distractions concession is in the lobby.

So we are suspended in a null space, bringing with us a certain habit of the affections. We have come to do work that we enjoy. We have come to watch *this*.

The projector is turned on.

So and so many kilowatts of energy, spread over a few square yards of featureless white screen in the shape of a carefully standardized rectangle, three units high by four units wide.

The performance is flawless. The performer, is a precision machine. It sits behind us, out of sight usually. Its range of action may be limited, but within that range it is like an animal, infallible.

It reads, so to speak, from a score that is both the notation and substance of the piece.

It can and does repeat the performance, endlessly, with utter exactitude.

Our rectangle of white light is eternal. Only *we* come and go; we say: this is where I came in. The rectangle was here before we came, and it will be here after we have gone.

So it seems that a film is, first, a confined space, at which you and I, we, a great many people, are staring.

It is only a rectangle of white light? But it is all films. We can never see *more* within our rectangle, only *less*.

The red filter is placed before the lens at the word "red".

If we were seeing a film that is *red*, if it were only a film of the color red, would we not be seeing more?

No.

A red film would *subtract* green and blue from the white light of our rectangle.

So if we do not like this particular film, we should not say: there is not enough here, I want to see more. We should say: there is too much here, I want to see less.

The red filter is withdrawn.

Our white rectangle is not "nothing at all." In fact it is, in the end, all we have. That is one of the limits of the art of film.

So if we want to see what we call *more*, which is actually *less*, we must devise ways of subtracting, of removing, one thing and another, more or less, from our white rectangle.

The rectangle is generated by our performer, the projector, so whatever we devise must fit into it.

Then the art of making films consists in devising things to put into our projector.

The simplest thing to devise, although perhaps not the easiest, is nothing at all, which fits conveniently into the machine.

Such is the film we are watching. It was devised several years ago by the Japanese film-maker *Takehisa Kosugi*.

Such films, offer certain economic advantages to the film-maker.

But aside from that, we must agree that this one is, from an aesthetic point of view, incomparably superior to a large proportion of all films that have ever been made.

But we have decided that we want to see *less* than this.

Very well.

A hand blocks all light from the screen.

We can hold a hand before the lens. This warms the hand while we deliberate on *how much less* we want to see.

Not so much less, we decide, that we are deprived of our rectangle, a shape as familiar and nourishing to us as that of a spoon.

The hand is withdrawn.

Let us say that we desire to *modulate* the general information with which the projector bombards our screen. Perhaps this will do.

A pipe cleaner is inserted into the gate.

That's better.

It may not absorb our whole attention for long, but we still have our rectangle, and we can always leave where we came in.

The pipe cleaner is withdrawn.

Already we have devised four things to put into our projector.

We have made four films.

It seems that a film is anything that may be put in a projector, that will modulate the emerging beam of light.

For the sake of variety in our modulations, for the sake of more precise control of what and how much we remove from our rectangle, however, we most often use a specially devised material called: film.

Film is a narrow transparent ribbon of any length you please, uniformly perforated with small holes along its edges so that it may be handily transported by sprocket wheels. At one time it was sensitive to light.

Now, preserving a faithful record of where that light was, and was not, it modulates our light beam, subtracts from it, makes a vacancy, a hole, that looks to us like, say, Lana Turner.

Furthermore, that vacancy is doing something. It seems to be moving.

But if we take our ribbon of film and examine it, we find that it consists of a long row of small pictures which do not move at all.

We are told that the explanation is simple—*all* explanations are.

The projector accelerates the small still pictures into movement. The single pictures, or frames, are invisible to our failing sense of sight, and nothing that happens to any *one* of them will strike our eye.

And this is true, so long as all the frames are essentially similar. But if we punch a hole in only one frame of our film, we will surely see it.

And if we put together many dissimilar frames, we will just as surely see all of them separately. Or at least we can *learn* to see them.

We learned long ago to see our rectangle, to hold all of it in focus simultaneously. If films consist of consecutive frames, we can learn to see *them* also.

Sight itself is learned, a newborn baby not only sees poorly—he sees upside down.

At any rate, in some of our frames we found, as we thought, Lana Turner. Of course she was but a fleeting shadow—but we had hold of something. She was what the film was *about*.

Perhaps we can agree that the film was about *her* because she appeared oftener than anything else.

Certainly a film must be about whatever appears most often in it.

Suppose Lana Turner is not always on the screen.

Suppose further that we take an instrument and scratch the ribbon of film along its whole length.

Then the scratch is more often visible than Miss Turner, and the film is about the scratch.

Now suppose that we project all films. What are they about, in their great numbers?

At one time and another, we shall have seen, as we think, very many things.

But only one thing has *always* been in the projector.

Film.

That is what we have seen.

Then that is what all films are about.

If we find that hard to accept, we should recall what we once believed about mathematics.

We believed it was about the apples and peaches owned by George and Harry.

But having accepted that much, we find it easier to understand what a film-maker does.

He makes films.

Now, we remember that a film is a ribbon of physical material, wound up in a roll: a row of small unmoving pictures.

He makes the ribbon by joining large and small bits of film together.

It may seem like pitiless and dull work to us, but he enjoys it, this splicing of small bits of anonymous stuff.

Where is the romance of movie-making? The exotic locations, the stars?

The film artist is an absolute imperialist over his ribbon of pictures. But films are made out of footage, not out of the world at large.

Film, we say, is supposed to be a powerful means of communication. We use it to influence the minds and hearts of men. But the artist in film goes on building his ribbon of pictures, which is at least something he understands a little about.

The pioneer brain surgeon, Harvey Cushing, asked his apprentices: Why had they taken up medicine?

To help the sick.

But don't you enjoy cutting flesh and bone? He asked them. I can't teach men who don't enjoy their work.

But if films are made of footage, we must use the camera. What about the romance of the camera?

And the film artist replies: A camera is a machine for making footage. It provides me with a third eye of sorts, an acutely penetrating extension of my vision.

But it is also operated with my hands, with my body, and keeps them busy, so that I amputate one faculty in heightening another.

Anyway, I needn't really make my own footage. One of the chief virtues in doing so is that it keeps me out of my own films.

We wonder whether that interferes with his search for self-expression.

If we dared ask, he would probably reply that self-expression interests him very little.

He is more interested in reconstructing the fundamental conditions and limits of his art.

After all, he would say, self-expression was only an issue for a very brief time in history, in the arts or anywhere else, and that time is about over.

Now, finally, we must realize that the man who wrote the text we are hearing read, has more than a passing acquaintance and sympathy with the film-maker we have been questioning.

For the sake of precision and repeatability, he has substituted a tape recorder for his personal presence—a mechanical performer as infallible as the projector behind us.

There is still time for us to watch our rectangle awhile.

Perhaps its sheer presence has as much to tell us as any particular thing we might find inside it.

We can invent ways of our own to change it.

But this is where we came in.

Please turn on the lights.

HOLLIS FRAMPTON:

"A specter is haunting the cinema: the specter of narrative. If that apparition is an Angel, we must embrace it; and if it is a Devil, then we must cast it out. But we cannot know 'what' it is until we have met it face to face." To that end, then, I offer the pious:

A Pentagram for Conjuring the Narrative

I.

Lately, a friend has complained to me that his sleep is troubled by a recurrent nightmare, in which he lives through two entire lifetimes.

In the first, he is born a brilliant & beautiful heiress to an immense fortune. Her loving & eccentric father arranges that his daughter's birth shall be filmed, together with her every conscious moment thereafter, in color & sound. Eventually he leaves in trust a capital sum, the income from which guarantees that the record shall continue, during all her waking hours, for the rest of her life. Her own inheritance is made contingent upon agreement to this invasion of privacy, to which she is, in any case, accustomed from earliest infancy.

As a woman, my friend lives a long, active & passionate life. She travels the world, & even visits the Moon, where, due to a miscalculation, she gives birth to a normal female baby inside a lunar landing capsule. She marries, amid scores of erotic adventures, no fewer than three men: an Olympic decathlon medalist, a radio-astronomer, &, finally, the cameraman of the crew that follows her everywhere.

At twenty-eight, she is named a Nobel laureate for her pioneering research on the optical cortex of the mammalian brain; on her forty-sixth birthday, she is awarded a special joint citation by the Congress of the United States & the Central Committee of the People's Republic of China, in recognition of her difficult role in mediating a treaty regulating the mineral exploitation of Antarctica. In her sixty-seventh year, she declines, on the advice of her lawyers, a mysterious offer from the decrepit Panchen Lama, whom she once met, as a very young woman, at a dinner given in honor of the Papal Nuncio by the Governor of Tennessee. In short, she so crowds her days with experience of every kind that she never once pauses to view the films of her own expanding past.

In extreme old age—having survived all her own children—she makes a will, leaving her entire fortune to the first child to be born, following the instant of her own death, in the same city. . . .on the single condition that such child shall spend its whole life watching the accumulated films of her own. Shortly thereafter, she dies, quietly, in her sleep.

In his dream, my friend experiences her death; & then, after a brief intermission, he discovers, to his outraged astonishment, that he is about to be re-incarnated as her heir.

He emerges from the womb to confront the filmed image of 'her' birth. He receives a thorough but quaintly obsolete education from the films of 'her' school-days. As a chubby, asthmatic little boy, he learns (without ever leaving his chair) to dance, sit on a horse, & play the viola. During his adolescence, wealthy young men fumble through the confusion of 'her' clothing to caress his own unimaginable breasts.

By the time he reaches maturity, he is totally sedentary & reclusive, monstrously obese (from subsisting on an exclusive diet of buttered popcorn), decidedly homosexual by inclination (though masturbation is his only activity), hyperbolic, pallid. He no longer speaks, except to shout "FOCUS!"

In middle age, his health begins to fail, & with it, imperceptibly, the memory of his previous life, so that he grows increasingly dependent upon the films to know what he is to do next. Eventually, his entire inheritance goes to keep him barely alive: for decades he receives an incessant trickle of intravenous medication, as the projector behind him turns & turns.

Finally, he has watched the last reel of film. That same night, after the show, he dies, quietly, in his sleep, unaware that he has completed his task. . . .whereupon my friend wakens abruptly, to discover himself alive, at home, in his own bed.

II.

Whatever is inevitable, however arbitrary its origins, acquires through custom something like gravitational mass, and gathers about itself a resonant nimbus of metaphoric energy.

I can recall, from my childhood, a seeming infinitude of Japanese landscape photographs that included, inevitably, the image of Mount Fujiyama. Naively, I attributed this to native reverence for the holy mountain. The rare or imaginary exception ached mysteriously, in the distant planes of its illusion, for the absent mass,—as if a great truncated cone of displaced air could somehow refract the energy of consciousness, as surely as solid rock reflected more visible light.

Later on, I came to understand that Fujiyama is visible from absolutely every place in Japan, and that it looms from every direction at once. In that distant country, every single act of perception must include (must indeed be fused inextricably with) its proper coeval segment of an enterprise of the mind incomparably vast and continuous: the contemplation of the inevitable Mountain.

A stable pattern of energy had once locked granite and ice into a shape immutable beyond human recollection or surmise; that same pattern formed, over long ages, the very physical minds of its beholders, as magnetic forces trace in steel dust the outline of a rose. So that, eventually, all things were to be construed according to the number of qualities they could be seen to share with Fujiyama, the supreme metaphor.

Naturally enough, the Japanese themselves have known about this for centuries. Hokusai, in a magnificent inventory of the mind's ways of knowing through the eye, displays the whole compound of terror and humor: I refer to the "Hundred Views."

III.

Euclid is speaking: "Given a straight line, and a point exterior to that line, only one line may be drawn through the point that is parallel to the line." The West listens, nodding torpid assent: the proposition requires no proof. It is axiomatic, self-evident.

Is is not.

The famous Postulate rests upon two unstated assumptions concerning the plane upon which the geometer draws: that it is infinite in extent; and that it is flat. Concerning the behavior of those redoubtable fictions, the point and the line, in spaces that are curved, or bounded, Riemann and Lobachevsky have other tales to tell.

Thought seeks inevitable limits—irreducibly stable patterns of energy—knowing that it prospers best within axiomatic perimeters that need never be patrolled or repaired.

I am told that, in 1927, a Louisiana lawmaker (haunted by the ghost of Pythagoras, no doubt) introduced into the legislature of that state a bill that would have made the value of 'pi' equal to precisely 3. No actual circle could pass unscathed through that equation.

The Emperor Shih Huang Ti attempted an axiomatic decree of similar instability: his Great Wall, subject to entropy, never kept out an invader. Instead, the language and culture of China, an energy-pattern of appalling stability, simply engulfed one conqueror after another. Everyone who ventured South of the Wall became, in time, Chinese.

Marcel Duchamp is speaking: "Given: 1. the waterfall; 2. the illuminating gas." (Who listens and understands?)

A waterfall is not a "thing," nor is a flame of burning gas. Both are, rather, stable patterns of energy determining the boundaries of a characteristic sensible "shape" in space and time. The waterfall is present to consciousness only so long as water flows through it, and the flame, only so long as the gas continues to burn. The water may be fresh or salt, full of fish, colored with blood; the gas, acetylene or the vapor of brandy.

You and I are semistable patterns of energy, maintaining in the very teeth of entropy a characteristic shape in space and time. I am a flame through which will eventually pass, according to Buckminster Fuller, 37 tons of vegetables. . . .among other things. Curiously enough, then, I continue to resemble myself (for the moment at least). Thus reassured, I will try to ask a question.

What are the irreducible axioms of that part of thought we call the art of film?

In other words, what stable patterns of energy limit the "shapes" generated, in space and in time, by all the celluloid that has ever cascaded through the projector's gate? Rigor demands that we admit only characteristics that are 'totally redundant,' that are to be found in "all" films.

Two such inevitable conditions of film art come immediately to mind. The first is the visible limit of the projected image itself—the frame—which has taken on, through the accumulation of illusions that have transpired within its rectangular boundary, the force of a metaphor for consciousness itself. The frame, dimensionless as a figure in Euclid's "Elements," partitions what is present to contemplation from what is absolutely elsewhere.

The second inevitable condition of film art is the plausibility of the photographic illusion. I do not refer to what is called "representation," since the photographic record proves to be, on examination, an extreme abstraction from its pretext, arbitrarily mapping values from a long sensory spectrum on a nominal surface. I mean simply that the mind, by a kind of automatic reflex, invariably triangulates a precise "distance" between the image it sees projected and a "norm" held in the imagination. (This process depends from an ontogenetic assumption peculiar to photographic images, namely that every photograph implies a "real" concrete phenomenon (and 'vice versa!'); since it is instantaneous and effortless, it must be 'learned.')

Recently, in conversation, Stan Brakhage (putting on, if you insist, the mask of an 'advocatus diaboli') proposed for film a third axiom, or inevitable condition: narrative.

I admit that Brakhage's preferred argument in support of this intuition devolves upon a metaphor drawn from music. But I fear having my throat cut by Occam's Razor, so I'll stick to a figure of my own, stating, as compactly as possible:

> BRAKHAGE'S THEOREM: For any finite series of shots ["film"] whatsoever there exists in real time a rational narrative, such that every term in the series, together with its position, duration, partition and reference, shall be perfectly and entirely accounted for.

(An example: consider for a moment the equation
$$p=30$$
which may be expanded to yield

$$p=\frac{p}{3}+\frac{p}{5}+\frac{p}{6}+\frac{p}{10}+6$$

Here is a rational narrative that accounts for the expansion: "A necklace was broken during an amorous struggle. One-third of the pearls fell to the ground, one-fifth stayed on the couch, one-sixth was found by the girl, and one-tenth recovered by her lover: six pearls remained on the string. Say of how many pearls the necklace was composed." Such was the algebra of the ancient Hindus.)

An algorithm derived from Brakhage's Theorem has already been tested on a number of difficult cases, including Kubelka's "Arnulf Rainer," Conrad's "The Flicker," and the films of Jordan Belson. All have responded. At this writing, narrative 'appears' to be axiomatically inevitable.

"Whatever is inevitable, however arbitrary its origins, acquires through custom something like gravitational mass. . . ."

It is precisely universal 'gravitation' that makes the skills of the acrobat or aerialist both possible and meaningful. The levitation of our dreams confirms the gravity of our wakefulness.

IV.

Samuel Beckett gives us "Malone," a fiction with whom, (as we Facts must finally admit) we share at least one humiliating trait: we are all waiting to die. Malone waits, literally alone, comfortably supine but immobile, in a small room. How he came to be there, together with some odd bits of rubbish (a boot, for instance, and the cap of a bicycle bell,) is uncertain. We are not many pages into his company before we recognize our meeting-place: it is intolerably familiar.

"I" is the English familiar name by which an unspeakably intricate network of colloidal circuits—or, as some reason, the garrulous temporary inhabitant of that nexus—addresses itself; occasionally, etiquette permitting, it even calls itself that in public. It lies, comfortable but immobile, in a hemiellipsoidal chamber of tensile bone. How it came to be there (together with some odd bits of phantasmal rubbish) is a subject for virtually endless speculation: it is certainly alone; and in time it convinces itself, somewhat reluctantly, that it is waiting to die.

The wait turns out to be long, long. The presence, in its domed chamber, masters after a while a round of housekeeping and book-keeping duties. Then it attempts to look outside. Glimpses are confusing: the sensorium reports a fractured terrain whose hurtling bits seldom coalesce, "make sense," as pregnant idiom has it—and the sense they make is itself fugitive, and randomly dispersed throughout an unguessable volume of nothing in particular. What is to be done?

Beckett lets us overhear Malone promising himself to pass the time by telling himself stories. Then Malone proceeds to digress, with a fecundity that is clearly circumscribed only by the finite size of the book; we realize that we are being made privy to nothing less (or more) than the final cadence of a larger digression that extends, by extrapolation, back to the primal integer of Malone's consciousness.

And that integer is halved by an inevitable convention of story-telling: whatever is said implies not only a speaker, but also a listener. The fiction we call Malone divides, like an ovum fertilized by our attention, into two such complementary partners.

The speaker, a paragon of loquacity who calls himself "I," uses every rhetorical trick in the book to engage his listener's attention, even going so far as to ignore him; only rarely does he let slip his suspicion that he may be only a figment of the listener's imagination.

The listener, contrariwise, is a model of taciturnity, invincibly unnameable and invisible, whose presence is felt only in the numbing quietude we normally expect of any discerning auditor forced to listen to a long-winded joke in poor taste. . . . or of a reader who passes the time by skimming, for his own perverse reasons, the sort of confessional literature that remorselessly asserts its own authenticity in flat declarative sentences.

On the subject of who might be inventing whom, the listener maintains at all times a hissing silence, as of an open telephone line.

Listen, now: what you have just read is no invention of my own.

But I must prefer it to any matrix I myself might choose to generate (from more cheerful assumptions) in the hope of defining the predicament of consciousness, because 'it locates the genesis of story-telling among the animal necessities of the spirit.' Whereas received opinion seems always to represent the story-teller as insinuating his views into the mind of another party, preferably for commercial purposes.

V.

One cannot escape the feeling that these mathematical formulae have an independent existence and an intelligence of their own, that they are wiser than we are, wiser even than their discoverers, that we get more out of them than was originally put into them.

—Heinrich Hertz

One fine morning, I awoke to discover that, during the night, I had learned to understand the language of birds. I have listened to them ever since. They say: 'Look at me!' or: 'Get out of here!' or: 'Let's fuck.' or: 'Help!' or: 'Hurrah!' or: 'I found a worm!' and that's 'all' they say. And that, when you boil it down, is about all 'we' say.

(Which of those things am I saying now?)

Joseph Conrad insisted that any man's biography could be reduced to a series of three terms: "He was born. He suffered. He died." It is the middle term that interests us here. Let us call it "X." Here are four different expansions of that term, or true accounts of the suffering of "X," by as many story-tellers.

Gertrude Stein: $\quad x = x$

Rudyard Kipling: $\quad x = \dfrac{c-b}{a}$

Ambrose Bierce: $\quad x = 3\sqrt{\dfrac{2c(c-b)}{a^2}}$

Henry James: $\quad x = \dfrac{2c(c^2 - 2bc + 2b^2)}{c^3 - 3bc^2 + 3b^2c - b^3}$

Any schoolboy algebraist will readily see that all four are but variations upon the same hackneyed plot:

$$ax + b = c$$

which may also be solved for the viewpoint of any of its other main character, thus:

$$a = \frac{c-b}{x} \quad \text{or, } b = c - ax \quad \text{or, } c = ax + b$$

or for that of the Supreme Unity:

$$1 = \frac{c-b}{a} - x$$

Manipulation will even yield us the unbiassed spectator:

$$0 = \frac{c-b}{ax}$$

All right. Any discerning reader will be finding this a long-winded pointless joke in poor taste. (It is possible, even to approach my examples with seriousness. The equation I attribute to Miss Stein may be inverted to read as follows:

$$x - x = 0$$

That says, in English, that anything diminished by something of its own magnitude amounts to nothing. If we care to personify, it suggests that, in the absence of equals, any man is diminished to a cipher. And 'that' smacks painfully enough of folk wisdom to have interested Gertrude Stein. . . . even if I can't state it in her own idiom.)

The algebraic equation

$$ax + b = c$$

is our name for a stable pattern of energy through which an infinity of numerical tetrads may pass. A story is a stable pattern of energy through which an infinity of personages may pass, ourselves included.

The energy-patterns we call physical laws are named after their discoverers: Avogadro, Boyle, Snell. The energy-patterns we call stories are named after their protagonists: Faust, Jesus, Philoktetes. Certain stories seem related to one another, as though the same general equation had been solved for successive roots. We might call such a general equation a 'myth.'

But instead, let us imagine every myth as a crystalline regular 'Polyhedron,' suspended, weightless, in a void, with each of its vertices touching, in perfect geodesic equilibrium, the surface of an iridescent imaginary sphere. The existence of the whole body is utterly dependent upon the integrity of all its facets: every facet represents a story.

Near the cliptic of our universe we find, for example, the mythic 'Polyhedron of the Father and the Son': on it, the stories of Odysseus and Hamlet occupy adjacent facets, since they are really the same story, told in the former instance from the point of view of the father, and in the latter, from that of the son. Nearly opposite these two, on the dark side, the stories of Oedipus and Agamemnon are nearly contiguous.

The center of the cosmos is occupied by the 'Polyhedron of the Story-Teller.' Here we find, imaged upon various facets, the stories of Malone, waiting to die; of Scheherazade, waiting to be killed; of the 'Decameron,' whose narrators wait for others to die; of the "Canterbury Tales," told to ease a passage through space as well as time.

The universe is but sparsely populated by these 'Polyhedra,' enormous though they are. Here and there, a faint nebula marks, perhaps, the region where a new myth struggles to cohere; elsewhere, dark cinders barely glow, remnants of experience lost forever to consciousness. A hole torn in the very fabric of space, whence no energy escapes, is rumored to mark the place where AGNOTON, the black 'Polyhedron of the Unknowable,' vanished.

Nor do all the facets bear images. Some are dusty, some cracked; some are filled with senseless images of insects, or else with a vague, churning scarlet, shot with sparks. Some are as transparent as gin. Some are bright as mirrors and reflect our own faces. . . . and then our eyes. . . . and behind our eyes, distantly, our polyhedral thoughts, glinting, wheeling like galaxies.

(From *Form and Structure in Recent Film,* Vancouver Art Gallery, 1972)

INDEX